In GALLIPOLI Alan Moorehead omits no detail of the maudlin waste, the physical horror, the sheer heartbreaking folly of three quarters of a million men committed to fight for impossible objectives with inadequate means on unknown, unmapped terrain. But if the generals bungled, the men fought magnificently. . . .

Intrepid submarine commanders slipping through the Narrows in their primitive ships to shell the railway lines of Constantinople. . . .

The fantastic Anzacs landing on the wrong beach and digging on the steep hillside to hold off Turkish attacks— for which they earned their name of "Diggers." . . .

The fanatical courage of Mustafa Kemal, who fought like a tiger and led his men in bayonet charges against the British lines. . . .

"GALLIPOLI is an account of that World War I campaign written as Bruce Catton might write of the Civil War. . . . It adds up to one of the great tragedies of our tragic times, both softened and at the same time made more poignant by the navieté and humanity that went into it."

—Walter Millis

GALLIPOLI

Alan Moorehead

BALLANTINE BOOKS • NEW YORK

TO LIONEL FIELDEN

NOTE

I SHOULD like to record my particular thanks to General Lüfti Güvenc, of the Historical Branch of the Turkish General Staff, who gave me the fullest access to official archives in Ankara, and to Colonel Sükrü Sirer, who prepared many maps and accompanied me over the battlefield itself: to Major T. R. Molloy of the British Embassy in Ankara, who translated Mustafa Kemal's war diaries for me: to Brigadier-General Cecil Aspinall-Oglander and Captain Basil Liddell Hart, who, in reading through the text, have saved me from much error: to General Hamilton's literary executor, Mrs. Mary Shield, who has allowed me to make use of the General's private papers: and to my wife, who has worked with me on the book in all its stages.

Among the many others who have most kindly helped me with their reminiscences and their advice are Sir Harold Nicolson, Lord Hankey, Field-Marshal Sir John Harding, Field-Marshal Sir William Slim, Lady Violet Bonham-Carter, Mr. H. A. J. Lamb, Mrs. Helen Hugo, Lieut.-General Lord Freyberg, V.C., and Major Tasman Millington. I am also most grateful for the help I have received from the Admiralty, the War Office, the Imperial War Museum, the staffs of the London Library, and the British Embassy in Ankara.

A large library exists on the subject of the Gallipoli campaign, and while I cannot pretend to have read it all I must acknowledge here my especial indebtedness to Brigadier-General Aspinall-Oglander's official history, Sir Winston Churchill's *World Crisis,* Sir Ian Hamilton's *Gallipoli Diary,* and the memoirs of Admiral of the Fleet Lord Keyes.

The spelling of Turkish names has presented difficulties which I have been unable to resolve. Gallipoli, for example, is to the Turks Gelibolu, and Chanak is more correctly spelt Canak. Other places have changed their names since the campaign, notably Constantinople which is now Istanbul. However, since this book is written in English, it seemed best to adopt the names which are most familiar to English-speaking readers, and so in general I have followed the spelling used in the British military maps of the time.

ALAN MOOREHEAD

Library of Congress Catalog Card Number: 56-6028

ISBN 0-345-30772-0

This edition published by arrangement with Harper & Brothers

Manufactured in the United States of America

First Ballantine Books Edition: May 1958
Second Printing: December 1982

PLANS AND MAPS

The Eastern Mediterranean

ONE

'Essentially the great question remains: Who will hold Constantinople?'—NAPOLEON

EVEN as late as August 1914 it was by no means certain that Turkey would come into the first world war on the German side. There was no need for her to go to war, nobody seriously threatened her, and in fact at that time it was the policy of the Allies and the Central Powers alike to keep her neutral if they could. Certainly the country was in no condition to fight. In the five years that had elapsed since the Young Turks had first come to power the Ottoman Empire had very largely disintegrated: Bulgaria was independent, Salonika, Crete and the Ægean islands had gone to Greece, Italy had seized Tripoli and the Dodecanese, and Britain had formally proclaimed the protectorate of Egypt and the annexation of Cyprus.

Since the previous year the German Military Mission had made great improvements in the Turkish army, but the long series of defeats in the Balkan wars had done enormous harm. At many places the soldiers had gone unpaid for months, and morale had sunk almost to the point of mutiny. Except in a few *corps d'élite* they were ragged, hungry and short of nearly every kind of weapon required for a modern war. The fleet too was hopelessly out of date, and the garrison at the Dardanelles was far too weak, its guns too obsolete, to stand a chance against a determined attack from any one of the great powers.

Politically the situation was chaotic. The Young Turks with their Committee of Union and Progress had begun

1

well enough when they had deposed the Sultan in 1909, and their democratic ideas had had the support of all liberal-minded and progressive people everywhere. But five years of wars and internal troubles had been too much for them. The ramshackle government of the empire had run down too far to be revived in another and a better way, and inevitably the energies of the Young Turks had become swallowed up in the simple and desperate struggle for their own political survival. Now there was no longer any talk of democratic elections and the freedom and equality of all races and creeds under the Crescent. The bloom had long since worn off the Committee: it was revealed as a ruthless party machine which was almost as sinister and a good deal more reckless than anything Abdul the Damned had contrived. Financially the Government was bankrupt. Morally it had reverted to the old system of force and corruption; there were Committee cells in every sizeable town in what was left of the empire in Asia, and no political appointment could be obtained without their support. Local government at the outlying centres like Baghdad and Damascus was in an appalling state, and Constantinople had so little hold over them that it was always possible that some local chieftain might set himself up in yet another independent state.

It was this very helplessness both abroad and at home that made Turkey turn to the outside world for allies, and in effect it came down to a choice between Germany and Britain. The German alliance was, tactically, the obvious one, since the Kaiser was eager for it and was in a position to put the Turkish army back on its feet. But the Germans were not liked. Lewis Einstein, the special minister at the American Embassy in Constantinople, was probably right when he said that the Turks preferred the English to all other foreigners—and this despite the fact that the British officials in Turkey tended to regard as 'good' Turks only those who prayed five times a day and turned to the English for advice. England had the money, she had command of the seas, and she had France and Russia on her side. The presence of Russia in the alliance was, of course, an embarrassment, since Russia was the traditional enemy of Turkey, yet even this might not have been too much for the Young Turks to have accepted had the English been enthusiastic. But they were not. They did not think at all highly of this government of young revolutionaries, and suspected that it might be put out of office at any moment. When the Young Turks came to London with a proposal for an Anglo-Turkish alliance they were politely turned aside.

And so by August 1914 things had drifted into a compromise that was rather weighted on the German side. The British Naval Mission continued to serve at Constantinople, but it was counterbalanced—perhaps over-balanced—by the German Military Mission which was actively filtrating through the Turkish army; and while the British and the French continued to give their tacit support to the older more conservative politicians in Constantinople, the Kaiser firmly nobbled the younger and more aggressive leaders of the Committee. It was, then, very largely a question of which side had backed the right horse: if the Young Turks were turned out the Allies could count on a friendly neutral government in Constantinople and the end of the German threat in the Near East. If on the other hand the Young Turks remained in office then the British and the French would be in the uncomfortable position of having to switch, of being obliged to try and get their money on the winner before the race was over.

It was a situation which had extreme attractions for the oriental mind, and the Young Turks made the most of it. Moreover the setting could hardly have been better for the complicated intrigues that now began: the foreign ambassadors, installed like robber barons in their enormous embassies along the Bosphorus, the Young Turks in the Yildiz Palace and the Sublime Porte, and everywhere through the sprawling decaying beautiful capital itself that hushed and conspiratorial air which seems to overtake all neutral cities on the edge of war. It was the atmosphere of the high table in the gambling casino very late at night when every move takes on a kind of fated self-importance, when everyone, the players and the watchers together, is engrossed, and when for the moment the whole world seems to hang on some chance caprice, some special act of daring, the turning of a card. In Constantinople this false and artificial excitement was all the more intense since no one really knew the rules of the game, and in the uncertain jigsaw of ideas which is created by any meeting between the East and the West no one could ever look more than a move or two ahead.

But it was the personalities of the protagonists that

3

counted, above all the personalities of the Young Turks. Even in a place with so lurid a reputation as Constantinople it would be hard to imagine a stranger group of men. There is a dramatic quality about the Young Turks, a wild and dated theatricality, which is familiar and yet quite unreal. One tends to see them in the terms of a gangster movie, half documentary and half extravagant make-believe, and it would be very easy to dismiss them to that convenient limbo that envelops most political adventurers had they not, just for this instant, had such power over so many millions of men.

Sir Harold Nicolson, who was then a junior secretary in the British Embassy, remembers them all coming to dinner at his house one day. 'There was Enver,' he wrote, 'in his neat little uniform, his hands resting patiently upon his sword-hilt, his little hairdresser face perked patiently above his Prussian collar. There was Djemal, his white teeth flashing tigerish against his black beard: there was Talaat with his large gypsy eyes and his russet gypsy cheeks: there was little Djavid who spoke French fluently, and who hopped about, being polite.'

The odd thing, of course, was that they should have been there at all, that power should ever have reached them in a world which still knew nothing of Nazis and Fascists in uniform, of communist officials at a banquet.

Talaat was an extraordinary man: yet there is a certain earthiness about him that makes him rather easier to understand than any of the others. He is the party boss, gross, hard and good-tempered, who has his tendrils everywhere, and in place of faith possesses an instinctive understanding of the weaknesses of human nature. He began life as a post office telegraphist, and he never really made much of an outward show of being anything more. Even now when he was Minister of the Interior, a post for which he might have been designed by nature, and virtually controller of the Committee machine, he still had his telegraphist's keyboard on his desk, and, with his enormous wrists on the table, he liked to tap out messages to his colleagues on it. Long after the others, with their uniforms and their bodyguards, had moved into splendid villas along the Bosphorus, Talaat continued to live in a rickety three-storied wooden house in one of the poorer districts of Constantinople. Henry Morgenthau, the American Ambassador, called upon

4

him there unexpectedly one afternoon, and found him in thick grey pyjamas with a fez on his head. He was surrounded by cheap furniture, bright prints on the walls, worn rugs on the floor; and his Turkish wife kept peeping nervously at the two men through a latticed window while they talked.

Most of those foreigners who knew Talaat during this summer regarded him highly and even with some liking. Morgenthau always found it possible to make him laugh, and then the animal craftiness would subside, the dark gypsy face would relax, and he would talk with great frankness and intelligence. He had, Aubrey Herbert says, 'strength, hardness and an almost brutal bonhomie, and a light in his eyes rarely seen in men, but sometimes in animals at dusk'. Yet Talaat with all his sagacity and his powers of unemotional concentration seems to have felt the need of men of action like Enver.

Enver was the prodigy of the group, the terrible child who shocked and bewildered them all. He was distinguished by the kind of dark and composed good looks that never seem to age or reveal the mind beneath; and indeed, if Talaat is represented by Wallace Beery of the silent films, then Enver most certainly, for all his pertness, is Rudolph Valentino.

He was born at Adano on the Black Sea coast, the son of a Turkish father who was a bridge-keeper and an Albanian mother who followed one of the lowest occupations of the country—that of laying out the dead. It is possible that the boy's exceptional good looks descended to him from a Circassian grandmother, but his other qualities seem to have been peculiarly his own, and were in a state of remarkable balance with each other. He was extremely vain, but it was a special kind of vanity which was overlaid by an air of shyness and modesty, and his reckless bravery in action was offset by an appearance so cool, so calm and unhurried, that one might have thought him half asleep. In office he exhibited this same quiet distinction of manner, so that no disaster ever appeared to flurry him, and no decision, however important, caused him more than a few moments' hesitation. Even his ambition was disguised by a certain ease with which he moved among people who belonged to a much more cultivated society than his own. With this fluency and this charm it was no wonder that

5

he was made so much of by the hostesses of the time; here was the young *beau sabreur* in real life, an unassuming young hero. All this was a most effective cover for the innate cruelty, the shallowness and the squalor of the megalomania that lay beneath.

From the age of twenty-five or so, when he had graduated from the military staff college in Constantinople, Enver's career had been tumultuous. His speciality was the overturning of governments by physical violence, the sudden armed raid on cabinet offices. In later wars he would have made an admirable commando leader. In 1908 he was one of the small band of revolutionaries who marched on Constantinople and forced Abdul Hamid to restore the constitution, and a year later when Abdul had defaulted in his promises, Enver was back again in the capital, storming the barricades in a torn uniform, with a four days' growth of beard and a bullet wound on his cheek; and this time Enver and his friends disposed of Abdul forever.

Then in the following years, when half the countries of Eastern Europe were demolishing the carcase of the Ottoman Empire, there was no front, however remote, at which Enver did not appear, dramatically and suddenly, to lead the counter-attack. From his post of military attaché in Berlin he rushed to the Libyan desert to fight the Italians outside Benghazi. Then in 1912 he was back on the Continent again holding the Bulgars off Constantinople. Nothing dismayed him, no defeat exhausted his endless energy. At the end of the first Balkan war in 1913, when everything was lost and Constantinople itself in danger of falling, Enver was the one man who would not accept an armistice. He led a band of two hundred followers into the capital, burst in upon the peace-making cabinet at their deliberations, shot dead the Minister for War, and then, having established a new government which was more to his liking, he returned to the front again. Finally he emerged gloriously at the end of the second Balkan war leading the tattered Turkish battalions back into Adrianople.

As an administrator his methods were very similar. In the summer of 1913, when he was at the Ministry of War, he dismissed 1200 officers from the Turkish army in a single day, among them no fewer than 150 generals and colonels. In Enver's view they were politically unsound.

6

There were other leaders among the Young Turks who were probably just as able as Enver: Mahmad Shevket, who led the 1909 march on Constantinople, Djavid, the Jewish financier from Salonika, Djemal, the Minister for Marine, and several others; but none could compete with Enver's peculiar brand of political audacity. He outmanœuvred them by doing the outrageous, the impossible thing. By the summer of 1914, when he was thirty-four and looking as youthful and composed as ever, he had reached a position of great power in Constantinople. He had married a princess and was settled in a palace with a personal bodyguard and a retinue of attendants. He was Minister for War and Commander-in-Chief of the army. In cabinet and in the Committee of Union and Progress not even Talaat cared to oppose him, and it was becoming increasingly evident that he had even larger designs for his own future. Foreign ambassadors coming to call on the young minister in his office would find him sitting there in his uniform, very spruce and smiling. On the wall behind his desk there were portraits of Frederick the Great and Napoleon.

There was one name, more important than all the rest, that is missing from the list of guests at Harold Nicolson's dinner party. Indeed, it could hardly have occurred to the British Embassy to have invited Mustafa Kemal, for he was still unknown in Turkey. Yet there is a striking parallel in Kemal's and Enver's lives, and it can only have been by accident—the accident of Kemal's solitary and introverted mind—that he was not already a member of the group. The two men were of the same age; Kemal like Enver had been born in a poor family, had entered the army, had joined the revolutionary movement, and had been in all the wars. But a uniform greyness hangs over this early part of Kemal's career. He had none of Enver's flair, his quickness and spontaneity. A private rage against life seemed to possess him, and he had no talent for compromise or negotiation. Being contemptuous of other people's opinion and impatient of all authority he seems somehow to have been trapped within his own mind. He waited in a resentful claustrophobia for the opportunity that never came, and while he waited the others so easily outstripped him.

From 1909 onwards Kemal had been constantly in

Enver's shadow; he took part in the revolutionary march on the capital that year, but was in the rear planning the administration of the army while Enver was rushing over the barricades. He served under Enver in the Tripoli campaign and again in the Balkan wars. He was even present at Enver's triumph at Adrianople. At every stage the two men quarrelled, as they were inevitably bound to do; for while Kemal was a military commander of genius, Enver must surely be judged as one of the most inept and disastrous generals who ever lived. It is not evident that Enver ever learned the first principles of warfare or ever profited by the experience of any of the appalling disasters which he so confidently planned. Through all these chaotic years it was Kemal's galling fate to take orders from this man.

By 1913 Kemal had reached the low point in his career; he was an unemployed lieutenant-colonel in Constantinople, and Enver had gone far above his head. As yet there was no sign whatever of the strange reversal which was shortly to take place in their fortunes; and no one in his wildest dreams would have imagined that half a century later Kemal's name would be reverenced all over Turkey, that every child at school would know by heart the gaunt lines of his face, the grim mouth and the washed eyes, while his spectacular rival would be all but forgotten. Indeed it is even remarkable that either of them should have survived the five years that lay immediately ahead.

The Young Turks were surrounded by hatred. They were hated by the older politicians of the Abdul Hamid régime whom they had displaced. They were hated by the army officers whom Enver had expelled; and, beyond anything, they were hated and feared by the foreign minority groups in Constantinople, the Armenians, the Greeks and to some extent the Jews. Any one of these factions would have done anything, would have accepted any foreign domination in Turkey, in order to have got the Young Turks out of office.

For the moment, however, Talaat and Enver and their friends had control and they were determined to keep it by any kind of ruthlessness, by any kind of bargaining.

These then were the young men who in August 1914 were putting Turkey up to auction, and they were opposed

—perhaps abetted is an apter word—by the group of professional western diplomats who were making the bidding. Unlike the Young Turks, the men at the foreign embassies in Constantinople were not strange at all. Here everything was perfectly distinct and familiar. One knows at sight the Ambassador, the Dragoman (the political adviser), the Military Attaché, the head of Chancery, and the swarm of secretaries, just as one knows the pieces in chess and what moves they are capable of making. All is in order and the different nationalities are as easily distinguished as red is from black.

Yet in one respect at least the Ambassador of 1914 differed from his counterpart of the present time: he had more authority, much more freedom of action. It was not often that he was overshadowed by the sort of international conferences which now occur every other week, nor was his work being constantly overlooked by cabinet ministers and politicians coming out from home. His brief may have been prepared for him, but he interpreted it in his own way. It was a long journey from Western Europe to Turkey, and the approaching war had made Constantinople doubly remote. It really was possible for an ambassador by some gesture, by some decision taken on his own authority, to alter the balance of things, perhaps even to retard or to accelerate Turkey on the path to war. Then too the 'eastern-ness' of the Ottoman Empire, its differences of every kind in religion and in manners and culture, were much more exaggerated then than they are now. The Embassy became an outpost, a stronghold, the one really solid physical symbol of a nation's place in the world. It had to be large—larger if possible than the other rival embassies—and the ambassador must have the presence of an important man. He must have his flag, his servants in livery, his yacht in the Golden Horn, and his summer embassy at Therapia in addition to his more formal palace in Constantinople. All this tended to set the diplomats in Constantinople very much apart from Turkey, and no doubt they felt more at home with one another than they did with the Turks. The ambassadors and their staffs, indeed, were often to be seen together at the international club: and the attitudes which they took towards the Turks were much as one would have expected.

9

'Sir Louis Mallet, the British Ambassador,' says Morgenthau, 'was a high-minded and cultivated English gentleman: Bompard, the French Ambassador, was a singularly charming honourable Frenchman, and both were constitutionally disqualified from participating in the murderous intrigues which then comprised Turkish politics. Giers, the Russian Ambassador, was a proud and scornful diplomat of the old régime. . . . It was apparent that the three ambassadors of the Entente did not regard the Talaat and Enver régime as permanent, or as particularly worth their while to cultivate.'

There was one other man who was extremely influential in the Allied camp. This was Fitzmaurice, the Dragoman of the British Embassy. T. E. Lawrence had met Fitzmaurice in Constantinople before the war and wrote the following note about him:[1]

'The Ambassadors were Lowther[2] (an utter dud) and Louis Mallet who was pretty good and gave fair warning of the trend of feeling. I blame much of our ineffectiveness upon Fitzmaurice, the Dragoman, an eagle-mind and a personality of iron vigour. Fitzmaurice had lived half a lifetime in Turkey and was the Embassy's official go-between and native authority. He knew everything and was feared from end to end of Turkey. Unfortunately he was a rabid R.C. and hated Freemasons and Jews with a religious hatred. The Young Turk movement was fifty per cent crypto-Jew and ninety-five per cent Freemason. So he regarded it as the devil and threw the whole influence of England over to the unfashionable Sultan and his effete palace clique. Fitzm. was really rabid . . . and his prejudices completely blinded his judgment. His prestige, however, was enormous and our Ambassadors and the F.O. staff went down before him like nine-pins. Thanks to him, we rebuffed every friendly advance the Young Turks made.'

With Baron von Wangenheim, the German Ambassador, however, it was quite different. After two world wars it is becoming a little difficult to focus this powerful man, for he was the prototype of a small group of Junkers which has almost vanished now. He was a huge man, well over six

[1] Published in *T. E. Lawrence to his Biographer—Liddell Hart.*
[2] Sir Gerard Lowther, who preceded Mallet.

feet in height, with a round cannonball of a head and staring arrogant eyes, and his belief in the Kaiser was absolute. He was not a Prussian, but his character and attitudes were almost a caricature of what foreigners imagine a Prussian aristocrat to be: an utter ruthlessness, an ironclad and noisy confidence in himself and his caste, a contempt for weakness and, underneath the heavy dignity, a childish excitement with his own affairs. He spoke several languages with fluency, and was possessed of a certain gargantuan good humour. He was a man at once dangerous, accomplished and ridiculous: the animal in a tight sheath of manners.

Wangenheim stood very high in the Wilhelmstrasse. He had more than once been to stay with the Kaiser in his villa at Corfu, and he could speak for Germany with some authority. It was now his mission so to cajole, flatter and bewitch the Young Turks that they could see nothing in the political horizon but the vast technical might of the German army. Wangenheim's argument seems to have run as follows: Russia was the immemorial enemy of Turkey, and since Russia was the ally of Britain and France there was no question of their coming down on that side of the fence. Moreover, Germany was bound to win the war. The British might control the seas, but this was to be a land battle, and if there were to be a revolution in Russia—a thing that might easily happen—then France alone could never withstand the concentrated weight of the Wehrmacht. Turkey's only hope of regaining her lost provinces—of recovering Egypt and Cyprus from the British, Salonika and Crete from the Greeks, Tripoli from the Italians, of subduing Bulgaria and driving back the Serbs—was to join Germany now when she was about to show her strength.

Wangenheim's trump card was the German Military Mission. In the summer of 1913 the Young Turks had asked for this mission, and by the beginning of 1914 it had arrived in overwhelming measure. German officers, technicians and instructors began to appear at first in scores and then in hundreds. They took over control of the munitions factory in Constantinople, they manned the guns along the Bosphorus and the Dardanelles, and they reorganized the tactics and the training of the infantry. By August 1914 the Mission had already been able to produce a sample of what it could do: a regiment of Turkish soldiers, newly equipped with uniforms and rifles, went goose-stepping across a parade ground before an admiring group of the Sultan's court, the Young Turkish cabinet, and such foreign ambassadors as did not find it embarrassing to be present.

Liman von Sanders, the head of the Mission and the author of these drastic changes, was an inspired choice for the Germans to have made in sending a general to Turkey. He was a calm and steady man with all the impressive authority of an intelligent soldier who has the trained habit of command. The army was his life, and he did not look beyond it; not being distracted by politics he was genuinely absorbed in the technique of tactics and strategy. He might not have been considered brilliant, but he was not easily to be upset, and by holding fast to his excellent training he was not likely to make mistakes. Watching him at work it is not surprising that the Young Turks were more than ever convinced that if war should break out with Germany and Austro-Hungary on the one side, and Britain, France and Russia on the other, it was not Germany who would lose.

Enver certainly needed very little persuading. As a military attaché in Berlin he had been much cultivated by the German General Staff, and there was something in the awesome precision of the Prussian military machine and the ruthless *realpolitik* of the German leaders that fulfilled his need for a faith and a direction. He had learned to speak German well, and even the mannerisms of the country seemed to captivate him; by now he had begun to affect a fine black Prussian moustache with the ends turned upward, and a punctilious air of cold wrath on the parade ground. He was determined, he said, upon the Germanization of the army; there was no other way.

Talaat was not quite so sure about all this. He could see that a resuscitated Turkish army gave them a strong bargaining point against both the Germans and the Allies, but he would rather have waited a little longer before entirely committing himself. He hesitated, and while he hesitated Enver prodded him on. Finally, in that odd state of apathy and half fear which seems to have overtaken him in all his dealings with Enver, he submitted; it was secretly agreed between them that, if they were to go to war at all, it would be on the German side.

12

The other members of the cabinet were less easy to handle. At least four of them said that they did not like this growing German encroachment, and if it ended in bringing them into the war they would resign. Djemal, the Minister of Marine, was still looking to the French who had been very friendly to him on a recent visit to Paris. Djavid, the financier, could see no way out of bankruptcy through war. And behind these there were others, neither pro-German nor pro-Allied, who floated vaguely in a neutral fear.

Enver dealt with this situation in his usual fashion. In the Ministry of War he was quite strong enough to go ahead with his plans without consulting anybody, and it was soon observed that Wangenheim was calling there almost every other day. The activities of the German Mission steadily increased, and by the beginning of the summer had become so marked that the British, French and Russian ambassadors protested. Enver was quite unmoved; he blandly assured Mallet and Bompard that the Germans were there simply to train the Turkish army, and when they had done their work they would go away—a statement that became increasingly dubious as more and more technicians and experts continued to arrive by every train. Presently there were several hundreds of them in Constantinople.

It was the Russians who were chiefly concerned. Ninety per cent of Russia's grain and fifty per cent of all her exports came out through the Bosphorus and the Dardanelles, and a corresponding volume of trade came in by this route from the outside world. Once hostilities broke out there would be no other outlet, no other place where she could join hands with her allies, England and France; Archangel was frozen over in winter, Vladivostok lay at the end of 5,000 miles of tenuous railway from Moscow, and the Kaiser's fleet was bound to blockade the Baltic.

Up to this time it had suited Russia very well to have the Turks as neutral caretakers of the straits at Constantinople, but a Turkey dominated by Germany was another matter. Giers, the Russian Ambassador, felt so strongly that at one moment, apparently on instructions from Moscow, he threatened war. But he subsided. One by one they all subsided as the hot summer weeks of 1914 dragged by. A European war was unthinkable, and even if it did come

13

then Turkey was still too corrupt and weak to make much difference either way. Sir Louis Mallet went off on leave to England.

While he was away—it was the last uneasy month of peace that followed the assassination of the Archduke Ferdinand at Serajevo at the end of June—Enver and Wangenheim prepared their final plans. Enver seems to have had very little trouble with the reluctant members in cabinet; he is said to have laid his revolver on the table at the height of their argument, and to have invited the other members to continue with their protests. Talaat did nothing but watch and wait. On August 2, two days before Britain presented her ultimatum to the Germans, a secret alliance was signed between Turkey and Germany. It was directed against Russia.

This still did not commit Turkey to war, and there was still no real feeling of belligerence anywhere in the country. But now in the charged atmosphere of these last few hours of European peace there occurred one of those incidents which, though not vitally important in themselves, yet somehow contrive to express and exacerbate a situation and finally push peoples and governments to the point where, suddenly and emotionally, they make up their minds to commit all their fortunes regardless of what the consequences are going to be. This was the incident of the two warships Britain was building for Turkey.

To understand the importance of these two vessels one has to cast one's mind back to the conditions of 1914, where air-power was virtually non-existent and road and rail transport in the Balkans was limited to a few main routes. Overnight the arrival of one battleship could dominate an enemy fleet and upset the whole balance of power among minor states. With the Russian Black Sea fleet to the north of them, and Greece in the south negotiating with the United States for possession of two dreadnoughts, it had become urgently necessary for Turkey to acquire warships of her own, and of at least equal strength to those of her neighbours. The order for the two vessels was placed in England, the keels were laid down, and something of a patriotic demonstration was made out of the whole affair.

In every Turkish town people were asked to contribute to the cost of this new venture. Collection boxes were put up on the bridges across the Golden Horn, special drives were made among the village communities, and no doubt in the end there was a warm feeling among the public that this was its own spontaneous contribution to the revival of the Turkish Navy. By August 1914 one of the ships was completed at Armstrong's on the Tyne, and the other was ready for delivery within a few weeks.

At this point—to be precise on August 3, the eve of the outbreak of war—Winston Churchill, the First Lord of the Admiralty, announced to the Turks that he could not make delivery; in the interests of national security the two ships had been requisitioned by the British Navy.

One does not need much imagination to understand the indignation and disappointment with which this news was received in Turkey: the money had been paid, the two ships had been given Turkish names, and Turkish crews were actually in England waiting to man them and bring them home. And now suddenly nothing. Rarely before had von Wangenheim been allowed such an opportunity. He lost no time in repeating to Enver and Talaat the warning he had been giving them all along—the British were not to be trusted—and he came out with a dramatic offer: Germany would make good Turkey's loss. Two German warships would be dispatched to Constantinople at once.

The ensuing adventures of the *Goeben* can be told very briefly. Possibly by accident but much more probably by design she was in the Western Mediterranean with her attendant light cruiser, the *Breslau*, on this vital day. She was a battle-cruiser recently built in Germany with a displacement of 22,640 tons, ten 11-inch guns and a speed of 26 knots. As such she could dominate the Russian Black Sea fleet and, what was more important at the moment, she could outdistance (though not out-gun) any British vessel in the Mediterranean.

The British knew all about the *Goeben*. They had been watching her for some time, for they feared that on the outbreak of war she would attack the French army transports coming across from North Africa to the continent. On August 4 the British commander-in-chief in the Mediterranean signalled the Admiralty in London: '*Indomitable, Indefatigable,* shadowing *Goeben* and *Breslau* 37° 44' North 7° 56' East', and the Admiralty replied, 'Very good. Hold her. War is imminent.' Throughout that afternoon the two British battleships continued closely in the *Goeben's* wake.

15

At any moment they could have knocked her out with their 12-inch guns, but the British ultimatum to Germany did not expire until midnight, and the cabinet in London had expressly forbidden any act of war until that time. It was an unbearably tantalizing situation. Churchill has related that at five o'clock in the evening Prince Louis of Battenburg, the First Sea Lord, observed to him at the Admiralty that there was still time to sink the *Goeben* before dark. But there was nothing to be done but to wait.

As night fell the *Goeben* increased speed above 24 knots and vanished. It was not until two days later, when the war had already begun, that the British discovered that she was coaling with the *Breslau* at Messina, in Italy, and they still did not know that Admiral Souchon, who was in command of the vessel, had there received a message instructing him to proceed directly to Constantinople. At 5 p.m. on August 6 the *Goeben* and the *Breslau* emerged from Messina with their bands playing and their decks cleared for action. Still under the impression that they would either turn west to attack the French transports or north to the friendly port of Pola, the British fleet had disposed itself to the west of Sicily and at the mouth of the Adriatic. The *Goeben* and the *Breslau* turned south-east, and when the British light cruisers of the Adriatic squadron failed to engage they got clean away. Two days later, still undetected, they were hanging about the Greek islands waiting for permission from the Turks to enter the Dardanelles.

The excitement in Constantinople was now intense. To allow the German vessels to pass through the straits was virtually an act of war. But Wangenheim was ready with a solution: once the ships arrived in Turkish waters they would cease to be German and instead become part of the neutral Turkish Navy. But would they arrive? That was the point. On August 8 there was still no news of the two vessels in Constantinople, and it seemed possible that they had been sunk by the British Fleet.

Curiously it was Enver who lost his nerve, and he attempted to restore the situation by performing a simple double-cross. He sent for the Russian Military Attaché and proposed to him the terms of a Russian-Turkish alliance which would have cancelled out the agreement with Wangenheim which had been signed only a week before. Indeed, under one clause, Liman von Sanders and all German officers were to be dismissed from the Turkish service.

The Germans were quite unaware of this duplicity when on the following day one of the officers on Liman's staff arrived at the Ministry of War with the news that the *Goeben* and the *Breslau* were outside the Dardanelles and waiting to enter. Enver said he must consult his colleagues. The German officer, however, insisted that an answer must be given at once. There was a slight pause. Then Enver said, 'Let them come in.' The following evening the *Goeben* and the *Breslau* steamed through the Dardanelles and the proposed alliance with Russia was forgotten.

But it was not the end. Germany still had no wish to bring Turkey actively into the war, since, as a friendly neutral, she was performing a very useful purpose in tying up a British squadron at the mouth of the Dardanelles, and in threatening the British lines in Egypt. Moreover, if, as everyone expected, the war was going to be over in a few months there was no point in contracting additional obligations to Turkey.

For the Russians, the British and the French, on the other hand, the situation was becoming intolerable. Here was the *Goeben* anchored in the Bosphorus, here was Admiral Souchon and his crew going through the farce of dressing-up in fezzes and pretending that they were sailors in the Turkish Navy, and here was Liman von Sanders with his Military Mission re-organizing the Turkish Army. At night the cafés in Pera and Stamboul were filled with roistering Germans; staff cars embellished with the Kaiser's eagles drove ostentatiously through the streets, and Enver's Ministry of War became every day more like a German military headquarters. A rueful pun went round the foreign colony: '*Deutschland über Allah*'.

Sir Louis Mallet protested repeatedly about the *Goeben* but he was assured that she was now a Turkish ship. Then, he argued, the German crews should be dismissed. But they were no longer Germans, Enver told him, they were part of the Turkish Navy; and in any case Turkey was short of sailors. Her best men had been sent to England to man the two British-built battleships which were never delivered. Nothing could be done until these men returned. The Turkish crews returned, but still nothing was done, beyond putting a handful of them on board the *Goeben*; the German crew remained.

The Allies were now thoroughly alarmed, for they desired even more than the Germans, that the Turks should remain neutral. For a time Mallet and his Russian and French colleagues kept pointing out to Enver and the war party that Turkey had been exhausted by the Balkan Wars and that she would be ruined if she took up arms again so soon. Then towards the end of August they adopted a much stronger line: they proposed in return for Turkish neutrality that Britain, France and Russia should guarantee the Ottoman Empire from attack.

This was a momentous proposal, and had it been put forward before the war it must have been decisive. But now an entirely new factor entered the scene: on September 5, 1914, the Battle of the Marne had been fought in France, and with every succeeding week it became more and more apparent that the first German onrush across France had been stopped. In the east as well the Russians were making headway against the Austrian forces. It was no longer so evident that this was to be a short war ending in a German victory; Germany was beginning to need allies. She now wanted Turkey in the war.

One of the earliest indications of this changed attitude was in the treatment of the British Naval Mission. This Mission, under the command of Admiral Limpus, had for some years past undertaken the training of the Turkish Navy. With the arrival of the *Goeben* its position had become at first embarrassing and then insupportable. Early in September it was clearly impossible for Admiral Limpus to go on. On the 9th the Mission was withdrawn, and the Germans now controlled the Turkish Navy as well as the Army. Then on September 26 something much more serious happened. A Turkish torpedo-boat was stopped at the mouth of the Dardanelles by the British squadron lurking there, and when it was found that there were German soldiers on board the vessel was ordered to go back to Turkey. On hearing this news a certain Weber Pasha, the German soldier commanding the fortifications, took it on himself to close the Dardanelles. New mines were laid across the channel, lighthouses were extinguished, and notices were put up on the cliffs warning all vessels that the passage was blocked. This was by some way the boldest thing that the Germans had attempted yet, for the free passage of the Dardanelles was governed by an international convention which affected both belligerents and neutrals alike, and any interference with international shipping there was an act of war.

The Turks themselves received no warning that this step was to be taken by the Germans, and there was an agitated meeting of the cabinet in Constantinople on September 27. But by now Enver and Talaat had delivered the country into German hands. The other members of the government might protest and threaten to resign, but there was nothing they could do to alter the situation. Russia's lifeline was cut. For some weeks merchantmen from the Black Sea ports filled with Russian grain and other exports piled up in the Golden Horn until there were hundreds of them there, and a motor boat crossing the harbour could hardly find a way between them. When at last it was evident that the blockage was permanent the ships one by one sailed back to the Black Sea, never to return.

One can judge the importance of this day from the fact that the great maritime trade of the Dardanelles has never again been revived. When the straits were reopened in 1918 the revolution had already taken place in Russia, and in the years since then the Soviet Empire has effectively cut itself off from the seaborne trade of the West. The consulates of all the great powers which used to line the foreshore at Chanak with their fluttering flags have been closed, and nothing now passes except the local caiques, a thin stream of ocean traffic on the Constantinople run, and, just occasionally, some solitary communist vessel that goes by with a silent and rather fated air, as though it were a visitor from some other planet.

The last few weeks of peace in Turkey ran out very quickly. More and more German technicians arrived, and all night long a constant clanging sounded from the naval yard where the old Turkish ships were being fitted out for war. Most of the German naval officers were quartered in the *General*, a depot ship tied up near the Galata Bridge in the Golden Horn, and it was common knowledge that in the nightly drinking parties there these officers boasted that if Turkey did not soon move then the Germans themselves would take a hand. Admiral Souchon was constantly sending the *Goeben* into the Black Sea on manœuvres. Once, being moved by a sense of humour which is a little difficult to gauge at this distance, he brought his ship to a standstill

19

before the Russian Embassy on the Bosphorus. The sailors appeared on deck in their German uniforms and treated the enemy ambassador to a concert of German national songs. Then, putting on their fezzes, they sailed away again.

The end came in the last days of October. On the 29th the *Goeben,* the *Breslau* and a Turkish squadron which was manned in part by German sailors steamed through the Black Sea, and on this and the following day they opened fire without warning on Odessa harbour, on the Russian fortress at Sevastopol and on Novorossiisk, sinking all shipping they could reach and setting the oil tanks on fire. Djemal, the Turkish Minister for Marine, was playing cards at his club in Constantinople at the time, and when the news was brought to him he declared that he had not ordered the raid and that he knew nothing about it. Whether this be true or not, it seems hardly likely that Enver and Talaat were not informed. Moreover, at that same moment a Turkish column at Gaza, in the Palestinian desert, was about to set out on a major raid on the Suez Canal.

On October 30 the Russian, British and French ambassadors at Constantinople delivered a twelve-hour ultimatum to the Turkish government, and when it was unanswered, asked for their passports. Hostilities began on the following day.

Mustafa Kemal had no part in these events. He had, in the previous year, chosen to send a strong letter to Enver inveighing against Liman von Sanders and the German Mission. Turkey, Kemal argued, needed no help from foreigners of any kind; only the Turks themselves could find their own salvation.

Enver could afford to be lenient, for it was inconceivable that Kemal could ever become a rival. He posted him off as military attaché to the Turkish Embassy at Sofia.

There is a lurid legend of how Kemal employed his time in this semi-banishment. He is said to have made a gauche attempt to learn dancing, and to enter the social life of the Bulgarian capital; then, when he failed dismally in this enterprise, he is reputed to have reverted to debauchery. There may be some truth in the story. Yet he acted very promptly when he heard that his country had gone to war: he wired from Sofia for permission to return to active service. He had no answer for a time—an anti-German man was not wanted in the new Turkish Army—and was on the point of deserting his post and of making his way back to Turkey when orders came through for him from Constantinople. He was posted to Rodosto, at the head of the Gallipoli peninsula. It was an event which, passing quite unnoticed at the time, was to change the whole course of the campaign that lay ahead.

TWO

~~~~~~

'The whole hog. Totus Porcus.'—ADMIRAL
FISHER

BY their daring—perhaps even because they had to dare in
order to keep in office—the Young Turks had got their
country into a war which was much too big for them.
They were small gamblers in a game of very high stakes,
and, as it usually happens in such cases, their presence was
hardly noticed by the other players for a while. They
watched, they waited, they made their anxious little bids,
they tried desperately to understand which way the luck
was going, and they put on an air of being quite at ease
which was very far from being the case.

October, November and December went by and their
small army had still not been risked, nor had they cared
to expose their borrowed warships in any way. Two expe-
ditions had set out: one to the east headed by Enver himself, and the other to the south commanded by Djemal, the
Minister of Marine; and their objectives were nothing less
than the conquest of the Caucasus from the Russians and
the ejection of the British from Egypt. But as yet nothing
had been heard of either of these two enterprises, and a
certain cynicism was beginning to develop in the other
Balkan states which had not dared to risk their fortunes
in the war. Nothing would have given greater pleasure in
Greece, Bulgaria and Rumania than the humiliation of the
Turks in some major battle, and they waited hopefully for
the Allies to move.

There were one or two skirmishes at sea. A squadron of

British and French warships was patrolling the Ægean in the hope that the *Goeben* would emerge, and in November the ships opened up their guns on the forts of Sedd-el-Bahr and Kum Kale on either side of the entrance to the Dardanelles. It was all over in twenty minutes, and there was no reply from the Turks. Then on Sunday, December 13, Lieutenant Norman Holbrook penetrated through to the Narrows in the submarine B 11. Entering the straits as soon as the Turkish searchlights were extinguished at dawn, he found his way through the minefields and after four hours hoisted his periscope. He saw a large two-funnelled vessel, the Turkish battleship *Messudieh,* at anchor in Sari Sigla Bay, and fired his torpedoes at her from 600 yards away. Waiting just long enough to see that his target was destroyed, Holbrook dived steeply and bumped along the bottom until he reached deep water and the open sea. He was awarded the Victoria Cross.

But these actions were nothing more than local raids, and no attempt was made to follow them up. In London, it is true, there was a general feeling that something ought to be done about Turkey, and the question was revived from time to time. Even before hostilities began Lord Kitchener, the Secretary of State for War, and Winston Churchill, the First Lord of the Admiralty, had discussed whether they might not persuade the Greeks to land an army on the Gallipoli peninsula. Once the Turkish garrison there had been defeated the fleet would sail through the straits, sink the *Goeben,* and then turn its guns on Constantinople. It was an intriguing project, and the Greeks on being sounded out were at first quite eager; they were to be given the island of Cyprus as a reward. Later, however, they changed their minds, and the British too soon cooled.

The vast killing match in France overwhelmed them all. By the end of November, barely three months after the fighting began, the Allies had suffered nearly a million casualties, a fantastic figure never to be eclipsed in so short a period throughout the entire war. It was so terrible that it seemed that it must soon produce some result; somehow, if only sufficient men were got to the front, if they charged just once more against the machine-gun bullets and the barbed wire, they were bound to get through.

To kill Germans—that was the thing; to go on killing them until there were no more left, and then to advance into Germany itself.

At the end of December Lieut.-Colonel Hankey, the Secretary of the War Council, produced a paper in which he pointed out that the Allies were not in fact advancing, nor were they killing Germans at a greater rate than they were being killed themselves. The trenches were now dug for 350 miles from the North Sea to the Swiss Alps, and Hankey suggested that it was time to consider whether this impasse might not be broken by making some broad flanking movement around the line—perhaps through Turkey and the Balkans.

These ideas had been canvassed already in a general way by Churchill, Lloyd George and others, and Lord Fisher, the First Sea Lord, had a scheme for breaking into the Baltic and landing a Russian army on Germany's northern coast. But there was determined opposition from the French and British generals in France—the killing-Germans school of thought; in their view not a man could be spared from the vital theatre in the west. They argued that to divide the allied forces, to set off on some experimental expedition in the east, would endanger the safety of their whole position in France and expose England to the risk of invasion.

Kitchener at first supported these views, but then in the last days of the year a message arrived from Sir George Buchanan, the British Ambassador in Petrograd, saying that the Russians were in difficulties. The Grand Duke Nicholas, the commander-in-chief of the Russian armies, had asked, Sir George said, 'if it would be possible for Lord Kitchener to arrange for a demonstration of some kind against the Turks elsewhere, either naval or military, and to so spread reports as to cause Turks, who he says are very liable to go off at a tangent, to withdraw some of the forces now acting against the Russians in the Caucasus, and thus ease the position of the Russians.'

This was a matter that could not be ignored. After the tremendous blows of Tannenberg and the Masurian Lakes the Russian armies were beginning to falter everywhere along the line. They were reported to have suffered over a million casualties, and their supplies of rifles and ammunition were giving out. A new German offensive in the spring might prove disastrous.

Kitchener came across to the Admiralty to discuss the message with Churchill, and the following day, January 2, 1915, in a letter to Churchill, he said: 'The only place that a demonstration might have some effect in stopping reinforcements going east would be the Dardanelles. Particularly if, as the Grand Duke says, reports could be spread at the same time that Constantinople was being threatened.'

And the following telegram was sent off to Petrograd:

'Please assure the Grand Duke that steps will be taken to make a demonstration against the Turks. It is, however, feared that any action we can devise and carry out will be unlikely to seriously affect numbers of enemy in the Caucasus, or cause their withdrawal.'

Gloomy as this message was, it committed the British to action, and at the Admiralty both Churchill and Fisher got down to the question of just what action it should be. Fisher was all for taking up Hankey's plan at once. 'I CONSIDER THE ATTACK ON TURKEY HOLDS THE FIELD!' he wrote (in capital letters), 'BUT ONLY IF IT'S IMMEDIATE!' and he went on to define exactly what should be done. All the Indians and 75,000 of the British troops in France were to be embarked at Marseilles and landed, together with the Egyptian garrison, on the Asiatic side of the Dardanelles; the Greeks were to attack the Gallipoli peninsula, and the Bulgarians to march to Constantinople. At the same time a squadron of old British battleships of the *Majestic* and *Canopus* class were to force the Dardanelles.

This was all very well in its way, but Kitchener had said emphatically in the course of the discussion that he could not spare a man for any new expedition, and there was certainly no question of taking troops from France; if there was to be any demonstration at all it would have to be a naval affair. Churchill was particularly struck by Fisher's reference to the forcing of the straits with old battleships. It was an exploit which had captivated British naval strategists for at least a century, and in fact it had once been done, and in very similar circumstances to those that now prevailed. In 1807 when Napoleon was advancing to the east, the Russians had asked for assistance against Turkey, and the British sent a naval squadron to the Dardanelles. Sir John Moore, who was second-in-command of the British garrison in Sicily, urged that troops should accompany the expedition, but was told that there were none to spare (which was not, in fact, true). 'It would have been well,' Sir John wrote after the ships had sailed, 'to have sent 7,000 or 8,000 men with the fleet to Constantinople, which would have secured their passage through the Dardanelles and enabled the admiral to have destroyed the Turkish fleet and arsenal, which, from the want of such a force, he may not be able to effect.' The expedition, however, opened very well. Admiral Duckworth with seven ships of the line ran the gauntlet of the Turkish batteries along the straits, destroyed a Turkish squadron and was within eight miles of Constantinople when the wind failed. He waited for a week, unable to bring his guns to bear on the city, and then decided to retire. The return journey proved more difficult. He lost no ship but the Turkish guns at the Narrows inflicted 150 casualties among his sailors.

Since then the problem had been studied anew on several occasions and in the light of steam navigation. Fisher himself had twice considered making the attempt in the first years of the twentieth century, but had decided that it was 'mightily hazardous'. There were now, however, good arguments for taking up the matter again. The battleships of the *Majestic* and *Canopus* class were all due for scrap within the next fifteen months. Already they were so out of date they could not be used in the first line of battle against the German fleet, but they were perfectly adequate to deal with the Turkish batteries at the Dardanelles. The Germans in their recent advances across Belgium had given a striking demonstration of what modern guns could do against old forts—and the Turkish forts were very old indeed. The British had had their naval mission in Turkey for years, and they knew all about them, gun by gun. It was also known that there was barely a division of Turkish soldiers on the Gallipoli peninsula. These were widely scattered and very badly equipped; and presumably they were still subject to the inertia and the confusion of command which had lost Turkey all her battles in the past five years.

As for Fisher's other proposal—the bringing in of Greek and Bulgarian soldiers to attack Turkey—there was a good deal to be said for it. Once the fleet was in the Sea of Marmara it was quite likely that Greece and Bulgaria would abandon their neutrality in the hope of gaining still more territory from the Turks. Italy and Rumania too would be greatly influenced, and thus you might end with a grand alliance of the Balkan Christian states against Turkey. But it was the aid that would be brought to Russia that was the really vital thing. Directly the Dardanelles was forced and Constantinople taken, arms and ammunition could be sent to her across the Black Sea, and the 350,000 tons of shipping which had been bottled up would be released.

Russia's grain would once more become available to feed the Allies in the west.

With these ideas in mind Churchill sent off the following message to Vice-Admiral Sackville Carden, who was commanding the squadron outside the Dardanelles:

'Do you consider the forcing of the Dardanelles by ships alone a practical operation?

'It is assumed older battleships fitted with mine-bumpers would be used, preceded by colliers or other merchant craft as mine-bumpers and sweepers.

'Importance of results would justify severe loss.

'Let me know your views.'

Both Fisher and Sir Henry Jackson (who was attached to the Admiralty staff as an adviser on the Turkish theatre), saw this telegram before it went, and approved it. On January 5 Carden's answer arrived: 'With reference to your telegram of 3rd instant, I do not consider Dardanelles can be rushed. They might be forced by extended operations with large number of ships.'

Up to this point nobody, either in the Admiralty or at the War Office, had reached any definite conclusions or made any plan as to what was to be done. But here for the first time was something positive: the Admiral on the spot believed that he might get through the straits, and by a method that had not been broached before: that of a slow progress instead of a rush, a calculated shelling of the forts one by one. Having consulted Sir Henry Jackson and his Chief-of-Staff, Admiral Oliver (but not Fisher), Churchill telegraphed again to Carden:

'Your view is agreed with by high authorities here. Please telegraph in detail what you think could be done by extended operations, what force would be needed, and how you consider it should be used.'

Admiral Carden's plan arrived in London on January 11 and it envisaged the employment of a very large force: 12 battleships, 3 battle-cruisers, 3 light cruisers, 1 flotilla leader, 16 destroyers, 6 submarines, 4 seaplanes, 12 mine-sweepers and a score of other miscellaneous craft. He proposed in the first place to take on the forts at long range and by indirect fire and then, with his minesweepers in the van, to sail directly into the range of the Turkish guns and demolish them *seriatim* as he went along. Meanwhile a diversionary bombardment would be carried out on the Bulair Lines at the base of the Gallipoli Peninsula and on

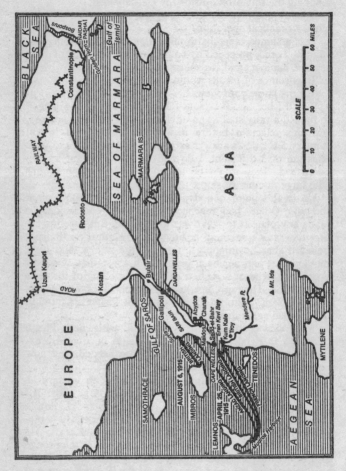

The Gallipoli landings of April 25th and August 6th

Gaba Tepe on the western coast. He would require much ammunition, he said, and once he had emerged into the Sea of Marmara he proposed to keep open the straits in his wake by patrolling them with a part of his force. He added,

'Time required for operations depends greatly on morale of enemy under bombardment; garrison largely stiffened by the Germans; also on weather conditions. Gales now frequent. Might do it all in a month about.'

This plan was discussed and approved in detail at the Admiralty and one very important addition was made to it. The *Queen Elizabeth,* the first of five new battleships and one of the most powerful vessels afloat, was about to set off for the safe waters of the Mediterranean for her calibration exercises. It was now decided that, if the plan went through, she should proceed to the Dardanelles and calibrate her 15-inch guns on the Turks—a thing she could very easily do without ever coming into the range of the hostile batteries on shore.

The vital meeting of the War Council took place on January 13. Churchill had now become an ardent enthusiast for the plan, and with the aid of a map he explained it to the other members. He argued, Lloyd George says, 'with all the inexorable force and pertinacity, together with the mastery of detail he always commands when he is really interested in a subject'.

There appears to have been very little discussion. Lord Fisher and Admiral of the Fleet Sir Arthur Wilson had come to the meeting but did not speak. 'Lord Kitchener,' it is recorded in the Council's Minutes, 'thought the plan worth trying. We could leave off the bombardment if it did not prove effective.' And finally the decision was made without a dissenting voice: 'That the Admiralty should prepare for a naval expedition in February to bombard and take the Gallipoli Peninsula with Constantinople as its objective.'

In the years that followed great play was made over the wording of this resolution. 'It is impossible,' the Dardanelles Commissioners wrote in their report in 1917, 'to read all the evidence, or to study the voluminous papers which have been submitted to us, without being struck by the atmosphere of vagueness and want of precision which seems to have characterized the proceedings of the War Council.' How, it was asked, can a fleet 'take' a peninsula?

And how could it have Constantinople as its objective? If this meant—as it apparently did mean—that the Fleet should capture and occupy the city, then it was absurd.

Yet in point of fact this is precisely what everyone at the War Council did hope; and it may not have been altogether absurd. Turkey's position was very weak. Twice within the last five years Constantinople had been thrown into chaos by political revolution. It had the reputation of being an hysterical place, and it was known to be divided against itself. For the moment Enver and the Young Turks might have control, but anything could happen with the appearance of an Allied fleet in the Golden Horn. One had to consider the condition of the crowded streets with their tumbledown wooden houses once the guns had begun to fire—or even at the threat of the guns firing. On past occasions the mob had run loose under far less provocation than this, and Turkish governments had been known to bolt very easily. There existed only two munition factories in Turkey, and both these were on the shore, where they could have been quickly destroyed by naval gunfire along with such military objectives as the naval dockyards, the Galata bridges and the Ministry of War. Constantinople was the centre of all Turkish affairs, economic, political and industrial as well as military. There was no other city in the country to replace it, no network of roads and railways which would have enabled the Army and the government to have rapidly regrouped in another place. The fall of Constantinople was in effect the fall of the state, even though resistance might have been maintained indefinitely in the mountains. If the arrival of one battle-cruiser, the *Goeben*, had been enough to bring Turkey into the war then surely it was not altogether too much to hope that the arrival of half a dozen such ships would get her out of it.

These then were the arguments which Churchill used among his colleagues, and up to the middle of January there appears to have been no dispute. Kitchener was satisfied because none of his soldiers, except a few who were to be employed as landing parties, were to be engaged. Grey, the Foreign Secretary, saw great political prospects. Arthur Balfour said it was difficult to imagine a more useful operation. The Russians on hearing of the plan spoke of the possibility of sending troops to support it, and the French offered four battleships with their auxiliaries to serve under Carden's command.

Towards the end of the month the enterprise was fairly under way; the ammunition was assembled, the final instructions drafted, and from as far away as the China station ships were under orders to proceed to the Mediterranean. It was arranged that the whole armada should gather in the Ægean Sea in the neighbourhood of the island of Lemnos at the end of the first week in February. All that was needed was the final approval of the War Council, and the action would begin.

It was at this point that a new and wholly unexpected factor came into the scene: Fisher turned against the whole design. His motives for doing this were so unusual that one can only hope to understand them—and the famous quarrel that followed—by recalling the strange position into which they had all drifted at this time. It is as strange in some ways as any of the inner manœuvrings of the Russian Government at the present day.

On the outbreak of war a War Council had been formed, and it consisted of the Prime Minister (Asquith), the Lord Chancellor (Lord Haldane), the Secretary of State for War (Lord Kitchener), the Chancellor of the Exchequer (Lloyd George), the Foreign Minister (Sir Edward Grey), the Secretary of State for India (Lord Crewe) and the First Lord of the Admiralty (Winston Churchill). Fisher and Sir James Wolfe Murray, the Chief of the Imperial General Staff, also attended the meetings to give their technical advice, Lieut.-Colonel Hankey was the secretary, and there were others who were called in from time to time. Ostensibly this body as a whole was responsible for the higher conduct of the war. In fact, it was dominated by three men —Asquith, Churchill and Kitchener—and of these three Kitchener was incomparably the most powerful. Churchill himself summed up the position when he came to give evidence to the Dardanelles Commission in 1916:

'Lord Kitchener's personal qualities and position,' he said, 'played at this time a very great part in the decision of events. His prestige and authority were immense. He was the sole mouthpiece of War Office opinion in the War Council. Everyone had the greatest admiration for his character, and everyone felt fortified, amid the terrible and incalculable events of the opening months of the war, by his commanding presence. When he gave a decision it was invariably accepted as final. He was never, to my belief, overruled by the War Council or the cabinet, in any military matter, great or small. No single unit was ever sent or withheld contrary, not merely to his agreement, but to his advice. Scarcely anyone ever ventured to argue with him in Council. Respect for the man, sympathy for him in his immense labours, confidence in his professional judgment, and the belief that he had plans deeper and wider than any we could see, silenced misgivings and disputes, whether in the Council or at the War Office. All-powerful, imperturbable, reserved, he dominated absolutely our counsels at this time.'

Twenty-five years were to elapse before such a figure, in Winston Churchill himself, was to reappear in England; and it is even doubtful if Churchill in the nineteen-forties enjoyed quite the same prestige, the air of almost infallible right and might, which Kitchener possessed during these winter months in 1915 when the country had still not recovered from the first shock of the war. Kitchener was not only thought to be as resolute as Churchill later became in the Battle of Britain; he really knew, people felt, precisely how he was going to win the war. The famous poster of the Field Marshal with the pointing finger and the legend 'Your country needs YOU' was, possibly, the most effective recruiting propaganda ever devised. All over the country, on the hoardings and the railway stations, in the shops and the buses, the commanding eyes never left one's face, and the pointing finger followed everywhere. This was Big Brother, protective and all-wise, the face of Mars himself, but there was no evil in him, only strength and the stern sense of duty.

Inside Whitehall, at close range, the effects were just as remarkable. Asquith, the most urbane of men, came under the influence, and Churchill, an extremely youthful First Lord of forty, was in no position to challenge the colossus, even if he had wanted to. Certainly at this stage Lloyd George had not begun to murmur that Kitchener's handling of affairs was less than perfect.

The point was of course that while the others were civilians, and unused to taking decisions in the awful physical presence of war, Kitchener, the professional soldier, was presumably in his very element. He knew the mysteries of war and they did not. Inside the War Office his power was absolute, for by now the ablest generals and the best of the regular soldiers had been sent to France, and the General Staff had been virtually disbanded. Under the new system there was the Minister who decided everything, and a group of secretaries who supplied him with information and saw to it that his orders were carried out. There was no discussion, no pooling of brains and experience to make a plan, and more often than not his subordinates did not have the vaguest idea of what was passing through his mind until he announced his decisions. Then the scurry began to catch up with the Minister's mind, to arrange the details which were necessary for his broad designs. Sir James Wolfe Murray, the general who had recently and hastily been put into the position of Chief of the General Staff, was in no different case from the others; although he attended the meetings of the War Council he did not speak, and indeed he often heard there from Kitchener's lips the first news of some new military plan that was to be carried out.

This system was all the more complicated by the fact that Kitchener had an oddly feminine way of thinking. Most of his big decisions appeared to be based upon a kind of flair, a queer mixture of technical experience and instinctive divination; in other words, the calculated hunch. When all the world was saying that the war would be over in six months he would suddenly come out with the announcement that they must prepare for three years at least. These oracles, which were often proved right, and if wrong became confused and forgotten in other events, added immensely to his reputation.

Fisher's position was entirely different. He was not a minister and he had no power to decide on policy. Yet to the public and even inside Whitehall he was something more than the First Sea Lord: he was the expression of the Navy itself. With his curiously gnarled face, which gave him almost an oriental appearance, his irreverence and drive, his tremendous knowledge of the Navy, he answered every requirement in the conception of what a great British sailor ought to be. In the past the Admiral's pugnacity had caused serious disputes inside the Navy, but all that was done with now. He was as solid and tried as one of his own dreadnoughts, and if his authority was not as great as Kitchener's he had one thing the Field Marshal lacked, a shrewd, fresh, humorous mind that enabled him to come to the heart of a problem in language that everyone could enjoy and understand. Kitchener was respected, but Fisher one really liked.

It was Churchill who brought Fisher back from his retirement to the Admiralty at the age of seventy-four, shortly before the war began, and an intimate relationship had grown up between the old Admiral and the young Minister. Together they were a formidable team. A new wind blew through the Navy. Fisher had but to produce a plan and Churchill promptly put it through the cabinet and the House of Commons for him. In this way together they had got Jellicoe the command of the Grand Fleet, they had secured the Navy's supply of oil by inducing the government to finance the Persian wells, and they had embarked on a ship-building programme which made Britain the strongest maritime power in the world.

Churchill liked to work late at night, Fisher in the early morning. Thus there was a continuous control at the Admiralty; a stream of minutes, notes and letters passed between the two, and no move of any consequence was made by one man without the other having given his agreement. Fisher, coming to work at four or five in the morning, would find the fruits of Churchill's labour of the previous night on his desk; and Churchill, arriving at his office later in the day, was sure to have a letter waiting for him with the famous green F scrawled on the bottom.

They quarrelled at times—as when Fisher in an outburst of rage against the Zeppelin raids wanted to take reprisals among the Germans interned in England—but these commotions were soon over, and at the beginning of 1915 Fisher was still ending his letters to his friend, 'Yours to a cinder', 'Yours till hell freezes over'.

One wonders, naturally, how far Churchill's very forceful personality may have pushed Fisher and the other admirals beyond the point where they themselves really wanted to go. In the Navy especially men were trained since boyhood to believe in the established system and to obey orders; one did not argue, the senior officer knew best. Discipline and loyalty—those were the two imperative things. Fisher and his brother admirals considered it their duty never to express any open disagreement with their Minister in a cabinet or War Council meeting. No matter whether they agreed with him or not they sat silent: and this silence was accepted as assent. Inside the Admiralty the admirals were of course free to state their views, but it may not always have been easy to do this. Churchill was young while they were older, he made the pace hot and the very brilliance and energy of his mind may not have encouraged his colleagues to express those half-formed ideas, those vague inconsequential questionings which sometimes contain the beginnings of an understanding of the real truth, the truth that is not always revealed by logic.

This, at any rate, is the real core of the mistrust of Churchill over the Dardanelles—that he bamboozled the admirals—and no matter how much he proves that he was right and they were wrong there will always be an instinctive feeling among some people that somehow or other he upset the established practices of the Navy at this time, and not in the Nelson manner, but as a politician. It is the old story of the conflict between the experimenter and the civil servant, the man of action and the administrator, the ancient dilemma of the crisis where, for the moment, the trained expert is dumbfounded and only the determined amateur seems to know the way ahead.

Churchill himself, in *The World Crisis,* makes it clear that he was perfectly well aware of this issue. He says, 'The popular view inculcated in thousands of newspaper articles and recorded in many so-called histories is simple. Mr. Churchill, having seen the German heavy howitzers smash the Antwerp forts, being ignorant of the distinction between a howitzer and a gun, and overlooking the difference between firing ashore and afloat, thought that the naval guns would simply smash the Dardanelles forts. Although the highly competent Admiralty experts pointed out these obvious facts, this politician so bewitched them that they were reduced to supine or servile acquiescence in a scheme which they knew was based upon a series of monstrous technical fallacies.

'These broad effects,' he adds pleasantly, 'are however capable of refinement.'

Refine them he does, and with devastating force. Yet still, against all logic, the doubt remains: somewhere, one feels, there was a break in the flow of ideas between the young Minister and the sailors.

Up to the middle of January the admirals certainly had nothing to complain of. They had been consulted about the Dardanelles plan at every step of the way. They never liked the idea of going ahead without the backing of the Army, yet they gave their consent. But now, all at once, after the January 13 meeting, Fisher is beset with the deep empirical misgivings of old age. He cannot explain precisely what it is that causes this change of mind, but he is not Kitchener,

35

he cannot just bluntly say, 'No, I have decided not to go ahead with the matter'; he must give reasons. Moreover, he must give them to Churchill whom he likes and with whom he is on terms of almost emotional intimacy and to whom he must be loyal. There can be no half-measures between them: they must go into the thing wholeheartedly together or they must part.

And so, within the narrow room of his own conscience, caught as he is between his respect and friendship for Churchill and his loyalty to his own ideas, the old Admiral suffers a considerable strain. He chops and changes. He tries to fix his vague forebodings about the Dardanelles adventure on some logical argument, on any convenient pretext which will establish his general sense of danger and uneasiness. And Churchill, naturally, has no difficulty in proving him wrong.

The argument began over the strength of the Grand Fleet in the North Sea. Fisher's point was that it was being so seriously weakened by the demands of the Dardanelles that it was losing its superiority over the German Fleet, and might find itself exposed to an attack under disadvantageous conditions. Churchill was able to reply that, far from this being the case, the Grand Fleet had been so strengthened since the outbreak of the war that its superiority over the Germans had been actually increased; and this would continue to be so after all the requirements of the Dardanelles had been met.

Fisher still persisted; he suggested that a flotilla of destroyers should be brought back from the Dardanelles, a move which in Churchill's opinion would have crippled the venture at the outset. Then there was the question of the Zeebrugge Canal. For some time past there had been under discussion a plan for the Navy to sail in and block the canal to German shipping. Fisher began to express his doubts about this operation as well. He was indeed, he now revealed, against aggressive action of any kind, until the German Fleet had been defeated.

Matters came to a head on January 25, when Fisher put down his views in writing and sent them to Churchill with this note: 'First Lord: I have no desire to continue a useless resistance in the War Council to plans I cannot concur in, but I would ask that the enclosed may be printed and circulated to members before the next meeting. F.'

The document expressed complete opposition to the

whole Dardanelles scheme. In it Fisher wrote, 'We play into Germany's hands if we risk fighting ships in any subsidiary operations such as coastal bombardments or the attack of fortified places without military co-operation, for we thereby increase the possibility that the Germans may be able to engage our Fleet with some approach to equality of strength. The sole justification of coastal bombardments and attacks by the Fleet on fortified places, such as the contemplated prolonged bombardment of the Dardanelles Forts by our Fleet, is to force a decision at sea, and so far and no further can they be justified.'

The fact that it was intended only to use semi-obsolete battleships to force the Dardanelles, he went on, was no reassurance; if they were sunk the crews would be lost and these were the very men who were needed to man the new vessels coming out of the dockyards.

So then, Fisher argued, Britain should revert to the blockade of Germany and be content with that. 'Being already,' he concluded, 'in possession of all that a powerful fleet can give a country we should continue quietly to enjoy the advantage without dissipating our strength in operations that cannot improve the position.'

Here then was a fundamental difference on policy, a reversal, it seemed to Churchill, of the whole spirit in which they had planned the Dardanelles operation together.

One does not know how far Fisher had consulted the other members of the Admiralty Board before he committed himself to these views. Fisher himself denied that he had any such support. He said later, 'Naval opinion was unanimous. Mr. Churchill had them all on his side. I was the only rebel.' Churchill, however, felt that without Fisher's support he was in an impossible position, and he persuaded the Admiral to come with him to the Prime Minister twenty minutes before the Council meeting began on the morning of January 28, so that they could have the matter out. The discussion went off very quietly at 10 Downing Street. Fisher stated his objections to both the Dardanelles and the Zeebrugge operations, and Churchill answered that he was prepared at any rate to give up Zeebrugge. Asquith, being left to decide, fell in with Churchill's proposal: Zeebrugge should be stopped but the Dardanelles was to go forward. Fisher said no more and the three men went into the War Council together.

It appeared to Churchill that Fisher had accepted the

decision, but here he was quite wrong, for the Admiral, in silence and rage, was preparing his protest. Directly Churchill had finished explaining to the Council the latest position of the Dardanelles plan, Fisher said that he had understood that this matter would not be raised that day: the Prime Minister knew his views.

To this Asquith replied that in view of the steps which had already been taken, the question could not very well be left in abeyance.

Fisher at once got up from the table, leaving the others to carry on the discussion, and Kitchener followed him over to the window to ask him what he was going to do. Fisher replied that he would not go back to the table: he intended to resign. Kitchener's answer to this was to point out to Fisher that he was the only one in disagreement; the Prime Minister had taken the decision and it was his duty to abide by it. After some further discussion he eventually persuaded the Admiral to come back to the table again.

Churchill had noticed this incident, and as soon as the Council rose he invited Fisher to come to his room at the Admiralty in the afternoon. There is no record of the conversation that then took place, but it appears, in Churchill's phrase, to have been 'long and very friendly', and at the end of it Fisher consented to undertake the operation.

'When I finally decided to go in,' Fisher said later, 'I went the whole hog, *totus porcus*.' Nothing, not even this extremity of his affairs, could quite upset that robust spirit; he even added two powerful battleships, the *Lord Nelson* and the *Agamemnon*, to the Dardanelles Fleet.

Returning with the Admiral to the afternoon meeting of the Council, Churchill was able to announce that all at the Admiralty were now in agreement, and that the plan would be set into motion. From this point onwards there could be no turning back. Turkey, the small gambler, was in the thick of the big game at last.

THREE

SOMEWHAT more than half way down the Gallipoli Peninsula the hills rise up into a series of jagged peaks which are known as Sari Bair. Only the steepest and roughest of tracks leads to this spot, and except for an occasional shepherd and the men who tend the cemeteries on the mountainside, hardly anybody ever goes there. Yet the view from these heights, and especially from the central crest which is called Chunuk Bair, is perhaps the grandest spectacle of the whole Mediterranean.

On first reaching the summit one is quite unprepared for the extreme closeness of the scene which seemed so distant on the map and so remote in history; an illusion which is partly created, no doubt, by the silence and the limpid air. To the south, in Asia, lie Mount Ida and the Trojan plain, reaching down to Tenedos. To the west, the islands of Imbros and Samothrace come up out of the sea with the appearance of mountain tops seen above the clouds on a sunny morning; and one even fancies that one can descry Mount Athos on the Greek mainland in Europe, a hundred miles away. The Dardanelles, which split this scene in two, dividing Asia from Europe, are no more than a river at your feet.

On a fine day, when there is no movement on the surface of the water, all this is presented to the eye with the clear finite outlines and the very bright colours of a relief map modelled in clay. Every inlet and bay, every island, is exactly defined, and the ships in the sea below float like toys in a pond. From this point too the Gallipoli Peninsula is laid out before you with the intimate detail of a reef uncovered by the tide, and you can see as far as the extreme tip at Cape Helles where the cliffs fall sharply downward, their contours still visible beneath the water, into the unbelievable blue of the Ægean. It is not the flat pattern one sees from an aeroplane: Chunuk Bair is only 850 feet high, and therefore you yourself are part of the scene, slightly above it and seeing all, but still attached.

This illusion of nearness, this compression not only of space but of time, is very much helped by the fact that, through the centuries, hardly anything has been done to change the landscape. There are no new towns or highroads, no advertisements or tourist haunts, and this rocky soil can support only a light crop of wheat and olives, a few flocks of sheep and goats. Very probably this same coarse scrub covered the broken ground when Xerxes crossed the Hellespont below Chunuk Bair, and although since the siege of Troy the Scamander may have changed its windings and its name (it is now called the Mendere), it still meanders down to its ancient mouth at Kum Kale on the Asiatic side.

From our perch on Chunuk Bair the Hellespont—the Dardanelles—does not appear to be a part of the sea at all: it looks more like a stream running through a valley, an estuary scarcely wider than the Thames at Gravesend. In the course of an afternoon one might take a motor boat from one end to the other, for the distance is just over forty miles. The mouth at Cape Helles in the Mediterranean is 4,000 yards wide, but then the banks on either side open out to a distance of four and a half miles until they gradually close in again at the Narrows, 14 miles upstream. Here the passage is only 1600 yards across. Above the Narrows it again opens out to an average width of four miles until the Sea of Marmara is reached just above the town of Gallipoli.

There is no tide, but the Black Sea rivers and the melting snows create a four to five knot current, which at all times of the year sweeps down through the Dardanelles to the Mediterranean. In a severe winter this current can be blocked with great chunks of floating ice. The depth of the water is easily enough to accommodate any ship afloat.

Although there is no point in the whole forty miles where a hostile vessel cannot be reached by direct or even pointblank fire from either shore, the key to the whole military position is, of course, the Narrows. It was just upstream from this point that Xerxes built the bridge of boats on which his army crossed into Europe, and here too Leander is supposed to have swum by night from Abydos to meet Hero in Sestos, on the European shore.[1]

Two ancient fortresses, one a square crenellated building in the town of Chanak on the Asiatic side, and the other an odd heart-shaped structure tilted towards the sea at Kilid Bahr on the opposite bank, stand guard over the Narrows, and it was here that the Turks established their main defences at the outbreak of war. These consisted of eleven forts with 72 guns, some of them new, a series of torpedo tubes designed to fire on vessels coming upstream, a minefield and, later on, a net of wire mesh to block sub-

---

[1] The poem which Lord Byron wrote when he himself accomplished this feat in 1810 is well known, but he added to it the following footnote which is seldom printed, and which gives a livelier impression of the Narrows than any statistics can provide.

'On the 3rd of May, 1810, while the *Salsette* (Captain Bathurst) was lying in the Dardanelles, Lieutenant Ekenhead of that frigate and the writer of these rhymes swam from the European shore to the Asiatic—by-the-by, from Abydos to Sestos would have been more correct. The whole distance from the place whence we started to our landing on the other side, including the length we were carried by the current, was computed by those on board the frigate at upwards of four English miles; though the actual breadth is barely one. The rapidity of the current is such that no boat can row directly across, and it may in some measure be estimated from the circumstance of the whole distance being accomplished by one of the parties in an hour and five, and by the other in an hour and ten, minutes. The water was extremely cold from the melting of the mountain snows. About 3 weeks before in April, we had made an attempt, but having ridden all the way from the Troad the same morning, and the water being of an icy chilliness, we found it necessary to postpone the completion till the frigate anchored below the castles, when we swam the straits, as just stated; entering a considerable way above the European, and landing below the Asiatic fort. Chevalier says that a young Jew swam the same distance for his mistress; and Oliver mentions it having been done by a Neapolitan; but our consul, Tarragona, remembered neither of these circumstances, and tried to dissuade us from the attempt. A number of the *Salsette's* crew were known to have accomplished a greater distance; and the only thing that surprised me was that, as doubts had been entertained of the truth of Leander's story, no traveller had ever endeavoured to ascertain its practicability.'

41

marines. They had in addition other heavier guns in forts at Kum Kale and Sedd-el-Bahr at the mouth of the straits, and various intermediate defences further upstream. After the first Allied bombardment of November 1914, the Germans made certain additions to this armament—notably eight 6-inch howitzer batteries which could change position fairly rapidly, and the number of searchlights was increased to eight. Nine lines of mines were laid in the vicinity of the Narrows. Along the whole length of the straits there were in all something like 100 guns.

These defences, however, were less formidable than they sound, since barely a score of the guns were of modern design, and ammunition was in short supply. Two divisions of infantry—one in the Gallipoli Peninsula and the other on the Asiatic side—were responsible for holding all the ground from the Gulf of Saros to the Asiatic coast opposite Tenedos in the event of the Allies making a landing.

The fleet which the Allies assembled to attack these obstacles was the greatest concentration of naval strength which had ever been seen in the Mediterranean. Apart from the cruisers, destroyers, minesweepers, and lesser craft, the British had contributed fourteen battleships, two semi-dreadnoughts, the *Lord Nelson* and the *Agamemnon*, the battle-cruiser *Inflexible* and the newly completed *Queen Elizabeth*. The French squadron, under Admiral Guépratte, consisted of four battleships and their auxiliaries.

Although most of these battleships had become semi-obsolete their 12-inch guns were, of course, immensely superior to anything the Turks had on shore, and the *Queen Elizabeth* with her 15-inch guns was a more formidable opponent still. It was quite possible for the Fleet to fire on the forts at the mouth of the Dardanelles without ever coming into the range of the Turkish batteries. The only question was just how accurate this long range fire was going to be: how many forts would be knocked out before the Allied vessels closed in, as it were, for the kill?

Admiral Carden, flying his flag in the *Queen Elizabeth*, deployed his force in three divisions:

Inflexible	*Vengeance*	*Suffren*
Agamemnon	*Albion*	*Bouvet*
Queen Elizabeth	*Cornwallis*	*Charlemagne*
	Irresistible	*Gaulois*
	Triumph	

The attack itself was planned in three parts: a deliberate long-range bombardment followed by a medium-range bombardment, and finally an overwhelming fire at very close range. Under the cover of this attack minesweepers were to clear the channel up to the entrance of the straits. For the moment, the rest of the Fleet which was not engaged on diversionary missions was held in reserve.

At 9.51 a.m. on February 19 (which happened to be the 108th anniversary of Duckworth's exploit), the assault began. A slow bombardment continued all morning, and at 2 p.m. Carden decided to close to six thousand yards. Up to this time, none of the Turkish guns had replied, but at 4.45 p.m. the *Vengeance,* the *Cornwallis* and the *Suffren* went closer still and drew the fire of two of the smaller forts. The other batteries were enveloped in dust and smoke and appeared to be deserted. By now, however, the light was failing, and Carden sounded the general recall. Vice-Admiral de Robeck in the *Vengeance* asked for permission to continue the attack, but this was refused as the ships were now silhouetted against the setting sun.

The results of this short winter day were not entirely satisfactory. It was observed that the firing was not very accurate so long as the ships were moving, and only 139 12-inch shells had been used. To be really effective it was evident that the Fleet would have to go in much closer and engage the individual Turkish guns one by one with direct fire.

There was, however, no immediate opportunity of putting these tactics to the test, because the weather broke that night, and rough seas continued for the next five days. Bitterly cold sleet and snow flew in the wind. Aware of the impatience at the Admiralty in London, and a little troubled by it, Carden sent off a message which Roger Keyes, his chief-of-staff, had drafted for him: 'I do not intend to commence in bad weather leaving result undecided as from experience on first day I am convinced given favourable weather conditions that the reduction of the forts at the entrance can be completed in one day.'

It was almost true. When the storm quietened on February 25 Vice-Admiral de Robeck in the *Vengeance* led the attack right up to the mouth of the straits, and the Turkish and German gunners, unable to keep up the unequal struggle any longer, withdrew to the north. During the next few days, through intermittent gales, parties of marines and bluejackets were put on shore, and they roamed at will across the Trojan plain and the tip of the Gallipoli peninsula, blowing up the abandoned guns, smashing the searchlights and wrecking the enemy emplacements. There were one or two skirmishes with the Turkish rearguard, but for the most part the countryside around Cape Helles and Kum Kale was deserted. The minesweepers were having some difficulty in making headway against the current, but they penetrated for a distance of six miles into the straits without finding any mines, and although the warships were repeatedly hit by the mobile guns on shore no vessel was lost or even seriously damaged. The casualties were trifling. On March 2 Admiral Carden sent a message to London saying that, given fine weather, he hoped to get through to Constantinople in about fourteen days.

This news was received with elation at the Admiralty, and in the War Council. All earlier hesitations vanished; now everyone wanted to be associated with the adventure, and Lord Fisher even spoke of going out to the Dardanelles himself to take command of the next stage of the operations: the assault on the main enemy forts at the Narrows. In Chicago the price of grain fell sharply in expectation that, on the arrival of the Allied fleet in Constantinople, Russia would soon resume the export of her wheat.

But now difficulties appeared. The Turkish soldiers on shore were beginning to recover their confidence, for they returned to Kum Kale and Cape Helles and drove off the British landing parties with heavy rifle fire. At the same time the Turks had much more success against the Fleet with their howitzers and small mobile guns; they lay low until each bombardment from the Fleet was over and then, emerging from their emplacements, moved to other hidden positions in the scrub; and so it often happened that the batteries which the British thought they had silenced in the morning had to be dealt with all over again in the afternoon. This hardly affected the battleships, but it was a serious matter for the unarmed minesweepers, especially at night in the narrow waters below Chanak where they were instantly picked up by searchlights and exposed to a harassing fire.

None of these things amounted to a definite reverse, but by March 8, when the weather worsened again, it was evident that the first impetus of the attack had spent itself. It was an exasperating position for the Admirals: they were being held up, not by the strength of the enemy, but by his elusiveness. The minesweepers could not go forward until the guns were silenced, and the battleships could not get near enough to silence the guns until the mines were out of the way. The Fleet's seaplanes with their new wireless equipment might have solved the problem for the naval gunners by acting as spotters, but each day the sea proved either too rough or too smooth for the machines to take off. In this dilemma Carden began to hesitate and delay.

Roger Keyes, who was constantly up at the front of the attack, was convinced that it was all the fault of the civilian crews of the minesweepers who had been recruited from the North Sea fishing ports of England. Their officers told him that the men 'recognized sweeping risks and did not mind being blown up, but they hated the gunfire, and pointed out that they were not supposed to sweep under fire, they had not joined for that'.

Well then, Keyes suggested, let us call for volunteers from the regular Navy, and in the meantime offer the civilian crews a bonus if they will go in again tonight. This was on March 10, and as soon as he had got the Admiral's rather reluctant consent, Keyes himself went in with the flotilla under the cover of darkness. Five brilliant searchlights burst out at them directly they entered the straits, and the battleship *Canopus,* following behind, opened fire.

'We were fired at from all directions,' Keyes says. 'One saw stabs of light in the hills and in the direction of the 6-inch battery covering the minefields on both sides of the straits, followed by the whine of little shells, the bursting of shrapnel, and the scream of heavy projectiles which threw up fountains of water. It was a pretty sight. The fire was very wild, and the *Canopus* was not hit, but for all the good we did towards dowsing the searchlights we might just as well have been firing at the moon.'

It was too much for the minesweepers. Four of the six passed over the minefield below Chanak without getting their kites down, and one of the remaining pair soon struck a mine and blew up. For a time a tremendous fire poured down on the survivors, and it was an astonishing thing that, with so many mines cut loose and drifting about in the darkness, only two men were wounded before the flotilla got away.

Next night Keyes tried again without the assistance of the

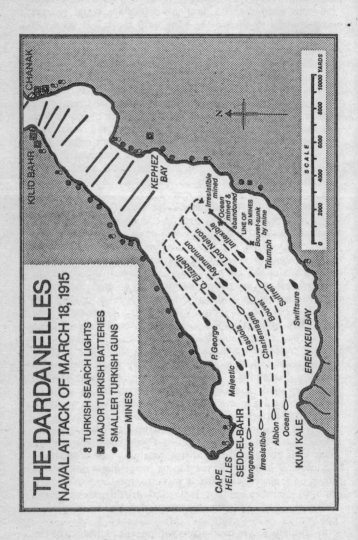

THE DARDANELLES
NAVAL ATTACK OF MARCH 18, 1915

8   TURKISH SEARCH LIGHTS

◼   MAJOR TURKISH BATTERIES

●   SMALLER TURKISH GUNS

—   MINES

CHANAK

KILID BAHR

KEPHEZ BAY

SCALE

0   2000   4000   6000   8000   10000 YARDS

Irresistible

Ocean mined & abandoned

LINE OF 20 MINES

Bouvet sunk by mine

Inflexible

Lord Nelson

Agamemnon

Q. Elizabeth

Triumph

Swiftsure

Suffren

Bouvet

Charlemagne

Gaulois

P. George

Majestic

Vengeance

Irresistible

Albion

Ocean

CAPE HELLES

SEDD-EL-BAHR

KUM KALE

EREN KEUI BAY

battleship, hoping to steal up on the Turks unawares. 'The less said about that night the better,' he wrote later. 'To put it briefly, the sweepers turned tail and fled directly they were fired upon. I was furious and told the officers in charge that they had had their opportunity, there were many others only too keen to try. It did not matter if we lost all seven sweepers, there were twenty-eight more, and the mines had got to be swept up. How could they talk of being stopped by heavy fire if they were not hit? The Admiralty were prepared for losses, but we had chucked our hand in and started squealing before we had any.'

And so too it seemed to Churchill in London. On this same day, March 11, he sent the following telegram to Carden:

'Your original instructions laid stress on caution and deliberate methods, and we approve highly the skill and patience with which you have advanced hitherto without loss. The results to be gained are, however, great enough to justify loss of ships and men if success cannot be obtained without. The turning of the corner at Chanak may decide the whole operation. . . . We do not wish to hurry you or urge you beyond your judgment, but we recognize clearly that at a certain point in your operations you will have to press hard for a decision, and we desire to know whether you consider that point has now been reached.'

By March 13 new crews had been assembled for some of the minesweepers—just as Keyes had anticipated there had been an immediate response to the call for volunteers —and that night the attack was renewed with great resolution. The enemy gunners waited until the trawlers and the picket boats were in the middle of the minefield and then, turning on all their searchlights together, opened up with a concentrated fire. This time the trawlers stuck to it until all but three were put out of action, and the effect of this was seen on the following morning when many mines came floating down with the current and were exploded. From this time forward it was decided that the sweeping should be done by day, and it was hoped that sufficient progress would be made for the Fleet to close in for the full scale attack on the Narrows on March 17 or 18.

Carden meanwhile had still not replied to the Admiralty's message, and on March 14 Churchill telegraphed again. 'I do not understand,' he said, 'why minesweepers should be interfered with by firing which causes no casualties. Two

47

or three hundred casualties would be a moderate price to pay for sweeping up as far as the Narrows. I highly approve your proposal to obtain volunteers from the Fleet for minesweeping. This work has to be done whatever the loss of life and small craft and the sooner it is done the better.

'Secondly, we have information that the Turkish forts are short of ammunition, that the German officers have made despondent reports and have appealed to Germany for more. Every conceivable effort is being made to supply ammunition, it is being seriously considered to send a German or an Austrian submarine, but apparently they have not started yet. Above is absolutely secret. All this makes it clear that the operation should now be pressed forward methodically and resolutely at night and day. The unavoidable losses must be accepted. The enemy is harassed and anxious now. The time is precious as the interference of submarines is a very serious consideration.'

To these messages Carden now replied that he fully appreciated the situation, and that despite the difficulties he would launch his main attack as soon as he could: probably March 17.

Carden was ill. Under the increasing strain of the operations he was unable to eat and he slept very little at night. He was worried about the failure of the seaplanes, about the mines and about the weather. It had taken him two days to make up his mind as to how he was to reply to Churchill's messages, and now that he had pledged himself to this drastic all-out attack his confidence began to ebb away. He did not explicitly lose faith in the adventure, but in his weakened condition he seems to have felt that he no longer had the personal power to command it.

In fairness to Carden it ought perhaps to be remembered that it was only by chance that he had ever come to the Dardanelles at all; this was a post that should have gone to Admiral Limpus, the head of the former British Naval Mission to Turkey, the man who knew all about the Dardanelles. But at the time when Limpus left Constantinople Turkey was still a neutral, and the British did not wish to irritate the Turks by deliberately sending the man who knew all their secrets to blockade the Dardanelles. So Carden had been lifted out of his post as Superintendent of Malta Dockyard, and he had already had a long winter at sea off the straits before this action had begun. The enterprise had not been exactly thrust upon him—indeed, he himself had suggested the method of attack—but in agreeing to it in the first place one can imagine that he was influenced by the knowledge that he was going the way the young First Lord wanted him to go. And now this highly dangerous operation had built itself up around him into a tremendous thing. It had gathered an impetus out of all proportion to its beginnings, and since as yet he had fought no major action, had lost no ship and scarcely any men, he felt bound to go on. But he dreaded it.

On March 15, after another bad night, Carden told Keyes he could continue no longer. This meant the end of his career, and both Vice-Admiral de Robeck and Keyes begged him to reconsider. However, on the following day a Harley Street specialist who was serving with the Fleet announced after an examination that Carden was on the edge of a nervous collapse; he must sail for home at once.

The attack was now due to be launched within forty-eight hours, and a new Commander had to be found in haste. Admiral Wemyss, the commandant of the base on the island of Lemnos, was the senior officer on the station, but he at once offered to stand down in favour of de Robeck, who had been involved in the fighting from the beginning. On March 17 Churchill cabled his agreement to this arrangement, and sent de Robeck the following message:

'Personal and Secret from First Lord. In entrusting to you with great confidence the command of the Mediterranean Detached Fleet I presume . . . that you consider, after separate and independent judgment, that the immediate operations proposed are wise and practicable. If not, do not hesitate to say so. If so, execute them without delay and without further reference at the first favourable opportunity. . . . All good fortune attend you.'

De Robeck replied that weather permitting he would attack on the following day.

There is an excitement about the attack on the Narrows on March 18, 1915, a sense of natural adventure, which sets it apart from almost any other battle in the two world wars. Those who took part in it do not remember it with horror, as one might remember poison gas or the atomic bomb, or with the feeling of futility and waste that eventually surrounds most acts of war. Instead they look back on this battle as a great day in their lives: they are delighted that the risk was taken, delighted that they themselves were there, and the vision of the oncoming ships with great fountains of spray about them, and the gunfire echoing along the Dardanelles, is still an exhilaration in their memory.

In our time most decisive naval actions have been fought far out at sea, and often in rough weather and over a large area of water so that no one man's eye could command the whole scene. But here the land was near, the area of action very closely confined, and from morning until dusk a brilliant sun shone down on the calm sea. An observer, whether in the fighting tops of a battleship or standing on any of the hills on either side of the straits, could have seen precisely what was going on as the struggle unfolded itself from hour to hour; and even when night fell the battlefield was still illuminated by the beams of the searchlights constantly sweeping across the water.

In another sense this struggle was unusual, for it was essentially a naval attack upon an army, or at any rate upon artillery. From first to last the Turkish and German warships never appeared, and no aircraft were employed by either side. Then too, there was no element of surprise. Every fine morning had brought the Turks and the Germans the prospect of this attack. The forces on either side were very largely known—just how many ships and guns and mines—and the object of the struggle was perfectly obvious to everybody from the youngest bluejacket to the simplest private. All hung upon that one thin strip of water scarcely a mile wide and five miles long at the Narrows: if that was lost by the Turks then everything was lost and the battle was over.

De Robeck arranged his fleet in three divisions. Line A, steaming abreast, consisted of the four most powerful British ships which were to open the attack—*Queen Elizabeth*, *Agamemnon*, *Lord Nelson* and *Inflexible*—and they were accompanied on either flank by two more battleships, *Prince George* and *Triumph*.

In Line B, following about a mile astern, was the French squadron—*Gaulois*, *Charlemagne*, *Bouvet* and *Suffren*—with two more British battleships, *Majestic* and *Swiftsure*, on either side. The other six battleships and the destroyers and minesweepers which were also committed to the engagement were to wait their turn outside the straits. It was hoped that in the course of the day the forts at the Narrows would be so battered that the minesweepers would be able to clear a channel that same evening. Then with luck the battleships might pass through into the Sea of Marmara on the following day.

The morning of March 18 broke warm and sunny, and soon after dawn de Robeck gave orders for the Fleet to clear for action. Then with the crews at action stations down below and only the commanders and the men controlling the guns on deck the ships moved off from their anchorage at Tenedos.

At 10.30 a.m., when the morning haze had lifted sufficiently for the Turkish forts to be clearly seen, the first ten battleships entered the straits, and at once came under the fire of the enemy howitzers and field guns on either side. For about an hour the *Queen Elizabeth* and her companions steamed steadily forward under this barrage, getting in a shot with their lighter guns where they could but making no other reply. Soon after 11 a.m. Line A reached its station, a point about eight miles downstream from the Narrows, and without anchoring remained stationary, stemming the current. At 11.25 a.m. the assault began. The *Queen Elizabeth's* targets were the two fortresses on either side of the town of Chanak on the Narrows, and on these she turned her eight 15-inch guns. Almost immediately afterwards the *Agamemnon, Lord Nelson* and *Inflexible* engaged three other forts at Kilid Bahr on the opposite bank.

After their first few shots in reply the Turkish and German gunners at the Narrows realized that they were out of range, and the forts fell silent; and in silence they endured the fearful bombardment of the four British ships for the next half hour. All five forts were hit repeatedly, and at 11.50 a.m. there was a particularly heavy explosion in Chanak. The British meanwhile were entirely exposed to the Turkish howitzers and smaller guns which were nearer at hand, and these poured down a continuous barrage on the ships from either side. This fire could never be decisive against armour, but the unprotected superstructure of the battleships was hit again and again and a certain amount of minor damage was done.

A few minutes after midday de Robeck, who was in the *Queen Elizabeth,* judged that the time had come to engage the Narrows at closer range, and he signalled for Admiral Guépratte to bring the French squadron forward. This was a mission for which Guépratte had expressly asked on the ground that it was now the turn of the French, since it was de Robeck himself who had carried out the close-range attack on the outer defences.

Admiral Guépratte has a personality which refreshes the whole Gallipoli story. He never argues, he never hangs back: he *always* wishes to attack. And now he took his old battleship through the British line to a point about half a mile further on where he was well within the range of all the enemy guns and in constant danger of being hit. On reaching their station the French ships fanned out from the centre so as to give the British astern of them a clear field of fire, and there then ensued through the next three-quarters of an hour a tremendous cannonade.

One can perhaps envisage something of the scene: the forts enveloped in clouds of dust and smoke, with an occasional flame spurting out of the debris, the ships slowly moving through a sea pitted with innumerable fountains of water, and sometimes disappearing altogether in the fumes and the spray, the stabs of light from the howitzers firing from the hills, and the vast earthquake rumbling of the guns. Presently *Gaulois* was badly holed below the waterline, the *Inflexible* had both her foremast on fire and a jagged hole in her starboard side, and the *Agamemnon*, struck twelve times in twenty-five minutes, was turning away to a better position. These hits though spectacular had scarcely touched the crews—there were less than a dozen casualties in the whole fleet—and as yet no ship was seriously affected in its fighting powers.

With the enemy at the Narrows, on the other hand, a critical situation had developed. Some of the guns were jammed and half buried in earth and debris, communications were destroyed between the fire control and the gunners, and those few batteries which managed to continue became more and more erratic in their fire. Fort 13 on the Gallipoli side had been obscured by an internal explosion, and it was clear to the British and the French that even though the forts were not yet destroyed the enemy gunners were for the moment demoralized. Their fire grew increasingly spasmodic until at 1.45 p.m., after nearly two and a half hours of continuous engagement, it had practically died away altogether.

De Robeck now decided to retire the French squadron with the rest of Line B and bring in his six battleships waiting in the rear. The movement began shortly before 2 p.m. and the *Suffren*, turning to starboard, led her sister ships out of the action along the shores of Eren Keui Bay on the Asiatic side. They were almost abreast of the *Queen Elizabeth* and the British line at 1.54 p.m. when the *Bouvet*, lying immediately astern of the *Suffren*, was observed to be shaken with an immense explosion, and a column of smoke shot up from her decks into the sky. She heeled over, still going very fast, capsized and vanished. It was all over in two minutes. According to one observer the vessel 'just slithered down as a saucer slithers down in a bath'. At one moment she had been there, perfectly safe and sound. Now there was nothing left but a few heads bobbing about in the water. Captain Rageot and 639 men who were trapped between decks had been drowned.

It seemed to those who watched that the *Bouvet* had been struck by a heavy shell which had reached her magazine, and now the Turkish gunners, heartened by what they had seen, renewed their attack on the other ships. The next two hours were largely a repetition of the morning's events. Moving in pairs, *Ocean* and *Irresistible*, *Albion* and *Vengeance*, *Swiftsure* and *Majestic*, came in and closed the range to ten thousand yards. Under this new barrage the heavy guns at the Narrows began firing wildly again, and by 4 p.m. they were practically silent once more.

Now at last it was time for the minesweepers to go in, and de Robeck called them forward from the mouth of the straits. Two pairs of trawlers led by their commander in a picket boat got out their sweeps and they appeared to be going well as they passed by *Queen Elizabeth* and the rest of A Line. Three mines were brought up and exploded. But then, as they drew forward to B Line and came under enemy fire, something like a panic must have occurred: all four trawlers turned about, and despite all the efforts of their commander to drive them back, ran out of the straits. Another pair of trawlers, which was supposed to take part in the operation, vanished without getting out their sweeps at all.

This fiasco was followed by something much more serious. At 4.11 p.m. the *Inflexible*, which had held her place in A Line all this time, despite the fire in her foremast and other damage, was seen suddenly to take a heavy list to starboard. She reported that she had struck a mine not far from the spot where the *Bouvet* had gone down and now she left the battle line. She was observed to be down by the bows and still listing considerably as she steamed for the mouth of the straits, with the cruiser *Phaeton* attending her. It seemed likely that she would go down at any moment. The explosion of the mine had flooded the fore torpedo flat and besides killing the twenty-seven men stationed there had done other extensive damage. Flames and poisonous fumes began to spread; not only were the ship's electric lights extinguished but the oil lamps, which had been lit for just such an emergency, failed as well. At the same time the ventilator fans stopped running and the heat below deck was intolerable. In these circumstances Phillimore, the captain, decided that it was not necessary to keep both steaming watches on duty, and he ordered one of the watches up to the comparative safety on deck. All, however, volunteered to stay below. They worked in darkness amid the fumes and the rising water until all the valves and watertight doors were closed. The remainder of the ship's company stood to attention on the upper deck as they passed back through the rest of the Fleet. It seemed to those who saw them that none of these men had been defeated by the day's events, or were shaken by the imminent prospect of drowning; and they got the ship back to Tenedos.

Meanwhile the *Irresistible* had been struck. Not five minutes after *Inflexible* had left the line, she too flew a green flag on her starboard yard arm, indicating that she believed she had been torpedoed on that side. She was on the extreme right of the Fleet at the time, close to the Asiatic shore, and at once the Turkish gunners began to pour their shells into her. Unable to get any answer to his signals, de Robeck sent off the destroyer *Wear* to render assistance, and presently the *Wear* came back with some six hundred of the *Irresistible*'s crew, several dead and eighteen wounded among them. The senior executive officers of the *Irresistible* had stayed on board with ten volunteers in order to make the ship ready for towing.

It was now 5 p.m., and three battleships were out of action: the *Bouvet* sunk, the *Inflexible* limping back to Tenedos and the *Irresistible* drifting towards the Asiatic shore under heavy Turkish fire. There was no clear explanation of these three disasters. The area in which the ships had been operating all day had been swept for mines on a number of occasions before the operations began. On the previous day a seaplane had been over and had confirmed that the sea was clear—and some reliance could be placed on this report for it had been demonstrated in tests off Tenedos that aircraft could spot mines as deep as eighteen feet in this limpid water. What then was doing the damage? It was hardly likely to have been torpedoes. The only conclusion that remained was that the Turks were floating mines down with the current. In fact, as we shall see later, this conclusion was not correct, but it was near enough as to make no odds, and de Robeck felt he could do no other than to break off the action for the day. Keyes was instructed to go aboard the *Wear* and proceed to the salvage of the *Irresistible* with the aid of two battleships, the *Ocean* and *Swiftsure*. In addition, a division of destroyers was ordered forward into the straits and placed under Keyes's command. The rest of the Fleet retired.

One can do no better now than follow Keyes in his own account of what happened at the end of this extraordinary day. He says that salvo after salvo was hitting the *Irresistible*, and he could see no sign of life in her when he came alongside at 5.20 p.m. He concluded, therefore, that the captain and the skeleton crew had already been taken off—and rightly so because the ship was in a desperate condition. She had got out of the main current sweeping down the straits and a light southerly breeze was drifting her in towards the shore. With every minute as she drew nearer to them the Turkish gunners were increasing their fire. Nevertheless, Keyes decided that he must attempt to save her and he signalled to the *Ocean*. 'The Admiral directs you to take *Irresistible* in tow.' The *Ocean* replied that there was not sufficient depth of water for her to do so.

Keyes then directed the captain of the *Wear* to get his torpedoes ready for action so that he could sink the helpless ship before she fell into the hands of the enemy; but first he wished to make quite certain that the water was too shallow for the *Ocean* to come in and take her in tow. The *Wear* then ran straight into the enemy fire to take soundings—she came so close to the shore that the Turkish gunners could be seen around their batteries, and at that point-blank range the flash of the guns and the arrival of the shells seemed to be simultaneous. The *Wear*, however, was not hit, and presently Keyes was able to signal to the *Ocean* that there were fifteen fathoms of water for half a mile inshore of the *Irresistible;* and he repeated de Robeck's

55

order that the ship should be taken in tow. To this he got no reply. Both the *Ocean* and the *Swiftsure* were now hotly engaged, and the *Ocean* in particular was steaming back and forth at great speed, blazing away with all her guns at the shore. It seemed to Keyes that she was doing no good whatever with all this activity and was needlessly exposing herself. For some time the heavy guns at the Narrows had been silent, but it was quite possible that they would open up again at any minute. He therefore signalled the *Ocean* once more: 'If you do not propose to take the *Irresistible* in tow the Admiral wishes you to withdraw.' With the *Swiftsure* Keyes could afford to be more peremptory—her captain was junior to him—and he ordered her to go at once. She was an old ship and much too lightly armoured to have undertaken the salvage in the present circumstances.

Meanwhile things had begun to improve with the *Irresistible;* she had lost her list and although she was down by the stern she was still no lower in the water than she had been an hour previously when the *Wear* first arrived. Keyes now decided to go full speed to de Robeck and suggest that trawlers might be brought back after dark to tow her into the current so that she would drift out through the straits. He was actually on his way and was drawing close to the *Ocean* so that he could repeat the order for her to withdraw when the next disaster occurred. A violent explosion shook the water and the *Ocean* took a heavy list. At the same time a shell hit her steering gear and she began to turn in circles instead of escaping down the straits. The destroyers which had been standing by for the last two hours raced in and took off her crew. Now the Turkish gunners had a second helpless target close at hand.

With this bad news Keyes returned to de Robeck in the *Queen Elizabeth* which was lying just outside the straits. The captains of both the *Irresistible* and the *Ocean* had already been taken off their ships and were with the Admiral when Keyes arrived. A sharp discussion ensued. Keyes said exactly what he thought about the loss of the *Ocean* and her failure to take the *Irresistible* in tow, and he asked for permission to go back and torpedo the *Irresistible*. The *Ocean*, he thought, might be salvaged. De Robeck agreed, and after a quick meal Keyes set off again in one of the *Queen Elizabeth's* cutters. It was now dark and he was unable to find the *Wear* but fell in with the *Jed* instead, and in this destroyer he steamed back into the straits.

The scene in the Dardanelles now was extremely eerie. All was silent on either shore, and except for the Turkish searchlights that kept sweeping back and forth across the water there was no sign of life anywhere. For four hours the *Jed* cruised about hunting for the two lost battleships. She crept close in to the Asiatic shore, and with the aid of the enemy searchlights probed into every bay where the *Irresistible* and the *Ocean* might have gone aground. But there was nothing to be seen or heard: nothing but this extraordinary silence, the utter lassitude of the battlefield after the day's fighting is done. To Keyes it was an exhilarating experience.

'I had,' he wrote later, 'a most indelible impression that we were in the presence of a beaten foe. I thought he was beaten at 2 p.m. I knew he was beaten at 4 p.m.—and at midnight I knew with still greater certainty that he was absolutely beaten; and it only remained for us to organize a proper sweeping force and devise some means of dealing with the drifting mines to reap the fruits of our efforts. I felt that the guns of the forts and batteries and the concealed howitzers and mobile field guns were no longer a menace. Mines moored and drifting must, and could, be overcome.'

In the early hours of the morning Keyes, in this uplifted state of mind, steamed back to the *Queen Elizabeth*.

FOUR

~~~~~~

THE attack on the Dardanelles could hardly have happened at a worse time for the Turks. In the five months that had elapsed since they had gone to war nothing had gone well with them. In the south Basra, at the head of the Persian Gulf, had fallen to the British, and the expedition into Egypt had ended in a miserable fiasco; a few exhausted and bewildered troops managed to reach the Suez Canal but they were easily driven off and not many of them got back to the oases of Palestine alive.

In the east things were even worse. It was Enver's notion that Turkey should launch an offensive against Russia in the Caucasus with the Third Army stationed at Erzerum, and he decided to lead the expedition himself. Before leaving for the front he discussed his plan with Liman von Sanders, and the antagonism between the two men seems to have gathered impetus from this moment. Liman pointed out that Enver was proposing to take his troops across the mountains at Sarikamish in mid-winter, when the passes were blocked with snow, and that he had made no arrangements for his lines of supply. All this had no effect whatever upon Enver; he would proceed according to his plan, he said, and after the Russians had been defeated he would advance upon India through Afghanistan. Liman von Sanders has written a sober account of his experiences in Turkey, and he rarely permits himself an emotional expression. This last piece of information, however, undermined his calm. 'Enver,' he said, 'gave utterance to fantastic ideas.'

The details of the battle of Sarikamish, on January 4,

1915, have never been fully known, for there was no one to record them and the news of what had happened was suppressed in Turkey at the time. The official figures, however, reveal that of the ninety thousand Turks who set out on the expedition only twelve thousand returned. The others were killed, captured, died of hunger or were frozen to death. Enver, a sad travesty of the Napoleon he so longed to emulate, abandoned what was left of the army in the field and came back through the winter snow across the Anatolian plain to resume his post at the Ministry of War in Constantinople. Outwardly he remained as calm as ever, and nothing was said about the disaster at Sarikamish or the subsequent outbreak of typhus in the broken army.

There followed in Constantinople a ludicrous attempt to proclaim a Jehad—a Holy War—against all Christians in the Near East (Germans and Austrians excepted), and German missions were sent as far off as Afghanistan to intrigue against the British. But nothing now could disguise the fact that Turkey's war effort had come to a standstill. The Treasury was empty, the Army's requisitions of private property were becoming more and more severe, and among civilians there was apathy everywhere. According to Lewis Einstein, the American Minister, the Germans were in some considerable anxiety that at the next blow the Turks might start negotiating in secret for a separate peace.

It was in these low circumstances that the news of the bombardment of the Dardanelles arrived.

In a time of crisis the morale of the civilians in a city which has not yet been touched by war is seldom as high as it is among the soldiers in the frontline; but in March Constantinople excelled itself. In the absence of any reliable information from the Dardanelles rumours began to spread, and they gathered an astonishing virulence as they went along. Forty thousand British soldiers were about to land on the Golden Horn. The women would be raped. The whole city was about to go up in flames.

'It seems so strange now,' Henry Morgenthau wrote later on, 'this conviction in the minds of everybody then—that the success of the Allied Fleets against the Dardanelles was inevitable, and that the capture of Constantinople was a matter of only a few days.'

For two centuries the British Fleet had gone on from one victory to another, it was the one wholly unshakeable power

59

in the world; what hope was there that a handful of old guns on the Dardanelles could hold it back?

In early March the exodus from Constantinople began. The state archives and the gold in the banks were sent to Eski-Shehr, and some attempt was made to bury the more valuable art treasures underground. The first of two special trains, one for the Sultan and his suite, the other for the foreign diplomats, stood ready at Haidar Pasha on the Asiatic shore, and the more well-to-do Turks began to send their wives and families into the interior, by every means they coud find.

They were hardly to blame for these precautions, for Talaat himself was utterly despondent. As early as January he had called a conference of Liman von Sanders, Admiral Usedom, the German who was in command of the coastal defences, and Bronsart, the German chief-of-staff of the Army. All had agreed that when the Allied Fleet attacked it would get through. Now in March, Talaat had requisitioned a powerful Mercedes car from the Belgian Legation, and it was packed and equipped with extra petrol tanks, ready for his departure. Since the distance from Gallipoli to Constantinople was only 150 miles it was judged that the first British warships would appear off the Golden Horn within twelve hours of their arrival in the Sea of Marmara.

Among the diplomats too there was much apprehension. The German Embassy, a huge yellow pile of stone, stood on a particularly exposed point at the head of the Bosphorus, and Wangenheim, all his earlier courage gone, was convinced that it would be shelled. He had already deposited some of his baggage with Morgenthau for safe keeping on neutral American ground. 'Let them dare to destroy that Embassy,' he exclaimed to Morgenthau one day. 'I'll get even with them. If they fire a single shot at it we'll blow up the French and the British Embassies. Go tell the British Admiral that, won't you? Tell him also that we have the dynamite ready to do it.'

Wangenheim was in an awkward position. If he retired with the Sultan into the interior of Asia Minor and the Turks signed a peace with the Allies he would be cut off from Germany and the West. For a time he had tried to persuade Talaat to move the government to Adrianople, whence he would have an opportunity of escaping across the Bulgarian border; but Talaat had refused on the grounds that it was more than likely that Bulgaria would attack Turkey once Constantinople fell.

Next Bedri, the Chief of Police, came to Morgenthau to arrange for the departure of the American Embassy. Morgenthau told him that he was not going to move, and suggested instead that they should draw up a map of the city showing the areas which were likely to be bombarded. It was agreed that the two ammunition factories, the powder mills, the offices of War and Marine, the telegraph office, the railway stations and a number of other public buildings were all legitimate targets. These were marked off, and Morgenthau telegraphed the State Department in Washington with a request that the British and French should be approached and asked to spare the other purely residential districts.

This plan, however, was hardly more than a straw in the wind, for the more ruthless of the Young Turks had already made their own arrangements for destroying the city rather than let the Allies have it. If they themselves had to go then all should go. They cared nothing for the Christian relics of Byzantium, and regarded patriotism as a higher thing than the lives of the hundreds of thousands of people who lived in the tumbledown wooden houses in Galata and Stamboul and along the Golden Horn. If one did not remember the burning of Moscow by the Russians after Borodino, and Hitler's last days in Berlin, it would be difficult to credit the arrangements that were now made. Petrol and other inflammable material were stored in the police stations. St. Sophia and other public buildings were made ready for dynamiting.

Morgenthau pleaded for St. Sophia at least, but Talaat answered him, 'There are not six men in the Committee of Union and Progress who care for anything that is old. We all like new things.'

The truth was that by March the Young Turks had something to fear which was even worse than the approach of the Allied Fleet. Placards had begun to appear in the streets denouncing their government. With every day that went by it became more evident that a great part of the population —and not only the Greeks and the Armenians—looked upon the arrival of the Allied warships, not as a defeat but as a liberation. Bedri was able to do something to check this increasing unrest by deporting a number of men whom he judged to be dangerous, but it was perfectly clear that riot-

61

ing would break out directly the British and French ships appeared.

For the rest, all was concealed muddle and a silent confusion. Outwardly the city was quiet and normal, inwardly it was possessed by a coma of suspense. The shops were open, the government departments at work; but everyone, with divided hopes and different fears, had fixed his attention on the Dardanelles, and even the great mass of minor people who aspire to nothing but their own safety and who submerge their imaginations in the routine of their daily lives were eager for the latest rumour, the least scrap of information from the front.

It was that ominous quietness that precedes a riot. Everywhere in Constantinople soldiers were marching about or standing at the street corners, and they had that curious appearance of aimlessness, of menace that has not yet quite decided upon its target, that seems to overtake armed forces in a city when the officers have no orders, when nothing certain is known and each new rumour cancels out the last. The *Goeben* made ready to steam out into the Black Sea before the *Queen Elizabeth* arrived.

'These precautions,' Liman remarks dryly, 'were justified.' Turkish General Headquarters, he says, were convinced that the Fleet would break through, and meanwhile the orders issued by Enver for the disposition of the troops along the Dardanelles were such that a successful defence against an Allied landing there would have been impossible. 'Had these orders been carried out,' Liman goes on, 'the course of the world war would have been given such a turn in the spring of 1915 that Germany and Austria would have had to continue the struggle without Turkey.'

Meanwhile at the Narrows in the Dardanelles, the last obstacle between the Fleet and the Sea of Marmara, the Turkish and German gunners were reaching the end of their resources. Up to March 18 they had been able to hold their own, and in the excitement of the struggle they had come to regard with almost a casual air the slim dark silhouettes of the battleships which appeared each day so clearly before them at the southern approaches to the straits. Soon they knew all the names: 'There's the *Agamemnon;* there's the *Elizabeth*,' and they longed only for the ships to come within range so that they could begin to shoot. But each day drained away a little more of their energy and their ability to fight. The massed attack of

March 18 had been a devastating thing. By midnight, just as Keyes had guessed, they had reached a point of crisis.

Their courage had not gone—it had been a tremendous thing to see the enemy battleships go down, and in all the day's fighting they had suffered only 118 casualties—but half their ammunition had been fired away, and there was no possibility of getting any more. In particular the heavy guns had been left with less than thirty armour-piercing shells, which alone had power to destroy the battleships. When these were gone it was simply a question of how long the lighter guns and howitzers could keep the mine-sweepers off the minefields; some thought one day, others two. The mines themselves offered no particular difficulty once the guns were dominated; there were 324 of them arranged in ten lines, but they were spaced ninety yards apart, many of them were old, and after six months in the water had broken from their moorings and drifted away.[1] Apart from another thirty-six mines which had not yet been put into the water there was no other reserve, and it was now quite possible for the British to sweep a channel through to the Sea of Marmara in a matter of hours. Beyond the Narrows there were no other defences of any kind to impede the battleships, except a few old guns which were aimed the wrong way.

The Narrows on this night presented an appearance that was not unlike the scenes that followed the air raids in the second world war. Chanak, a town of 16,000 people, was now very largely deserted and in ruins. Fires had started during the bombardment and although they had died down after nightfall rubble still blocked the streets and the quays. Everywhere around the forts shell craters had broken up the ground, and at the Dardanos, a little further downstream on the Asiatic shore, the hillsides were pitted and scarred like the surface of the moon. Coins and pieces of pottery which had lain in the earth since classical times had been flung up into the air. Only eight of the heavy cannon had been put out of action, but there was much serious damage in the emplacements, and soldiers worked through-

---

[1] The Turks in fact were so short of mines that they had been collecting those the Russians had been floating down the Bosphorus from the Black Sea in the hope of destroying the *Goeben* and the *Breslau*. In Constantinople these mines had been picked up, transshipped to the Dardanelles, and put into the minefields there.

out the night rebuilding the parapets, repairing the telephone lines and righting the guns which had jammed and had shifted their position among the falling debris.

The behavior of the soldiers throughout the long seven hours' bombardment had been admirable. Those who watched the Turkish gunners at Kilid Bahr on the Gallipoli side of the straits say that they fought with a wild fanaticism, an Imam chanting prayers to them as they ran to their work on the gun emplacements. This was something more than the usual excitement of battle; the men were possessed, apparently, with a religious fervour, a kind of frenzy against the attacking infidel. And so they exposed themselves quite indifferently to the flying shrapnel and the bursting shells.

The Germans at Hamidieh Fort and the other batteries on the opposite bank displayed a different kind of courage. Many of these men were gunners who had been taken off the *Goeben* and the *Breslau,* and so they had the precise and technical discipline of the sea. In addition they had improvised with great skill. In the absence of motor transport and horses they had requisitioned teams of buffaloes to drag their mobile howitzers from place to place, so that the British could never find the range. Field guns were sited on the skyline in such a way as to create the maximum of optical illusion. They had too a primitive but effective device by which black puffs of smoke were made to emerge out of pieces of piping each time the guns fired, and this had drawn some scores of British and French shells away from the batteries.

But none of these makeshifts, nor the discipline and the fanaticism of the defenders, could alter the fact that they had so much ammunition and no more. So long as it lasted they were quite confident that they could keep the Fleet at bay—and probably this confidence governed every other feeling at this high point of the attack. But if the battle went on and no unforeseen reinforcements arrived it was obvious to the commanders that the moment would come when they would be bound to order their men to fire off the last round and then retire. After that they could do no more.

They were convinced that the Fleet would attack again on the following day. They knew nothing of the alarming mystery which had been created among the British and the French by the loss of the *Bouvet,* the *Irresistible* and the

Ocean. This was a matter which the Germans and the Turks could have explained in two minutes. What had happened was that on the night of March 8 a Lieut.-Colonel Geehl, who was a Turkish mine expert, had taken a small steamer called the *Nousret* down into Eren Keui Bay and there, parallel to the Asiatic shore and just inside the slack water, he had laid a new line of twenty mines. He did this because he had seen British warships manœuvring there during the previous day. Somehow in the ten days before the March 18 attack the British mine-sweepers had never found these mines; three of them, it is true, had been swept up, but it was not realized that there was a whole line of them; nor had they been noticed by the British aerial reconnaissance. For these ten days the destiny of the Fleet and much else besides had been lying quietly there in the clear water.

To the Turks and the Germans it hardly seemed likely that the enemy warships would make this mistake a second time. And so through this night of March 18 they worked and waited for what the morning would bring, not over-elated by the success of the day or indifferent to their danger, but simply determined to fight on.

The British knew nothing of all this—of the plight of the gunners at the Narrows or of the preparations which the Turkish government was making to abandon Constantinople. A few of the leaders like Keyes at the Dardanelles and Churchill in London might have divined that they had now come up to the crisis of the battle, but they had nothing definite to go on, they simply felt the presence of victory very near at hand. The others felt nothing of the kind. And in fact, through all these weeks while the bombardment had been going on, the old misgivings about the whole adventure had been revived in London. It was not that the commanders wanted to abandon it; they were eager to push on and believed that it could be made to succeed. But it was increasingly felt, at first at the Admiralty and then in the War Office, that the Navy would not be able to do the job alone. Somehow an army would have to be provided.

As early as February, before ever Carden had begun the bombardment, Venizelos, the Greek Prime Minister, had been privately approached over the matter. As an inducement for Greece to come in on the side of the Allies he was offered two divisions, one British and one French, to stiffen his northern flank at Salonika. Venizelos judged that this reinforcement would be just enough to bring his enemies down on top of him and not enough to hold them off, and he therefore declined the offer. At the end of February however he changed his mind. Carden's bombardment was going very well and it looked as though he might be in the Sea of Marmara at any moment. On March 1 the Greeks offered to send a force of three divisions to occupy the Gallipoli peninsula and then advance, if possible, upon Constantinople.

There is a fatuity about the negotiations which followed that still has power to cause surprise across the gulf of two world wars. It was to everybody's interest—Russia's more than anyone's—that Greece should come in with her army and buttress the Fleet at the critical moment; yet the arrangements that were now made were precisely calculated to keep her out and almost lose her allegiance altogether. Britain and France would have accepted the Greek offer at once. But to Russia it was a matter of great alarm. It revived all her old fears about the guardianship of the Bosphorus and the Dardanelles, her one vital outlet to the south. She by no means wished to have the Greeks in Constantinople when she might be there herself. Blind to the fact that his own military situation was desperate, and that the revolution and his own death were not far off, the Czar permitted himself to say to the British Ambassador on March 3 that in no circumstances would he see Greek soldiers in Constantinople. In particular, King Constantine was not to appear there.

When this news reached Athens the Venizelos Government fell and was replaced on March 7 by a new ministry of pro-German views. Britain and France meanwhile, with an eye to bolstering Russia's morale, informed the Czar that he should have control of the Bosphorus as soon as Constantinople fell, and an agreement to that effect was signed in the middle of March. With this all the Navy's hopes of getting an army quickly into the Gallipoli peninsula were gone. It remained to be seen what could be done by Britain and France.

In London the chief advocate for an army for Gallipoli was Lord Fisher. 'The Dardanelles,' he cried in a note to Lloyd George. 'Futile without soldiers!' and he remarked very sensibly, 'Somebody will have to land at Gallipoli some time or other.' The decision on this matter, however, did not rest with the Admiralty; it rested with Kitchener, and Kitchener had been saying all along that he had no soldiers to spare. In point of fact he did have soldiers who were not then employed—notably the 29th Division, which was a very fine unit of the regular Army standing idle in England. Through February a lively argument developed between the western front generals and the supporters of the Dardanelles scheme as to who should get possession of this valuable force. By the middle of the month Kitchener was coming round to the Dardanelles side, and on the 16th he announced that the division could sail for the Ægean. It would assist the marines already on the spot in mopping up the Gallipoli peninsula, and later in occupying Constantinople. This brought so sharp a protest from the generals in France that on February 18, the day before the naval bombardment began, the Field Marshal revoked his decision and said that the Australian and New Zealand divisions then in Egypt should go instead. At this the ships which the Admiralty had assembled for the transport of the 29th Division were dispersed.

But now a new factor came into the scene. General Sir William Birdwood was sent out to the Dardanelles to report on the military position there, and one of his earliest messages to Kitchener on March 5 was disturbing. He did not believe, Birdwood said, that the Fleet would get through by itself; the Army would have to come in.

One sympathizes with Kitchener, for the situation was complicated. At one moment he is offered a Greek army and at the next it is snatched away. On March 2 Carden says he can get through. On March 5 Birdwood says he cannot. Nobody at this stage, not even Carden who is ill or Fisher who dislikes the whole design, suggests that the operations should be abandoned. As Churchill wrote later, 'Everybody's blood was up': the excitement of a naval battle, the sudden vision of spectacular success it had conjured up, the historic ground, the daring of the enterprise —all these things had captivated people's minds, and Kitchener himself at last fell under the Gallipoli spell. On March 10 he announced that the 29th Division was to go after all, and that he had arranged for the French to send a division as well. This meant that, with the Anzac divisions, there would be an Army Corps of some seventy thousand men in the field.

No one knew yet what this large force was to do or precisely where it was to go, or what allies and enemies it would gather on its way. Despite Birdwood's report it was still thought that the Navy would break through alone, and still no one suggested that it should suspend its operations until the Army arrived so that the two forces could attack together.

Something of the confusion and the vagueness—the remarkable blending of precipitancy and hesitation—that governed the situation in London at this time can be glimpsed from the circumstances in which General Ian Hamilton, an old comrade of Kitchener's from the South African war, was appointed to command this new army that had drifted into being. It was on the morning of March 12 that Hamilton was told of his appointment. He himself has described the scene:

'I was working at the Horse Guards when about 10 a.m. K. sent for me. I wondered. Opening the door I bade him good morning and walked up to his desk where he went on writing like a graven image. After a moment, he looked up and said in a matter-of-fact tone, "We are sending a military force to support the Fleet now at the Dardanelles, and you are to have command. . . ."

'K., after his one tremendous remark, had resumed his writing at the desk. At last, he looked up and inquired, "Well?"

' "We have done this sort of thing before, Lord K.," I said; "We have run this sort of show before and you know without saying I am most deeply grateful and you know without saying that I will do my best and that you can trust my loyalty—but I must say something—I must ask you some questions." Then I began.

'K. frowned; shrugged his shoulders; I thought he was going to be impatient, but although he gave curt answers at first he slowly broadened out, until at the end no one else could get a word in edgeways.'

Lord Kitchener, however, was not able to be very explicit, for until the Navy had launched its attack on March 18 neither he nor anybody else had any clear notion of what Hamilton was to do. General Caldwell, the Director of Military Operations, was called in and although he was able to produce a map of the Gallipoli area (which subsequently turned out to be quite inaccurate), the sum of his knowledge of the situation appeared to be confined to a plan for a landing on the southern part of the Gallipoli peninsula which had been worked out by the Greek General

68

Staff some years before. The Greeks, Caldwell said, had estimated that they would require 150,000 men.

Kitchener dismissed this idea at once. Half that number, he said, would do Hamilton handsomely. The Turks were so weak on the peninsula that if a British submarine managed to get through the Narrows and wave the Union Jack outside the town of Gallipoli the whole enemy garrison would take to its heels and make a beeline for Bulair.

At this point General Wolfe Murray, the Chief of the Imperial General Staff, and General Archibald Murray, the Inspector of Home Forces, came into the room together with General Braithwaite, who had been appointed Hamilton's chief-of-staff. None of them had heard of this plan for a Gallipoli campaign before and the Murrays were so taken aback that neither of them ventured to comment.

However, Braithwaite spoke. According to Hamilton: 'He only said one thing to K. and that produced an explosion. He said it was vital that we should have a better air service than the Turks in case it came to fighting over a small area like the Gallipoli peninsula; he begged, therefore, that whatever else we got, or did not get, we might be fitted out with a contingent of up-to-date aeroplanes, pilots and observers. K. turned on him with flashing spectacles, and rent him with the words, *"Not one"*.'[1]

Returning to the War Office next morning Hamilton found Kitchener 'standing at his desk splashing about with his pen at three different drafts of instructions'. There were but three or four essential points in the document that finally emerged; Hamilton was to hold back his troops until the Fleet had made its full-scale attack on the forts at the Narrows. If this attempt failed he was to land on the Gallipoli peninsula; if it succeeded he was to hold the peninsula with a light garrison and advance directly upon Constantinople, where it was hoped he would be joined by a Russian corps which would be landed on the Bosphorus.

In no circumstances was Hamilton to proceed until his whole force was assembled and he was not to fight on the Asiatic side of the Dardanelles.

'He toiled over the wording of his instructions,' Hamilton says in his diary. 'They were headed "Constantinople Expeditionary Force". I begged him to alter this to avert Fate's evil eye. He consented and both this corrected draft

---

[1] It was left to the Navy to supply aircraft for the operation.

and the copy as finally appproved are now in Braithwaite's dispatch box more modestly headed "Mediterranean Expeditionary Force". None of the drafts helps us with facts about the enemy; the politics; the country, and our allies, the Russians. In sober fact these "instructions" leave me to my own devices in the East.

'So I said good-bye to old K. as casually as if we were to meet together at dinner. Actually my heart went out to my old chief. He was giving me the best thing in his gift and I hated to leave him among people who were frightened of him. But there was no use saying a word. He did not even wish me luck and I did not expect him to, but he did say, rather unexpectedly, *after* I had said good-bye and just as I was taking up my cap from the table, "If the Fleet gets through, Constantinople will fall of itself and you will have won, not a battle, but the war".'

By now there had been assembled some thirteen officers who were to act on Hamilton's staff. Most of these were regular soldiers, but there were one or two who, Hamilton says, had hastily put on uniform for the first time in their lives: 'Leggings awry, spurs upside down, belts over shoulder straps! I haven't a notion of who they all are.' Others again who were to handle the administration and quartermastering of the headquarters he failed to meet at all, since they had not heard of their appointments as yet.

However, the paramount need now was haste, and at 5 p.m. on Friday, March 13, the party, armed with the instructions, the inaccurate map, a three-years-old handbook on the Turkish Army and a pre-war report on the Dardanelles defences, proceeded to Charing Cross station. Churchill, who had been pressing strongly for their immediate departure, had made all the arrangements; a special train was waiting to take them to Dover where they were to cross to Calais on H.M.S. *Foresight*. At Calais another special express would take them through the night to Marseilles, where H.M.S. *Phaeton*, a 30-knot unarmoured cruiser, was commissioned to convey them to the Dardanelles.

Churchill himself with his wife came down to Charing Cross to see the party off, and there was some last minute conversation on the subject of Hamilton's reports from the front. They would all have to go directly to Kitchener, Hamilton said; to address Churchill separately at the Admiralty would be disloyal. With that he was off. As the train drew out Hamilton said to Captain Aspinall, the young officer who was to plan the operations, 'This is going to be an unlucky show. I kissed my wife through her veil.' Four days later the party was at the Dardanelles.

They were just in time. Next day, March 18, Hamilton watched the assault on the Narrows from the decks of the *Phaeton*.

So now at midnight they were all gathered in the arena: the Turks and the Germans at the Narrows preparing to make a desperate stand, the British and French sailors with their battered but still powerful fleet, and the new Allied Commander-in-Chief who had arrived without an army and without a plan.

Having satisfied himself that both the *Ocean* and the *Irresistible* were safe from the Turks at the bottom of the sea, Keyes on the night of March 18 went directly in the *Jed* to the *Queen Elizabeth* to see de Robeck. He was astonished to find the Admiral much upset. He was sure, de Robeck said, that because of his losses he would be dismissed from the command on the following day. Keyes answered with some spirit that de Robeck had judged the situation quite wrongly: Churchill would not be discouraged. He would send reinforcements at once and back them up in every way. Apart from the 639 men drowned in the *Bouvet*, the casualties had been amazingly small: not seventy men in the entire Fleet. All three lost battleships were old vessels due for scrap, and even if the *Gaulois* and the *Inflexible* were withdrawn for repairs the great power of the Fleet was substantially intact.

For a time the two officers discussed the problem of the mines, and it was agreed that they should immediately set about organizing a new force to deal with them. The civilian crews of the trawlers would be sent home, and volunteers from the lost battleships would take their place. Destroyers would be equipped with sweeping apparatus, and at the next attempt an attack would be finally driven home.

On this encouraging note the Admiral and his chief-of-staff finally went to their cabins for a few hours' rest.

Keyes rose next morning, March 19, and having shaved, as was his custom, with a copy of Kipling's 'If' propped up before him, went out to survey the condition of the Fleet, which had spent the night sheltering about Tenedos.

It was clear that a day or two must elapse before the attack could be resumed—the wind was again rising to a gale and there was much to be done in organizing the new minesweeping force—but everywhere the captains and the crews were eager to renew the fight.

In the course of the morning a message arrived from the Admiralty condoling with de Robeck over his setback but urging him to press on with the attack.

His losses were to be made good by four more battleships—the *Queen, Implacable, London* and *Prince of Wales* —which would sail at once. In addition the French Ministry of Marine was replacing the *Bouvet* with the *Henri IV*.

The damage to the French squadron had been severe: *Gaulois* had been forced to ground herself on Rabbit Island to the north of Tenedos, and the *Suffren* was leaking from the effects of a plunging shell. The *Gaulois*, however, was soon pumped out and refloated, and with the *Inflexible* and the *Suffren* she went off to Malta for repairs. Meanwhile the organization of the new minesweeping force began. One hundred and fifteen men from the trawler crews were sent home and there was an overwhelming response from the crews of the *Ocean* and the *Irresistible* for volunteers to replace them. Kites, wire mesh, and other tackle were ordered from Malta, and at Tenedos Greek fishermen were engaged to help the British crews in equipping the destroyers as minesweepers. All day in heavy seas this work was pressed forward, and on March 20 de Robeck was able to report to the Admiralty that fifty British and twelve French minesweepers, all manned by volunteers, would soon be available. Steel nets would be laid across the straits to deal with floating mines when the attack was renewed. 'It is hoped,' he added, 'to be in a position to commence operations in three or four days.'

Now too an efficient squadron of aircraft under the command of Air Commodore Samson began to arrive. With this the Navy hoped greatly to improve their spotting of the enemy guns.

De Robeck also wrote to Hamilton, who had gone to Lemnos to inspect the 2,000 marines and the 4,000 Australian and New Zealand soldiers who had already arrived there. He urged Hamilton not to take these troops back to Egypt for re-grouping as he proposed to do, since it might create a bad impression in the Balkans just at the moment

72

when the Navy was about to resume its attack. 'We are all getting ready for another go,' he said, 'and not in the least beaten or down-hearted.'

Hamilton did not share this confidence. He had been deeply moved by what he had seen of the battle on March 18, and perhaps he was affected by the sight of the damaged *Inflexible* creeping back to Tenedos. Perhaps he was influenced by Birdwood, who from the beginning had never believed that the Fleet could do the job alone. Other considerations—even a simple chivalrous desire to help the Navy—may have weighed with him; but at all events he sent the following message to Kitchener on March 19:

'I am most reluctantly driven to the conclusion that the straits are not likely to be forced by battleships, as at one time seemed probable, and that, if my troops are to take part, it will not take the subsidiary form anticipated. The Army's part will be more than mere landing parties to destroy forts; it must be a deliberate and prepared military operation, carried out at full strength, so as to open a passage for the Navy.'

Kitchener had replied with surprising energy: 'You know my view, that the Dardanelles must be forced, and that if large military operations on the Gallipoli peninsula by your troops are necessary to clear the way, those operations must be undertaken, after careful consideration of the local defences, and must be carried through.'

This then was the situation on March 21—a Naval Command that believes that the Fleet can still get through alone, and an Army Command convinced that it cannot.

The following morning, March 22, de Robeck decided to take the *Queen Elizabeth* over to Lemnos for a conference with Hamilton. There is something of a mystery about this meeting, for none of the subsequent accounts of what took place are in agreement with each other. Keyes was occupied with the arrangements for the new naval attack and was not present, but he assures us that he believed that nothing more than future military movements were to be discussed. Those who assembled in the *Queen Elizabeth* were Hamilton, Birdwood and Braithwaite from the Army, and de Robeck and Wemyss from the Navy.

Hamilton's version is as follows: 'The moment he sat down de Robeck told us that he was now quite clear *he could not get through without the help of all my troops.* Before ever we went on board, Braithwaite, Birdwood and

73

I agreed that, whatever we landsmen might think, we must leave the seamen to settle their own job, saying nothing for or against the land operations or amphibious operations until the sailors themselves turned to us and said that they had abandoned the idea of forcing the straits by naval operations alone. They have done so. The fat (that is us) is fairly in the fire.

'No doubt we had our views. Birdie (Birdwood) and my own staff disliked the idea of chancing mines with million pound ships. The hesitants who always make hay in foul weather had been extra active since the sinking of the three men-of-war. Suppose the Fleet *could* get through with the loss of another battleship or two—how the devil would our troopships be able to follow? And the store ships? And the colliers?

'This had made me turn contrary. During the battle I had cabled that the chances of the Navy pushing through on their own were hardly fair fighting chances, but since then de Robeck, the man who should know, had twice said that he *did* think that there was a fair fighting chance. Had he stuck to that opinion at the conference, then I was ready, as a soldier, to make light of military croaks about troopships. Constantinople must surrender, revolute or scuttle within a very few hours of our battleships entering the Marmara. Memories of one or two obsolete six-inchers at Ladysmith helped me to feel as Constantinople would feel when her rail and sea communications were cut and a rain of shell fell upon the penned-in populace from de Robeck's terrific batteries. Given a good wind that nest of iniquity would go up like Sodom and Gomorrah in a winding sheet of flame.

'But once the Admiral said his battleships could not fight through without help, there was no foothold left for the views of a landsman.

'So there was no discussion. We at once turned our faces to the land scheme.'

This account does not square with what Keyes knew of de Robeck's views up to the time of this meeting; and it does not square with a message the Admiral sent to London after the meeting was over.

'I do not hold the check on 18th decisive,' he wrote, 'but, having met General Hamilton on 22nd and heard his proposals, I now consider a combined operation essential to obtain great results and object of campaign. . . . To attack Narrows now with Fleet would be a mistake, as it would jeopardize the execution of a better and bigger scheme.'

In other words, it is only after he has heard Hamilton's proposals that he decides to abandon the naval attack.

Whatever may be the truth of this matter—whether Hamilton enticed de Robeck away from the naval attack or whether de Robeck himself suggested that the Army should come in and help—the important thing is that on March 22 the Admiral changed his mind; nothing more was now to be done by the Fleet until the Army, now scattered along the Mediterranean, was assembled and ready to land.

One can perhaps glimpse something of what was going on in de Robeck's mind. The wounds of March 18 were beginning to stiffen and hurt. To sailors of de Robeck's generation it was an appalling thing to lose battleships, no matter how old and out of date they were. Most of their lives had been spent on these decks; these ships had been their home, and through the years they had developed for them not only affection but pride as well. The whole tradition of the Navy was that the ship was more important than the man: no matter what the cost in lives the captain must always try to save his ship. And now in a few hours three of the largest vessels of the Fleet with their famous names had gone to the bottom.

Then again de Robeck was perfectly aware of Fisher's opposition to the Dardanelles adventure. For the moment Churchill might be holding the old Admiral in line, but young and enthusiastic First Lords did not last for ever. Fisher stood for the Navy, its permanence and its traditions, and he was a formidable man. He had said all along that the Fleet was not likely to get through without the aid of the Army, and now here were three sunken battleships to prove his point. Suppose another three ships were lost when the attack was renewed? It could very easily happen. What was Fisher going to say to that?

There was one other point. De Robeck had very much hoped that once he was in the Marmara Hamilton would land at Bulair on the neck of the peninsula, and that the Turkish Army, finding itself cut off, would surrender. Thus there would no longer be any threat to the lifeline of the Fleet through the Dardanelles. But at the meeting Hamilton had announced that it could not be done. He had been up to Bulair himself aboard the *Phaeton*, and had seen the network of entrenchments there. Hamilton now proposed that he should land instead at the tip of the peninsula and fight his way up it. This altered the Fleet's situation entirely. It meant that there would be no sudden collapse of the Turks; they would continue to hold the Narrows and threaten the supply ships coming through. It was true that from the Marmara the Fleet could attack the Turkish forts from the rear. But how long would it take to destroy them? How long could the Fleet remain isolated in the Marmara without coal and ammunition; and with the *Goeben* still intact? A fortnight? Three weeks?

There were of course grave dangers in delaying the renewal of the naval attack until the Army was ready. With every day that went by the Turks were recovering from the bombardment of the 18th, and one had only to look at the new entrenchments that appeared every morning on the cliffs to know that reinforcements were arriving. Well then, how much delay would there be? Hamilton thought it would be about three weeks before he was ready. Had Kitchener allowed the 29th Division to sail at the beginning of February as he had originally intended, the troops would be here now, and it would have been a very different story. But the 29th was still at sea, far down the other end of the Mediterranean,[1] and Hamilton did not believe he could attack without them—and in fact Kitchener had expressly forbidden him to do so.

Birdwood disagreed with Hamilton over this. He said that it might be worth while taking a chance and landing there and then with whatever forces they could scrape together at Lemnos. But on going into the matter it was found that every sort of equipment from guns to landing craft was missing. Moreover, the transports coming out from England had been stowed in the wildest confusion: horses in one ship, harness in another: guns had been packed without their limbers and isolated from their ammunition. Nobody in England had been able to make up their minds as to whether or not there were roads on the Gallipoli peninsula, and so a number of useless lorries had been put on board. To have landed on hostile beaches in

[1] Actually the first transports had just reached Malta, where that day the officers were being entertained at a special performance of the opera *Faust*.

these conditions would have been a hazardous thing. Nor were there any facilities for repacking the ships at Lemnos. So now there was nothing for it but to take everything back to Alexandria in Egypt, and there re-group the whole force and its equipment in some sort of battle order. Provided his administrative staff arrived in good time, Hamilton judged that the Army might be ready to land on Gallipoli somewhere about the middle of April—say, April 14. Then the Army and the Navy could attack together.

Upon this the meeting of March 22 broke up.

Keyes was appalled when he got back to the *Queen Elizabeth* and heard the news. He pleaded with de Robeck not to change his plans. The new minesweeping force, he said, would clear all their difficulties away, and they were bound to get through. To delay for the Army would be fatal.

De Robeck was still uneasy in his mind and he agreed to see Hamilton again. In the afternoon the two sailors went across to the *Franconia* where the General was living and Keyes set out his arguments again. He was asked when his minesweepers would be ready, and he replied that it would be in about a fortnight's time: April 3 or April 4. De Robeck then pointed out that since Hamilton would be ready on April 14 this only meant a delay of ten days. 'So', says Keyes, 'the matter was finally settled.' He adds, 'I must confess I was fearfully disappointed and unhappy.'

To this theme Keyes returned again and again in later days, and it finally emerges in an unrepentant counter blast in the memoirs he published in 1934: 'I wish to place on record that I had no doubt then, and have no doubt now—and nothing will ever shake my opinion—that from the 4th of April onwards the Fleet could have forced the straits and, with losses trifling compared with those the Army suffered, could have entered the Marmara with sufficient force to destroy the Turco-German Fleet.'

By 1934 Keyes was an Admiral of the Fleet and a great man in the world, with a fighting record that put him almost in the Nelson class. But in 1915 he was no more than an exceptionally promising young commodore, and he was no match for the steady conservatism of the Navy personified by de Robeck. De Robeck was no weakling—he was a kindly, firm, courageous and fair-minded man—but he had had his training and he was the one who bore the responsibility. That sudden flash of inspiration that will sometimes

77

transport a commander past all the accepted rules of warfare into a field of daring that carries everything before it was perhaps lacking in the Admiral's character, but he can hardly be blamed for that. His 'no' was a definite no; it only remained now to learn how London would view this change of plan.

Churchill says he heard the news with consternation. He told the Dardanelles Commission later: 'I regarded it (the battle of March 18) as only the first of several days' fighting, though the loss in ships sunk or disabled was unpleasant. It never occurred to me for a moment that we should not go on, within the limits of what we had decided to risk, till we had reached a decision one way or another. I found Lord Fisher and Sir Arthur Wilson in the same mood. Both met me that morning (March 19) with expressions of firm determination to fight it out.'

But now, on March 23, Churchill has a telegram from de Robeck saying that he will not move without the Army, and not for another three weeks. At once—and one can imagine with what pugnacity—Churchill sat down and drafted a telegram ordering the Admiral to 'renew the attack begun on March 18 at the first favourable opportunity'. Then, convening a meeting of Fisher and the War Group at the Admiralty, he placed the telegram before them for their approval.

Describing this meeting, Churchill says: 'For the first time since the war began, high words were used around the octagonal table.' To Fisher and the other admirals it seemed that with de Robeck's telegram the situation at the Dardanelles had entirely altered. They had been willing, they said, to support the purely naval attack so long as the admiral on the spot had recommended it. But now both de Robeck and Hamilton had turned against it. They knew the difficulties; they had the responsibility. To force them to attack against their own judgment would be entirely wrong.

Churchill could make no headway against these views though he appears to have argued with great energy that morning. When finally the meeting broke up without a decision he still persisted in his opinion. But it was evident that he was defeated. Asquith said that he agreed with Churchill, but he would not give the order against the advice of the admirals. De Robeck in a further exchange of telegrams proved immovable. At the Dardanelles the bad weather continued, and Hamilton went off with his staff to

Egypt. In London Kitchener informed the War Council that the Army was now quite willing to take over from the Navy the task of opening the straits. With this there was nothing more to be said, and Churchill gave up at last. With good grace he sent off a message to de Robeck saying that his new plans had been approved.

A silence now settled on the Gallipoli peninsula: no ship entered the straits, no gun was fired. The Fleet lay at anchor in the islands. The first part of the great adventure was over.

FIVE

~~~~~~~~~~~~~~~~~~~~~~~~~~~~~~~~~~~~

> *'The Turks belong to the Turanian race which comprises the Manchus and Mongols of North China: the Finns and the Turks of Central Asia.'*
> —WHITAKER'S ALMANAC

> *'The epithet popularly associated with the Turk in the English mind is "unspeakable": and the inevitable reaction against the popular prejudice takes the form of representing the Turk as "the perfect gentleman" who exhibits all the virtues which the ordinary Englishman lacks. Both these pictures are fantastic. . . .'*
> ARNOLD TOYNBEE and KENNETH P. KIRKWOOD
> in a study of Turkey written after the war.

ALTHOUGH they knew they had inflicted great damage on the Allied Fleet on March 18 it never occurred to the German and Turkish gunners on the Dardanelles that the Allied warships would not resume their attack on the following day. The men stood to their guns all through the morning of March 19, and when there was still no sign of the enemy they presumed that it was the gale that was preventing the ships from coming back. But the rough weather subsided and as day followed day without any sign of the Fleet their sense of dazed relief began to change into hope. By the end of the month this hope had developed into certainty.

There was one man in Constantinople who could claim that he had never been in the slightest doubt about this astonishing result. As early as February Enver had been saying to his friends in the capital that it was all nonsense; there was nothing to be afraid of, the enemy would never get through. In March he went down to the Dardanelles to watch the battle, and on his return he announced that the defences were absolutely solid; the gunners had plenty of ammunition, the minefields were intact. 'I shall go down in history,' Enver said, 'as the man who demonstrated the vulnerability of the British Fleet. Unless they bring up a large army with them they will be caught in a trap. It seems to me a foolish enterprise.'[1]

Since Enver's military judgments in the past had been spectacularly unsound, few people, either among the diplomats or his colleagues, had been much reassured by this. Yet nothing could shake him. He confided to Morgenthau one day that when he was in England before the war he had seen many of the leading men—Asquith, Churchill and Haldane—and had pointed out to them that their ideas were out of date. Churchill had argued that England could defend herself with her Navy alone, and Enver had replied that no great empire could last that did not have an Army as well. Now here was Churchill sending his Fleet to the Dardanelles so that he could prove to Enver that he was wrong. Well, they would see.

Turning to the Ambassador at the end of this interview, Enver said seriously: 'You know, there is no one in Germany with whom the Emperor talks as intimately as I have talked with you today.'

It was not entirely ridiculous. Already Enver was ruling as a dictator in the Ministry of War. No one dared to take a decision in his absence, and the oldest and most distinguished of politicians and generals were obsequious before him. He thought nothing of keeping the Sultan waiting half an hour or more at a ceremony or a parade, and even Wangenheim was becoming alarmed at the little colossus he had raised, especially when, after March 18, Enver's position became more powerful than ever.

In the many histories of the Gallipoli campaign it is argued that the abortive naval attack on the Dardanelles

---

[1] Enver reversed this opinion after March 18. Some time later, when it was safe to do so, he admitted: 'If the English had only had the courage to rush more ships through the Dardanelles they could have got to Constantinople.'

was a cardinal error, not only because it failed but because it warned the Turks of the approaching invasion and gave them time to fortify the peninsula. This, as we shall see in a moment, was true enough; yet it seems possible that the political and psychological effect of March 18 was even more important. It was the Turks' first victory for many years. Since the beginning of the century the country had never known anything but defeat and retreat, and they had grown used but not reconciled to the demoralizing spectacle of the refugees streaming back after nearly every battle. To take only one case out of millions, Mustafa Kemal's mother had been forced to decamp from Macedonia, and he found her penniless in Constantinople. Salonika, the city in which he had grown up and which he regarded as Turkish by right, was now Greek.

One particularly appalling winter in Constantinople Aubrey Herbert had been moved to write:

'There falls perpetual snow upon a broken plain,
And through the twilight filled with flakes the white
    earth joins the sky.
Grim as a famished wounded wolf, his lean neck in a
    chain,
The Turk stands up to die.'

Kemal, no doubt, really did see himself in this light, and there must have been many others like him.

Herbert wrote again: 'In 1913, when the Balkans gained one smashing victory after another over the unequipped and unorganized Turkish forces every Greek café in Pera shouted its song of triumph.'

Nor was it only the Greeks, the Armenians and the other foreign minorities who were witnessing the Turks' humiliation; the great Christian powers had established sovereign prerogatives in Turkey. They controlled her foreign trade, they administered her armed services and the police, they granted loans to the bankrupt government according to their judgment of its behaviour, and their own nationals residing in Turkey were above the law: under the system of capitulations Western Europeans could only be tried for offences in their own courts. The obvious implication was that the Turk was not only incompetent to manage his own affairs, he was not yet civilized. He was Caliban, a dangerous but now docile monster; and the Christian powers were Prospero, controlling him for his own good.

For the first five months of the war there had been very little change in these conditions. However much their religion and their instincts taught them to regard foreigners and Christians as unclean slaves, lower than animals, the Young Turks still desired to be modern, to be Western, and they still affected to despise the methods of Abdul Hamid. Enver, it is true, had talked about abolishing capitulations and of making foreign residents pay special taxes, but he soon dropped these ideas when he heard Baron von Wangenheim was against him.

The security measures taken in Constantinople and the other cities, therefore, had not been excessive. Greeks and Armenians were deprived of their arms and were conscripted into the labour battalions of the Army. In some cases their property was requisitioned but this was a fairly general thing, and it probably fell as heavily upon the Moslem peasant as upon anyone else, since his stock and grain were seized to feed the Army. Bedri, the police chief in Constantinople, had gone out of his way to try and humiliate Sir Louis Mallet and the French Ambassador when they left the country on the outbreak of war by holding up their special trains and making other difficulties. But some 3,000 British and French nationals who had made their homes in Turkey had remained behind and they were not interned.

In Constantinople the street signs which for years had been written in French were obliterated; no shop could display a placard in a foreign language; merchants were required to dismiss their foreign employees and take on Turks instead. There was a mild spy hunt. Nobody in time of war could have seriously objected to these and the other measures that were imposed, since very much the same sort of thing, or worse, was happening in the other belligerent countries in western Europe.

But March 18 changed all this. Now at last the Turkish soldier was something in the world again. The British battlefleet was the strongest armament in existence, its very name had been enough to strike terror among its enemies in every ocean, and no one had given the Turks the ghost of a chance against it. Yet by some miracle they had driven it away. Constantinople had been saved at the last moment. The Turk could hold up his head again.

Not unnaturally and perhaps not unfairly Enver and Talaat claimed the credit for all this, and indeed the victory of March 18 was for them absolutely vital. Up to this time they had never been really secure in office, they had steered a breathless course from day to day, and they had been very largely driven by events. But now they found themselves borne up on a wave of popularity and patriotic pride. The Army's success was their success. At last they represented Turkey. It was even more than this: they stood for the Turk himself, for Islam with all its xenophobia and its hunger for revenge on the patronizing, dominating foreigner.

And so in their elation—their sudden emotional transition from fear to not-fear, from weakness and doubt to strength and certainty—they did a thing which was nothing new in the East, or anywhere else for that matter: they set about hunting down their racial and political opponents. They were now strong enough to express their hatred and they wanted victims.

At this stage there could be no question of attacking the British and French nationals: the American ambassador was looking after their interests, and in any case there was still the possibility that the Allies might win the war. The Greeks too could count on some sort of protection from the neutral government in Athens. But the Armenians were in a very different case. In nearly every way they fitted the role of the perfect scapegoat. The Armenians were Christians and yet there was no foreign Christian government which was responsible for them. For years they had hoped to set up an independent Armenian state in Turkey, and no matter how quiet they might be lying at the moment, it was obvious that they staked their future on the victory of the Allies. Herbert probably went too far when he said, 'though the Armenians had a future before them in the development and the improvement of Turkey, they were seduced by Europe and flattered to suicide.' Yet there were grounds for the Turkish belief that the Armenians were a fifth column inside the country, and that, no less than the Greeks, they had gloated over every Turkish reverse in the Balkan wars.

Then too the Armenians were supposed to be rich: they lent money, a thing forbidden to the Moslems, and many of them handled commerce in the city while the Turkish peasant remained on the land. They had a reputation for cleverness, for outwitting the lazier, less efficient Turks, and they had not always disguised the fact that they regarded themselves as a superior race, better educated than the Moslems, more Westernized. A long skein of trivial jealousy was woven around these gifted people in every village.

These things applied of course in equal measure to the Greeks and the Jews, but the Turks had another particular grudge against the Armenians. It was thought that they had been disloyal in the recent campaign in the Caucasus, that they had sent information across to the Russians, and that some of their young men had even crossed the border to join the Russian army. Soon a rumour spread that the Armenians were secreting arms with the idea of raising a revolution.

There had been massacres in Turkey before this, but nothing could compare with the ferocity, the organized brutal hatred with which the Turks now launched themselves in their revenge. In some places like Smyrna the massacres were comparatively mild; in others like Van, where the Armenians did put up a successful defence for a while, the slaughter was complete. The system used—and it was entirely a system planned by Talaat and the Committee—was to goad the Armenians to the point where they attempted to resist. At first their goods were requisitioned, then the women were molested, and finally the shooting began. It was customary, once an Armenian village had been quelled, to torture the men so that they would reveal where their arms and money were hidden, then to take them out into the country, tied together in batches of four, and shoot them dead. In some cases the women were given the opportunity of becoming Moslems, but more usually the attractive ones were simply taken off to the harems by the local Turkish garrison. The remainder, with the old men and the boys, were then assembled with what goods they could carry and put on the road to the Mesopotamian deserts in the south. Very few of them arrived; those who were not waylaid and stripped naked by marauding bands soon died of hunger and exposure.

To Morgenthau and other Western observers in Turkey who were confronted with the full horror of these events at the time it seemed that what they were witnessing was a reversion of the Turks to their nomadic and barbaric ancestry of the fourteenth and fifteenth centuries. Now at last, after two hundred years of interference in Constantinople, the Russians, the British and the French were out of the way, and the Germans, the only Christian people with any influence left in the country, soon made it clear that they had no intention of interfering. Indeed, it was believed that Wangenheim, or at any rate someone on his staff, had suggested the refinement of adding wholesale deportation to local massacre. The Germans at this moment had a good interest in the Turkification of Turkey, the doctrine of Pan-Turkism; it inflamed the Turks' military spirit, it made them much more formidable allies in the struggle against Russia and the rest of Europe.

Protests by Morgenthau and even by the Bulgarians had no effect whatever upon the Young Turks. Talaat, who was so often reasonable on other matters, was ferocious on this subject. 'I have accomplished more towards solving the Armenian problem in three months,' he said, 'than Abdul Hamid accomplished in thirty years.' The Armenians were disloyal, he declared, they had enriched themselves at the expense of the Turks, they had helped the Russians, they were plotting to set up a separate state.

Morgenthau pointed out that Talaat had even turned on his friends among the Armenians.

'No Armenian,' Talaat answered, 'can be our friend after what we have done to them.'

Clearly there was some fundamental thing at work in the Turkish mind, something which was beyond all reason, some terrible instinct that made them feel that they had to persecute somebody in order to establish their own security. The very helplessness of the Armenians seemed to be an incitement. Having once raised their hand, the Turks appear to have felt, with a crazed and guilty logic, that they must go on and on until the very enormity of their cruelty was its own justification. If they *could* do this thing then they must be in the right. This was the only way to compensate for the unexpressed resentment of so many years.

'The Turk,' Aubrey Herbert wrote, 'was unbusinesslike, placid, and lazy or easy-going. But when he turned in his rage he poured out death in a bucket, and guilty and innocent suffered in his blind anger.'

Before March there were about two million Armenians in Turkey, and it was the Young Turks' intention to exterminate or deport them all. This task, however, was never completed; barely three-quarters of a million were dead or dying by the time the frantic rage of their tormentors had exhausted itself.

It would be absurd, of course, to argue that the Allies' failure in the Dardanelles was the only cause of the Armenian massacre; the root instinct of the Turks to destroy this unprotected minority was always there. But March 18 offered them the opportunity, the massacre followed the victory, and the psychological effect on the Turks was immense. From this time onwards the soldiers felt that they were utterly committed; the traitors at home had been stamped out and now they were Moslems together in a common cause. There was no longer any question of surrender or defeat. It was the defiance of the wounded wolf. He had wreaked his vengeance on the weak and now he stood at bay against the world.

Thus before ever the land battle had begun there were decisive influences at work on the Gallipoli campaign, and perhaps in the long run they counted for more than armaments and strategy; March 18 had brought the Turks together, and the *auto-da-fé* of the Armenian massacres had added a certain desperation, the desperation which presumably the outlaw feels. And it was one more complication in this strange mental web that while the Turks were now quite determined to resist the coming invasion they did not really hate the British and the French—not at any rate in the intimate personal way in which they hated the Armenians and perhaps the Russians. It was opposition of a more dangerous kind. For the Turks the Allies were, quite simply, invaders from outer space, and they prepared to meet them as one prepares to face some tremendous natural upheaval like an earthquake or a hurricane at sea. In other words, they got ready to fight not with passion but simply to survive; they were Turks fighting for Turkey, Moslems against the infidel. The battle, as they saw it, was a straight clash of opposites, a trial of strength and skill which could only end in their own extermination or in victory. Such opponents are probably the most formidable of all—and especially so in this case because these things were not really understood in the Allied camp at the time.

The Turks were seriously underrated by the Allies. They had only been known in retreat and in battles outside their own country. They were expected to fight as they fought the Armenians, recklessly and viciously but not as disciplined soldiers who knew the science of modern war. It was even hoped in the War Office in London that once the Allied expeditionary forces were ashore at Gallipoli the enemy would turn tail and make for Constantinople. There might be moments of difficult guerrilla fighting, but it remained in effect for the British and the French a minor operation.

These were very serious delusions, for the Turks in fact were making the most sensible arrangements for the defence of their country. Directly the bombardment of March 18 was over Enver sent a message to Liman von Sanders saying he wanted to see him in his office. Arriving soon afterwards, he offered the Field Marshal the command of the forces at the Dardanelles.

It must have caused Enver some little heartburning to reach this decision, for his relations with Liman had been getting steadily worse from the moment when, three months before, the German general had derided his plans for the invasion of the Caucasus. To Enver, no doubt, this foreign technician was a solemn bore. In his capacity of Inspector-General of the Turkish Forces Liman had been a persistent nuisance; one day it was a complaint about the hospitals (they were in an appalling state, with spotted typhus spreading everywhere), and the next it was a demand for better food for the men, for rifles, for blankets, for uniforms. Enver at least had been able to settle the matter of the uniforms. Just a few soldiers in Constantinople were presentably equipped, and as soon as it was learned that Liman was about to make an inspection this squad was hurried to the spot with freshly polished boots and shining buttons. But Liman soon found out about this and complained again.

The real argument between the two men, however, had arisen over the disposal of the forces in the south. Enver, as commander-in-chief, had drawn a line through the Dardanelles and the Sea of Marmara, and had set up a command on either side, one in Asia, the other in Europe. This arrangement might have been sound enough at the time when Xerxes crossed from east to west in his advance on Europe, but to Liman's mind it was precisely calculated to lead to the complete annihilation of the army as soon as an enemy attacked from the south. In short, the defences were placed exactly the wrong way round; the line should have been drawn east and west through the Sea of Marmara and all the forces to the south of it should have been prepared, under one command, to meet an invasion from the Mediterranean. When Liman advanced this view, Enver had replied calmly that he was wrong and the dispositions were going to stay as they were. By the end of February things had drifted towards an open breach, and Enver had even been intriguing for Liman's recall to Germany.

But now in March when a renewal of the Allied attack on the Dardanelles was expected any minute, it was another matter. Something had to be done quickly about the fortification of Gallipoli.

Liman lost no time in taking up his new command. Having asked for and got the reinforcement of an extra division, he set off on March 25 for the peninsula—the very day on which Hamilton was sailing away from it to regroup his forces in Egypt. Liman's departure indeed was so rapid that in many ways it resembled Hamilton's hurried exit from London twelve days earlier; he waited neither for his staff nor his reinforcements, but took the first available boat and landed in Gallipoli town on the morning of March 26. There he set up his headquarters in the bare rooms of the French consular agent's house and got to work.

The defence of the Gallipoli peninsula and the Dardanelles does not present any great mystery, at all events in its broader aspects. The peninsula juts out into the Ægean Sea for a distance of fifty-two miles, and it has a misshapen lozenge formation—very narrow at the neck, widening out to twelve miles in the centre, and then tapering off again to the tip at Cape Helles. The hills and the beaches are the important features, since an invading army presumably would first want to land, and then as quickly as possible get on to the heights whence it could dominate the Dardanelles. There were four beaches: at Bulair at the neck, at Suvla Bay half way down the peninsula, at Ari Burnu, still further south, and at the tip at Cape Helles. Behind all these landing places there was high ground—it almost formed a spine running down the centre of the peninsula—but the really important eminences were the Tekke Tepe ridge which made a semi-circle around Suvla

Bay, the Sari Bair chain which rose to 1,000 feet just to the north of Ari Burnu, and Achi Baba, a rounded, gently-sloping hill 709 feet high, which was about six miles north of the Cape Helles beaches and dominated them entirely.

Similar beaches and hills existed on the eastern side of the peninsula along the Dardanelles, but it was hardly likely that an enemy would attempt a landing there, since he would come under fire from the Turkish guns in Asia, and so from Liman's point of view they could be disregarded.

There remained the Asiatic side—the danger that the enemy might come ashore somewhere opposite the islands of Tenedos and Mytilene and make his way north across the plains of Troy towards the Narrows.

It was, then, a question of guessing just where the invader was going to strike: at Bulair, where he could cut off the peninsula at the neck, at Suvla and Ari Burnu, half way down, where he could rapidly cross over to the Narrows, at Cape Helles, where his naval guns could dominate the land on three sides, or in Asia, where he had space to manœuvre: or at two or three or all these places?

Liman found that he had six divisions known as the Fifth Army under his command, and at the time of his arrival they were scattered along the coastline in a way which he considered bizarre if not downright dangerous. 'The enemy on landing,' he observed, 'would have found resistance everywhere, but there were no reserves to check a strong and energetic advance. I ordered the divisions to hold their troops together and send only the most indispensable security detachments to the coast.'

It seemed to the new commander that the point of most danger was the Asiatic shore, and he accordingly posted two divisions there to the south and west of Troy—the 11th, and later, the 3rd, which he had trained himself and which was now on its way from Constantinople. Next in priority he placed Bulair, and here two more divisions, the 5th and the 7th, were disposed. A fifth division, the 9th, was sent to Cape Helles. To the sixth and last division, which was now under the command of Mustafa Kemal, there was assigned a special role: it was to remain grouped near Maidos on the Narrows, directly under the commander-in-chief's orders, and would stand ready to go north to Bulair, south to Cape Helles, or across the straits to Asia, according to where the danger most threatened. Liman knew all about Kemal's anti-German views, but he regarded him as an efficient and intelligent soldier; and there may even have been some grudging respect for the new commander-in-chief from Kemal's side. At all events, this mobile assignment suited Kemal admirably.

Liman's headquarters staff in Gallipoli town was Turkish, but he had, scattered through his divisions, a number of German officers in senior commands; and the German gunners and other technicians remained at the Narrows under a German admiral.

Having placed his forces where he wanted them—and these dispositions have been applauded by almost all experts who have studied them—Liman next got his men into training. They had grown stiff, he says, in their garrisons, and he now instituted a programme of drilling and digging. By day the men marched. By night they came down to the coast and worked on new roads and entrenchments. There was a shortage of every kind of material, and much improvisation was required. Spades and other implements were taken from the peasants, and the soldiers even dug the earth with their bayonets. When the supply of barbed wire gave out they ripped up the fences of the farms; and on the most likely landing places this wire was spread beneath the surface of the water. Land mines were constructed out of torpedo heads.

This work was pressed on with great haste, for there were many signs that the Allied attack would not be much longer delayed. Before the end of March Liman learned that four British officers had arrived in Piræus in Greece, and had there bought for cash forty-two large lighters and five tugs. The British apparently were not very successful in keeping watch on spies in Lemnos and the other Greek islands, for a stream of information about the Allies' preparations kept reaching Constantinople by way of Egypt and Greece. General Hamilton's arrival had been reported. It was known that a landing pier had been built in the harbour of Mudros, on Lemnos, and that stores and equipment were being unloaded there. Most of these reports came from the Balkans, but even as far off as Rome German agents were hearing rumours of the coming offensive, and these were duly relayed to the headquarters in Gallipoli. At one time it was said that 50,000 British soldiers had assembled on Imbros and Lemnos. Then the total was increased to 80,000 with 50,000 French in addition. Though confusing, all this intelligence pointed in the same direction: there was not much time left.

Each day, too, there was a good deal of enemy activity which Liman could see with his own eyes. Allied aircraft of a newer, faster pattern had begun to fly over the peninsula on reconnaissance. Like cruising sharks, grey, silent and sinister, the silhouettes of British warships kept ceaselessly moving back and forth far out to sea.

Then in the third week of April there occurred a sudden flurry of activity in the straits themselves.

Shortly after dawn on April 17 Turkish sentries at Kephez Point saw a submarine come to the surface. Apparently it was heading for the Narrows with the intention of passing through to the Sea of Marmara, but suddenly it was caught in a violent eddy and began to drift towards the shore. At once every Turkish gun in the neighbourhood was turned on to the helpless vessel, and as it touched the shore the crew came on deck and were swept into the sea by machine-gun fire. During the next two days and nights an erratic duel took place between the Turks and the British for the abandoned hulk. In turn British submarines, aircraft and warships came rushing into the straits in an attempt to destroy it before the Turks got possession, but their torpedoes went astray, the bombs fell wide, and the warships were driven off by the shore batteries. Finally on the third night a little British patrol boat came sailing straight into the glare of the searchlights and with a lucky shot got one of its torpedoes home.

According to Lewis Einstein, the American Minister in Constantinople, the Turks behaved very well over this incident. When the submarine was first abandoned and the British sailors were struggling in the water the Turkish soldiers on the shore jumped in and rescued them. The dead were first buried on the beach and then taken to the English cemetery at Chanak, where a service was said over them. 'The Turks are extraordinary in this,' Einstein wrote. 'One moment they will murder wantonly, and the next surprise everyone by their kindness. Thus when the first English submarine prisoners were led into the hospital at Chanak, shivering in their wet clothes, the Turkish wounded called them guests, and insisted on their being given everything new, and such few delicacies as they possessed.'

It was only later when the prisoners were sent to filthy prisons in Constantinople that ill-treatment began, but even then in most cases it was the ill-treatment of indifference, of the squalor and callousness of the East rather than an act of deliberate revenge.

Meanwhile another warning had sounded on the Dardanelles. On April 19 a company of Turkish soldiers had made their camp in a fold of the hills on the western side of the peninsula. It was the usual early morning scene: the soldiers asleep on the ground, the smoke of the first cooking fires rising upwards and the lines of horses and mules tethered nearby. Then without warning the terrible searing rush of shells filled the sky and everything was in an uproar of cascading earth and bursting shrapnel. Some thought it was an earthquake and lay still in terror, others ran to the lines of screaming animals and tried to mount and get away, others again who kept their wits went to their guns. But they could see nothing on the flat and deserted sea, nothing but a tiny yellow balloon on the far horizon. It was not until after the campaign that the Turks learned that this was the *Manica*, the first of the British kite-balloon ships, trying out a new artillery spotting device. While the vessel still lay below the horizon out of sight from the land two observers had gone up in a wicker basket attached to the balloon at the end of a long vertiginous swaying cable, and, with the first light of the morning, had seen through their binoculars the peaceful encampment in the hills. It was an easy matter then for the encampment's position to be fixed on the map and the news to be telephoned down to the *Manica's* bridge below; and it was the shells of the cruiser *Bacchante* lying unseen still further out at sea that fell, so miraculously, out of the empty sky on to the sleeping Turks.

And then, a day or two later, a heavy British air-raid, the first of the campaign, fell on Maidos at the Narrows. Seven 100-lb. bombs, an unheard-of kind of missile in the Mediterranean at this time, set the town on fire.

After this there was silence again. No more ships attempted to enter the straits and no gun was fired on either side. The weather continued to be unsettled and cold. Among the Turks, who had now been given almost five weeks in which to prepare their defences, nothing remained

93

to be done but to wait—to post their watchers on the hill tops and the cliffs, to keep gazing out to sea by day and sweeping the straits with their searchlights at night. The dread of the coming invasion was everywhere about them; but where it would fall, and at what hour of the day or night, and what it would look like when it came—of all this they had no notion at all.

SIX

~~~~~~~~~~~~~~~~~~~~~~~~~~~~~~~~~~~~~~

> '*A voice had become audible, a note had been
> struck, more true, more thrilling, more able to do
> justice to the nobility of our youth in arms en-
> gaged in this present war, than any other. . . . The
> voice has been swiftly stilled.*'
>
> WINSTON CHURCHILL in a letter to *The
> Times*, April 26, 1915.

THERE was a fever of excitement about the 'Constantinople
Expedition' among young men in England. 'It's too wonderful for belief,' Rupert Brooke wrote as he was setting
out. 'I had not imagined Fate could be so kind. . . . Will
Hero's Tower crumble under the 15-inch guns? Will the
sea be polyphloisbic and wine-dark and unvintageable?
Shall I loot mosaics from St. Sophia, and Turkish Delight
and carpets? Should we be a Turning Point in History?
Oh God! I've never been quite so happy in my life I think.
Never quite so pervasively happy; like a stream flowing
entirely to one end. I suddenly realize that the ambition
of my life has been—since I was two—to go on a military
expedition against Constantinople.'

Rupert Brooke, with his romanticism, his eagerness and
his extreme physical beauty, is the symbolic figure in the
Gallipoli campaign. One feels that he was destined to be
there, that among all these tens of thousands of young men
this was the one who was perfectly fitted to express their
exuberance, their secret devotion, their 'half joy of life and
half readiness to die'.[1]

---

[1] A phrase of Desmond McCarthy's in a preface to *Ben Ken-
dim* by Aubrey Herbert.

He was just twenty-seven at this time, and the circumstances of his life were almost too good to be true. There had been his lyrical schooldays at Rugby, where he was liked by everybody and where he was in all the teams, and all the literary honours were his. Then Cambridge with the dabblings in socialism, the amateur theatricals, the sittings-up all night, the ramblings through the countryside talking of Oscar Wilde and singing all the way. Like T. E. Lawrence later on he had met and captivated almost everyone who counted in London, from the Asquiths and the Churchills to the Shaws and Henry James. He had travelled everywhere (though always at the end of a thread that tied him to England), and just before the war had been searching for lost Gauguins in Tahiti in the South Pacific. It was Churchill who had obtained for him his commission in the Royal Naval Division which had gone first to Antwerp and was now committed to Gallipoli. More than ever, on the eve of this new adventure, the poet was the hero of Mrs. Cornford's poem:

> *A young Apollo, golden-haired,*
> *Stands dreaming on the verge of strife,*
> *Magnificently unprepared*
> *For the long littleness of life.*

Brooke's own war sonnets were soon to be on everybody's lips:

> *Now, God be thanked who has matched us with His*
> *   hour,*
> *And caught our youth, and wakened us from*
> *   sleeping. . . .*
>
> *Blow out you bugles, over the rich Dead!*
>
> *If I should die think only this of me;*
> *That there's some corner of a foreign field*
> *That is for ever England.*

All this—the charmed life, the beauty, the immense promise of his talents—was now to be risked in battle in the classical Ægean. It was indeed almost too wonderful for belief.

As always, Brooke was surrounded by his friends. There

was young Arthur Asquith, the Prime Minister's son; Aubrey Herbert, the orientalist who 'went to the East by accident as a young man may go to a party, and find his fate there'; others like Charles Lister and Denis Browne who would certainly have been something in the world had they not been about to die. To these, new friends were constantly being added; men like Bernard Freyberg, who was in California when war broke out and came back to England to enlist. He joined the Naval Division.

Soon they were all together in Egypt, living in tents, driving out to the desert to see the pyramids by moonlight, a dedicated group ringed about with its own code and its excitement in the adventure that lay ahead; and they were completely happy. Then Rupert Brooke went down with sunstroke, and the Commander-in-Chief (whom of course he had known in England) called on him in his tent. When Hamilton offered him a place on the headquarters staff Brooke refused; he wanted to be at the landing on Gallipoli with his men.

'He looked extraordinarily handsome,' Hamilton wrote in his diary, 'quite a knightly presence stretched out there on the sand with the only world that counts at his feet.'

Compton Mackenzie in his *Gallipoli Memories* relates how he too was caught up in the Gallipoli fever. He was living at Capri at the time, had just published *Sinister Street* (which had made his name), and was working on the concluding chapters of *Guy and Pauline*. Directly he heard of the expedition he was in a frenzy of impatience to get to Egypt. Friends in Whitehall found him a job on Hamilton's staff, and presently he was off down the Mediterranean on the first available boat out of Naples, appalled that as yet he had no uniform, and beset with anxiety that he would not arrive in time.

Almost all these young men—and thousands of others less imaginative but just as ardent—were facing the prospect of battle for the first time, and their letters and diaries reveal how strongly the sense of adventure communicated itself through the Army. For the moment the constricting fear of the unknown was overlaid by the newness and the excitement of the occasion, the feeling that they were isolated together here in this remote place and entirely dependent upon one another. They were determined to be brave. They were convinced that they were committed to something which was larger and grander than life itself,

97

perhaps even a kind of purification, a release from the pettiness of things.

'Once in a generation,' Hamilton wrote in his diary, 'a mysterious wish for war passes through the people. Their instinct tells them that *there is no other way* of progress and of escape from habits that no longer fit them. Whole generations of statesmen will fumble over reforms for a lifetime which are put into full-blooded execution within a week of a declaration of war. There is *no other way*. Only by intense sufferings can the nations grow, just as a snake once a year must with anguish slough off the once beautiful coat which has now become a strait jacket.'

In the long tradition of British poet-generals Hamilton remains an exception of an extremely elusive kind. One knows everything and nothing about him. Whether one is dealing with the poet or the general at any given point it is almost impossible to tell. Somewhere about this time— April 1915—there was a remarkable photograph taken of the General on board the *Triad,* and this perhaps reveals him more intimately than all the diaries and the opinions of his friends. One recognizes the other figures in the group at once. Admiral de Robeck stands with his feet firmly planted on the deck, his arms clasped behind his back, and his steady, carved, admiral's face belongs to gales at sea. Keyes, at his side, is exactly as he ought to be: a slim, angular figure, alas not a beautiful face with those big ears, but most engaging. Braithwaite, the Chief of Staff, is the handsome professional; he fills his uniform like a soldier and he knows where he is. But it is upon Hamilton that one inevitably fixes one's eye. Everything about him is wrong. He has adopted an almost mincing attitude, his shoulders half-turned in embarrassment towards the camera, one hand resting on a stanchion in a curiously feminine way and the other grasping what appears to be a scarf or a piece of material at his side. The fingers are long, shapely and intensely sensitive,[1] the face quite firm and patrician but somehow nervous and ill-at-ease. His uniform does not fit him—or rather he gives the impression that he ought not to be in uniform at all. His cap is a disaster. Braithwaite has the right kind of cap and it suits him; Hamilton's perches like a pancake on his head, his tunic is bus-conduc-

---

[1] Actually his hand was partly paralysed and he is holding a fly-whisk.

torish, his breeches too tight for his wilting bow legs. Physically he is the last possible man one can imagine as a commander-in-chief. He simply does not inspire confidence.

And yet it is clear beyond any doubt from this photograph that here is an exceptionally intelligent man—much more intelligent than any of the others. One looks again and finds oneself hoping that this intelligence, this sensitivity and bird-like quickness, also contains a germ of resolution, perhaps some special sort of refined courage which we had missed before; and still one remains uncertain.

It is left to his record to reassure us. The General was sixty-two when this picture was taken. He was born in the Mediterranean on the island of Corfu, and had spent the whole of his adult life in the Army—indeed, he had seen more active service than almost any other senior general. He had fought the tribesmen on the north-west frontier of India, had served throughout the Boer War, and had been with the Japanese in Manchuria in the Russo-Japanese war. In recent years he had held the appointments of commander-in-chief in the Mediterranean and Inspector-General of Overseas Forces. According to his contemporaries, Hamilton was one of those unusual men who apparently are quite indifferent to danger. His left hand had been shattered early in his career, and more than once he had been recommended for the Victoria Cross.

There was one other thing that set him apart, and that was his exceptional talent as a writer. He read and wrote much poetry and he loved to keep diaries in a kind of French shorthand which he had invented himself; these jottings, he said, cleared his mind and put events into perspective when he was in command in the field. As a staff officer he had been full of ideas. His *Staff Officer's Scrapbook*, for example, had foretold the disappearance of cavalry in favour of trench warfare.

There is a theme running through his life, and that is Lord Kitchener. Kitchener was Hamilton's star. Fifteen years before Hamilton had served as the Field Marshal's chief-of-staff in South Africa, and the intimacy that had grown up between them was a good deal more than the relationship of the admiring junior to his chief; there was a strength in Kitchener, a massiveness, which appears to have deeply satisfied something which was wanting in

99

Hamilton's own life. He was quite shrewd enough to see Kitchener's weaknesses, and in his diaries he occasionally permitted himself to fret about them as a woman will fret about her husband. But Kitchener had only to speak out and Hamilton dissolved at once. Old K. In the end he was bigger than them all. One had to protect him from the fools and the critics. Never for an instant does Hamilton challenge his chief's authority. Never does he fail to pause before taking a major decision and ask himself, 'What would K. have done?' And Kitchener on his side promotes his follower, occasionally favours him with his confidence, and now sends him off to Constantinople.

Henry Nevinson, the war correspondent, has an interesting note on Hamilton's character: 'From a mingled Highland and Irish descent he had inherited the so-called Celtic qualities which are regarded by thorough Englishmen with varying admiration and dislike. His blood gave him so conspicuous a physical courage that after the battles of Caesar's Camp and Diamond Hill the present writer, who knew him there, regarded him as an example of the rare type which not merely conceals fear with success, but does not feel it. Undoubtedly he was deeply tinged with the "Celtic charm"—that glamour of mind and courtesy of behaviour which create suspicion among people endowed with neither.'

After the war Hamilton was criticized for being so much under Kitchener's thumb, for being a weak commander, a commentator on battles instead of a man of action. But it is only fair to remember that he was respected and liked by Winston Churchill and a great many other demanding people in London. At Gallipoli none of his contemporaries speak against him—not Keyes nor any of the Admirals, not any of the French. The one man who attacks him is a corps commander whom Hamilton dismissed. Under Hamilton's command there is never any dispute between the Army and the Navy, and all the Allied contingents serve him with the utmost loyalty.

This in itself was something of an achievement, for the force that was now assembling itself in Egypt was a very mixed bag indeed. There were the French, a splendid sight on the parade ground, their officers in black and gold, the men in blue breeches and red coats. There were Zouaves and Foreign Legionaries from Africa, Sikhs and Gurkhas from India, and the labour battalions of Levantine Jews and Greeks. There were the sailors of the British and French Navies. There were the Scottish, English and Irish troops. And finally there were the New Zealanders and the Australians.

These last were an unknown quantity. They were all volunteers, they were paid more money than any of the other soldiers, and they exhibited a spirit which was quite unlike anything which had been seen on a European battlefield before. A strange change had overtaken this transplanted British blood. Barely a hundred years before their ancestors had gone out to the other side of the world from the depressed areas of the United Kingdom, many of them dark, small, hungry men. Their sons who had now returned to fight in their country's first foreign war had grown six inches in height, their faces were thin and leathery, their limbs immensely lithe and strong. Their voices too had developed a harsh cockney accent of their own, and their command of the more elementary oaths and blasphemies, even judged by the most liberal army standards, was appalling. Such military forms as the salute did not come very easily to these men, especially in the presence of British officers, whom they regarded as effete, and their own officers at times appeared to have very little control over them. Each evening in thousands the Australians and New Zealanders came riding into Cairo from their camp near the pyramids for a few hours' spree in the less respectable streets, riding on the tops of trams, urging their hired cabs and donkeys along the road—and the city shuddered a little.

This independent spirit was a promising thing in its own way, but for Birdwood, the British officer who was put in command of the Anzac[1] corps, there was a problem here which could not be easily solved. The men were nearly all civilians, and who could say how they would behave when they came under enemy fire for the first time? A period of intensive training began, but there was not much time.

Indeed, there was very little time for any of the matters which Hamilton had to attend to if he was to honour his undertaking that the attack would be launched by the middle of April. He did not reach Alexandria until the after-

[1] ANZAC: Australian and New Zealand Army Corps. The word bears an unfortunate resemblance to the Turkish 'ANSAC' which means 'almost'.

noon of March 26, and this meant he had barely three weeks in hand. The job that lay before the General was, in effect, nothing less than the setting up of the largest amphibious operation in the whole history of warfare. No similar exploit in the past bore any real comparison: in 1588 the Spanish Armada never did succeed in landing its men on England; neither Napoleon in Egypt in 1799 nor the British and the French in the Crimea in 1854 had had to face such entrenched positions as Liman von Sanders was now establishing at Gallipoli. In fact the only operation that could be compared with this lay thirty years ahead on the beaches of Normandy in the second world war; and the planning of the Normandy landing was to take not three weeks but nearly two years.

Hamilton's mind went back to classical times. 'The landing of an army upon the theatre of operations I have described,' he wrote in one of his despatches, '—a theatre strongly garrisoned throughout and prepared for any such attempt—involved difficulties for which no precedent was forthcoming in military history, except possibly in the sinister legends of Xerxes.'

There were some 75,000 men at the General's disposal: 30,000 Australians and New Zealanders divided into two divisions, the 29th British Division of 17,000 men, one French division of 16,000, and the Royal Naval Division of 10,000. All these forces, together with 1,600 horses, donkeys and mules and 300 vehicles, had to be so assembled on board the ships that they would be able to land together on the enemy coast under the direct fire of the Turkish guns.

It is a matter of some surprise that the expedition ever got to sea at all. On March 26 Hamilton's administrative staff had still not arrived from England (it did not get to Alexandria until April 11), many of the soldiers were still at sea, no accurate maps existed, there was no reliable information about the enemy, no plan had been made, and no one had yet decided where the Army was to be put ashore.

The simplest of questions were unanswered. Was there water on the shore or not? What roads existed? What casualties were to be expected and how were the wounded men to be got off to the hospital ships? Were they to fight in trenches or in the open, and what sort of weapons were required? What was the depth of water off the beaches and what sort of boats were needed to get the men, the guns and the stores ashore? Would the Turks resist or would they break as they had done at Sarikamish; and if so how were the Allies to pursue them without transport or supplies?

It was perhaps the very confusion of this situation which made it possible for the staff to get things done. Since no one could really calculate what the difficulties were going to be it was simply a matter of taking the material that came to hand, and of hoping for the best. A period of hectic improvisation began. Men were sent into the bazaars of Alexandria and Cairo to buy skins, oildrums, kerosene tins—anything that would hold water. Others bought tugs and lighters on the docks; others again rounded up donkeys and their native drivers and put them into the Army. There were no periscopes (for trench fighting), no hand grenades and trench-mortars; ordnance workshops set to work to design and make them. In the absence of maps staff officers scoured the shops for guide-books.

On the Alexandria docks lamps were set up so that the work of unloading and repacking the ships could go on all night, and soon the harbour was filled with vessels of every kind from Thames tugboats to requisitioned liners. There was a shortage of almost everything—of guns, of ammunition, of aircraft and of men—and Hamilton sent off a series of messages to Kitchener asking for reinforcements. He had found a brigade of Gurkhas in the Egyptian garrison—could he have those? Where were his reserves of artillery and shells? These requests were met either with terse refusals or no reply at all. Hamilton felt that he was hardly in a position to press the point; Kitchener had been known to be ruthless with subordinates who nagged him, and once he had even taken troops away from an officer who had asked for reinforcements. Then too Hamilton remembered that he had promised Kitchener before he left that he would not embarrass him with requests of this kind. Churchill of course would have helped, but the General had deliberately cut himself off from the First Lord. De Robeck also was chary about asking for too much since his messages were bound to go directly to Fisher in the Admiralty.

'Even more than in the Fleet,' Hamilton wrote, 'I find in

the Air Service the profound conviction that, if they could only get into direct touch with Winston Churchill, all would be well. Their faith in the First Lord is, in every sense, *touching*. But they can't get the contact and they are thoroughly imbued with the idea that the Sea Lords are at the best half-hearted; at the worst, actively antagonistic to us and the whole of our enterprise.'

Hamilton's own divisional commanders were very far from being enthusiastic. Before drawing up his plans for the invasion the General asked them for their views, and he received a most discouraging series of replies. Hunter-Weston, the commander of the 29th Division, thought that the difficulties were so great that the expedition ought to be abandoned altogether. Paris, the commander of the Naval Division, wrote, 'To land would be difficult enough if surprise were possible but hazardous in the extreme under present conditions.' Birdwood changed his ground; he no longer wanted to go ashore at the tip of the peninsula but at Bulair or somewhere in the neighbourhood of Troy. The French too were all for Asia. Even the Egyptian sultan at a ceremonial luncheon at the Abdin Palace in Cairo offered his opinion. The Turkish forts at the Dardanelles, he assured Hamilton, were absolutely impregnable.

There were other worries which were no less serious. The security position was almost entirely out of hand. Greek trading caiques were noting every preparation in the islands and carrying the news back to enemy agents in Athens. Letters were arriving in Alexandria by the ordinary post from England marked, 'Constantinople Force, Egypt.' And the *Egyptian Gazette* in Cairo not only announced the arrival of each new contingent but openly discussed the chances of the expedition at the Dardanelles. Hamilton protested in vain; he was told that since Egypt was a neutral country the British authorities could not interfere with the newspapers. The best therefore that could be hoped was that the Turks would regard all this publicity as an elaborate bluff, and Intelligence was instructed to spread a rumour through the Near East that the actual landing would be made at Smyrna.

All this was very depressing. But Kitchener had said that the attempt must be made, and so there could be no question of turning back. In the first week of April, therefore, Hamilton and his staff set about drawing up their plans at

104

their headquarters in the Metropole Hotel in Alexandria. Even if they had faltered—and Hamilton seems to have been at his best during these days, patient, optimistic and extremely energetic—there now began to grow up around him an atmosphere that made it all the more imperative for him to go on. The expedition began to develop a life of its own. However gloomy the commanders might be, a communal will for action had spread itself through the Army. The men were eager to be off, and it was becoming perfectly clear that they would go into the first assault with great determination. The very sight of the ships gathering in Alexandria harbour, the hammerings in the workshops, the long lines of marching men in the desert, the heavy booming of the artillery at practice—all these things seemed to make it inevitable that they must go forward, and that once they attacked they were bound to win. This auto-suggestion, this mass-will towards adventure, presently began to take effect upon the generals. As the date of the assault grew nearer their earlier misgivings were swallowed up in the practical and stimulating work of getting the Army ready to fight. D'Amade, the French commander, drops his ideas on Asia. Birdwood is now sure that he can get his Australians and New Zealanders ashore. Paris sees chances he overlooked before. And Hunter-Weston, having studied the maps and the forces, declares that his earlier appreciation was wrong—the thing is very possible and he particularly likes the role that he himself is to play.

By April 8 Hamilton judged that the arrangements were moving forward at a sufficient pace to enable him to get away and place his plan before de Robeck and the Admirals. The *Arcadian,* a liner which normally made pleasure cruises to the Norwegian fjords, had been fitted up as a headquarters ship, and in her he sailed for Lemnos. He arrived in Mudros Harbour on April 10, and at once proceeded to his vital conference with the admirals aboard the *Queen Elizabeth.*

Hamilton's plan, though complicated in its details, amounted to a simple assault upon the Gallipoli peninsula itself. The main striking force was to be his best division, the British 29th, under Hunter-Weston. It was to go ashore on five small beaches at Cape Helles at the extreme tip of the peninsula, and it was hoped that by the end of the first day the crest of Achi Baba, six miles inland, would be in its hands. Meanwhile Birdwood was to land with the Anzac Force about thirteen miles up the coast between Gaba Tepe and Fisherman's Hut. Striking across the peninsula through the Sari Bair hills he was to make for Mal Tepe—the mountain on which Xerxes is supposed to have sat while he reviewed his fleet in the Hellespont. Thus the Turks fighting Hunter-Weston at Cape Helles would be cut off in their rear, and the hills dominating the Narrows would be overcome.

Simultaneously, two main diversions were to be carried out. The Royal Naval Division was to make a pretence at landing at the neck at Bulair, and the French were to go ashore for a large armed raid on Kum Kale on the Asiatic side of the Straits. Later these two forces would be brought back to Cape Helles and put into the main attack. By the second or the third day it was hoped that the lower half of the peninsula would be so overrun that the Fleet with its minesweepers could safely pass through the Narrows into the Sea of Marmara.

De Robeck, Wemyss and Keyes were delighted with this plan. They agreed with Hamilton that he was right in rejecting Bulair. It was much too dangerous, despite all its attractions. Directly the Army advanced inland it would lose the support of the naval guns and expose itself to attack on both its flanks—one Turkish army coming down from Thrace and another coming up from Gallipoli. There was also the possibility that Bulgaria might declare war and threaten Hamilton in his rear. The same kind of difficulties would apply if the Allies made their main assault in Asia.

On the peninsula itself no beach was large enough to allow the Army to concentrate for one hammer blow, but the Fleet would be there to cover the assault at every point, and in any case there was a certain virtue in dispersal: Liman von Sanders would get reports of landings from half a dozen different places at once, and for the first twenty-four hours at least he would not know which was the main one. Therefore he would hold back his reserves until the Allies were securely ashore.

There was to be one important refinement of the plan, and this was a stratagem put forward by a Commander Unwin, who seems to have been inspired by the story of the wooden horse at the siege of Troy. He proposed to secrete 2,000 men in an innocent looking collier, the *River Clyde*, and run her aground at Cape Helles. Directly she touched, a steam hopper and two lighters were to be brought round to her bows and lashed together to form a bridge to the shore. The men would then issue from two sallyports which were to be cut in the ship's sides. Running along two gangplanks to a platform at the ship's bows, they would drop on to the bridge and make their way to the beach. It was hoped in this way to empty the ship within a few minutes. In addition, machine guns were to be mounted behind sandbags in the bows, and these were to hold the enemy down while the disembarkation was taking place.

The Navy indeed had been extremely busy with a number of such devices and improvisations. Quite apart from Keyes' new fleet of destroyer-minesweepers which was now ready, three dummy battleships had arrived. These were ordinary merchantmen enlarged and disguised with wooden guns and superstructure. From a distance the silhouette they presented was exactly that of a battleship, and it was hoped that their presence here in the Ægean might induce the German Fleet to come out and fight in the North Sea.[1]

Air Commodore Samson was now established on Tenedos, and the seaplane carrier *Ark Royal* had joined the Fleet. Samson's difficulties had been almost crippling. When his thirty aircraft were uncrated only five were found to be serviceable, and their equipment was not such as to inspire confidence. Bombs were either released from a primitive rack under the pilot's feet or simply flung overboard by the observer once the safety tabs had been removed. No machine-guns had been fitted at this stage, but instead, there was available a supply of iron spikes; these the pilot or the observer could aim at such of the enemy who appeared below, rather in the manner of a hunter spearing a bear. Although these spikes emitted an unpleasant whirring noise as they descended, and no doubt created a feeling of extreme insecurity among the infantry below, they seldom hit anything. For the rest, Samson's pilots carried a revolver, binoculars and a lifebelt or an empty petrol can to hold

[1] One of them was subsequently torpedoed by a U-boat near Malta, and must have occasioned some surprise to the Germans. As the ship settled her wooden turrets and her 12-inch guns floated away on the tide.

on to in case they fell into the sea. The observers were equipped with a rifle, charts and a watch.

On Tenedos an airfield 800 yards long had been constructed with the aid of Greek workmen who uprooted a vineyard and with oil drums filled with cement rolled the ground moderately flat. But it was not altogether a satisfactory base. From the island the Gallipoli peninsula could be clearly seen, but Cape Helles was seventeen and a half miles away, and Gaba Tepe, where the Australians and New Zealanders were to land, thirty-one miles, and these were formidable distances for an aircraft in those days. Constantinople, of course, was out of the question.

Despite these hazards Samson, doing a great deal of flying himself, was already beginning to produce useful results. Carrying volunteer naval officers as observers—usually lightweight midshipmen—he got his new radio-telephone into use, and the spotting for the Fleet's guns greatly improved. Since the radio-telephone was a one-way system the warships checked back the messages they received with a searchlight. Several bombardments had been carried out in this way, notably the raid on Maidos on April 23.

Much the most important part of Samson's work, however, in these last days before the attack was his photography of the enemy entrenchments. Hamilton and Keyes together made a close study of these photographs, and were not reassured. At all but one or two places where the landings were to be made there were abundant signs of barbed-wire. This wire was becoming a nightmare in all their minds, and Hamilton privately confided to Samson that he feared that the casualties might be as high as fifty per cent in the first landing. Had they been able to get hold of some of the Navy's new armoured invasion boats it might have been a different story—but these were a closely guarded secret in the Admiralty at the time, and not even Kitchener was supposed to know anything about them.

When Hamilton had left the Dardanelles in March it had been understood that the Navy would keep harassing the Turks with a series of bombardments along the coast; but now it was found that all such operations were impossible. The entire energies of the Fleet were consumed in the arrangements for the landing. It was decided that the bulk of the invasion force should assemble in Mudros Harbour in the island of Lemnos, with subsidiary bases on Imbros,

Tenedos and Skyros. Forty-eight hours before the landing the Fleet with the Army on board would start to move towards its battle stations off the Gallipoli peninsula. A mile or two from the coast the soldiers would be transferred to lighters and small boats and these, in groups of four, would be towed by launches to the shore. The actual landing would take place in the first light of dawn, the assaulting troops carrying with them nothing more than 200 rounds of ammunition, their rifles and trenching tools and three days' rations.

All this required elaborate preparation: the construction of tows and wharves and barges; the training of midshipmen in piloting launches to fixed points on the strange coast in darkness; the study of the currents and the weather; the arrangements for getting animals on shore and the piping of fresh water from the ships to the beaches; the fixing of signals and codes; the allotting of targets to the battleships and cruisers which would support the landing; the working-out of the whole vast time-table for the movements of the Fleet. Every problem was new or at any rate unusual; there was even a plan for evacuating the Army in case the assault miscarried either in part or altogether.

Meanwhile Hamilton's 75,000 men had to be transported from Egypt to the islands, a distance of some 700 miles.

Astonishingly—even miraculously—these arrangements and many others went forward without any major setback. Just once the crew of a transport on its way to Lemnos was forced to abandon ship when a Turkish destroyer appeared, but the enemy torpedoes went clean under the vessel's keel and soon the men were scrambling back on board. Chased by British destroyers the Turkish ship ran for the shore, and beached herself off Chios. Even the weather seemed to prove that Hamilton had been wise to delay, for there were hardly two fine days together in the first fortnight in April. Provisionally the day for the assault was fixed on April 23, which was St. George's Day; the moon then was due to set two hours before dawn, and thus the armada would be able to approach the coast in the darkness. But on April 21 half a gale set in, and the attack was postponed, at first twenty-four and then forty-eight hours. Finally Sunday, April 25, was chosen as the day.

The island of Lemnos, which had been loaned to the Allies by the Venizelist government in Greece, is reputed to be the abode of Vulcan, and the Argonauts are said to have rested there for a time. By the standards of the Ægean Sea it is not, however, a beautiful place. Few trees can be made to grow, and the local inhabitants have never been able to scratch much more than a bare living from the harsh volcanic rock and the surrounding sea. An uneventful timeless life goes by.

This island now became, in April 1915, the scene of one of the great maritime spectacles of the war. Ship after ship steamed into Mudros Harbour until there were some two hundred of them anchored there, and they made a city on the water. In addition to the warships, every possible variety of vessel had been pressed into service to transport the troops: brightly-painted Greek caiques and pleasure steamers, trawlers and ferryboats, colliers and transatlantic liners. Among the long lines of great battleships and cruisers some vessels, like the Russian cruiser *Askold,* became great objects of wonder. The *Askold* carried five extremely tall perpendicular funnels, and the soldiers at once renamed her the Packet of Woodbines. Then there was the ancient French battleship *Henri IV,* which had scarcely a foot of freeboard and a superstructure so towered and turreted that she looked like a medieval castle, a Braque drawing in heavy grey. These antiquities found themselves lying side by side with the latest submarines and destroyers.

A detached observer might have found the scene almost gay and regatta-like. From shore to ship and from ship to ship swarms of motor-boats and cutters ran about. Every vessel flew its flag, the smoke from hundreds of funnels rose up into the sky, and from one direction or another the sound of bugles and military bands was constantly floating across the water. There was movement everywhere. On the crowded ships the men who were to make the first assault were exercised in getting down rope ladders into boats. Others drilled on deck. Others again exercised the animals on shore. By night thousands of lights and signal lamps sparkled across the bay.

In the midst of this scene, dominating it and imparting an air of great strength and resolution, rode the flagship, the *Queen Elizabeth,* in which Hamilton had decided to make his headquarters with de Robeck until he was able to set up on shore on the Gallipoli peninsula.

An immense enthusiasm pulsated through the Fleet. With

the sight of so many ships around them it seemed to all but a few sceptics more certain than ever that they could not fail. Everyone was delighted when the men scrawled slogans across the sides of their transports: 'Turkish Delight'; 'To Constantinople and the Harems'. They lined the decks shouting and cat-calling to one another, cheering each ship that arrived or departed from the harbour. Finally the excitement of the adventure had seized upon everybody's mind, and the inward choking feeling of dread was overlaid by an outward gaiety, by the exaltation and otherworldness that chloroforms the soldier in the last moments of waiting.

The morning of April 23 broke fine and clear, and de Robeck gave orders for the operations to begin. All that day and on the day following the slower transports amid cheers moved out of Mudros and steamed toward their rendezvous off the beaches. By the evening of Saturday, April 24, the 200 ships were in motion, those carrying the Royal Naval Division headed for the Gulf of Saros, the Anzac contingent making for Imbros, the British and the French for Tenedos. The sea was again unsettled, and a sharp wind blew. As dusk fell a wet three-quarter moon with a halo round it was seen in the sky, but presently this halo cleared away, bright moonlight flooded the night, and the waves began to subside to perfect calm.

Hamilton, going aboard the *Queen Elizabeth*, found a signal waiting for him. Rupert Brooke was dead. His sunstroke had developed into blood poisoning, and he had died on a French hospital ship at the island of Skyros, just a few hours before he was due to set off for Gallipoli. Freyberg, Browne, Lister and others of his friends had carried him up to an olive grove on the heights of the island, and had buried him there with a rough pile of marble on the grave.

Towards midnight the warships with the assault troops on board were beginning to reach their battle stations. When they were still out of sight of land the ships came to a dead stop, all hands were roused, and a meal of hot coffee and rolls was given to the soldiers. In silence then, with their rifles in their hands and their packs on their backs, the men fell in on numbered squares on deck. There seems to have been no confusion as each platoon went down the ladders hand over hand, and directly the boats were filled they were towed by pinnaces in groups to the stern. The moon had

111

now set, and there remained only a faint starlight in the sky. The battleships, each with four lines of boats behind it, steamed slowly forward again towards the shore. Soon after 4 a.m. the outline of the coast became visible through the early morning mist. An utter stillness enveloped the cliffs; there was no sign of life or movement anywhere.

SEVEN

A STRANGE light plays over the Gallipoli landing on April 25, and no matter how often the story is retold there is still an actuality about it, a feeling of suspense and incompleteness. Although nearly half a century has gone by, nothing yet seems fated about the day's events, a hundred questions remain unanswered, and in a curious way one feels that the battle might still lie before us in the future; that there is still time to make other plans and bring it to a different ending.

Hardly anyone behaves on this day as you might have expected him to do. One can think of half a dozen moves that the commanders might have made at any given moment, and very often the thing they did do seems the most improbable of all. There is a certain clarity about the actions of Mustafa Kemal on the Turkish side, and of Roger Keyes with the British, but for the others—and perhaps at times for these two as well—the great crises of the day appear to have gone cascading by as though they were some natural phenomenon, having a monstrous life of its own, and for the time being entirely out of control.

For the soldiers in the front line the issues were, of course, brutally simple, but even here the most implausible situations develop; having captured some vital position a kind of inertia seizes both officers and men. Fatigue overwhelms them and they can think of nothing but retreat. Confronted by some quite impossible objective their lives suddenly appear to them to be of no consequence at all; they get up and charge and die. Thus vacuums occur all along the line; while all is peace and quiet in one valley a frightful carnage rages in the next; and this for no apparent reason, unless it be that men are always a little mad in battle and fear and courage combine at last to paralyse the mind.

Even the natural elements—the unexpected currents in the sea, the unmapped countryside, the sudden changes in the weather—have a certain eccentricity at Gallipoli. When for an instant the battle composes itself into a coherent pattern all is upset by some chance shifting of the wind, some stray cloud passing over the moon.

And so no programme goes according to plan, never at any moment through the long day can you predict what will happen next. Often it is perfectly clear to the observer that victory is but a hairsbreadth away—just one more move, just this or that—but the move is never made, and instead, like a spectator at a Shakespearean drama, one is hurried off to some other crisis in another part of the forest.

The movements of both the commanders-in-chief were very strange. Instead of putting himself aboard some fast detached command vessel like the *Phaeton*, with adequate signalling equipment, Hamilton chose to immure himself in the conning tower of the *Queen Elizabeth*, and thereby he cut himself off both from his staff and from direct command of what was happening on shore. The *Queen Elizabeth* was a fighting ship with her own duties to perform quite independently of the commander-in-chief, and although she was able to cruise up and down the coast at the General's will, she could never get near enough to the beaches for him to understand what was going on; and the firing of her huge guns can scarcely have been conducive to clear thinking. Hamilton, in any case, had resolved before ever the battle began not to interfere unless he was asked—all tactical authority was handed over to his two corps commanders, Hunter-Weston with the British on the Cape Helles front, and Birdwood with the Anzac forces at Gaba Tepe. Since these two officers also remained at sea through the vital hours of the day they too were without accurate information. Signalling arrangements on the shore began to fail as soon as the first contact with the enemy was made, and very soon each separate unit was left to its own devices. Thus no senior commander had any clear picture of the battle, and battalions divided by only a mile or two from the main front might just as well have

114

been fighting on the moon for all the control the commanders exercised upon them.

On several occasions Hamilton might have committed a mobile reserve of troops with the most telling consequences, but it never occurred to him to do this without his subordinates' approval, those same subordinates who were almost as much in ignorance as he was, and in no position to approve or disapprove of anything. And so all day the commander-in-chief cruises up and down the coast in his huge battleship. He hesitates, he communes with himself, he waits; and it is not until late that night that, suddenly and courageously, he intervenes with a resolute decision.

Liman von Sanders' actions on April 25 were more understandable but hardly more inspired. He was at his headquarters in the town of Gallipoli when, at 5 a.m., he was woken with the news that the Allies had landed. There were, he says, many pale faces around him as the reports came in. The first of these reports arrived from Besika Bay, south of Kum Kale in Asia: a squadron of enemy warships was approaching the coast there with the apparent intention of putting a force ashore. This was quickly followed by news of the actual landing of the French at Kum Kale, and of heavy fighting on the peninsula, both at Cape Helles and near Gaba Tepe. Still another part of the Allied Fleet had steamed up into the Bay of Saros and had opened fire on the Bulair lines. Which of these five advances was the main attack?

Liman judged that it must be at Bulair. This was the point where he could be most seriously hit, and he felt bound to safeguard it until he knew more clearly which way the battle was going to go. Ordering the Seventh Division to march north from Gallipoli (that is to say *away* from the main battle) he himself with two adjutants galloped on ahead to the neck of the peninsula. While the early sun was still low on the horizon he drew rein on a high patch of ground near the Tomb of Suleiman the Magnificent and looked down on to Saros Bay. There he saw twenty Allied warships firing broadsides on the shore, with the shells of the Turkish batteries erupting in the sea around them. It was not possible to estimate how many soldiers the enemy had brought to this attack, because a high wall made of the branches of trees had been laid along the decks of the ships, but boats filled with men were already being lowered into the sea. They came on towards the beaches until the Turkish machine-gun fire thickened about them. Then they turned and retired out of range, as though they were waiting for reinforcements before renewing the assault.

Liman was studying this scene when Essad Pasha, one of his Turkish corps commanders, brought him the news that the troops in the toe of the peninsula, some forty miles away to the southwest, were being hard pressed and were urgently calling for reinforcements. Essad Pasha was ordered to proceed at once by sea to the Narrows and take command there. But Liman himself lingered on at Bulair. Even when Essad reported later in the day from Maidos that the battle in the south was growing critical, Liman still could not bring himself to believe that the landings near Gaba Tepe and Cape Helles were anything more than a diversion. However, he dispatched five battalions by sea from Gallipoli to the Narrows, while he himself remained behind in the north with his staff.

That night the fire from the enemy warships off Bulair died away, and when no further action followed in the morning Liman was persuaded at last that the real battle lay in the peninsula itself. He then took a major decision: the remainder of the two divisions at Bulair were ordered south, and he himself proceeded to Mal Tepe, near the Narrows, to take command.

Thus on both sides the opening phases of the battle were fought in the absence of the commanders-in-chief; each having made his plan stood back and left the issue to the soldiers in their awful collision on the shore.

The behaviour of the Turks is another part of the mystery. It is true that they were defending their own soil against a new Christian invasion from the west. They had their faith, and their priests were with them in the trenches inciting them to fight in the name of Allah and Mahomet. For many weeks they had been preparing for this day; they were rested and ready. But when all this is said, one still finds it difficult to understand their *esprit de corps*. For the most part they were illiterate conscripts from the country, and they fought simply because they were ordered to fight. Many of them had been without pay for months, they were poorly fed and badly looked after in every way; and the discipline was harsh.

One would have thought that these things would have

been enough to have broken their spirit when the first dreadful barrage fell upon them from the sea. Yet, with one or two exceptions, the Turks fought with fantastic bravery on this day, and although they were always out-gunned and outnumbered their steadiness never forsook them. They were not in the least undisciplined in the way they fought; they were very cool and very skilful.

Nor is the conduct of the Allied soldiers very easily explained. Certainly they had the expedition feeling; they were young and consequently they believed that they could do anything. Yet very few of Hamilton's troops had ever come under fire before or had ever killed a man or seen death around them. The midshipmen who took the boats to the shore were hardly more than children, and even the professional French and British soldiers had little conception of the nature of a modern battle, let alone so strange and perilous an operation as this. In the case of the Australians and New Zealanders there was not even a tradition to guide them, for there had been no wars at all in their country's past. They had no immediate ancestors to live up to—it was simply a matter of proving themselves to themselves, of starting a tradition here and now.

The unknown, which is the real destroyer of courage, pressed more heavily on the Allies than the Turks, for these young men were a long way from their homes, most of them had lived much more protected lives than the Anatolian peasant, and now, at this first experience of war, they were the ones who had to get up into the open and expose themselves while the Turks remained in their safe and familiar trenches. Everything before the Allied soldiers was unknown: the dark sea, the waiting enemy, the very coast itself and all that lay beyond. And it was perhaps not very helpful that General Hunter-Weston should have made a proclamation to the 29th Division before the battle saying, 'heavy losses by bullets, by shells, by mines and by drowning are to be expected.' But none of this made any difference.

A wild exuberance seems to have seized upon everybody's mind. The Australians rush ashore shouting 'Imshi Yallah', a phrase they had picked up in more careless days in Cairo. The sixteen-year-old British midshipman, standing up very straight at the tiller, grounds his boat on the sand, cries out some phrase from the football field, and

117

such of his men who are still alive follow him ashore. The French doctor, operating in a ghastly welter of blood, makes a note in his diary, 'I have sublime stretcher-bearers.'

They probably were sublime, for nearly everyone seems to have been possessed with an inhuman recklessness and selflessness on this day. On one beach alone no fewer than five Victoria Crosses were won within a few hours of the landing.

Still another decoration[1] was awarded to Lieut.-Commander Bernard Freyberg in circumstances which, though hardly typical of the fighting, do manage to convey perhaps as well as anything the curiously dedicated courage of the men. Freyberg, who was one of the party who had buried Rupert Brooke on Skyros two days before, came north with the Royal Naval Division, and as part of the pretended landing which was so successful in delaying Liman von Sanders at Bulair he was chosen to lead a boatload of soldiers ashore in the darkness. At the last moment, however, he pointed out that it was unwise to risk the lives of a whole platoon when one man would suffice. Accordingly he had himself taken towards the land in a naval cutter, and when the boat was still two miles from the coast he slipped naked into the icy midnight sea and swam ashore carrying on his back a waterproof canvas bag containing three oil flares and five calcium lights, a knife, a signalling light and a revolver. Reaching the beach after an hour and a half's hard swimming, he lit his first flare, and then entering the water again swam on for another 300 yards to the east. Landing again he lit another flare and crept into some bushes to await developments. Nothing happened. He then crawled into the Turkish entrenchments, and finding no one about went back to the shore and ignited the third flare.

Freyberg's chances of being picked up again in the expanse of black water in the bay were not very good, and by now he was suffering from cramp. But he loathed the idea of being made a prisoner of war; and so he went back into the sea and swam out into the darkness. He did not drown. When he was about half a mile from the shore the crew of the cutter caught sight of his brown oil-painted

---

[1] The D.S.O. It was in the following year that Freyberg was awarded the V.C. in France.

body in the waves. He was hauled on board and restored to life again.

Finally, among all these imponderables there remains the perplexing nature of the battlefield itself. Hamilton naturally made some effort to carry out a reconnaissance of the peninsula beforehand. Some of his senior officers had been taken up the coast in a destroyer to study the beaches and the cliffs, one or two of them had been flown over the scene; and there were Samson's photographs. But none of these measures succeeded in conveying any real idea of the difficulties of the country, and the maps which were supplied to the officers were incomplete, if not downright inaccurate. In the case of the southern landing around Seddel-Bahr at Cape Helles there was at least some guidance to be had from the reports of the marines who had gone ashore during the naval bombardments in February and March. But the Gaba Tepe region, where the Anzac troops were to land, was unmapped and almost wholly unknown. It is still the most savage part of the whole peninsula.

From Chunuk Bair a hopeless maze of scrub-covered ridges drops almost sheer into the sea, and some of the ravines are so precipitous that nothing will grow upon their sides. There is no general lie to the land; dried-up watercourses abruptly change direction and end in walls of gravel, each scarred crest leads on to another tangle of hills and formless valleys. Even with a map the eye quickly grows tired; by the very nature of their endless disparity the outlines dissolve and all shapes become one shape like the pieces of a jigsaw puzzle. There is, too, something unwanted and desolate in this scene; one feels that it has become a wasteland without any purpose or design in nature.

The Turks naturally made no arrangements to defend this part of the coast, since it was inconceivable that an enemy force would land there, or, having landed, would be able to fight in such difficult ground. There is however a good beach just to the south. It runs for a mile or two in a shallow curve to the Gaba Tepe headland, and the country inland is much less broken. Here the Turks posted part of a battalion of infantry. This was not a strong force, but it was well dug in, and from Gaba Tepe the soldiers commanded a fair field of fire along the shore.

It was upon this beach that Hamilton directed his first attack for the conquest of the peninsula, very early on April 25.

119

Shortly after 2 a.m. three battleships, the *Queen*[1], *Prince of Wales* and *London,* reached their sea rendezvous off Gaba Tepe and stopped to lower their boats. The 1500 Australians who were to make the first assault assembled very quietly on deck. They had their last hot drink, and then, with their heavy packs on their backs and their rifles slung on their shoulders, they went down the Jacob's ladders in the darkness. They sat tightly packed together in the boats, neither smoking nor talking, as they were towed on towards the shore. Presently they could see the dark smudge of the cliffs on the horizon ahead of them, and beyond this, reflected in the sky, the flash of the Turkish searchlights sweeping the Dardanelles on the other side of the peninsula.

At 4 a.m. when they were still 3,000 yards away, the tows were cast off, the black shapes of the battleships slid slowly astern, and a line of pinnaces, their engines sounding unnaturally loud, went on with the boats towards the shore. There was still no sign of life there. Once a signalman cried out, 'There's a light on the starboard bow.' But it proved to be nothing more than a bright star and there was still no sound but the throbbing of the pinnace engines, the slow fall of the sea on the rocks. When they were within two or three hundred yards of the beach the pinnaces in their turn cast off, and the bluejackets took to the oars. The dawn was breaking.

The men had now been in the boats for several hours, their limbs had grown stiff and cramped, and the tension of waiting was becoming unbearable. It was inconceivable that they had not been seen. Suddenly a rocket soared up from the cliffs, and this was instantly followed by a sharp burst of rifle fire. Here finally was the moment for which they had been trained: the men jumped out of the boats and began wading the last fifty yards to the land. A few were hit, a few were dragged down by the weight of their packs and drowned, but the rest stumbled through the water to the beach. A group of Turks was running down the shore towards them. Forming themselves into a rough line and raising their absurd cry of 'Imshi Yallah' the Dominion soldiers fixed their bayonets and charged. Within a few minutes the enemy before them had dropped their rifles and fled. The Anzac legend had begun.

[1] Not to be confused with the *Queen Elizabeth.*

And now suddenly everything seemed to go wrong. The men had been told that they would find level ground and fairly easy going for the first few hundred yards inland from the beach. Instead of this an unknown cliff reached up before them, and as they hauled themselves upward, clutching at roots and boulders, kicking footholes into the rocks, a heavy fire came down on them from the heights above. Soon the air was filled with shouts and cries. Men kept losing their grip and tumbling down into gullies from which apparently there was no egress. Those who gained the first heights went charging off after the enemy and were quickly lost; and those who followed on behind, not knowing where to go, followed new paths of their own in other directions. Officers lost touch with their men, units became hopelessly mixed up and signals failed altogether.

Sunrise revealed a scene which had never been envisaged in Hamilton's or anybody's plans. Over an area of several thousand square yards a dozen isolated skirmishes were going on. Small groups of the Australians had penetrated inland for a mile or more; but most of the others were still pinned to the coast where they stumbled about among the rocks and the prickly scrub of the ravines. It was now apparent to everyone that they had not landed on the Gaba Tepe beach at all. In the darkness an uncharted current had swept the boats about a mile north of the intended landing-place and they were now in the midst of the moon landscape of the Sari Bair range.

The situation was almost as bewildering for the Turks as it was for the Dominion troops. They had made no plans whatever to meet this kind of attack. From the Gaba Tepe headland they still commanded the beach, and they drove back any of the Australians who attempted to come along it, but the small cove at which the boats had chanced to make their landfall was blocked from their field of fire and partly screened by jutting cliffs from the heights above. In the hills themselves there was no properly organized defence at all, and it was largely a matter of how far and how fast the Anzac troops could make their way over the tortuous ground—and in some cases this was very far and fast indeed. By 7 a.m. one young officer and two scouts had succeeded in climbing the first three ridges on the coast, and they were able to look down on the calm waters of the Narrows, only three and a half miles away, the object of the whole offensive. Another party was half way up the

121

dominating peak of Chunuk Bair. By 8 a.m. eight thousand men had come ashore, and although there was great confusion everywhere it was clear that at many places the Turks were on the run. The horrors of the dark and the fear of facing bullets for the first time were now over, and an exuberant relief began to spread through the Anzac troops. The officers set about gathering them together for a more coherent advance.

It was at this point that Mustafa Kemal arrived. We have Kemal's own account of his actions on this day, and there appears to be no reason to doubt his facts since they are confirmed by other people. Since dawn, he says, he had been standing by with his reserve division at Boghali in the neighborhood of the Narrows, and it was not until 6.30 a.m. that he received an order to send off one battalion to meet the Anzac attack. The march from Boghali was slow and difficult, for the Turks themselves did not know this ground. Two guides who were sent on ahead got lost, and it was Kemal himself who, with a small compass and map in hand, found a way up to the crest of Sari Bair. From here he looked down and saw the warships and the transports in the sea below, but of the actual battle in the broken hills along the shore he could make out nothing at all. His troops were tired after the long hot march, and he gave orders for them to rest while he himself, accompanied by two or three officers, went forward on foot to get a better view. They had reached the slopes of Chunuk Bair when they saw a party of Turkish soldiers running towards them, evidently in full retreat. Kemal shouted to them to stop and asked them why they were running away. 'Sir, the enemy.' The men pointed down the hill, and at that moment a detachment of Australian soldiers emerged through the scrub. Already Kemal was a good deal nearer to them than to his own battalion, and he ordered the frightened soldiers about him to stand and fight. When they protested they had no ammunition he forced them to fix their bayonets and lie down in a line on the ground. Seeing this, the Australians also took cover, and while they hesitated Kemal sent his orderly officer running back to bring up his battalion which was waiting out of sight on the other side of the ridge.

In his report, Kemal remarks cryptically, 'The moment of time that we gained was this one,' and he goes on to describe how his battalion came up and drove the Australians from the hill.

It seems possible that Kemal's astonishing career as a commanding general dates from this moment, for he saw what neither Liman von Sanders nor anybody else had seen —that Chunuk Bair and the Sari Bair ridge had become the key to the whole southern half of the peninsula. Once established on these heights the Allies would dominate the Narrows and direct their artillery fire where they wished for a dozen miles around. Indeed, the whole system of the Turkish defence was based upon the principle that they must hold the hills so that they could overlook the enemy and constantly force him to attack; and these were the most important hills of all. It was not distance that counted on Gallipoli, nor even the number of soldiers or the guns of the Fleet; it was a simple issue of the hills. Later on fifty thousand men were to lose their lives around Chunuk Bair in establishing this fact.

From the Allies' point of view it was one of the cruellest accidents of the campaign that this one junior Turkish commander of genius should have been at this particular spot at this moment, for otherwise the Australians and New Zealanders might very well have taken Chunuk Bair that morning, and the battle might have been decided then and there.

After the war the Turkish General Staff noted in its history of the campaign: 'Had the British been able to throw stronger forces ashore at Gaba Tepe either by reinforcing more rapidly those first disembarked, or by landing on a broader front, the initial successful advance of 2.500 yards in depth might have been extended so as to include the ridges overlooking the straits, and a serious, perhaps fatal, blow struck at the heart of the Turkish defences.'

Kemal realized at once that his single battalion was quite inadequate in this situation. He therefore ordered up the whole of his best regiment, the Turkish 57th, and then when heavy fighting developed he committed one of his Arab regiments as well. As a divisional commander he had no authority whatever to do this—these were the only reserves Liman possessed, and their position would have been hopeless if the Allies had planned yet another landing in another place. It was not until the end of the morning, however, that Kemal galloped back to Corps Headquarters and informed Essad Pasha of what he had done. At the same time he asked for permission to throw in the third and last regiment of the 19th Division. The battle had now grown so furious and threatening that Essad had no choice but to agree, and Kemal came back to assume command along the whole Anzac front. He never again left it until the campaign was virtually over.

There is an air of inspired desperation about Kemal's actions this day, and he even seems to have gone a little berserk at times. Instinctively he must have realized that his great chance had come, that he was either going to die here or make his name at last. He was constantly at the extreme front, helping to wheel guns into position, getting up on the skyline among the bullets, sending his men into attacks in which they had very little hope of survival. One of his orders was worded: 'I don't order you to attack, I order you to die. In the time which passes until we die other troops and commanders can take our places.' The soldiers got up from the ground and ran into the rifle and machine-gun fire; and presently the 57th Turkish Regiment was demolished.

It was the most confused of battles, for the Anzac troops were also determined to attack, despite the disorder of their first landing and the mixing up of their units, despite the fact that nowhere could the guns of the Fleet bring them any help in this bewildering country. There was no front line. The men landing on the beach were as much exposed to the snipers' bullets as those a mile inland. Advancing up a gully the soldiers would suddenly find themselves in the midst of the Turks, and hand-to-hand fighting with the bayonet began. Ridges were stormed and lost, and then abandoned by both sides. Units fighting side by side lost touch not only with their headquarters but with each other, and there were times when the bullets like cross-currents in the wind seemed to be coming from several different directions at once.

And so all through the midday hours the wild scramble went on and no one could be sure of anything except that the Allies were ashore and building up their reinforcements with every hour that went by.

Meanwhile a battle of a very different kind was being fought by the British at Cape Helles, some thirteen miles away to the south. It will be remembered that the 29th Division (with some additional troops) under Hunter-

Weston was to make five separate landings around the toe of the peninsula in the vicinity of the village Sedd-el-Bahr. This was regarded as the spearhead of the whole Allied offensive. Sedd-el-Bahr had been scanned many times from the sea, and it presented a perfect target for the naval guns. To the right of the little cove there was a ruined medieval fortress with a minuscule village behind it. Beside this fortress the land sloped quite gently down to a small gravelly beach no more than 300 yards long and 10 yards wide. Although it was known that this natural amphitheatre had been entrenched and sown with barbed wire it seemed likely that the whole area could be so savaged and cut about by the naval barrage that very little fight would be left in the defenders by the time the first British troops got ashore.

Accordingly at 5 a.m. in the uncertain first light of the morning the battleship *Albion* opened up a tremendous bombardment on the village and the cove. There was no reply from the shore. After an hour it was judged that the Turks there must either be demoralized or dead, and the *River Clyde* with her two thousand men on board was ordered to the shore. About twenty small boats all filled with men went with her. There was some little delay in the programme, for the current setting down the Dardanelles was much stronger than anyone had guessed, and the launches with the small boats in tow made slow headway against it. At one time the *River Clyde* got ahead of them and had to be brought back into position.

Thus it was in broad daylight and on the calmest of seas that the soldiers approached the shore. An unnatural stillness had succeeded the barrage. Neither on the beach nor in the fortress nor on the slopes above was there movement of any kind. At 6.22 a.m. the *River Clyde* grounded her bows without a tremor just below the fortress, and the first of the boats was within a few yards of the shore.

In that instant the Turkish rifle fire burst out. It was a frightful fire, and it was made more shocking by the silence that had preceded it. Far from being demoralized, the Turks had crept back to their trenches as soon as the bombardment was over, and they were now firing from a few yards away into the packed mass of screaming, struggling men in the boats. Some few among the British jumped into the water and got to the shelter of a little bank on the far side of the beach, and there they huddled while the storm of bullets passed over their heads. The others died in the boats just as they stood, crowded shoulder to shoulder, without even the grace of an instant of time to raise their rifles. When all were dead or wounded—the midshipmen and sailors as well as the soldiers—the boats drifted helplessly away. This was the beach on which the Marines had walked in perfect safety two months before.

Many strange scenes occurred because the men persisted in trying to do the things they had been told to do. A sailor from the *Lord Nelson,* for example, managed to pole his cutter up to the beach, but when he turned to beckon his passengers to the shore he found that they were no longer alive. The boy was observed to be standing there in wonder when he too was struck and his boat slid back into the sea.

Meanwhile Commander Unwin was having difficulty aboard the *River Clyde.* Her bows were still divided by an expanse of deep water from the shore, and when they tried to bring the steam hopper round to fill the gap it was swept away to port by the current and lay broadside to the beach, where it was useless. It was vital now that the two lighters should be brought round from the stern to make the causeway between the ship and the shore. Unwin left the bridge and dived overboard with a tow rope in his hand. He was at once followed into the water by an able seaman named Williams. Together the two men swam to the shore, and while still standing waistdeep in water and under heavy fire they managed to get the lighters lashed together and placed before the bows. Bracing himself against the current, Unwin held the more landward of the two lighters in position and shouted to the soldiers in the *River Clyde* to come ashore.

The men at once came running down the gangways along the ship's sides, and as they ran they presented a target which was not unlike the line of moving objects one sees sometimes in a shooting gallery at a village fair. Having beaten off the smaller boats the Turks were now able to give all their attention to this new assault. They opened up their fire from both sides of the ship, and soon the gangways became jammed with dead and dying. Those of the British who succeeded in reaching the lighters found themselves exposed to an even closer fire, and presently Williams was hit. Not knowing that he was dead, Unwin propped him up in the water and in doing so let go his grip on the

126

lighter. Immediately it was swept away in the current, spilling its cargo of wounded into the sea.

Air Commodore Samson came flying over Sedd-el-Bahr at this moment, and looking down saw that the calm blue sea was 'absolutely red with blood' for a distance of fifty yards from the shore, 'a horrible sight to see.' Red ripples washed up on the beach, and everywhere the calm surface of the water was whipped up into a ghastly discoloured foam by thousands of falling bullets. The sun was shining brightly.

The British had now reached that point in a battle which is the most terrible of all—the point where the leaders feel they must persist in attacking although all hope has gone. Just for a short time they live in this meaningless and heroic limbo which is at the edge of panic, and which makes a kind of welcome to death. It is a feeling which perhaps the parachutist knows when for the first time he jumps from the aircraft into the sky. The senseless attack had to continue for a little longer until it was sufficiently demonstrated that the thing was impossible, until enough of the general pool of courage had vanished with the dead, and shock and exhaustion had overcome them all. And so they kept pulling the lighters back into position, and the men kept running out of the ship and the Turks kept killing them.

When Commander Unwin collapsed in the water through cold and exhaustion a naval lieutenant and two midshipmen jumped in to take his place. After an hour's rest aboard the *River Clyde* Unwin was back in the water again, dressed in a white shirt and flannel trousers (his uniform had been ripped off his back), and there he remained, struggling with the lighters, bringing the wounded off the beach, until again he collapsed and was carried away.

By 9.30 a.m., when the casualties were being numbered in many hundreds, it was becoming apparent to the soldiers at last that they could do no more. Barely two hundred had reached the shelter of the little bank on the beach, and the barbed wire before them was hung with the corpses of the men who had tried to cut a way through to the Turkish trenches. A thousand others remained inside the *River Clyde*, and they were safe enough there with the bullets hammering on the armoured plates of the ship, but directly they showed themselves at the sallyports the killing began

127

again. Only the machine-guns mounted behind sandbags in the bows of the ship were able to keep firing.

General Hunter-Weston was at sea aboard the cruiser *Euryalus* all this time, and he knew little or nothing of what was going on. Accordingly he put the next part of the plan into action: Brigadier-General Napier was ordered to the shore with the main body of the troops. The transports steamed slowly forward to the point where they had a rendezvous with the boats which had taken the first assault troops to the shore. Had this meeting ever taken place a massacre of far greater proportions would certainly have occurred. But of the original assault force there remained barely half a dozen boats with living crews. These now came up to the transports and having emptied out their dead and wounded, the sailors stood by to return to the shore. There was room only for Napier, his staff and a few of his soldiers. As they approached the beach, the General was hailed by the men on the *River Clyde* who wanted to warn him that it was useless to continue. Napier, however, did not understand the situation. He came alongside the lighters, and seeing them filled with men sprang on board to lead them to the shore. But they made no response to his orders and he realized then that they were all dead. From the decks of the *River Clyde* they called to the General again, 'You can't possibly land.' Napier shouted back, 'I'll have a damned good try.' He tried, but he was dead before he reached the beach.

With this the assault landing at Sedd-el-Bahr came to an end.

Meanwhile the other four landings at Cape Helles had been going forward and with much better success. After heavy fighting near Tekke Burnu, about a mile away to the west, considerable numbers of soldiers were ashore on two beaches there, and towards midday Hunter-Weston began to divert his reinforcements to this point. To the east, in Morto Bay, another force had scrambled up the cliffs with trifling loss at Eski Hissarlik Point, and was securely ensconced. But the commander at Eski Hissarlik had no orders to go to the relief of Sedd-el-Bahr—indeed, he had no knowledge of what was going on there—so he stayed where he was and entrenched.

An even stranger situation had developed at the fifth landing place, a point which had been called 'Y' beach, about four miles up the coast on the western side of the peninsula. This landing was Hamilton's own idea; he had planned to spring a trap on the Turks by getting 2,000 men ashore in this isolated spot. Their mission was to take the Turks in the rear and perhaps even cut them off entirely by marching across the tip of the peninsula and joining up with the other landings in the south. There was no actual beach at this point, but a cleft in the cliffs seemed to offer a fairly easy way up to the heights 200 feet above, and reconnaissance from the sea had revealed that the Turks had established no defences on the shore.[1]

This enterprise opened with astonishing success. The 2,000 men landed and climbed up the cliffs without a single shot being fired at them. At the top there was no sign of the enemy at all. While their senior officers strolled about through the scrub inspecting the position the men sat down to smoke and brew themselves a cup of morning tea. And so the morning was whiled away. Less than an hour's march to the south their comrades at Sedd-el-Bahr and Tekke Burnu were being destroyed but they knew nothing of this. They heard the distant sounds of firing through the clear sunlit air, but they made no move in that direction. Had they but known it these troops at Y beach were equal in numbers to the whole of the Turkish forces in the tip of the peninsula that morning; they could have marched forward at will and encircled the entire enemy position. By midday they might have cleared the way to Achi Baba and turned a massacre into a brilliant victory.

It is doubtful however whether the soldiers at Y beach would have acted with very much initiative even if they had known these things, for their operation had been planned in circumstances of the utmost confusion. Two colonels had been landed with the force, and each thought he was in command. No one had bothered to tell Colonel Koe that he was in fact subordinate to Colonel Matthews, and in any case neither of the two men had been given any clear instructions. Both seem to have imagined that, far

---

[1] The following verse written by Jack Churchill, Winston Churchill's brother, appeared later in any Army broadsheet:

'Y Beach, the Scottish Borderer cried,
While panting up the steep hillside,
       Y Beach!
To call this thing a beach is stiff,
It's nothing but a bloody cliff.
       Why beach?'

from exploiting the enemy's rear, his mission was to stay where he was until the British who had landed in the south came up and made contact, and so all would march forward safely together. Messages were sent off from Y beach to the *Euryalus* through the day asking for information and instructions, but there was no reply from Hunter-Weston, and neither of the two colonels felt that he could take things into his own hands.

Quite early in the day Hamilton came by in the *Queen Elizabeth* and saw the peaceful bivouac on Y beach. Roger Keyes begged him to put more troops in there at once: the Royal Naval Division then making a demonstration at Bulair (the demonstration that was deceiving Liman von Sanders) could, he said, be brought down and landed before sunset. But Hamilton felt that he could not give the order without Hunter-Weston's consent. He sent off a signal to him: 'Would you like to get some more men ashore on Y beach? If so, trawlers are available.' To this there was no answer, and the message had to be repeated an hour or two later before Hunter-Weston finally replied: 'Admiral Wemyss and principal transport officer state that to interfere with present arrangements and try and land men at Y beach would delay disembarkation.'

Thus by midday an extraordinary situation had come about. The main assault of the British in the centre was being held up and was in danger of failing altogether, while two subsidiary forces which were perfectly capable of destroying the whole Turkish garrison of 2,000 men sat by in idleness on either flank. Under the existing system of command there was no immediate way out of this impasse. Hamilton was beginning to understand the position, but he refused to intervene. Hunter-Weston might have put things to rights, but he failed to do so because he did not comprehend what was happening. All his three brigade commanders at Cape Helles had by now become casualties, and two of the colonels who had replaced them had been instantly killed. Therefore there was no senior officer on shore, no tactical headquarters which could rally the men and keep the corps commander informed. It was left to the junior officers and the men themselves to make what shift they could out of whatever resources of courage and discipline remained to them in the bewildering chaos of the battle.

This tragic situation continued throughout the day. The naval gunners yearned to intervene and kept asking the soldiers for targets. But only the most confusing signals came out from the shore, and so for long periods at a stretch the ships were forced to stand helplessly by in the hateful security of the sea. Often the ships were so close that the sailors could see the Turks running about on the shore. Then they fired with a will. But they could not always be certain that they were not firing on their own men. The captains kept asking one another on the wireless, 'Are any of our troops dressed in blue? Have we landed any cavalry?'

At Sedd-el-Bahr another attempt was made to get the remaining soldiers off the *River Clyde* at 4 p.m., and this time a few did manage to get to the beach. They were cheered on by the little group who had huddled under the protection of the bank all day. But then the Turkish rifle fire made things impossible again. At 5.30 p.m. the village burst into flames under a new bombardment from the sea; thick smoke rolled over the battlefield and a red glare filled the evening sky. But it was clear that nothing more could be done until night fell. At Tekke Burnu things improved somewhat as more troops came ashore, but there was still no help from either flank: at Eski Hissarlik the British commander still judged himself too weak to make the two-mile march around to Sedd-el-Bahr, and in fact he was expressly forbidden to attempt it. And at Y beach, where the troops had been left undisturbed for eleven hours, retribution had at last begun: the Turks fell upon the bridgehead from the north in the evening light, and finding the British had not bothered to entrench themselves properly, continued the attack all night.

The rest of the Y beach story is brief and bitter, and can be conveniently told here. By dawn the following day there were 700 casualties, and many of the men began to straggle down the cliffs to the shore. Colonel Koe was now dead and in the absence of any clear authority a panic began. Frantic messages asking for boats were sent out to the Navy, and the Navy, believing that an evacuation had been ordered, began to take the men off. Colonel Matthews with the rest of his force on the cliff above knew nothing of all this. He fought on. At 7 a.m. he drove off a heavy Turkish attack with the bayonet, and in the lull that followed he made a tour of his position. He then discovered for the first time that a whole section of his line had been abandoned. His position was now so insecure that he felt he had no choice but to acquiesce in the retirement, and a general evacuation began. At this very moment the Turks, on their side, decided that they had been beaten, and they too withdrew; and so the British came off Y beach in the same way as they had arrived, without another casualty, without the sound of a shot being fired. In the afternoon of April 26 Roger Keyes's brother, Lieutenant-Commander Adrian Keyes, went ashore in a boat to look for wounded men who might have been left behind. He climbed the cliff and walked about for an hour among the abandoned British equipment. No one answered his calls. A perfect silence had settled on the air and the battlefield was empty.

All this, of course, was unknown and unguessed at on the other parts of the Cape Helles front as night at last began to fall on April 25. The night was the friend of the attackers. Little by little the Turkish fire began to slacken, and the aim of their gunners became uncertain. At Seddel-Bahr the men under the bank on the beach were able to put up their heads at last. Tentatively at first, and then with growing confidence, they crept out of their hiding-places to clear away the dead from the lighters and gather up the wounded from the beach. As the night advanced all the remaining men on the *River Clyde* were brought off without a single casualty. Everywhere along the line a furtive movement began under the cover of the darkness. Men crawled through the scrub to safer positions, and dug themselves entrenchments in the rocky ground. Others went forward to the barbed wire which had held them up all day and cut pathways through it. From out at sea the naval guns opened up again, and boats filled with fresh troops and stores of food and water began to reach the shore. Midshipmen and even the captains of ships took a hand in carrying boxes of ammunition up the cliffs.

By midnight the British no doubt might have gone forward again and perhaps overwhelmed the Turks in the tip of the peninsula. But there was still no senior officer ashore who was able to give them a lead. It was feared that an enemy counter-attack might start at any moment, and no one as yet had the slightest notion that they now outnumbered the enemy in Cape Helles by six to one. A dullness, a kind of mental paralysis, had followed the shock of the violent battles of the day, the unknown still loomed before them in the darkness.

The Turks in fact were in no position even to consider a

counter-attack. Of their original 2,000 men who opposed the five Cape Helles landings half were casualties. A Turkish message captured on the following day gives an idea of their condition in the frontline trenches. 'Captain,' it runs, 'you must either send up reinforcements and drive the enemy into the sea or let us evacuate this place because it is absolutely certain that they will land more troops tonight. Send the doctors to carry off my wounded. Alas alas, Captain, for God's sake send me reinforcements because hundreds of soldiers are landing. Hurry. What on earth will happen, Captain?'

Nothing happened. Fusillades of shots broke out and died away. Men fired at shadows. A light rain began to fall. Confused, exhausted, isolated in the small circle of their own experiences, the soldiers waited for the morning.

'Should the Fates so decree', Hamilton wrote in his diary, 'the whole brave Army may disappear during the night more dreadfully than that of Sennacherib; but assuredly they will not surrender; where so much is dark, where many are discouraged, in this knowledge I feel both light and joy. Here I write—think—have my being. Tomorrow night where shall we be? Well; what then; what of the worst? At least we shall have lived, acted, dared. We are half way through—we shall not look back.'

There were on the whole, he decided, fair grounds for optimism. Hunter-Weston should certainly be in a position to attack towards Achi Baba on the morrow. Reassuring messages had been coming in from Birdwood through the afternoon: he was engaged in heavy fighting all along the Anzac front, but 15,000 men had been landed there during the day. They should certainly be able to hold on. Not the least cheering news had come in from the French, who, remote from all the world, had been fighting a private battle of their own on the Asiatic side of the Straits. They had gone ashore a little late but in grand style near Orkanie Mound (the reputed tomb of Achilles), with a regiment of native African troops, and with a spirited bayonet charge had actually seized the ruined fortress of Kum Kale. That operation, at least, had been a complete success. The French, having completed their diversion, were ready now to be re-embarked and landed as reinforcements for the main offensive at Cape Helles. For a while Hamilton pondered the wisdom of this: since they had done so well should they not remain? But in the end he decided to

133

stick to the plan; Kitchener had forbidden him to fight in Asia.[1]

So then, in general, things were not too bad. Except at Kum Kale, none of the first day's objectives had been taken, but they were ashore with nearly 30,000 men. Along the whole front there had been frightful casualties, but that was to be expected on the first day and no doubt the Turks had suffered heavily as well. At all costs they must push on both from Anzac and Helles as soon as day broke.

Heartened by this review of the situation Hamilton went to his cabin towards 11 p.m. and fell asleep.

He was woken an hour later by Braithwaite shaking him by the shoulder and calling, 'Sir Ian. Sir Ian.' When he opened his eyes he heard his chief-of-staff saying, 'Sir Ian, you've got to come right along—a question of life or death —you must settle it.'

Putting a British warm over his pyjamas Hamilton crossed to the Admiral's dining saloon, and there he found de Robeck himself, Rear Admiral Thursby, Roger Keyes and several others. A message had arrived from Birdwood asking for permission to abandon the whole Anzac position at Gaba Tepe.

Mustafa Kemal had kept up his fanatical attack on the Anzac beach-head all afternoon. At 4 p.m. the Dominion troops began to fall back towards the coast from the out-lying positions they had taken in their first rush. By night-fall they were in a state of siege. But this alone had not caused the crisis in Birdwood's lines: the fatal error of the original misplaced landing was beginning to take its effect. Birdwood had expected to seize a strip of coast at least a mile in length, instead of which he found himself in pos-session of one small beach barely 1000 yards long and 30 yards wide. Everything coming ashore had to be fed through this bottleneck. Earlier in the day a small jetty had been built. But in the afternoon the congestion on the shore became intense. Animals, guns, ammunition and stores of every kind were dumped together in confusion on the sand, and there was no question of dispersing them until more territory had been gained. The whole Anzac

[1] The French actually forced the Turkish garrison at Kum Kale to surrender that night and when they were taken off on the following day they brought 450 Turkish prisoners with them.

134

position was less than two miles long and about three-quarters of a mile deep. No one could get inland. Bridges and Godley, the two divisional commanders, and their staffs were crammed together in a gully a few yards from the beach, and the headquarters of the brigades were almost on top of them. Hospitals, signalling units, artillery batteries and even prisoners' cages perched where they could among the rocks.

The wounded meanwhile were coming down from the hills in an endless stream, and were dumped in their stretchers in rows along the shore. Soon the whole of one end of the beach was covered with them, and there they lay, many of them in great pain, waiting to be taken off to the ships. While they waited a constant storm of bullets and shrapnel broke over their heads; and indeed, everyone on that crowded beach from generals to donkey drivers was under fire, for the Turks overlooked them from three sides. In desperation one of the officers in charge on the beach ordered every boat that came ashore to help in taking the casualties away, and this not only disorganized and delayed the disembarkation programme, it exposed the wounded to further suffering as well. Some were taken from transport to transport only to be sent away since there were no medical facilities on board; all the doctors and their staffs had gone to the shore.

On the front line—or rather at the changing points of contact with the enemy—the soldiers had had little opportunity of digging in. Their light trenching tools were not very effective among the rocks and the tough roots of the scrub, and at some places the slopes were too steep for them to dig in at all. They were in desperate need of artillery support, but because of the ragged nature of the country and the uncertainty of the front line there was very little the naval guns could do. By nightfall the situation was not yet critical but it was becoming so. It had been a long exhausting day, and the men were beginning to feel the intense psychological strain of always being looked down upon from above, their every move watched, their smallest gestures attracting the snipers' bullets.

Many stragglers began to come down to the tiny beach on which already 15,000 men had been landed that day. For the most part these men were simply those who had lost touch with their units, and believing themselves isolated had returned to the only rallying point they knew.

Some were in search of food and water. Others considered that they were entitled to a breather after a hard day. They dropped in exhaustion on any level piece of ground they could find, oblivious of the bursting shrapnel, and when they woke they were unable to return to the front because they could not find their way. These leaderless men added to the confusion and created an atmosphere of doubt and discouragement around the headquarters.

By nightfall, from almost every point of the bridgehead, desperate calls were coming in for more reinforcements, for ammunition, for artillery fire and for men to take the wounded away. The front line, it seemed, was breaking. It was in these circumstances that at 9.15 p.m. Bridges and Godley sent a message to General Birdwood aboard the *Queen*, asking him to come ashore at once. Birdwood, who had been on shore all afternoon, returned to the beach, and there he learned with astonishment that his two divisional generals, both Bridges the Australian, and Godley the Englishman, were in favour of an immediate evacuation.

Birdwood at first refused to accept this proposition, but he was persuaded as the conference went on: the troops were worn out and in the appalling terrain there was no reasonable chance of making any headway. If the Turks developed a counter-attack and a heavy bombardment next day the situation might get out of control.

Huddled together around candles in an improvised dug-out and with the rain falling outside and the wounded all about them, it cannot have been easy for the commanders to have taken a very hopeful view of the situation. In the end Birdwood sat down and dictated to Godley the following message for the Commander-in-Chief:

'Both my divisional generals and brigadiers have represented to me that they fear their men are thoroughly disorganized by shrapnel fire to which they have been subjected all day after exhaustion and gallant work in the morning. Numbers have dribbled back from the firing line and cannot be collected in this difficult country. Even the New Zealand Brigade, which has only recently been engaged, lost heavily and is, to some extent, demoralized. If troops are subjected to shell fire again tomorrow morning there is likely to be a fiasco, as I have no fresh troops with which to replace those in the firing

136

line. I know my representation is most serious, but if we are to re-embark it must be at once.'

This was the message which was placed before Hamilton when he was woken aboard the *Queen Elizabeth* at midnight that night.

The scene in de Robeck's dining saloon was more oppressive than dramatic, and yet it has an oddly spot-lighted quality that sets it apart from any other such conference in the Gallipoli campaign: the General sitting there in his pyjamas reading Birdwood's message, the others gathered around him in silence, the orderlies waiting at the door. This was either to be the ending of the campaign or a new beginning. Just for these few moments the action of the battle stops like a moving picture that has been arrested on the screen, and one concentrates upon this single group. To gain time, Hamilton asked a question or two of the officers who had come from the shore, but they could tell him nothing more. Admiral Thursby, who was in charge of the naval side of the Anzac landing, gave it as his opinion that it would take several days to get the soldiers back into the ships. Braithwaite had nothing to say.

For Hamilton there was no escape; he alone *had* to take the decision and it had to be taken at once. Already all available boats had been ordered to stand by for the evacuation. Yet there was something missing in this unbearable proposition—some one hard definite factor that would enable him to make up his mind.

Turning to Thursby, Hamilton said, 'Well then, tell me, Admiral, what do *you* think?'

Thursby answered, 'What do I think? Well, I think myself they will stick it out if only it is put to them that they must.'

It was at this point that Keyes was handed a wireless message from Lieut.-Commander Stoker, the captain of the submarine AE 2, saying that he had penetrated the Narrows and had reached the Sea of Marmara. Keyes read the telegram aloud and turning to Hamilton added, 'Tell them this. It is an omen—an Australian submarine has done the finest feat in submarine history, and is going to torpedo all the ships bringing reinforcements into Gallipoli.'

Upon this Hamilton sat down, and in a general silence wrote to Birdwood:

137

'Your news is indeed serious. But there is nothing for it but to dig yourselves right in and stick it out. It would take at least two days to re-embark you as Admiral Thursby will explain to you. Meanwhile, the Australian submarine has got up through the Narrows and has torpedoed a gunboat at Cunuk.[1] Hunter-Weston despite his heavy losses will be advancing tomorrow which should divert pressure from you. Make a personal appeal to your men and Godley's to make a supreme effort to hold their ground.

Ian Hamilton

P.S. You have got through the difficult business, now you have only to dig, dig, dig, until you are safe.

Ian H.

In an instant, with this message the action starts moving forward again. Aboard the *Queen Elizabeth*, back on the beach at Anzac Cove, among the soldiers in the front line, everyone suddenly feels an immense relief, everyone perversely finds his courage all over again. Now that they have got to fight it out the dangers appear to be half as formidable as they were before.

It was the postscript of the letter which contained the required touch of inspiration, for when it was read out to the soldiers on shore they began at once, quite literally, to dig. Here was something definite to do; you dug your way down to safety. Officers and men alike, on the beach and in the hills, set about hacking at the ground, and as the hours went by and still no Turkish counterattack came in, all the seaward slopes of the Sari Bair range began to resemble a vast mining camp. It was not long after this that the Australian soldiers became known as Diggers, and that name has remained with them ever since.

But there was, in fact, no possibility of a serious Turkish counter-attack at Anzac Cove that night or even on the following day. With 2,000 casualties in his ranks not even Mustafa Kemal could do more than launch a series of heavy raids that were never quite strong enough to push Birdwood into the sea. Everywhere along the front, at Cape Helles as well as Anzac, the first phase was already over. The moment of surprise had gone. Hamilton had declared his plan and Liman was reacting to it. Both sides

---

[1] Chanak.

now began to mass men on the two main battlefields, the Turks still convinced that they could throw the Allies into the sea, the Allies still believing that they could advance upon the Narrows. At this moment nobody could have persuaded either of the two generals or their soldiers that they were wrong. So long as their hopes held they were committed to a vast slaughter.

From this point onwards the element of the unexpected gradually dies away from the battle, the chances are calculated chances, the attacks and the counter-attacks foreknown, and only exhaustion can put an end to the affair.

EIGHT

'The terrible "Ifs" accumulate.'
—Winston Churchill

The news of the landing at Gallipoli was not released for publication until two days after the event, and it made no great stir in England. *The Times* in the leading article on April 27 put the matter very clearly: 'The news that the fierce battle in Flanders which began on Thursday (April 22) is being continued with unabated fury is coupled this morning with the news that the Allied troops have landed in Gallipoli. But the novel interests of that enterprise cannot be allowed to distract us from what is, and will remain, the decisive theatre of operations. Our first thoughts must be for the bent but unbroken line of battle in the West.'

A new and terrible phase of war in Europe had begun. In the very battle which *The Times* was describing the Germans used poison gas for the first time. This was soon followed by the news of the collapse of the Russian front in Galicia, and of the failure of the new British offensive in Aubers Ridge in France. The Aubers Ridge battle was typical of the kind of fighting which was to dominate the Western Front for the next three years: Sir John French attacked a German fortified line in full daylight on a two-mile front, and the action was not broken off until nightfall when 11,000 men had fallen. Not a single yard of ground was gained.

It was the lack of shells which was thought to be the cause of this disaster. 'British soldiers,' *The Times* said, 'died in vain on Aubers Ridge on Sunday because more shells were needed. The Government, who have so seriously failed to organize adequately our national resources, must bear their share of the grave responsibility.'

But it was the loss of the *Lusitania* in the Atlantic which made the deepest impression on people in England through these weeks. The ship was sunk off the Irish coast on May 7, 1915 by the U-boat 20, and more than half of the 2,000 civilians on board were drowned. Now finally it seemed that the enemy was prepared to descend to any barbarity, and the ancient idea that civilians should not be involved in wars was gone for ever. From this point onwards the hatred of Germany in England rose to a pitch which was hardly equalled in the second world war, except perhaps at the height of the flying-bomb raids of 1944. Revenge, the desire to kill Germans, became a major object in itself, and with this there was an increasing uneasiness, a feeling that somehow the Asquith Government was mishandling things, and that the war, instead of being short and victorious, might be long and lost. If shells were needed to get the enemy out of his trenches in France, then why were there not enough of them? Why had the U-boats not been stopped? Why were the Zeppelins still coming over London? Compared to these issues, the novel enterprise against the Turks at Gallipoli seemed rather insignificant and very far away.

Then too very little information about the Gallipoli campaign reached the public during these early days. A full month went by before the *Illustrated London News* was able to publish photographs from the peninsula, and the official communiqués were not very helpful. From France a stream of soldiers, either wounded or on leave, returned to England, and their descriptions of the fighting in the trenches were in everybody's mind. But Gallipoli was three thousand miles away and no soldier on leave ever got back as far as England, let alone Australia and New Zealand. To a great extent then it was left to the war correspondents to fill this gap.

Kitchener on principle was opposed to war correspondents, but he had, with some reluctance, permitted the English newspapers to send one man with the expedition, Mr. Ellis Ashmead-Bartlett. Ashmead-Bartlett was involved in difficulties from the moment of his arrival. Hamilton, though friendly, would allow him to send no messages until his own official cables had reached London, and this

141

sometimes meant a delay of days. No criticism of the conduct of the operations was allowed by the censor. Nor could there be any indication of set-backs and delays. Ashmead-Bartlett's lot seems really to have been a little too hard at times. He went ashore at Anzac Cove soon after the first assault wearing, for reasons best known to himself, a green hat, and was at once arrested as a spy. The Australians were about to shoot him when by chance a sailor whom he knew vouched for him. Soon afterwards he was nearly drowned when the ship in which he was travelling was torpedoed. The only other English correspondent at Gallipoli was a Reuter man who was somewhat handicapped by being so short-sighted that he could only see a hundred yards.

Hamilton's own despatches to Lord Kitchener tended at first to take an optimistic line. 'Thanks to God who calmed the seas,' he wrote on April 26, 'and to the Royal Navy who rowed our fellows ashore as coolly as if at a regatta; thanks also to the dauntless spirit shown by all ranks of both Services, we have landed 29,000 upon six beaches in the face of desperate resistance.' On April 27 he wrote again: 'Thanks to the weather and the wonderfully fine spirit of our troops all continues to go well.'

Meanwhile a great deal had happened. On the night of the landing the destroyers on the Anzac front came in close and shone their searchlights on the cliffs to prevent the Turks from making a surprise raid in the darkness. Then in the morning the *Queen Elizabeth* and two other battleships each took a section of the enemy line and bombarded it so heavily that it seemed for a time that the hills were erupting like active volcanoes. Spotters went up in the kite balloons to a height whence they could see over the top of the peninsula, and with one lucky shot the *Queen Elizabeth* destroyed a freighter in the Narrows, seven miles away. The cruisers meanwhile came so near to the shore that the sailors could see the Turks running along the cliffs above, and the Turks in their turn sniped down on to the British officers standing on deck. There was very little the Turks could do to injure the warships, but they kept up an incessant artillery fire on the beach, and every boat that tried to reach the shore with stores and reinforcements was forced to run through a curtain of bursting shrapnel and machine-gun bullets. Under this barrage the Dominion soldiers fought out their battle for survival.

142

It was extremely savage fighting, for at this early stage neither side had any real idea of what they could or could not do, and consequently both commanders committed everything they had to the battle. Kemal was still convinced that he could drive the Allies into the sea before they had had time to dig in, and Birdwood was still determined to advance against him. Often the Turks charged directly into the Anzac line, and wild hand-to-hand fighting with the bayonet took place in the half-dug trenches. Three days of this went by before it became apparent to the opposing commanders that both their propositions were wrong: the Anzac soldiers could not be dislodged; equally they could not advance. Hardly a thousand square yards of territory had changed hands: and the bridgehead remained there, congested and confined, every part of it swept by fire from the heights above, but apparently immovable. On the night of April 27, the fighting slackened, and both sides drew off to rest and gather their strength again.

Something of the same sort but on a wider front was happening at Cape Helles in the south. On the day after the landing the village of Sedd-el-Bahr fell, the scattered bridgeheads were joined together and the Turks drew back all along the line. Hamilton judged it to be absolutely vital to take Achi Baba before Liman von Sanders could bring reinforcements down to the toe of the peninsula, and on April 28, with the French on the right and the British on the left, a general forward movement began. It continued inland for a distance of about two miles against increasing opposition, and then came to a halt.

An extreme fatigue had now overtaken the soldiers. Many of them had been without sleep for two or even three nights, and their food, water and ammunition were running out. At Sedd-el-Bahr the *River Clyde* was firmly anchored to the shore, but the whole of the Allied position was under the fire of Turkish guns from across the straits and from the peninsula itself. The bulk of Hamilton's forces was now on land, but the beaches still looked like the scene of a gigantic shipwreck with vast piles of stores and military equipment scattered about on every side, and until some order could be got out of this confusion—until the troops were rested and supplied—there was no possibility of renewing the advance. By April 28 all impetus was lost and the firing began to die away along the line.

Thus at the very outset the pattern of the Gallipoli campaign was established: the action, the reaction and the stalemate. The objective is set, the attempt is made, and it falls just short of success. Already Achi Baba had begun to dominate everybody's mind. It loomed there on the skyline only a mile or two away, but as remote as Constantinople itself. It was not a spectacular hill in any way, for its height was only 709 feet and its sides sloped gently down to the Ægean through a pleasant countryside of olives and cypresses and scattered farms. But Hamilton was determined to take it. Once on the crest he believed that his guns would enfilade the straits as far as the Narrows, and the enemy line in the south would give way. On April 28 his position was particularly frustrating. He knew that time was running out. He saw the hill before him, and given another fresh division—perhaps even a brigade—he knew that he could have it. But there were no fresh divisions or brigades; everything he had was already committed to the battle, and for the time being the men were so worn out, so shocked and undermined by their casualties, that they could do no more. And so he returned to the questions which were destined to be endlessly repeated from this time onwards. Can he ask Kitchener for reinforcements? And even if Kitchener agrees to send them will they arrive in time?

Even before the expedition had sailed there had been a misunderstanding about this matter of reinforcements. Kitchener's attitude—and Hamilton was extremely conscious of it—seems to have been that he could spare so much and no more for Gallipoli, and Hamilton had better make the best of it. And so Hamilton's modest requests had been rebuffed or had remained unanswered. Yet in the end Kitchener had relented. On April 6 he had sent a cable to Sir John Maxwell, the commander of the Egyptian garrison: 'You should supply any troops in Egypt that can be spared or even selected officers or men that Sir Ian Hamilton may want for Gallipoli. . . . This telegram should be communicated by you to Sir Ian Hamilton.'

Hamilton knew nothing of this. It is one of the mysteries of the campaign that this telegram was never sent on to him, or if it was the copy was lost. And so now on April 28, when all the plans of the first assault had miscarried, when the exhausted army lay stranded just below the crest of Achi Baba, desperately in need of shells and ammunition of every kind, several divisions of fresh men were standing idly by in Egypt.

It was not from Hamilton but from the Admirals that Kitchener had the first news that the situation was becoming critical. On the day after the landing Admiral Guépratte had sent a message saying that reinforcements were needed immediately, and de Robeck had followed this with another signal which made it clear that the Army was in serious difficulties. Churchill and Fisher seized on de Robeck's message directly it arrived in the Admiralty in London, and they took it across to Kitchener at the War Office. The Field Marshal professed to be a good deal surprised. As far as he knew, he said, things were going well. Hamilton had not made any request for reinforcements. However, he at once instructed Maxwell in Egypt to embark the 42nd Division for the peninsula, together with an Indian Brigade—that same brigade of Gurkhas that Hamilton had pleaded for so unsuccessfully a month before. The French at the same time promised to embark another division at Marseilles.

On hearing this news Hamilton wrote in his diary, 'Bis dat qui cito dat. O truest proverb! One fresh man on Gallipoli today was worth five afloat on the Mediterranean or fifty loafing around London in the Central Forces. At home they are carefully totting up figures—I know them— and explaining to the P.M. and the Senior Wranglers with some complacency that the 60,000 effective bayonets left me are enough—seeing they are British—to overthrow the Turkish Empire. So they would be if I had that number, or anything like it, for my line of battle. But what are the facts? Exactly one half of my "bayonets" spend the whole night carrying water, ammunition and supplies between the beach and the firing line. The other half of my "bayonets", those left in the firing line, are up the whole night armed mostly with spades digging desperately into the earth. Now and then there is a hell of a fight, but that is incidental and a relief.'

While the Allies waited for their reinforcements a three days' lull settled down on the battlefield. The digging went on. On the front line the spring flowers were blooming wonderfully, cornflowers and scarlet poppies, tulips and wild thyme. A storm blew up and for some hours the Army was cut off from the Fleet, its one lifeline to the outer world. But this was the last of the winter; the snow began to melt

145

on Samothrace, and the sea lightened to its marvellous shade of transparent summer blue. On April 30 Hamilton transferred from the *Queen Elizabeth* to his command ship the *Arcadian,* and now for the first time his headquarters staff was gathered together. Some five thousand wounded men were sent off in hospital ships to Egypt, and the dead were buried.

Liman von Sanders was also carrying through a rapid reorganization. One of his Asiatic divisions was brought across the Straits in boats to the peninsula, and on April 30 two more divisions were sent down to him by sea from Constantinople. He could now count upon some seventy-five battalions against Hamilton's fifty-seven, and Enver in Constantinople ordered a full-scale attack at Cape Helles. This was to be a ruthless affair: the soldiers in the first assault were to charge with unloaded rifles so that they would be forced to advance right up to the Allied trenches with the bayonet, and inflammable material was to be carried by the troops to enable them to burn the British boats on the shore. At ten p.m. on May 1, the three days of comparative silence was broken by a Turkish artillery bombardment along the whole length of the line at Cape Helles, and immediately afterwards the enemy infantry came over the top.

There never was any hope for soldiers attacking in such circumstances in 1915, whether in Gallipoli or France or anywhere else, and it is impossible to follow the confused events of the next week without a feeling of despair at the useless waste. For three days the Turks kept it up, and when they had gained nothing, when their stretcher-bearers came out with the Red Crescent to gather up their wounded and bury the dead, it was Hamilton's turn.

By May 5 he had got his reinforcements from Egypt, and in addition he took six thousand men from Birdwood and put them into the British line at Cape Helles: a force of 25,000 men in all. Through most of May 6, 7 and 8 the fight went on and with the same heroic desperation as before. 'Drums and trumpets will sound the charge,' General d'Amade announced to the French, and out they went in their bright pale-blue uniforms and their white cork helmets, a painfully clear target against the dun-coloured earth. Each day they hoped to get to Achi Baba. Each night when they had gained perhaps 300 yards in one place and nothing in another a new attack was planned for the following day. Elaborate orders were got out by the staff for each new assault, but it often happened that the front-line commanders did not receive these orders until the very early hours of the morning, and only an hour or two before they had to go over the top. Soon, however, it hardly mattered whether the orders were issued or not, for the men were too exhausted to understand them, too bewildered to do anything but get up dumbly once again into the machine-gun fire. A wild unreality intervened between the wishes of the commanders and the conditions of the actual battle on the shore. The battle made its own rules, and it was useless for the generals to order the soldiers to make for this or that objective; there were no objectives except the enemy himself. This was a simple exercise in killing, and in the end all orders were reduced to just one or two very simple propositions: either to attack or to hold on.

In his extremity Hamilton cabled once more to the War Office for more shells to be sent out. The answer came when the fighting was at its height: he was told that the matter would be considered. 'It is important,' the message added, 'to push on.'

By all means Hamilton wished to push on, and he hardly needed a general in the War Office to tell him so, but by the afternoon of May 8 there was no question of his pushing anywhere. At Cape Helles he had lost 6,500 men, which was about a third of the force engaged, and his over-all casualties of British, French and Anzac troops on the two fronts were now over 20,000. Achi Baba, with a field of scarlet poppies on its crest, still stood before him unshaken on the skyline. All his reserves of men had gone. Most of his shells had been shot away. And his two bridge-heads scarcely covered five square miles between them.

Still sailing about in the *Arcadian* and unable to get his headquarters on shore, the General sent off a message to Kitchener saying he could do no more. 'If you could only spare me two fresh divisions organized as a corps,' he wrote, 'I could push on with great hopes of success both from Cape Helles and Gaba Tepe; otherwise I am afraid we shall degenerate into trench warfare with its resultant slowness.'

It was almost an admission of defeat, and to the sailors in the Fleet who had been mortified at the sight of the Army being cut up on the shore while the warships for the most part stood by watching, motionless in the blue,

Map of the
GALLIPOLI PENINSULA
AND
THE DARDANELLES

Scale

0 1 2   4   6

——— Main Roads
☆ Fortified Towns   ♦ Forts and Batteries

N

AEGEAN

GULF

Suvla Burnu
Beach A
Suvla Bay
Lala Baba

Karakol Dagh
KIZLAR DAGH
Mt. Turchenkeui
Kuchuk
Anafarta

(Chocolate Hill)   *Tekke*
Selvill

Fisherman's Hut
Ari Burnu
Anzac Cove

Biyuk Anafarta
KOJA CHEMEN
SARI BAIR
Kojadere

Kumkeui
Bilmaz D.

Yalova

Brighton Beach
Gaba Tepe

Boghali   Koje Tepe
Mersin Dagh   Ak Tepe
Bohali Kalessi

Ak Rashi D.

N

Kum Dere
Kion Tepe

Asmak D.

Sarda

Maghram

Maidos
Cham Kalessi

Nagara
Kalessi

Abydos Pt.

Dermaburnu Ft.
Kilid Bahr ☆

The Narrows

♦ Kosse Kale
♦ Medjidieh Batt

CHANAK
Hamidieh Ft. ♦

Beach Y

Tekke
Burnu

Helles
Burnu
Sedd-el-Bahr

Krithia
ACHI BABA
Haricot
Redoubt
DeTott's Batt
(Ruined)

Morto Bay

D A R

D A

N

Deurmen D.

Kum Kale

In Tepe Asmak

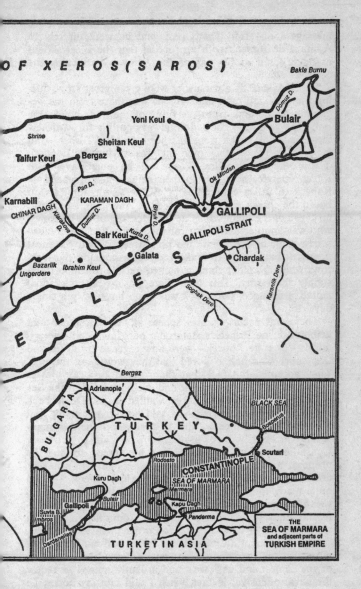

GULF OF XEROS (SAROS)

Bakla Burnu

Domuz D.

Bulair

Yeni Keul

Sheitan Keul

Shrine

Bergaz

Talfur Keul

Ok Mindan

Pan D.

Karnabili

KARAMAN DAGH

CHINAR DAGH

Kiarakova D.

Dumuz D.

Biyuk D.

Kuzla D.

GALLIPOLI

Bair Keul

GALLIPOLI STRAIT

Galata

Chardak

Bazarlik

Ibrahim Keul

Ungerdere

Soghak Dere

Karanlik Dere

G E L L E S

Bergaz

Adrianople

BLACK SEA

BULGARIA

T U R K E Y

Bosherus

Scutari

Rodosto

CONSTANTINOPLE

SEA OF MARMARA

Kuru Dagh

Marmara

Gallipoli

Bulair

Kapu Dagh

Suvla B.

Panderma

Imbros

Dardanelles

T U R K E Y I N A S I A

THE
SEA OF MARMARA
and adjacent parts of
TURKISH EMPIRE

it was unbearable. Roger Keyes saw a copy of Hamilton's message soon after it was sent, and he went directly to Admiral de Robeck with a proposal that the Fleet should at once come to the aid of the Army by attacking the Narrows again.

Keyes' talents as a persuader were given great scope during the Gallipoli campaign, for he was there from the beginning to the end, from the firing of the first shot to the last. He was always for action, always putting forward new ideas, most of which were anathema to Lord Fisher—and indeed, Fisher at this moment was saying in London, 'Damn the Dardanelles. They will be our grave.' But Keyes' energies now rose to their height: he persuaded de Robeck to call a conference of all the senior admirals on board the *Queen Elizabeth* on May 9. And then, having sat up through the night with Captain Godfrey of the Marines, who was another enthusiast for the naval attack, he placed a new plan before them: the minesweepers and the most powerful battleships to make a direct assault on the Narrows while the older ships remained outside to support and supply the Army. This time there was to be no gradual tentative advance; the attack was to go through in a single day.

There was a curious atmosphere at the conference that gathered in de Robeck's stateroom on May 9. All the admirals—even de Robeck—were now eager to try again and they more than half believed that they would get through. They accepted the fact that there might be heavy losses and that half the Fleet might find itself stranded in the Sea of Marmara; nevertheless they wanted to go. De Robeck still hung back somewhat—he said he did not think that the mere appearance of the battleships in the Marmara would necessarily force Liman von Sanders to retire or Constantinople to surrender—but he agreed to put the proposal to the Admiralty. The message that was sent was not a very enthusiastic document; it said in effect, 'We are quite ready to attack again but if we fail the consequences will be ruinous.' Yet when the admirals rose from the conference they fully expected that the Admiralty in London would decide to take the risk and order them to go ahead.

Admiral Guépratte was all for it. He had not been summoned to the conference, but, says Keyes, 'I knew he was of the same mind as I was, and ardently longed to renew the naval offensive; in fact, when I told him my hopes, he said, "Ah, Commodore, that would be *immortalité*." He was elated, and at once telegraphed to the Minister of Marine as follows: *"Afin d'assister l'Armée dans son action énergique et rude, nous méditons vive action flotte dans détroit avec attaque des forts. Dans ces conditions il me faut mes cuirassés* Suffren, Charlemagne, Gaulois *dans le plus bref délai possible."* '

These messages now set the whole issue of the Gallipoli campaign ablaze in London.

On the morning of May 11 Churchill and Fisher met at the Admiralty to discuss de Robeck's telegram, and Fisher at once made himself clear: he would have no part of any new attempt on the Narrows. Churchill's position was more complicated. Italy was about to enter the war, and as part of her price for joining the Allies she asked that four British battleships and four cruisers should be placed under her command in the central Mediterranean. Churchill himself had been over to the Continent early in May to conduct the negotiations, and thinking at that time that de Robeck had abandoned all idea of forcing the Dardanelles, he agreed that Italy should have the ships. They were to be taken from the Dardanelles. There was, too, another issue, and it was very urgent: news had been received at the Admiralty that German submarines had reached the Mediterranean and were on their way to the Ægean. De Robeck's fleet and the precious *Queen Elizabeth* were stationed in the open sea, and it did not seem practicable for him to undertake a new offensive with this new peril in his wake.

Churchill, however, was in favour of at least a limited advance; he wanted the minefields in the lower straits swept up so that the Fleet would be in a position to go through the Narrows once the Army had won the peninsula. Fisher's answer to this was that he was opposed to any action whatsoever until the Turkish Army was defeated.

The two men were in the midst of this discussion—perhaps argument is the better word, for they were now drifting steadily apart in their ideas—when news reached them that the battleship *Goliath* had been sunk in the Dardanelles. It was a brilliant manœuvre on the part of the enemy. In the very early hours of May 12 a Turkish destroyer commanded by a German lieutenant had emerged from the straits and had crept up upon the battleship at her anchorage about 100 yards offshore in Morto Bay. The quartermaster aboard the *Goliath* hailed the strange vessel through the darkness, and when he got a reply in English no alarm was given. An instant later three torpedoes struck, and the battleship heeled over and sank in two minutes. Although the French soldiers on the coast could plainly hear the cries of the crew as they struggled in the water, more than 500 men were drowned. The Turkish destroyer dashed away up the straits proclaiming her success over her radio.

The *Goliath* was not an important ship—she was fifteen years old and her tonnage was less than 13,000—yet the very fact that she had been sunk and in such difficult circumstances made the presence of the U-boats seem more menacing than ever. Fisher announced that he must retire the *Queen Elizabeth* from the Mediterranean at once. Churchill was ready to agree to this: new monitors with antitorpedo blisters on their sides were ready to sail, and there were other replacements which could be sent to de Robeck. But it was a very different matter with Lord Kitchener. On May 13 Churchill asked him to come to a conference at the Admiralty, and it was there that he was given the news of the withdrawal of the flagship. 'Lord Kitchener,' Churchill relates, 'became extremely angry. . . . Lord Fisher flew into an even greater fury. "The *Queen Elizabeth* would come home; she would come home at once; she would come home that night or he would walk out of the Admiralty then and there." ' Churchill did his best to mollify Kitchener by telling him of the new monitors and the other replacements, and at the breaking up of the meeting Fisher had his way. Orders were sent out recalling the *Queen Elizabeth,* and at the same time de Robeck was forbidden to renew his attack on the Narrows.

The meeting of the War Council on the following day, May 14, is described by Churchill as 'sulphurous'. Of all the men who gathered at 10 Downing Street that day only Churchill and Lord Hankey, who was the secretary of the Council, survive. Yet the scene has the contemporary quality which seems to characterize all the crises of the Gallipoli expedition.

Kitchener was very bitter. He had sent an army to Turkey, he said, because he had been assured that the Navy would force the Dardanelles, and because he had been led on by Churchill insisting upon 'the marvellous potentialities

152

of the *Queen Elizabeth*'. The Navy had failed, and now the *Queen Elizabeth* was being taken away at the very moment when the Army was struggling for its life on the edge of the peninsula. It so happened that *The Times* on this day had come out with its attack upon Asquith's Government over the shortage of the supply of shells. As he went on to deal with this matter, Kitchener became increasingly gloomy. No organization, he said, could keep pace with the expenditure of ammunition. No one could foresee what would happen. If the Russians cracked in the East it was quite possible that the Germans would bring back their armies to the West and set out upon the invasion of England.

Fisher's only comment on all this was that he had been against the Dardanelles adventure since the beginning, and this, he said, Lord Kitchener knew perfectly well. Everyone now seems to have been in an angry and despondent mood, and they listened without much patience as Churchill argued that the success of the campaign had never depended upon the *Queen Elizabeth*. The only thing to do now, he said, was to reinforce Hamilton, push the campaign through to a conclusion and forget their vague fears about the invasion of England. But with his First Sea Lord openly antagonistic to him Churchill was not in a strong position, and the meeting broke up without any decision being reached.

The crisis now moved quietly, almost stealthily, to its climax. In the afternoon there was a quite amicable meeting between Fisher and Churchill on the subject of the replacements that were to be sent to de Robeck. The list of ships was agreed, and Fisher went off to bed. Late that night Churchill went through the list again and decided to add two E-class submarines to it. His minute on the subject was sent off in the usual way to Fisher's office, so that the Admiral would see it on his desk when he arrived first thing on the following morning. Upon this the explosion erupted. Fisher appears to have reached his office about 5 a.m. on May 15, and on seeing Churchill's minute immediately decided to resign. The two submarines were, apparently, the last straw. 'First Lord,' he wrote, 'After further anxious reflection I have come to the regretted conclusion I am unable to remain any longer as your colleague. It is undesirable in the public interests to go into details—Jowett said "never explain"—but I find it increas-

153

ingly difficult to adjust myself to the increasing daily requirements of the Dardanelles to meet your views—as you truly said yesterday I am in the position of continually veto-ing your proposals.

'This is not fair to you besides being extremely distasteful to me.

'I am off to Scotland at once to avoid all questionings.

Yours truly,
Fisher.'

Churchill received this letter from his secretary as he was walking across the Horse Guards Parade later in the morning, and he did not take a serious view of the matter since Fisher had resigned or threatened to resign so many times before. The Admiral, however, was nowhere to be found, and Churchill went across to Downing Street to discuss the matter with the Prime Minister. Asquith's first move was to write out an order to Fisher commanding him to return to his duty in the name of the King, and secretaries were sent out to scour the town until they found him. Some went to the main railway stations, others hunted through the Admiralty. Several hours elapsed, however, before the Admiral was found in a room in the Charing Cross hotel, and for a time he refused to come out. In the end he agreed that he would at least see the Prime Minister.

Lloyd George was in the entrance lobby of 10 Downing Street when Fisher arrived for this interview. 'A combative grimness,' Lloyd George says, 'had taken the place of his usual genial greeting; the lower lip of his mouth thrust forward, and the droop at the corner was more marked than usual. His curiously oriental features were more than ever those of a graven image in an eastern temple, with a sinister frown. "I have resigned," was his greeting, and on my inquiring the reason he replied, "I can stand it no longer." He then informed me that he was on his way to see the Prime Minister, having made up his mind to take no further part in the Dardanelles "foolishness", and was off to Scotland that night.'

Fisher clearly was in a rage to have done with the formalities, and neither Asquith nor Churchill could move him.

In a last message to Churchill—and one can almost see the pen trembling in the Admiral's hand—he wrote: 'YOU

154

ARE BENT ON FORCING THE DARDANELLES AND NOTHING
WILL TURN YOU FROM IT—NOTHING. I know you so well
... *You will remain and I* SHALL GO—it is better so.' There
followed his defiant final ultimatum to Asquith demanding,
as a condition of his return, absolute control over the Navy
and the removal of Churchill and all others who, he
imagined, stood in his way. It was absurd, of course, even
crazy, and it meant that the old man had to be removed
from the scene as quickly as possible. A curt note from
Asquith accepting his resignation ended his career.

In more ordinary times Churchill perhaps might have
weathered Fisher's departure, but too much was happening
too quickly. The shell crisis alone was enough to bring the
Government down, or at any rate to lead to its reorganization. In some vague way it had begun to seem that the Gallipoli campaign was responsible for all their troubles, and
Churchill was regarded as the original author of it. He had
urged it from the beginning. He had lost the ships. He was
responsible for the disasters and delays in the Army's landing. He was the amateur who had dared to fly in the face
of the expert opinion of the Admirals—even Fisher, the
greatest of them all. All this was wildly unfair. 'It (Churchill's removal from the Admiralty) was a cruel and unjust
degradation,' Lloyd George wrote. 'The Dardanelles failure
was due not so much to Mr. Churchill's precipitancy as to
Lord Kitchener's and Mr. Asquith's procrastination.'

Directly they had word of Fisher's resignation Bonar
Law and the Opposition leaders gave notice to Asquith that
they would challenge the Government on the matter in the
House of Commons, and Asquith at once entered into
negotiations for a coalition. In the confused dealings of the
next few days Churchill had no part at all; for a time his
friends put up a show of a fight for him, but the Conservatives were absolutely determined to have him out. The
new cabinet was finally announced on May 26. Balfour
was to have the Admiralty with Sir Henry Jackson as his
First Sea Lord. Jackson was almost as much an opponent
of the Dardanelles as Fisher had been, and he later declared that he thought the forcing of the straits to be 'a
mad thing to do'. Churchill declined the Colonial Office,
and there was some discussion about his taking over a command in the Army in France, but in the end he was given
the minor office of Chancellor of the Duchy of Lancaster.

It was by some way his heaviest fall in politics since he had first entered the House of Commons fifteen years before. However, he was given a seat in the newly-formed Dardanelles Committee, and although he had no power to take decisions it was understood that he was to have a watching brief on the operations at Gallipoli. On May 26 he left the Admiralty, and he did not return there until twenty-four years later at the outbreak of the second world war.

Ashmead-Bartlett, who returned home from the peninsula for a few days about this time, gives a vivid picture of Churchill and his state of mind. 'I am much surprised,' he wrote in his diary, 'at the change in Winston Churchill. He looks years older, his face is pale, he seems very depressed and to feel keenly his retirement from the Admiralty. . . . At dinner the conversation was more or less general, nothing was said about the Dardanelles, and Winston was very quiet. It was only towards the very end that he suddenly burst forth into a tremendous discourse on the Expedition and what might have been, addressed directly across the table in the form of a lecture to his mother, who listened most attentively. Winston seemed unconscious of the limited number of his audience, and continued quite heedless of those around him. He insisted over and over again that the battle of March 18th had never been fought to a finish, and, had it been, the Fleet must have got through the Narrows. This is the great obsession of his mind, and will ever remain so. . . .'

Of these events little or nothing was known at Gallipoli. From day to day Hamilton waited for an answer to his message to Kitchener asking for the reinforcement of another Army corps. But nothing came beyond a promise of one Lowland division which was to sail from England. There was, however, an echo of the hesitation and the confusion in Whitehall in a cable which Hamilton received from Kitchener on May 19. In it Kitchener spoke of his disappointment at the progress at Gallipoli. 'A serious situation,' he said, 'is created by the present check, and the calls for large reinforcements and an additional amount of ammunition that we can ill spare from France.

'From the standpoint of an early solution of our difficulties, your views, as stated, are not encouraging. The question whether we can long support two fields of operation draining on our resources requires grave consideration. I know that I can rely on you to do your utmost to bring the present unfortunate state of affairs in the Dardanelles to as early a conclusion as possible, so that any consideration of a withdrawal, with all its dangers in the East, may be prevented from entering the field of possible solutions.

'When all the above is taken into consideration, I am somewhat surprised to see that the 4,500 which Maxwell can send you are apparently not required by you. With the aid of these I had hoped that you would have been in a position to press forward.'

Hamilton wrote in his diary: 'I can only surmise that my request made to Maxwell that these 4,500 men should come to me as drafts for my skeleton units, instead of as a raw brigade, has twisted itself going down some official corridor into a story that I don't want the men! K. tells me Egypt is mine and the fatness thereof; yet no sooner do I make the most modest suggestion concerning anything or anyone Egyptian than K. is got at and I find he is the Barmecide and I Schac'abac.[1] "How do you like your lentil soup?" says K. "Excellently well," say I, "But devil a drop is in the plate!" I have got to enter the joke; that's the long and short of it.'

There is a revealing quality about this grotesque little incident, for it was symptomatic of the general tug-of-war in which they were all engaged: Maxwell withholding troops from Hamilton, Fisher withholding ships from Churchill, the Conservatives withholding political support from Asquith. The setback at Gallipoli, in short, had brought out into the open, and more bitterly than ever, the great issue which in the end was to dominate all others before the end of the year: were they to fight in the East or the West?

Meanwhile on the peninsula the Army's store of ammunition had fallen so low that the guns were rationed to two shells a day. On the two fronts at Anzac and Cape Helles there was desultory fighting from time to time, but hardly more than a few yards of ground changed hands, and it seemed now that nothing could break the deadlock. Yet the situation could not remain as it was, some sort of decision would have to be taken. And, in fact, at this ul-

[1] A reference to the *Arabian Nights* tale in which a series of empty dishes is served to a hungry man.

timate moment of hesitation, a glimpse of reality was on its way. A few moments before dawn, on this same day, May 19, General Birdwood was woken in his dugout at Anzac with the news that, in a packed mass of many thousands, the Turks were streaming across to his trenches in the darkness.

NINE

THERE is some dispute as to who ordered the attack on the Anzac bridgehead on the night of May 18. Liman von Sanders says that he himself made the plan and he takes the responsibility for it; others believe that it was conceived by Enver when he first visited the peninsula on May 10, and the circumstances of the enterprise do, in fact, bear the impress of Enver's headlong cast of mind. There was no subtlety or caution about the matter: some 42,000 men under the command of Essad Pasha were assembled, and their orders were nothing less than to demolish the whole Anzac bridgehead at a single blow. By nightfall it was hoped that the last Dominion soldier would have been killed, captured or driven into the sea, and that the entire Turkish army would have then been free to turn south to deal with the remainder of Hamilton's forces at Cape Helles.

At this time the Australian and New Zealand Corps had dwindled to some 10,000 effective men, and it was only by luck that a brigade which had been sent round to Cape Helles earlier in the month was returned to Birdwood on the eve of the battle. This brought his numbers to a total of about 17,000, of which 12,500 were available for fighting in the front line. They were thus outnumbered by more than three to one.

The Anzac position had by now become very clearly defined: it was a shallow triangle, covering about 400 acres, its base, a mile and a half long, resting on the sea, its apex reaching to the slopes of Sari Bair about a thousand yards from the shore. In order to avoid the fire of the British

159

Fleet the Turks had dug their trenches almost on top of the Anzac lines, and at some places the two sides were divided by not more than ten yards. The situation at Quinn's and Courtnay's Posts in the centre of the line was fantastic; directly behind the Australian trench (which was kept packed with men by day and night), a steep cliff fell away to the gully below, and the Turks had only to make an advance of five yards in order to drive a wedge through the bridgehead to the sea. But this they never could succeed in doing, though they attacked repeatedly during the first half of May. No-man's-land at these and other points was no larger than a small room, and it was the easiest thing in the world for the Turks to toss a hand grenade into the Anzac trenches. The only real defence against this was to throw the grenade smartly back again before it exploded; except for a few jam tins which were filled with explosive at a makeshift workshop on the beach, the Australians had no such weapons of their own. No man could expose the smallest fraction of his body for an instant without being shot, and even a periscope hoisted for a moment above the parapet was immediately shattered. An extreme tension prevailed in the bridgehead; there was no hour when some new raid was not expected or delivered, no minute when shells were not crashing among them or bullets screaming overhead. The soldiers managed to sleep through this racket at odd hours of the day and night, but it was never a sufficient rest. No one was ever safe. On May 14 General Bridges, the commander of the Australian Division, was mortally wounded, and the following day Birdwood had his hair parted by a bullet while he was looking through a periscope. The wound turned septic and was very painful but he continued in command.

There was an intense hatred of the Turks among the Dominion soldiers. Most of them had grown up in a world of clear and obvious values; a fight was a fight, you knew who your enemy was and you stood up to him and had it out, fairly and squarely, in the open. It was in this spirit that they had volunteered for service in the Army. The charge was the thing, the quick and palpable blow in the face that knocked the man down. War, in fact, was an extension of the pub brawl and it had in it the elements of rioting, of street fighting, of instant physical revenge.

But nothing of the kind had happened at Gallipoli. From the day they had landed the soldiers had scarcely ever seen the enemy; he lurked unseen in the heights above, he sniped down on them and caught them unawares, he stood back at a safe distance with his guns and burst his shrapnel above their heads, and there seemed to be no effective way of retaliating. After more than three weeks of this the soldiers were beginning to feel an increasing sense of frustration and of impotent anger in their narrow bridgehead. A claustrophobia had developed; they felt that they had been caught in a trap, and there seemed to be something unfair in this kind of fighting in which they were never given a chance of showing their real courage and their strength.

Beyond this there was at this early stage another and perhaps deeper feeling that there was a monstrosity and inhumanity about the Turks: they were cruel and sinister fanatics, capable of any sort of vice and bestiality—in brief, it was the popular picture that had been drawn of them by Byron and the emotions of Gladstonian liberal England. The Turks were 'natives'—but natives of a peculiarly dangerous and subtle kind. And so the Australian and New Zealand soldiers fought, not an ordinary man, but a monster prefigured by imagination and by propaganda; and they hated him.

Despite these things, perhaps even because of them, an extraordinary cheerfulness and exaltation possessed the men in the front line. Living with the instant prospect of death, all pettiness, all the normal anxieties and jealousies of life, deserted them, and they developed an almost mystical feeling towards the extreme danger that surrounded them. The fighting became an elaborate and exciting game in which they were all immensely engrossed, and it was only when they were retired to rest for a while in some half-haven under the cliffs that they became aware again of the miseries of their situation, the monotonous food, the endless physical discomfort, the impossible limits of a life in which even a canteen of fresh water or a bathe in the sea were the utmost luxuries.

By now death had become a familiar, and they often talked about it in a half-derisive deprecating slang. In the same way as the Chinese will laugh at other people's pain it became a huge joke when the men bathing off the beach were caught in a burst of shrapnel, or when some poor devil had his head blown off while he was in the latrine. There had to be some sort of expression which would help to rationalize the unbearable circumstances of their lives, some

161

way of obtaining relief from the shock of it all, and since tears were impossible this callous hard-boiled laughter became the thing. They were not fatalists. They believed that a mistake had been made in the landing at Gaba Tepe and that they might easily have to pay for it with their lives; but they very much wanted to go on living, they were all for the battle and they hoped and believed obscurely that in the end they would win.

These high spirits, this fineness and integrity created by the powerful drug of risk, might not perhaps have continued indefinitely under such a strain, but there had certainly been no weakening in morale when, on May 18, the soldiers became aware that something unusual was happening in the enemy lines.

An unaccountable silence spread through the hills before them. For the first time since they had landed the fearful racket of the Turkish howitzers died away, and for several minutes at a stretch no rifle or machine-gun was fired. In this strange quiet most of the day went by. Then at five o'clock in the evening a tremendous artillery barrage broke out, and it continued for about half an hour. It chanced that on this day a naval aircraft had been sent out to fix the position of an enemy warship in the straits, and on his return the pilot reported that he had seen large numbers of men massing behind the Turkish lines. Later in the day this information was confirmed by a second pilot who had also seen enemy soldiers coming across the straits in boats from the Asiatic side; and from the battleship *Triumph* there was a further report that Turkish reinforcements were marching north from Cape Helles to the Anzac front. On hearing this, Birdwood sent a message to his two divisional commanders warning them to expect an attack that night; the men were to stand to arms at 3 a.m., which was half an hour before the usual time.

The night turned cold and misty, and when the moon went down at 11.35 p.m. there was hardly a sound along the front except for the breaking of the waves on the shore. Suddenly at fifteen minutes to midnight, a fusillade of rifle fire which was heavier than anything that had been heard before burst out from the Turkish trenches, and as it spread along the line the Anzac commanders kept telephoning to their outposts to ask if they were being attacked. But nothing followed, and presently the uproar dwindled into silence again. At 3 a.m. the men were roused, and they took their places on the firing steps with their bayonets fixed to their rifles. It was still cold and most of them were wearing their overcoats.

Hardly five minutes had gone by when a shout of warning went up from one of the outposts, and a company of Turks was seen advancing down a ravine known as Wire Gully in the centre of the line. There had been no preliminary bugle call, none of the usual shouts of Allah, Allah: merely these shadowy forms in the half-darkness and the long line of bayonets. The Australians opened fire from either side of the gully, and immediately the enemy bugles sounded and the charge began. Everywhere along the line the Turks jumped up from their hiding places and in a dark cloud swept forward over the broken ground.

At most places the oncoming enemy had to cross two or three hundred yards before they reached the Anzac entrenchments, and so there was half a minute or more when they were exposed in the open and quite defenceless. Very few of them survived even that amount of time. There was a kind of cascading movement in the battle; directly one line of soldiers had come over the parapet and been destroyed another line formed up, emerged into view and was cut down. For the first hour it was simply a matter of indiscriminate killing, but presently the Australians and New Zealanders began to adopt more systematic methods: when a Turkish officer appeared they deliberately withheld their fire until he had assembled the full company of his men in the open. Then all were destroyed together. At some points it became a kind of game to pick off the survivors as they ran back and forth across the battlefield like terrified rabbits in search of cover. Here and there some few of the Turks did manage to get into the Anzac trenches, but they survived only for a few minutes; there was a quick and awful bayoneting and then the tide receded again.

As daylight broke the battle assumed the character of a hunt, with the Turkish officers serving in the role of beaters driving the game on to the guns. A wild, almost berserk excitement filled the Australian and New Zealand ranks. In order to get a better view many of the soldiers jumped up and sat astride the parapets and from there they blazed away at the screaming mass of Turks before them. The Anzac soldiers who had been held in reserve could not bear to be left out of the fight; they came pressing forward offering to pay for a place on the firing line. In one trench two soldiers actually fought one another with their fists for a vacant position on the parapet, and there was a kind of mad surrealism in the shouts and cries along the line as each new Turkish rush came on. 'Backsheesh' 'Imshi Yallah', 'Eggs is cooked'.[1] Once an Australian was heard shouting to the Turks as they fell back from his trench, 'Saida (good-bye). Play you again next Saturday.'

By 5 a.m., when a hot sun was beginning to stream down on to the battlefield, the attack was broken. But the orders to the Turks were that they should continue the fight unil they got through to the sea, and so they went on with the struggle for another six hours, each new charge getting a little feebler than the last. Mustafa Kemal had been reduced to the command of a single division, the 19th, for the period of the offensive, and he alone, of the four divisional commanders engaged, had succeeded in making any headway. When at midday Essad Pasha decided to break off the action 10,000 of his men had fallen, and of these some 5,000 dead, dying and wounded, were lying out in the open between the trenches.

Other heavier battles than this were fought at Gallipoli, but none with such a terrible concentration of killing, none so one-sided, and none with so strange an aftermath. Through the long afternoon the wounded lay with the dead on the battlefield, and although the trenches on either side were only a yard or two away no one could go out and bring them in without taking the risk of being instantly shot.

'No sound came from that dreadful space,' the Australian history of the campaign relates, 'but here and there some wounded or dying man, silently lying without help or any hope of it under the sun which glared from a cloudless sky, turned painfully from one side to the other, or slowly raised an arm towards heaven.'

Birdwood was warned by his medical staff that, quite apart from any feelings of humanity, the dead should be buried as quickly as possible to prevent infection spreading through the Army. When the afternoon had passed without any sign of the Turks renewing the attack, he sent off Au-

---

[1] Or 'Eggs-a-cook', an expression used by the Egyptian vendors when they sold eggs to the Anzac troops during their stay in Egypt.

brey Herbert to ask Hamilton aboard the *Arcadian* if he might arrange an armistice.

Herbert was an odd figure on the Anzac bridgehead—indeed, he would have been odd in any army on any battlefield: a Member of Parliament turned soldier, an eccentric, a poet and a scholar who, far from hating the Turks, was captivated by them. This did not mean he was disloyal—he was determined that they should be defeated —but he knew Turkey and Turkish very well, and he believed that with better handling by the politicians they might have been converted into allies. Of all the band who had been with Rupert Brooke at Alexandria he was the one most possessed of ideas, and despite his short-sightedness, his impulsive and agitated manner, he was very brave and saw very clearly under the façade of things. Hamilton was glad enough to have him on his staff as an intelligence officer with the rank of lieutenant-colonel, but he noted in his diary that he was 'excessively unorthodox'.

Herbert chose to do his intelligence work in the front line at Anzac, and he proceeded to war in the manner of a nineteenth-century gentleman-adventurer. Servants were engaged at Lemnos, suitable horses and mules acquired, an adequate kit assembled, and off he went with an extraordinary assemblage of Greek and Levantine interpreters to the peninsula. There were staff troubles almost at once. A spy mania was raging through the Anzac bridgehead—the fear of spies seems to be endemic in every crisis in every military campaign—and his interpreters were arrested as many as four and five times a day. A terrible hail of shrapnel once fell on Herbert's dugout, and the cook, a Greek named Christopher of the Black Lamp, with the tears pouring down his face gave two hours' notice, though why it should be two hours and not two minutes he was unable to explain. Among these and other domestic anxieties Herbert continued with his work of questioning the Turkish prisoners and of acting as a kind of general confidant of the commanders in all questions relating to the habits and character of the enemy.

His methods of propaganda were very direct. He crawled into the foremost trenches and from there he addressed the enemy soldiers in their own language, urging them to desert, promising them good treatment and pointing out that the real quarrel of the Allies was not with Turkey but with the Germans. At times he actually got into trenches which communicated directly into the enemy emplacements, and lying on the dead bodies there, he called to the Turks through a single barrier of sandbags. Occasionally they would listen and enter into argument with him. More often they replied with hand-grenades—a thing which did not make Herbert very welcome with the Anzac troops—and in Constantinople one of the newspapers announced that there was someone in the Anzac bridgehead who was making a low attempt to lure the Turks from their duty by imitating the prayers of the muezzin.

It now fell to Herbert to put the case to Hamilton for an armistice. He argued that unless something was done quickly the situation would become intolerable: our own wounded as well as Turkish were still lying in the open, and in the hot sun the dead bodies were decomposing rapidly. Hamilton answered that he would not initiate any proposal himself, because the enemy would make propaganda of it, but if the Turks liked to come forward he was willing to grant them a cessation of hostilities for a limited period. It was agreed finally that notes could be thrown into the Turkish trenches telling them of this.

Meanwhile all May 20 had gone by and unknown to Hamilton and Herbert the soldiers at the front had already taken matters into their own hands. Towards evening an Australian colonel caused a Red Cross flag to be hoisted on a plateau at the lower end of the line. He intended to send out his stretcher-bearers to bring in a number of wounded Turks who were crying out pitiably in front of his trenches. Before they could move, however, the Turks put two bullets through the staff of the flag and brought it down. A moment later a man jumped up from the Turkish trenches and came running across no-man's-land. He stopped on the parapet above the Australians' heads, spoke a few words of apology, and then ran back to his own lines again. Immediately afterwards Red Crescent flags appeared above the enemy trenches, and Turkish stretcher-bearers came out. All firing ceased along the line, and in this eerie stillness General Walker, the commander of the 1st Australian Division, got up and walked towards the enemy. A group of Turkish officers came out to meet him, and for a while they stood there in the open, smoking, and talking in French. It was agreed that they should exchange letters on the subject of an armistice at 8 p.m. that night.

While this was going on another impromptu parley with

166

the enemy had opened on another section of the line. It was now growing late and Birdwood, as soon as he heard what was happening, issued an order that no further burials were to be made that night. A note signed by the General's A.D.C. was handed to a Turkish officer: 'If you want a truce to bury your dead,' it said, 'send a staff officer, under a flag of truce, to our headquarters via the Gaba Tepe road, between 10 a.m. and 12 noon tomorrow.'

At this stage neither side seems to have been absolutely sure of themselves; there was a tense feeling that some act of treachery might occur at any moment, that an attack might be launched under the cover of the white flags—and indeed, an Australian soldier who had been out in no-man's-land came back with the report that the enemy trenches were filled with men who were apparently ready to attack. Upon this the Australians opened fire on a party of stretcher-bearers who were still wandering about in the failing light. At once the Turkish artillery started up again and the bombardment continued intermittently all night.

Hamilton says he was very much annoyed when he heard of these irregular dealings with the enemy, and he dispatched Braithwaite to Anzac to handle the negotiations. The following letter, addressed to *Commandant en chef des Forces Britanniques*, Sir John Hamilton,' arrived from Liman von Sanders.

'Grand Quartier Général de la 5ème. Armée Ottomane. le 22 mai 1915.
Excellence,
J'ai l'honneur d'informer Votre Excellence que les propositions concernant la conclusion d'un armistice pour enterrer les morts et secourir les blessés des deux parties adverses, ont trouvé mon plein consentement—et que seuls nos sentiments d'humanité nous y ont déterminés.
J'ai investi le lieutenant-colonel Fahreddin du pouvoir de signer en mon nom.
J'ai l'honneur d'être avec assurance de ma plus haute considération.

Liman von Sanders,
Commandant en chef de la 5ème. Armée Ottomane.'

There is an air of fantasy about the conference that took place at Birdwood's headquarters on May 22. Herbert walked through heavy showers of rain along the Gaba Tepe beach, and a 'fierce Arab officer and a wandery-looking Turkish lieutenant' came out to meet him. They sat down and smoked in a field of scarlet poppies. Presently Kemal himself arrived on horseback with other Turkish officers, and they were blindfolded and led on foot into the Anzac bridgehead. The British intelligence officers were anxious to give the impression that a great deal of barbed-wire entanglement had been erected on the beach, and they forced Kemal to keep goose-stepping over imaginary obstacles as he went along. Presently the Turks were remounted and taken to Birdwood's dugout by the beach.

The conference in the narrow cave was a stiff and strained affair, the Turkish Beys in their gold lace, the British generals in their red tabs, each side trying to make it clear that it was not they who were eager for the armistice. But the atmosphere was relieved by one moment of pure farce: an Australian soldier, not knowing or caring about what was going on inside the dugout, put his head round the canvas flap and demanded, 'Have any of you bastards got my kettle?'

Herbert meanwhile had been taken into the Turkish lines as a hostage. He was mounted on a horse and blindfolded, and then led round and round in circles to confuse his sense of direction. At one stage the fierce Arab officer cried out to the man who was supposed to be leading the horse, 'You old fool. Can't you see he's riding straight over the cliff?' Herbert protested strongly and they went on again. When finally the bandage was taken from his eyes he found himself in a tent in a grove of olives, and the Arab officer said, 'This is the beginning of a lifelong friendship.' He ordered cheese, tea and coffee to be brought, and offered to eat first to prove that the food was not poisoned. They had an amiable conversation, and in the evening when Kemal and the other Turks came back from Birdwood's headquarters Herbert was blindfolded again and returned to the British lines.

The terms of the truce had been settled as precisely as possible; it was to take place on May 24 and was to continue for nine hours. Three zones were to be marked out with white flags for the burial of the dead—one Turkish, one British and the third common to both sides. Priests, doctors and soldiers taking part in the burials were to wear white arm-bands and were not to use field-glasses or enter enemy trenches. All firing was of course to cease along the line, and the soldiers in the opposing trenches were not to put their heads above their parapets during the period of the truce. It was also agreed that all rifles minus their bolts were to be handed back to whichever side they belonged to —but this move was circumvented to some extent by the Australians, who on the previous evening crept out into no-man's-land and gathered up as many weapons as they could find.

The morning of May 24 broke wet and cold, and the soldiers were in their greatcoats. Soon after dawn the firing died away, and at six-thirty Herbert set out again with a group of officers for Gaba Tepe beach. Heavy rain was falling. After an hour the Turks arrived—Herbert's acquaintance of two days before and several others, including a certain Arif, the son of Achmet Pasha, who handed Herbert a visiting card inscribed with the words, *Sculpteur et Peintre. Etudiant de Poésie.*

Together the two parties left the beach, and passing through cornfields flecked with poppies walked up to the hills where the battle had taken place. 'Then,' Herbert says, 'the fearful smell of death began as we came upon scattered bodies. We mounted over a plateau and down through gullies filled with thyme, where there lay about 4,000 Turkish dead. It was indescribable. One was grateful for the rain and the grey sky. A Turkish Red Crescent man came and gave me some antiseptic wool with scent on it, and this they renewed frequently. There were two wounded crying in that multitude of silence.'

Many of the dead had sunk to the ground in the precise attitude they had adopted at the moment when the bullets stopped their rush, their hands clasping their bayonets, their heads thrust forward or doubled up beneath them. Nothing was missing except the spark of life. They lay in mounds on the wet earth, whole companies of soldiers, like some ghastly tableau made of wax.

Among the living men there was at first some little friction. Everyone was nervous, everyone expected that even in these awful nightmarish surroundings some kind of treachery had been planned by the other side. There were complaints: the Australians were stealing arms: the Turks were coming too close to the Anzac trenches. At Quinn's Post, where the lines were only ten or fifteen yards apart, the tension was almost a palpable thing in the air, an inflammable essence that might explode at any moment.

169

Hands on their triggers the men watched one another across the narrow space, expecting at every minute that someone would make some foolish gesture that would start the fighting again. On the wider stretches of the battlefield, however, Turks and Anzac troops worked together in digging great communal graves, and as the hours went by they began to fraternize, offering cigarettes to one another, talking in broken scraps of English and Arabic, exchanging badges and gadgets from their pockets as souvenirs.

Herbert was kept busy settling points of difference. He allowed the Turks to extract for burial some bodies which had been built into their emplacements, and once he was even permitted to go into the enemy trenches to satisfy himself that the Turks were not using this lull to fortify and advance their positions. He found there a group of soldiers whom he had known previously in Albania. They gathered round him cheering and clapping, and he had to stop them because they were interrupting the burial services which were being conducted round about by the Moslem Imams and the Christian priests. From this time onwards, the Turks were constantly coming up to him for orders, and even getting him to sign receipts for money taken from the dead. Intervals of bright sunshine had now followed the rain.

Compton Mackenzie and Major Jack Churchill (the brother of Winston Churchill) had come over from the *Arcadian* for the day, and they stood on a parapet constructed chiefly of dead bodies to watch the scene. 'In the foreground,' Mackenzie writes, 'was a narrow stretch of level scrub along which white flags were stuck at intervals, and a line of sentries, Australians and Turks, faced one another. Staff officers of both sides were standing around in little groups, and there was an atmosphere about the scene of local magnates at the annual sports making suggestions about the start of the obstacle race. Aubrey Herbert looked so like the indispensable bachelor that every country neighbourhood retains to take complete control of the proceedings on such occasions. Here he was, shuffling about, loose-gaited, his neck out-thrust and swinging from side to side as he went peering up into people's faces to see whether they were the enemy or not, so that, if they were, he could offer them cigarettes and exchange a few courtesies with them in their own language. . . .

'The impression which that scene from the ridge by

Quinn's Post made on my mind has obliterated all the rest of the time at Anzac. I cannot recall a single incident on the way back down the valley. I know only that nothing could cleanse the smell of death from the nostrils for a fortnight afterwards. There was no herb so aromatic but it reeked of carrion, not thyme nor lavender, nor even rosemary.'

By three in the afternoon the work was practically done. There were two crises: it was discovered at the last minute that the Turks' watches were eight minutes ahead of the British, and a hurried adjustment had to be made. Then, as the hour for the ending of the truce was approaching, a shot rang out. Standing there in the open with tens of thousands of rifles pointed towards them the burial parties stood in a sudden hush, but nothing followed and they returned to their work again.

At four o'clock the Turks near Quinn's Post came to Herbert for their final orders, since none of their own officers were about. He first sent back the grave-diggers to their own trenches, and at seven minutes past four retired the men who were carrying the white flags. He then walked over to the Turkish trenches to say good-bye. When he remarked to the enemy soldiers there that they would probably shoot him on the following day, they answered in a horrified chorus, 'God forbid.' Seeing Herbert standing there, groups of Australians came up to the Turks to shake hands and say good-bye. 'Good-bye, old chap; good luck.' The Turks answered with one of their proverbs: 'Smiling may you go and smiling may you come again.'

All the remaining men in the open were now sent back to their lines, and Herbert made a last minute inspection along the front, reminding the Turks that firing was not to begin again for a further twenty-five minutes. He was answered with salaams, and he too finally dropped out of sight. At 4.45 p.m. a Turkish sniper fired from somewhere in the hills. Immediately the Australians answered and the roar of high explosive closed over the battlefield again.

There had been some irregularities. On both sides a good deal of surreptitious digging had been done, and both Turkish and British staff officers had strolled about no-man's-land, covertly studying the lie of each other's trenches. It was even said—and the story has never been denied in Turkey—that Kemal had disguised himself as a

171

sergeant and had spent the whole nine hours with various burial parties close to the Anzac trenches.

Much the most important result of the battle and the truce, however, was that from this time onwards all real rancour against the Turks died out in the Anzac ranks. They now knew the enemy from their own experience, and he had ceased to be a propaganda figure. He was no longer a coward, a fanatic or a monster. He was a normal man and they thought him very brave.

This camaraderie with the enemy—the mutual respect of men who are committed to killing one another—was not peculiar to Gallipoli for it existed also in France; but on this isolated battlefield it had a special intensity. The Australian and New Zealand troops refused to use the gas-masks that were now issued to them. When they were questioned about this they made some such reply as, 'The Turks won't use gas. They're clean fighters.'[1]

Had the soldiers known Enver a little better they might not have been so certain of this; yet perhaps they did know Enver, for politicians generally were held in contempt at Gallipoli and by both sides, and in a way that seldom occurred in the second world war. Soon many of the British began to feel as Herbert felt: that the campaign need never have been fought at all had only the politicians acted more responsibly in the beginning.

The extreme ferocity with which the battles were fought at Gallipoli gives no inkling of the compassion that the opposing soldiers in the front line felt for one another. In the periods of comparative calm which followed May 19 at Anzac, the most bizarre incidents occurred. Once a staff officer visiting the front saw with astonishment that a number of Turks were walking about behind their lines in full view of the Australians. He asked, 'Why don't you shoot?' and was answered, 'Well, they're not doing any harm are they? Might as well leave the poor beggars alone.' Later in the campaign there was an old Turk who apparently had been given the job of doing the washing for his platoon. Regularly each day he emerged from his trench and hung out the wet shirts and socks in a line along the parapet, and no Allied soldier would have dreamed of shooting him. The Turks on their side usually withheld their fire

---

[1] Gas was never used at Gallipoli.

from the survivors of wrecked ships, and in the front line at least their prisoners were treated with kindness.

There was a constant traffic of gifts in the trenches, the Turks throwing over grapes and sweets, the Allied soldiers responding with tinned food and cigarettes. The Turks had no great love for British beef. A note came over one day: 'Bully beef—non. Envoyez milk.' It became an accepted practice to wave a 'wash-out' to a sniper who missed: there would be the sudden crack of a rifle, the bullet screaming past the Turk's head, then the laugh from the enemy trench, the waving of a spade or a bayonet and the words in English softly shouted, 'Better luck next time, Tommy.'

Once or twice private duels were fought. While the rest of the soldiers on both sides held their fire an Australian and a Turk would stand up on the parapets and blaze away at one another until one or the other was wounded or killed, and something seemed to be proved—their skill, their wish 'to dare', perhaps most of all their pride. Then in a moment all would dissolve into the horror and frenzy of a raid or a set-piece battle, the inhuman berserk killing.

Between the two extremes, between the battles and the truce, between fighting and death, the men had to come to terms with their precarious existence. They soon developed habits that fitted their mad surroundings, and they did this very rapidly and very well. The rabbit warren of trenches and dugouts at Anzac became more familiar to them than their own villages and homes. By night ten thousand shaded fires were lit in niches in the cliffs, ten thousand crude meals were cooked; they slept, they waited for their precious mail, their one reminder of the lost sane world, they put the individual extra touch to their dug-outs—another shelf in the rock, a blanket across the opening, a biscuit tin to hold a tattered book. They knew every twist in the paths where a sniper's bullet would come thudding in, they accepted wounding as they might have accepted an accident on the football field, they argued about the war and the confined beehive politics of their battalions, they took the risk of bathing in the sea under the bursting shrapnel and nothing would stop them doing it. They cursed and complained and dreamed and this in fact was home.

No stranger visiting the Anzac bridgehead ever failed to be moved and stimulated by it. It was a thing so wildly out of life, so dangerous, so high-spirited, such a grotesque and theatrical setting and yet reduced to such a calm and almost matter-of-fact routine. The heart missed a beat when one approached the ramshackle jetty on the beach, for the Turkish shells were constantly falling there, and it hardly seemed that anyone could survive. Yet once ashore a curious sense of heightened living supervened. No matter how hideous the noise, the men moved about apparently oblivious of it all, and with a trained and steady air as though they had lived there all their lives; and this in itself was a reassurance to everyone who came ashore. The general aspect was of a vast mining camp in some savage desert valley. Close to the shore were the dug-outs of the generals, the wireless station, the telephone exchange, the searchlights, a factory for making bombs, a corral for Turkish prisoners, a smithy. Scores of placid mules sheltered in the gully until at nightfall they began their work of taking ammunition and supplies to the men in the trenches in the hills above—the water ration was a pannikin a day. There was a smoking incinerator near the jetty, and it erupted loudly whenever an unexploded bullet fell into the flames. An empty shellcase served as a gong for the headquarters officers' mess. They ate bully beef, biscuits, plum and apple jam, and just occasionally frozen meat; never vegetables, eggs, milk or fruit.

Above the beach a maze of goat tracks spread upward through the furze and the last surviving patches of prickly oak, and at every step of the way some soldier had made his shelter in the side of the ravine: a hole dug into the ground, the branches of trees or perhaps a piece of canvas for a roof, a blanket, a few tins and boxes, and that was all. As one progressed upward there were many crude notices of warning against the enemy snipers: Keep Well to Your Left. Keep Your Head Down. Double Across One at a Time. Then finally the trenches themselves, where all day long the men stood to their arms, watching and watching through their periscopes for the slightest movement in the enemy lines. Cigarettes dangled from their mouths. They talked quietly.

Hamilton came over to the bridgehead on May 30 and saw, 'Men staggering under huge sides of frozen beef: men struggling up cliffs with kerosene tins full of water; men digging; men cooking; men cardplaying in small dens scooped out from the banks of yellow clay—everyone wore a Bank Holiday air; evidently the ranklings and worries of mankind—miseries and concerns of the spirit—had fled the precincts of this valley. The Boss—the bill—the girl—envy, malice, hunger, hatred—had scooted away to the Antipodes. All the time, overhead, the shell and rifle bullets groaned and whined, touching just the same note of violent energy as was in evidence everywhere else. To understand that awful din, raise the eyes twenty-five degrees to the top of the cliff which closes in the tail end of the valley and you can see the Turkish hand-grenades bursting along the crest, just where an occasional bayonet flashes and figures hardly distinguishable from Mother Earth crouch in an irregular line. Or else they rise to fire and are silhouetted against the sky and then you recognize the naked athletes from the Antipodes and your heart goes into your mouth as a whole bunch of them dart forward suddenly, and as suddenly disappear. And the bomb shower stops dead—for the moment; but, all the time, from that fiery crest line which is Quinn's, there comes a slow constant trickle of wounded—some dragging themselves painfully along; others being carried along on stretchers. Bomb wounds all; a ceaseless silent stream of bandages and blood. Yet three out of four of "the boys" have grit left for a gay smile or a cheery little nod to their comrades, waiting for their turn as they pass, pass, pass, down on their way to the sea.

'There are poets and writers who see naught in war but carrion, filth, savagery and horror. The heroism of the rank and file makes no appeal. They refuse war the credit of being the only exercise in devotion on the large scale existing in this world. The superb moral victory over death leaves them cold. Each one to his taste. To me this is no valley of death—it is a valley brim full of life at its highest power. Men live through more in five minutes on that crest than they do in five years of Bendigo or Ballarat. Ask the brothers of these very fighters—Calgoorlie or Coolgardie miners—to do one quarter of the work and to run one hundredth the risk on a wages basis—instanter there would be a riot. But here—not a murmur, not a question; only a radiant force of camaraderie in action.'

From May onwards many of the men discarded their uniforms, and except for a pair of shorts, boots and perhaps a cap, went naked in the sun. Even in the frontlines they fought stripped to the waist, a girl, a ship or a dragon tattooed on their arms.

There was a toughness mixed with touchiness in this ant-heap life. Compton Mackenzie relates that on his visit

175

to Anzac he overtook Lieut.-Colonel Pollen, Hamilton's military secretary, who was talking to three Australians all well over six feet tall. 'Pollen, who had a soft, somewhat ecclesiastical voice, was saying, "Have you chaps heard that they've given General Bridges a posthumous K.C.M.G.?"

' "Have they?" one of the giants replied. "Well, that won't do him much good where he is now, will it, mate?"

'Poor Pollen, who was longing to be sympathetic and not to mind the way these Australians would stare at his red tabs without saluting, walked on a little depressed by his reception at making conversation, perhaps at the very spot where General Bridges had been mortally wounded. He looked carefully at the ground when he met the next lot, whereupon they all gave him an elaborate salute, and then because he had looked up too late to acknowledge it one of them turned to the others and said: "I suppose that's what they call breeding." They really were rather difficult.'

But it was the physical appearance of the Dominion soldiers—Colonials as they were then called—that captivated everybody who came to Anzac, and there is hardly an account of the campaign which does not refer to it with admiration and even a kind of awe. 'As a child,' Mackenzie wrote, 'I used to pore for hours over those illustrations of Flaxman for Homer and Virgil which simulated the effect of ancient pottery. There was not one of those glorious young men I saw that day who might not himself have been Ajax or Diomed, Hector or Achilles. Their almost complete nudity, their tallness and majestic simplicity of line, their rose-brown flesh burnt by the sun and purged of all grossness by the ordeal through which they were passing, all these united to create something as near to absolute beauty as I shall hope ever to see in this world.'

The soldiers themselves might not have thought of it in this way, but here perhaps, in this unlikely place, was the expression of Rupert Brooke's dream of war, the Grecian frieze, the man entirely heroic and entirely beautiful, the best in the presence of death. Just for this moment at the end of May and in the months that followed they were the living embodiment of the legend they were creating. This was the highest moment of their countries' short history; they had fought and won their first great battle, they were still in the glow of it, they knew suffering and they were not afraid. They had made a fortress of this wretched strip of foreign soil on which they had so haphazardly drifted, and they were quite determined to hold on. Never again in the whole course of the campaign did the Turks attempt an assault in force upon the Anzac bridgehead.

TEN

~~~~~~

DURING the first few weeks of the campaign the wildest rumours went about Constantinople; ten thousand British were said to have been killed at the landing, and another thirty thousand taken prisoner. At one moment the Allies were reported to be advancing on the city and at the next they had been driven into the sea. Once again there was talk of special trains that were to evacuate the Government into the interior, of bombardments and of riots. Yet it was not quite the same ferment, the near panic, that had followed the naval attack on the Narrows in March. The Allied Fleet then had been feared in much the same way as the Air Force bombers were feared at the start of the second world war, but a military campaign on land was something that everyone could understand, a slower and a more familiar thing; there was no question of the capital being demolished overnight.

Enver took a firm line from the outset; he announced flatly that the allies were already defeated, and to celebrate the event there was a ceremony at St. Sophia at which the Sultan was invested with the title of El Ghazi, the Conqueror, the driver of the Allies into the sea. Flags were hung out in all the principal streets and public squares.

It is doubtful if anyone was much impressed by this, but by the end of the first week in May it was clear at least that the invading army was not making much headway. An apathetic quiet settled on the streets, and the city began to accustom itself to the suspense, the misery and the occasional shocks of a long campaign. Presently the old familiar signs of war began to appear: the conscripts marching

178

through the streets in their shabby field grey uniforms and pyramidal hats, the Army communiqués that announced yesterday's victory all over again, the ferocious newspaper articles, the flags and the parades, the spy hunt and the renewed outburst of official xenophobia.

Once again the foreign minorities, the Armenians and the Greeks, went underground with their thoughts and, where they could, their belongings. Bedri, the Chief of Police, pursued them as persistently as he could, issuing worthless receipts for the goods he seized from their shops and houses, and extracting money by the simple process of keeping people in gaol until they bought themselves out. One day his men swooped on the Bon Marché and carried off all the boxes of toy soldiers in the shop on the ground that they had been manufactured in France.

After the first rush on the banks and the stores there was the usual shortage of coal and petrol. 'The bazaar is dead,' one of the foreign diplomats wrote in his diary. 'Nothing is bought or sold.' The Germans, meanwhile, managed to exercise a censorship on news since they controlled the newsprint that was imported into the country and issued it only to those newspapers which took a line that was strongly favourable to Germany.

For the rest, however, the rhythm of the city was not much changed, and travellers arriving there on the Orient Express were astonished at how normal it all was. The lights went on at night, the Pera Palace Hotel was open, the restaurants appeared to have plenty of food, and for the rich at least the war continued to rumble somewhere in the distance, unseen and only faintly heard like a far-off summer thunderstorm which yet might blow itself away. Even the bombardments of the Bosphorus by the Russian Black Sea Fleet caused very little alarm, for they were hit-and-run affairs and soon ceased altogether. At the international club where the foreign diplomats gathered Talaat was often to be seen serenely playing poker far into the night, and Enver continued to be very confident. He liked to show his visitors his latest trophy from the Dardanelles: an unexploded shell from the *Queen Elizabeth* mounted on a Byzantine column in his palace garden.

Wangenheim was a masterful figure in Constantinople during these weeks. He would come into the Club in the evening, huge, garrulous and assured, and when the other diplomats gathered round him he would retail the latest news from Potsdam: another 100,000 Russian prisoners taken, a break in the French line on the Marne, another British cruiser sunk in the North Sea. It was known that he had a wireless station attached to his Embassy, and was in direct touch with Berlin, if not with the Kaiser himself.

The other members of the Club were in no position to deny or check any of Wangenheim's stories; they had no wireless stations of their own and the Turkish newspapers told them nothing that they could believe. Without Wangenheim's daily bulletins they were forced to fall back on the small change of local gossip. The surprising thing about this gossip is not that it should have been so cynical, so entertaining and so futile in itself, but that it was so very nearly accurate. Thus someone would report that his doorman— or his cook or his butler—had positive information that the Italian Ambassadress had booked sleepers on the Orient Express; and this surely was a firm sign that Italy was about to declare war at last. Or again it would be some devious story of how Enver had quarrelled again with Liman von Sanders and was about to replace him at the front. There was much talk of peace: the Germans, it was said, had made a secret approach to Russia offering her Constantinople if she would abandon the Allies. Bulgaria, with her army of 600,000 men and her traditional hatred of Turkey was, naturally, very much on their minds, and there was a flurry in the foreign colony when it was learned that the Bulgarian students at the Robert College outside Constantinople had been recalled home by their Government. This, they argued, could hardly have happened unless Bulgaria, too, was about to come into the war. But on whose side? And when? Or was it just another move in the game of bargaining with her neutrality?

On such matters Wangenheim was always ready to comment, to correct and to inform. He was like the boy who has the crib with all the answers in it, and he spoke with a large air of frankness that seemed to put an end to all doubts and speculations.

As the spring advanced he developed the habit of sitting at the bottom of his garden at Therapia, on the Bosphorus, within nodding distance of all who passed by. He liked to stop his acquaintances when they were out walking in the morning and read them tit-bits from his latest telegrams. Soon Morgenthau noticed that when things were going well for the Germans the Ambassador was always there in his accustomed seat by the garden wall, but when the news was bad he was nowhere to be found. He told Wangenheim one day that he reminded him of one of those patent weather gauges equipped with a little figure that emerged in the sunshine and disappeared in the rain. Wangenheim laughed very heartily.

And, in fact, up to the middle of May, there were no reasons for the Germans to be apprehensive about Turkey. Instead of weakening and dividing the Government as in England, the Gallipoli landing had knitted the Young Turks together and made them stronger than ever. Unlike the Allies, the Turks were not obliged to advance in the peninsula; so long as the line held it was unlikely that Bulgaria or Rumania or even Greece would come in against them. The very strain of the war itself was useful; it gave them the right to requisition whatever property they liked, to call up more and more men for active service, to get a tighter control on everybody's lives. There were now over half a million Turks in the Army, and this force was becoming steadily stronger as the threat from Russia died away; already in May divisions were being withdrawn from the Caucasus to strengthen the front at Gallipoli. The Germans, too, were increasing their garrison in Constantinople and in the peninsula. They had various means of smuggling men and munitions through Bulgaria and Rumania; it was even said that on one occasion a bogus circus was sent from Germany by rail, and the clowns on arrival turned out to be sergeants and their baggage filled with shells. Taube aircraft were flown across from Austria, refuelling at secret landing-places on the way. Soon there was another munitions factory working at Constantinople under German supervision, and guns from the old Turkish warships were dismantled and sent down to the front. Wangenheim in his role of local Kaiser in the German garrison took good care not to expose the *Goeben* to the British fleet in the Dardanelles; occasionally she went off hunting the Russian fleet in the Black Sea, but for the most part she rode at anchor in the Bosphorus.

Enver, the chief sponsor of the Germans, had great credit for all this. As Minister for War he somehow contrived to make it appear that he personally was responsible for the successful resistance in the peninsula just as he had been responsible for the defeat of the Fleet on March 18. There was not very much that Wangenheim,

Talaat or anybody else could do to correct this impression. The young man ballooned up before them. However incredible it might be, the truth was that this boy, who had been born of a fifteen-year-old peasant girl on the Black Sea only thirty-five years before, was now virtually dictator of Turkey. He assumed all the trappings of dictatorship with apparent ease—the sudden tantrums and rages, the personal bodyguard, the uniform (the sword, the epaulettes and the black sheepskin fez), and the ring of subservient generals. Even the Germans in Turkey were becoming a little afraid of him, especially when he went over their heads and corresponded directly with the Kaiser.

There was a macabre incident about this time which shows very clearly how far Enver had travelled and how high he still hoped to go. Early in May he sent for Morgenthau and with a great show of anger told him that the British were bombarding helpless villages and towns in the Gallipoli peninsula. Mosques and hospitals had been burned down, he said, and a number of women and children had been killed. He proposed now to take reprisals; the 3,000 British and French citizens who were still living in Turkey were to be arrested and sent to concentration camps in the peninsula. Enver desired the Ambassador to inform the British and French governments through the State Department in Washington that henceforth they would be killing their own people at Gallipoli as well as Turks.

It was useless for Morgenthau to protest that towns like Gallipoli, Chanak and Maidos were military headquarters and that the Allies had a perfect right to bombard them; the best he could do was to get the women and children excluded from the order. A few days later, when the arrests began, an hysterical horde of French and British civilians descended on the American Embassy. Most of these people were Levantines who had been born in Turkey of British or French parentage and who had never seen either England or France. They gathered in hundreds round the Ambassador whenever he appeared, gesticulating and crying, clutching at his arms, imploring him to save them. After several days of this Morgenthau telephoned to Enver and demanded another interview. Enver replied smoothly that he was engaged in a council of Ministers but would be delighted to see the Ambassador on the afternoon of the following day. The hostages were due to be sent off to the peninsula in the morning, and it was only when Morgenthau threatened to force his way into the council room that Enver agreed to receive him at the Sublime Porte at once.

For one reason or another—perhaps because the Bulgarian Ambassador had just been in to protest against the arrests—Enver was excessively polite when Morgenthau arrived. He agreed after a while that perhaps he had made a mistake in this matter but it was too late to do anything about it: he never revoked orders. If he did he would lose his influence with the Army. He added, 'If you can show me some way in which this order can be carried out, and your protégés still saved, I shall be glad to listen.'

'All right,' Morgenthau said, 'I think I can. I should think you could still carry out your orders without sending *all* the French and English residents down. If you would send only a few you would still win your point. You could still maintain discipline in the Army and these few would be as strong a deterrent to the Allied Fleet as sending all.'

It seemed to Morgenthau that Enver seized on this suggestion almost eagerly. 'How many will you let me send?' he asked.

'I would suggest that you take twenty English and twenty French—forty in all.'

'Let me have fifty.'

'All right, we won't haggle over ten,' Morgenthau answered, and the bargain having been made Enver conceded that only the youngest men should go. Bedri, the Chief of Police, was now sent for, and these arrangements did not suit him at all. 'No, no, this will never do,' he said. 'I don't want the youngest; I must have the notables.'

The point was still unsettled when Bedri and Morgenthau drove back to the American Embassy where the selection was to be made. It was with some difficulty that they made their way through the frantic crowd to Morgenthau's office.

'Can't I have a few notables?' Bedri repeated.

There was an Anglican clergyman named Dr. Wigram, who, Morgenthau knew, was determined to be one of the hostages. 'I will give you just one,' he said.

Bedri had his eye on a Dr. Frew and several well-known men in the French colony, and he insisted, 'Can't I have three?'

'Dr. Wigram is the only notable you can have.'

In the end Bedri with a fairly good grace settled for the

183

clergyman and forty-nine young men, but he gave himself the pleasure of telling them that the British were in the habit of regularly bombing the town of Gallipoli to which they were to be sent. On the following morning, amid frenzied scenes, and accompanied by Mr. Hoffman Philip, the American counsellor, and a quantity of American food, the party set off.

Morgenthau at once began to agitate for their return, and his task was not made easier by the arrival of a message from Sir Edward Grey, the British Foreign Secretary, stating that Enver and his fellow Ministers would be held personally responsible for any injury to the hostages.

'I presented this message to Enver on May 9th,' Morgenthau writes. 'I had seen Enver in many moods, but the unbridled rage which Sir Edward's admonition now caused was something entirely new. As I read the telegram his face became livid, and he absolutely lost control of himself. The European polish which Enver had sedulously acquired dropped like a mask. I now saw him for what he really was —a savage, bloodthirsty Turk. "They will not come back," he shouted. 'I shall let them stay there until they rot. I would like to see those English touch me." And he added, "Don't ever threaten me." In the end, however, he calmed down and agreed that the hostages could come back to Constantinople.'

For a day or two this incident was the talk of Constantinople, but it was soon swallowed up in the general tide of half-truths and gossip, in the long, weary ennui of waiting for something definite to happen. Constantinople had a strange drifting existence at this time; it was in the war but not of it. It heard nothing and saw nothing and yet was ready to fear everything. The third week of May went by and still very few people had any real inkling of what was happening at the Dardanelles beyond the barren fact that the Allies were neither advancing nor being driven away. Nothing was published in the newspapers about the disastrous attack on the Anzac bridgehead on May 19, and the Ministry of War was careful to see that the increasing numbers of wounded returning from the front were taken through the city in the middle of the night when the streets were deserted. One quiet, uneasy day followed another, and it was not until May 25 that in the most unexpected and alarming way Constantinople was made to realize at last that the war was very near and very threatening. A British submarine surfaced in the Golden Horn.

The submarines in the second world war did far more damage than in the first, but they never re-created quite the same sort of helplessness, the sense of unfair lurking doom. In 1915 there were no depth charges and no asdic, and unless the submarine surfaced and exposed itself to ramming or to gunfire there was no sure means of detecting or destroying it. The unwieldy nets that were hung around the battleships were only a gesture of defence, and after the sinking of the *Lusitania* no merchantman ever felt safe, even in convoy, even at night.

Yet in 1915 the submarine service had still to prove itself. Everything about it was experimental, the size and armament of the vessel, its shape and speed, the way it should be used, and, perhaps most important of all, the endurance of the crews. How much could the men stand of this unnatural and claustrophobic life beneath the sea? And beyond this there was thought to be something ethically monstrous about the whole conception of submarines, a kind of barbarism which would end in the destruction of them all. The 'Submariners', in fact, were in much the same position as the young men in the Royal Air Force and the Luftwaffe in 1940; they were apart from the rest of the serving forces, a minority group with a strange, esoteric excitement of its own, and they were about to prove that they were capable of adventures which no one had ever dreamed of before. Far from cracking under the strain, they relished it; it was a new brand of courage, a controlled recklessness, a kind of joy in the power of the inhuman machine. It was not really a question of how much these men could stand, but of how far you could meet their demand for more speed, longer hours in action and more deadly gadgets.

But all this lay in the future in the early months of the first world war, and the submarine itself was still undergoing basic changes in design. The periscope, for example, was originally fixed in one set position, and its mirrors produced an inverted image, so the commander was obliged to bring the whole vessel close to the surface before he attacked, and his outlook was upon a strange world in which ships were for ever floating upside down. Even when the periscope became movable it was an unhandy device: as it rose upward the commander rose with it, beginning from a squatting position and ending on the tips of his toes. By 1915, however, most of these primitive inconveniences had been overcome, and the British E class (whose dispatch to the Dardanelles had so angered Lord Fisher) was a formidable instrument. It was a vessel of 725 tons, equipped with four torpedo tubes and oil engines which achieved a surface speed of about fifteen miles an hour. Submerged and running on its electric batteries it was capable of proceeding at ten knots for an hour, or even for periods of twenty hours at more economical speeds. In deep waters it descended by flooding its tanks until it had about a ton of buoyancy in hand, and the vessel, with its horizontal rudders depressed, was then driven down by its motors. Directly it stopped moving it rose to the surface again.

In shallow waters—and the E Class could descend to over 200 feet—the commanders had no fear of flooding their tanks entirely and of lying on the bottom so long as the air in the boat remained reasonably fresh—a period of some twenty hours. As they were not then moving there was still enough power in their accumulators to drive them to the surface again. The submarine's time of greatest danger was, of course, during the three or four hours when it was obliged to cruise about on the surface to replenish its batteries.

At Gallipoli these submarines were faced with an objective which was entirely new and fantastically dangerous. If they could once get through to the Sea of Marmara they knew that they could do pretty much what they liked with the Turkish shipping, more particularly with the vessels that were bringing down reinforcements and supplies to Liman's army on the peninsula. But how to get there, how to penetrate the Dardanelles?

The straits were swept all night by searchlights, and as soon as a submarine surfaced, as it was practically bound to do in the course of the forty-mile journey, it was not only fired on but ran the risk of being caught by the various currents that set towards the shore. Ten lines of mines off Kephez Point had to be negotiated, and beyond these there were the Narrows, under a mile wide, with guns on either side and patrol boats on the watch. There was another hazard: a stratum of fresh water about ten fathoms deep poured down the Dardanelles from the Sea of Marmara, and it was of much lighter density than the salt water below.

This made a kind of barrier in the sea, and as they passed through it the submarines were thrown violently out of control. It was not unlike the experiences of the first supersonic aircraft when they met the sound barrier in the sky; no one could make out why this strange, deadly disturbance should occur, and the commanders were forced to rise to the surface where they at once came under the fire from the enemy batteries on the shore.

Up to the time of the landing every attempt to force the Narrows had failed, and even the Australian E2 was to last only a few days before she was caught on the surface and sunk. A French submarine, the *Joule,* was destroyed before she even reached Chanak. Yet the exploit still seemed possible, and the young commanders of the E Class submarines who came out from England during April were eager to try again. Many of them had fought under Roger Keyes's command in the North Sea during the early months of the war, and their morale was very high. They believed they had only to try new tactics and they would get through.

For the German U-boats the problem at Gallipoli was quite different. Their target—and it was a superb target, almost a sitting duck—was the British battle fleet cruising along the shore of the peninsula in the open Ægean, and they were withheld from it not by the Narrows but by the wide expanse of the Atlantic and the Mediterranean. In April there was no German U-boat at Constantinople and none in the Mediterranean. The only way for the Germans to reach the scene of action was to sail round northern Europe and enter the Mediterranean through the Straits of Gibraltar; and this meant running the engines until almost the last ounce of fuel was gone. There was, it was true, a scheme for sending small U-boats in section by rail to Pola on the Adriatic coast, but nothing had come of this as yet.

And so at the opening of the campaign both sides were baulked in their undersea offensive. Each could see the prize plainly before it: for the British it was the helpless Turkish shipping in the Marmara, for the Germans the unprotected Allied battleships in the Ægean; and neither so far had been able to strike.

But now, at the end of April, there began a series of events which were to alter the whole character of the campaign. On April 25, the very day of the landing, Lieut.-Commander Otto Hersing, in the German U-boat 21, set out from Ems on the long journey around the north of Scotland for the Mediterranean. Two days later at Gallipoli, Lieut.-Commander Boyle, in the British E 14, slipped quietly into the Dardanelles and headed for the Narrows. From this moment both the Allied Fleet and the Turks on Gallipoli were in extreme danger.

Boyle had the idea of going through the Dardanelles on the surface under the cover of darkness, and he set off at two in the morning. He had not gone very far, however, before the Turkish searchlights and guns drove him down to a depth of ninety feet, and he continued there until he judged that he had passed under the Kephez minefield. Then he came up to twenty-two feet, intending to make the actual passage of the Narrows with his periscope raised. The disadvantage of this manœuvre was that the periscope made a distinct wash on the sea, and there was a desperate half-hour when the enemy guns around Chanak got his range. At one stage the crew of a Turkish patrol boat were grabbing at the periscope whenever Boyle brought it to the surface for a few seconds to see where he was going. Yet he got away, and soon after dawn came up unscathed in the Sea of Marmara. The passage had taken six hours.

For the next three weeks the E 14 cruised about at will. Her greatest success was the sinking of an old White Star liner that was bringing down from Constantinople 6,000 troops who were to join in the battle on the Cape Helles front. There were no survivors. It was a bigger victory than anything that had yet occurred on land, and there was immense elation in the Allied Fleet when Boyle came safely out again into the Ægean on May 18. Now at last they had found a way through. Admiral Guépratte had in the meantime lost a French submarine in the mysterious barrier in the straits, but that did not prevent him from congratulating the British; he sailed his flagship round the E 14 with his band playing Tipperary and the British national anthem.

Another submarine, the E 11, was waiting to take the E 14's place in the Marmara, and her young captain, Lieut.-Commander Nasmith, dined aboard the flagship on the night of May 18 with de Robeck, Keyes and Boyle. It was an animated party. Boyle had been recommended for an immediate award of the Victoria Cross. Keyes, who was still chafing at the withdrawal of the *Queen Elizabeth* and at the latest refusal of the Admiralty to allow the Fleet to resume its attack on the Narrows, thought he had begun to see a ray of light at last. Having heard Boyle's story, Nasmith set off that same night, and sixteen hours after leaving the Admiral's dining-table he was resting on the bottom of the Sea of Marmara. Unknown to anyone he had formed a plan which was more daring than anything which had been attempted before: a direct attack on Constantinople itself.

His first act on coming to the surface near the town of Gallipoli was to seize a Turkish sailing vessel and lash her to the E 11's side, so that she would act both as a disguise and a decoy. When after several days no target appeared he cast off this Trojan sea-horse and steamed directly up the Marmara.

On May 23 he sank a Turkish gunboat and several other smaller craft, and then on the following day he fell in with the *Nagara,* a transport that was making its way down to the Dardanelles. There was an American journalist on board the *Nagara,* Raymond Gram Swing of the *Chicago Daily News,* and he says he was on deck that morning chatting to a Bavarian doctor. Boyle's exploits of the previous weeks had become known in Constantinople, and Swing had just remarked to the doctor, 'It's a fine morning for submarines,' when he paused, gazed out to sea in astonishment, and added, 'And there's one.' E 11 broke the calm surface very gently about a hundred yards away, and four men appeared on the conning tower. One of them in a white sweater (it was Nasmith) used his cupped hands as a megaphone: 'Who are you?'

'I'm Swing of the *Chicago Daily News.*'

'Glad to meet you, Mr. Swing, but what I mean is what ship is that?'

'The Turkish transport *Nagara.*'

By now the ship's crew were in a state of extreme alarm, some coursing about the deck, others, with their fezzes still on their heads, jumping into the sea.

'Are those marines?' Nasmith asked.

'No, they're just sailors.'

'Well, I'm going to sink you.'

Swing asked, 'Can we get off?'

'Yes, and be damned quick about it.'

The confusion in the *Nagara* had now reached the point where everyone had begun to scramble over the sides, and the lifeboats were lowered so clumsily that they half filled with water. The Turks were frenziedly bailing with their fezzes. As Swing appeared to be the only calm man on board, Nasmith directed him in launching the last boat and in picking up the sailors and passengers who had jumped or fallen into the sea. Nasmith then closed with the ship, and an immense orange flame went up as he sank her: she was filled with ammunition.

Soon after this E 11 was driven away from the coast by a detachment of Turkish cavalry, but she managed to chase and sink another transport, and a third ship beached herself on the shore. By now the survivors of the wrecks had raised the alarm in Constantinople, and from early morning on May 25 the Turkish artillery on both sides of the Bosphorus were standing to their guns. In order to calm the population in the event of an action taking place, an announcement was made that there might be firing practice during the course of the day.

The submarine surfaced at 12.40 p.m., and Nasmith saw before him a large freighter, the *Stamboul,* berthed alongside the arsenal. His first torpedo ran in a circle and on its return narrowly missed the E 11 herself. His second, however, struck home, and he dived, heading through the city into the Bosphorus, while a barrage of artillery crashed over his head.

The panic that now broke out in Constantinople gives an indication of what might have happened had the Allied Fleet appeared there in March. While the *Goeben* hastily shifted her anchorage into the shelter of her attendant ships, a mob fled through the streets and everywhere the shops ran up their shutters. On the docks all activity ceased, and a contingent of soldiers which was embarking for Gallipoli was precipitately ordered back to the shore again. Now, in one moment, the powder factory on the wharves and the crowded wooden houses on the slopes above seemed utterly exposed, and it was apparent to everyone that there was very little that the fire brigade could do if this was to be the prelude to a serious attack.

Meanwhile, Nasmith and his men were struggling for their lives. The current in the Bosphorus was even stronger than in the Dardanelles, and for some twenty minutes the submarine was out of control, bumping from shoal to shoal along the bottom as far as Leander's Tower. She was righted eventually, and with great skill Nasmith turned back through Constantinople. 'The next day,' he reported later, 'was spent resting in the centre of the Sea of Marmara.'

Then on May 27 he resumed his attack, sinking ship after ship in the approaches to the Golden Horn. A terror spread through the Sea of Marmara, for it was thought that at least half a dozen submarines were operating. No vessel of any size was allowed to leave port without an escort of destroyers and gunboats, and these repeatedly tried to ram the E 11 whenever she rose to the surface to attack. Nasmith paused in his operations only when the air in the submarine became so foul that he was obliged to surface in order to allow the crew to come on deck and bathe.

Soon the shortage of torpedoes became the E 11's chief concern, and those that remained were set to run on the surface so that whenever they missed their targets Nasmith could dive into the sea and recover them. By June 5 a serious defect had developed in the port main motor, the starboard intermediate shaft had cracked, only two torpedoes were left, and Nasmith judged it time to go home. He entered the Dardanelles and steamed down as far as Chanak hunting for the Turkish battleship *Barbarossa Harradin*, upon which he had made an unsuccessful attack a few days before. He saw nothing, however, except a large transport anchored above Nagara. The E 11 was now in the most dangerous part of the Narrows, and in her crippled state was quite likely to be washed ashore. But it was unbearable to Nasmith that he should leave with two torpedoes still intact; he turned back up the Dardanelles, sank the transport, and then returned for the crucial dive through the Narrows. Off Chanak the trim of the boat became violently affected by the change in the density of the water, and Nasmith dived to seventy feet. About an hour later he heard a scraping noise which seemed to indicate that the keel was hitting the bottom, and since he knew this to be impossible he rose up to twenty feet below the surface to investigate. He saw then that about twenty feet ahead of the periscope a large mine had been torn from its moorings by the port hydroplane and was being towed along. Saying nothing to his crew, Nasmith continued for another hour until he was outside the entrance to the straits. He then went full speed astern with the bows of the submarine submerged and the rush of water from the screws carried the mine away.

There was another dinner aboard the flagship that night,

191

and at the end of it Boyle in E 14 set off again for the Marmara, while Lieut.-Commander Nasmith, V.C., sailed the E 11 to Malta for repairs.

An extreme crisis had overtaken the Allied Fleet while Nasmith had been away, and it was every bit as serious as the alarm which he had created in Constantinople. Towards the middle of May news had come through that a U-boat (it was Hersing in the U 21) had been sighted passing through the Straits of Gibraltar. It had been fired at but had got away, and was then presumably headed for Gallipoli.

During the next week, when Nasmith in the E 11 had vanished into the silence of the Sea of Marmara, there had been a growing depression in the Fleet. The *Queen Elizabeth* had been something of a symbol for the whole expedition, and it had seemed to the soldiers on shore as well as the sailors at sea that a good few of their hopes had gone with her when she sailed away. De Robeck had transferred his flag to the *Lord Nelson*, and had remained off the peninsula with the other battleships, but it was not the same thing. The Fleet had an apprehensive air. Each day the tension increased, and the men on watch kept seeing periscopes on every side. A gambolling porpoise was enough to raise the alarm, and so were the dead and bloated mules that floated out to sea from the battlefield on shore, their legs projecting to the sky.

In the very early dawn of May 24 a genuine emergency occurred: the old battleship *Albion* ran her bows on to a sandbank off Gaba Tepe and the Turks fired more than a hundred shells into her while the British tried to tow her off. Eventually the ship lightened herself by firing off all her heavy guns together, and in the recoil she got away. This incident had nothing to do with submarines, and there were under a dozen casualties, yet it was one more addition to the general feeling of insecurity.

Then on the following morning—at the very moment that Nasmith was gliding into the wharves at Constantinople —the *Vengeance* reported that a torpedo had passed across her bows while she was steaming between Anzac and Helles. It was true enough. Hersing had managed to get into the Austrian port of Cattaro before his oil ran out, and when he had refuelled he came straight through to Gallipoli.

A commotion spread through the Allied ships. De Robeck in haste transferred his flag again from the *Lord Nelson* to the *Triad,* a large yacht which had once been a pleasure-going ship along the Bosphorus, and all the more valuable battleships and transports were ordered to retire at once to Mudros. There was a feeling of desolation in the Army as the ships vanished over the horizon leaving behind them an unfamiliar, almost empty sea. Those few of the larger vessels that remained could not disguise the atmosphere of tension in which they waited, hour by hour, for the hidden attack which now seemed bound to come.

Commander Hersing struck at mid-day. He saw the old battleship *Triumph* near Gaba Tepe with a ring of destroyers circling round her, waited for his chance, and fired. The torpedo passed easily through the *Triumph's* nets and the ship at once took a heavy list. For eight minutes, while the destroyers came rushing in to the rescue, she remained at an angle of forty-five degrees, spilling her crew into the sea. Then she capsized and floated for a time with her green bottom upwards in the sunlight. The crews on the neighbouring ships stood to attention as she made her last plunge down to the bottom through clouds of smoke and steam. All this took place in full view of the two opposing armies on the shore, and while the Anzac soldiers watched in dismay a cheer came up from the Turkish trenches. This was the finest sight the enemy had seen since the campaign began, but they had no wish to be vindictive; after a few opening shots no further attempt was made to fire on the wreck or her survivors.

The *Triumph* was a twelve-years-old ship of 11,800 tons, and only seventy-one men had gone down with her, but this was the end of the security of all battleships at Gallipoli. De Robeck gave orders for a further retirement, and presently the *Majestic,* the oldest battleship of them all, was left alone with a screen of destroyers off Cape Helles. Admiral Nicholson, the commander of the flotilla there, came aboard her from the *Swiftsure* during the course of the afternoon. So eager were Nicholson and his staff to let the *Swiftsure* get away that they did not wait to pack their belongings; baggage, bedding, tinned preserves and an assortment of wines were dumped in a trawler and ferried across in a matter of minutes.

Few believed that the *Majestic* would survive, and the soldiers in their dugouts kept watching her all afternoon as she cruised along the shore. By nightfall, however, nothing had happened, and the old battleship went back to Imbros in the darkness. Some fishing nets had been erected across the mouth of the open harbour there, and these she carried away on her first attempt to enter; but otherwise no harm came to her through the night. Keyes went out in the destroyer *Grampus* hoping to ram the enemy submarine if she surfaced, but he saw nothing.

In the morning half a gale was blowing, and although the submarine scare was still at its height de Robeck felt that the Navy could not leave the Army entirely in the lurch. The *Majestic* was ordered back to Helles again, and she remained off-shore all through that day and the following night. A half-cynical fatalism prevailed on board; in the officers' wardroom the last of the champagne and the port was drunk on the grounds that it would have been a pity to see it go to the bottom.

At 6.40 the following morning the cry 'Torpedo coming' went up, and the sailors ran for the boats. The strike was made so low down on the port side there was scarcely a tremor on deck, but immediately afterwards a loud explosion shook the ship and she heeled over to port. The crew were given just fifteen minutes to get off before she sank bottom upward, her bows resting on a sandbank by the shore and exposing a fraction of her keel above the surface. A moment before the end a sailor ran the full length of the keel with the sea closing in around him. He reached the exposed bows just in time, and sat astride there until presently a boat came by and took him off. Forty-eight of his shipmates were lost. For the rest of the campaign the upturned hulk of the battleship remained there, like some stranded whale washed up on the shore.

For a few minutes it looked as though they were going to catch the U 21. Air Commodore Samson was circling overhead, and he dropped his bombs on the U-boat through the clear water. But Hersing dived under the French battleship *Henri IV*, and when Samson picked him up again, steaming up the Dardanelles in the sunshine, all his bombs were gone. But he permitted himself a gesture: he swooped and emptied his rifle on to her hull. The U 21 was last seen moving into the Narrows, and at some point in the Sea of Marmara must have passed Nasmith returning from Constantinople.

Thus on this one day, May 25, almost in one hour, two submarines, the German U 21 and the British E 11, brought an entirely new element into the campaign, and it was almost as important as the twenty Turkish mines which had been sown so fortuitously in Eren Keui Bay when the Allied Fleet attacked in March.

Nasmith's raid was, perhaps, the more telling of the two, for it caused the Turks to issue an immediate order that for the time being no further reinforcements were to be sent to the peninsula by sea. Instead of a short overnight voyage the soldiers were now faced with a roundabout train journey of 150 miles to Uzun Keupri on the Adrianople line. Thence a single road led down into the peninsula, another hundred miles away—a march of at least five days for the men, and of considerably more for the bullock carts and the camels that were now obliged to bring in their equipment. Other supplies had to be sent down the Sea of Marmara by small boats which hugged the coast and travelled only by night. All this meant a drastic slowing down of Liman's line of supply. 'Had the British managed to increase their undersea offensive,' he says in the study of the campaign which he wrote after the war, 'the Fifth Army would have starved.' And the German naval historian adds: 'The activity of the hostile submarines was a constant and heavy anxiety, and if communication by sea had been completely severed the Army would have been faced with catastrophe.' At one point the Turks on the peninsula were down to 160 rounds of ammunition per man.

Liman is a little tart about the activities—or rather the lack of activity—of the German Navy. The story was spread in Germany, he says, that the *Goeben* and the German submarines carried the main burden of the defence at Gallipoli; but the *Goeben* never took part at all, and the U 21, having got safely through to Constantinople and been much fêted there, emerged only once again. She came out of the straits on July 4 and sank the French transport *Carthage*. Finding that his return route was blocked, Hersing turned west and steamed for the Adriatic, to be seen no more. Yet he had achieved his purpose. The mere threat of his presence off Gallipoli had scattered the Allied battle fleet, and his two sinkings were enough to keep it in harbour in the islands ever afterwards.

For the British submarines, however, the situation was rather more difficult; in order to make good the work that had already been done by Boyle and Nasmith they had to keep up the pressure in the Sea of Marmara and if possible increase it; and indeed, in all the records of the Royal Navy there is hardly anything that quite compares with the undersea offensive that now began. In a world that has since grown used to the unearthly courage of young men with fantastic machines it is still difficult to credit some of the things that happened. Six-pounder guns were fitted to the decks of the submarines to help them eke out their supply of torpedoes, and two new arrivals, the E 12 and the E 7, ran up to Constantinople, where they bombarded the powder mills, put a torpedo into the arsenal, cut the railway line and chased the trains along the shore. Soon the commanders learned to handle the changing density of the water, and they even turned it to advantage; by lying on top of the layer of heavier specific gravity when they wished to hide or rest they saved themselves the danger and difficulty of diving great depths to the ocean floor.

It was on Boyle's third trip into the Marmara, on July 21, that a new hazard was discovered. As he passed through the Narrows he saw an obstruction under the water, and he reported this to Lieut.-Commander Cochrane in the E 7, when he met her in the Marmara next day. On July 24 Cochrane came out and he confirmed Boyle's report: the Germans were building a net. He himself had been entangled in it for half an hour, ninety feet down.

This was a much more formidable obstacle than anything the submarines had encountered before. By the end of July it was completed—a vast steel mesh of two-and-a-half-inch wire stretching entirely across the straits, and reaching 220 feet down to the floor of the channel. A line of buoys painted alternately red and black supported it on the surface, and one end was secured on the peninsula about a mile north of Maidos, the other on a steamer anchored near Abydos on the Asiatic side. Turkish motor-boats loaded with bombs patrolled the surface like spiders waiting at the edge of a web. Specially sited guns were set up on either bank.

There was a gate in the middle of the net, and unless the submarines were lucky enough to strike it their only way of getting through the wire was to ram it at full speed underwater and hope for the best. Boyle described this experience: 'I missed the gate and hit the net. I was brought up from eighty feet to forty-five feet in three seconds, but luckily only thrown fifteen degrees off my course. There was a tremendous noise, scraping, banging, tearing and rumbling, and it sounded as if there were two distinct obstructions, as the noise nearly ceased and then came on again, and we were appreciably checked twice. It took about twenty seconds to get through.'

But Cochrane on his next trip did not get through. Hopelessly entangled, he fought the net for twelve hours on the bottom of the straits while bombs exploded about him, and it was only when the hull was leaking and the lights had failed that he burned his papers and rose to the surface to surrender.

Nasmith, Boyle and the others were not deterred; they continued to pass through, and by the end of the year the net was so damaged by their repeated rammings it had almost vanished altogether. Up to the last, however, the passage through the Narrows remained an ordeal of the most frightening kind, and perhaps from that very fact it acted as a psychological stimulus on the crews. One seems to have read the story in some boyhood book of sea adventure: the pirates' cave with its treasure lies hidden in the cliffs, but one has to make a dangerous dive beneath the sea to reach it. And some get through and some get trapped halfway.

There is an almost dolphin-like air, a precise abandon, in the way the E-boats frisked about at times. On seeing a convoy, the commanders would deliberately surface and pretend to be in difficulties so as to entice the protective gunboats away. Then, diving deep, they would turn back and demolish the boats of the convoy one by one. They shot up the caravans of camels and bullock carts making their way down the Bulair isthmus with loads of barbed wire and ammunition. When they were short of fresh food they surfaced beside the Turkish trading caiques and provided themselves with fruit and vegetables. Wherever they could they saved their torpedoes and their ammunition by boarding enemy ships and simply opening the sea-cocks or placing a charge on the keel. Sometimes prisoners were carried around for days on end before they could be put ashore, and these were often very strange people—Arabs in their desert robes, sponge-divers and Turkish Imans, and once a German banker, wearing only a short pink vest, who complained that 5,000 marks in gold had just been sent to the bottom.

When more than one submarine was operating the commanders would make a rendezvous, and with their vessels tied up together far out in the Sea of Marmara they would exchange information for an hour or two, while their crews bathed in the sunshine; and then perhaps they would go off on a hunt together. Once there was a disaster. The French *Turquoise* ran aground and was captured. Enemy intelligence officers found in the captain's notebook a reference to a meeting which he was to have at sea in a few days' time with the British E 20. It was a German U-boat that kept the rendezvous, and she torpedoed E 20 directly she came to the surface. Only the British commander and eight of the crew who were on deck survived.

In August Nasmith sank the battleship *Barbarossa Harradin*. Expecting that she would come south to take part in a new battle on the peninsula, he lay in wait for her at the top of the Narrows—having, on the way through, scraped heavily against a mine. The battleship appeared in the early dawn escorted by two destroyers, and she was taken utterly by surprise. She capsized and sank within a quarter of an hour.

Nasmith then went on to Constantinople and arrived just at the moment when a collier from the Black Sea had berthed herself beside the Haidar Pasha railway station. Coal at this time had become more precious than gold at Constantinople, since it was so scarce and since everything depended upon it—the railways and the ships, the factories, the city's supply of light and water. A committee of officials was standing on the wharf discussing how the coal should be apportioned when E 11's torpedo struck and the ship blew up before their eyes.

Next the submarine turned into the Gulf of Ismid, where the Constantinople-Baghdad railway ran over a viaduct close to the sea, and there d'Oyly-Hughes, the first officer, swam ashore and blew up the line. Like Freyberg at the beginning of the campaign, he was half dead when the E 11 picked him up again.

There were in all 13 submarines engaged in the Sea of Marmara, and although 8 were destroyed the passage was made 27 times. The Turkish losses were 1 battleship (apart from the *Messudieh* sunk in the previous year), 1 destroyer, 5 gunboats, 11 transports, 44 steamers and 148 sailing boats. Nasmith's bag alone was 101 vessels, and he was in the Marmara for three months, including a stay of 47 days—a record that was never surpassed in the first world war. By the end of the year all movement of enemy ships by daylight had practically ceased, and with rare exceptions only the most urgent supplies were sent by sea to the peninsula.

It is doubtful if the success of the submarines was ever fully understood by the British while the campaign was going on. At Hamilton's and de Robeck's headquarters the sinkings seem to have been regarded more in the nature of a delightful surprise, a bonus on the side, than as the basis for a main offensive. It never seems to have occurred to them that they might have followed up d'Oyly-Hughes' adventure, that commandos might have been landed north of Bulair to have cut the Turkish land route to the peninsula.

Nor were the Germans any more imaginative. Five small U-boats were eventually assembled at Pola, and managed to get through to Constantinople, but apart from one or two lucky shots at transports coming out of Alexandria they made no further attempt on the Fleet at Gallipoli. By September forty-three German U-boats had been sent to the Mediterranean, but the bulk of the pack remained in the western half of the sea, and they failed to sink any of the ships bringing reinforcements out from England.

And so there was, even as early as May, some reasonable chance of the expedition gathering impetus again. If the Allies were being starved of supplies, so too were the Turks; the lost British battleships were being replaced by monitors, and with the arrival of the Lowland division Hamilton's forces outnumbered the enemy in the peninsula.

Hamilton in any case was an optimistic man. The sinking of the battleships had been a terrible blow, and on board the *Arcadian* the General himself was living in the most insecure conditions, so insecure indeed that two transports were lashed to the ship's side to act as torpedo-buffers. Dismayed but still buoyant, he wrote in his diary: 'We are left all alone in our glory with our two captive merchantmen. The attitude is heroic but not, I think, so dangerous as it is uncomfortable. The big ocean liners lashed to port and starboard cut us off from light as well as air, and one of them is loaded with Cheddar. When Mr. Jorrocks awoke James Pigg and asked him to open the window to see what sort of a hunting morning it was, it will be remembered that the huntsman opened the cupboard by mistake and made the reply, "Hellish dark and smells of cheese." Well, that immortal remark hits us off to a T. Never mind. Light will be vouchsafed. Amen.'

Useless now to reflect that the *Triumph* and the *Majestic* —and the *Goliath* too—might have gone to a better end by making a new attempt on the Narrows; or to think of how the great armada of battleships had been scattered and forced to retire into the harbour at Mudros whence it had so confidently set out a month before. The only thing to do now was to wait for news from London, to hope for reinforcements and to hold on.

ELEVEN

~~~~~~

DURING the months of June and July neither side made any serious attempt to attack at Anzac, and while an uneasy stalemate continued there five pitched battles were fought at Cape Helles. They were all frontal attacks, all of short duration, a day or two or even less, and none of them succeeded in altering the front line by more than half a mile.[1]

This fighting at Cape Helles was the heaviest of the campaign, and it followed the strict pattern of trench warfare: the preliminary bombardment, the charge of the infantry (sometimes as many as five men to four yards of front), the counter-attack, and then the last confused spasmodic struggles to consolidate the line. Nowhere at any time were any important objectives gained; at the end of it all the Turks were no nearer to driving the Allies into the sea and the Allies were hardly any closer to Achi Baba. Even in the killing of men neither side could claim the advantage, since it is estimated that for the period from the

[1] These engagements may be summarized:

June 4: Allied attack in the centre. Gain 250-500 yards on a one-mile front. Allies' casualties 6,500, Turkish 9,000.

June 21 and following days: French attack on the right. Gain of about 200 yards. French casualties 2,500, Turkish 6,000.

June 28: British attack on the left. Gain of half a mile. British casualties 3,800, Turkish unknown.

July 5: Turkish attack along the whole line. Nothing gained. Casualties, Turks 16,000, Allies negligible.

July 12/13: Allied attack on a one-mile front. Gain of 400 yards. Casualties, Allies 4,000, Turks 10,000.

201

first landings in April to the end of July the total casualties were about the same for each: some 57,000 men.

These battles were so repetitive, so ant-like and inconclusive, that it is almost impossible to discover any meaning in them unless one remembers the tremendous hopes with which each action was begun. The generals really did think that they could get through, and so for a while did the soldiers too. Hunter-Weston, the British Corps Commander, was an extremely confident man. 'Casualties,' he said one day, 'what do I care for casualties?' The remark might not have been particularly distressing to his soldiers; they too were quite prepared for casualties provided they defeated the Turks, and in any case it was nothing remarkable that the General still believed that victories could be achieved by this kind of fighting; with very few exceptions all the other generals, German, Turkish, French and British, in France as well as Gallipoli, believed the same thing. The artillery bombardment followed by the charge of the infantry was believed to be the surgical act that would bring success in the quickest way, and nobody had yet suggested any alternative to it except, of course, poison gas. The real answer to the problem was simple enough: they needed an armoured mobile gun that would break through the enemy machine-gun fire; in other words a tank. But in 1915 the tank was a year or more and several million lives away, and it seemed to both Turkish and Allied staffs alike that they had only to intensify what they were already doing—to employ more men and more guns on narrower fronts—and the enemy would crack.

Since the rules of the game, the actual methods of the fighting, were not in question, the generals had to find other reasons to explain their failure, and on the side of the Allies it usually boiled down to a matter of ammunition. If only they had had more shells to fire all would have been well. Just a few more rounds, another few guns, and the miracle would have happened. It had already been demonstrated at Gallipoli—and it was to be demonstrated over and over again on a much larger scale in France—that artillery bombardment was not the real way out of this suicidal impasse, but the British were strictly rationed in shells at Gallipoli, and this very shortage seemed to indicate that this was where their fatal weakness lay. Through June and July, there were times when Hamilton could think of nothing else, and he sent off message after message to Kitchener pointing out how badly served he was in the matter of ammunition compared with the armies in France.

'A purely passive defence is not possible for us,' he wrote: 'it implies losing ground by degrees—and we have not a yard to lose. . . . But, to expect us to attack without giving us our fair share—on Western standards—of high explosive and howitzers shows lack of military imagination.' He went on: 'If only K. would come and see for himself! Failing that—if only it were possible for me to run home and put my own case.' But he did not go. Sometimes his staff found him looking aged and tired.

Through these months a gradual change overtook the commanders at Cape Helles in the planning of their battles. They did not lose hope, they simply lowered their sights. In the beginning the Allies had envisaged an advance upon Constantinople itself and cavalry was held in reserve for that purpose. By June they were concentrating upon Achi Baba, and the more the hill remained unconquered the more important it seemed: the more it appeared to swell up physically before them on the horizon. By July they were thinking in still more restricted terms: of advances of 700 or 800 yards, of the capture of two or three lines of the enemy trenches. In the same way the Turks gradually began to give up their notions of 'pushing the enemy into the sea'. After July they tried no more headlong assaults; they were content to contain the Allies and harass them in their narrow foothold on the sea.

In the many books that were written about the campaign soon after the first world war, there is a constantly repeated belief that posterity would never forget what happened there. Such and such a regiment's bayonet charge will 'go down in history'; the deed is 'immortal' or 'imperishable', is enshrined forever in the records of the past. But who in this generation has heard of Lancashire Landing or Gully Ravine or the Third Battle of Krithia? Even as names they have almost vanished out of memory, and whether this hill was taken or that trench was lost seems hardly to matter any more. All becomes lost in a confused impression of waste and fruitless heroism, of out-of-dateness and little-ness in another age. And yet if one forgets the actual battles —the statistics, the plans, the place-names, the technical moves—and studies instead the battlefield itself in its quieter moments, the feelings of the soldiers, what they ate and wore and thought and talked about, the small circumstances of their daily lives, the scene does become alive again and in a peculiarly vivid way. There can scarcely have been a battlefield quite like it in this or any other war.

Usually one approached Cape Helles from either Imbros or Lemnos in one of the trawlers or flat-bottomed boats that provided a kind of ferry service to the beaches after the battleships had sailed away. By day it was a pleasant trip through a sea of cool peacock blue, and it was only when one was within about five miles of the shore that one saw that it was overhung by a vast yellowish cloud of dust. This dust increased during heavy fighting and diminished at night, and with sudden changes of the wind, but it was usually there through these months of early summer. And with the dust a sickly carrion smell came out across the sea, as far as three miles at times. A fringe of debris with the same implications of rottenness and decay washed along the shore. Yet on a quiet day there was a certain toy-like quality in the scene around Sedd-el-Bahr—toy-like in the sense that it was very busy, very crowded with ingenious imitations of ordinary life in other, safer places. The long green keel of the *Majestic* was still clearly visible beneath the sea, and the castle by the beach had a battered appearance as though someone had stamped on it with his foot. The *River Clyde* was still there, firmly moored to the shore with lighters and other small boats all about her, and she was joined now by another vessel, the old French battleship *Magenta*, which had been sunk about a quarter of a mile to the west to form a miniature harbour in the bay. Piers had sprung up, and around them thousands of men were bathing, unloading boats, stacking great piles of tins and boxes on the shore. A new road had been cut around the base of the cliff by Turkish prisoners, and lines of horses and mules stood waiting there.

'The comparison with a seaside resort on a fine bank holiday,' Compton MacKenzie wrote, 'arrived so inevitably as really to seem rather trite. Yet all the time the comparison was justifying itself. Even the aeroplanes on the top of the low cliff eastward had the look of an "amusement" to provide a sixpenny or threepenny thrill; the tents might so easily conceal phrenologists or fortune tellers; the signal station might well be a camera obscura; the very carts of the Indian Transport, seen through the driven sand, had an air of waiting goat-carriages.'

With this, however, all further comparison ended; the

dust covered all, billowing, choking and vile, and the Turkish shells came through it with the noise of express trains crashing in the sky. This noise was continuous at times, and the soldiers endured it, not as a temporary pain, but as a natural condition of life. It was as inevitable as the weather. You were hit or not hit. Eating, sleeping and waking the long scream went on. These slopes by the sea were supposed to be rest areas, but they were often more dangerous than the frontline trenches a mile or two inland, since they exposed such obvious targets to the enemy: the piers, the incoming boats, the men bathing. From their perch on Achi Baba the Turks overlooked the whole bridgehead, and when the dust lifted they could see every tent, every gun emplacement, every man and animal that moved above the cliffs. The horses and the mules were terribly exposed to this bombardment, but they appeared to notice nothing until they were actually hit. Some blessed lacuna in the brain allowed them to stand there calmly with unfrightened eyes when the bursting shrapnel had sent all human beings to the ground. 'Fountains of earth, fountains of water,' a French doctor wrote to his wife; 'shells cover us with a vault of steel, dissolving, hissing and noisy . . . without this radiantly beautiful light it would be frightfully sad.'

There were some—notably the more elderly men who were experiencing shellfire for the first time—who simply could not stand it and had to be invalided home: 'Weak minds were upset,' the doctor wrote. 'Few were able to keep a real and immediate notion of things. There is a physical exaltation which deforms and obscures everything and makes one incapable of reasoning.'

The cool weather had lasted until the end of May, and during that time the soldiers were perfectly healthy. May was an idyllic month that year with wild flowers blooming everywhere, even between the front lines, and tremendous sunsets fell on Imbros and the monolithic rock of Samothrace. The shelling was not really troublesome and the men slept in tents. Then in June when the Turks set up their big guns behind Achi Baba a furious digging began, and the Army went underground into trenches and dugouts, sometimes uncovered to the sky, sometimes with a sheet of galvanized iron and a layer of earth for a roof. At first there was no regular shelling from Asia and the side of the cliffs facing south and east was a favourite spot for a home; it was known as Sea View Terrace. Then one day new guns opened up from Kum Kale across the straits, and the shells burst directly at the front doors of the dugouts which had seemed so safe before. The French corps held the eastern tip of the peninsula opposite Asia, and they suffered worst of all: 2,000 quarts of irreplaceable wine went up one day. By the end of the month a network of trenches and sunken roads stretched outward from the beaches to the front line, and it was possible to walk for miles without showing one's head above the ground.

The colours of the landscape changed. Grass vanished from the ground, and in place of green crops there were now wide areas covered with the fading purple flowers of the wild thyme, the dried-up sticks of asphodel, an occasional dusty pink oleander, a green fig or a pomegranate with its little flame-coloured blossom on the fruit. All the rest was brown and bare and ankle-deep in dust, a semi-desert scene. With the increasing heat the summer insects and animals emerged, and many of the soldiers, their lives narrowed down to the few square yards of ground around them, became aware for the first time of tarantulas and centipedes, the scorpion and the lizard, the incessant mid-day racket of the cicadas in the trees. Mackenzie, straining his eyes through his binoculars to see an attack at the front, found a tortoise crawling across his line of vision.

By July the heat reached a steady eighty-four degrees in the shade. But there was no shade: from four in the morning until eight at night the sun glared down and made an oven out of every trench and dug-out. It was a fearful heat, so hot that the fat of the bully beef melted in the tins, and a metal plate would become too hot to touch. Some of the soldiers were supplied with topees, but most wore the same uniform which had been issued to the Army in France: a flat peaked cap, a thick khaki serge tunic and breeches, puttees and boots. There were no steel helmets.

On the heights above, the Turks had a constant supply of good drinking water, but with the exception of one or two springs in Gully Ravine there were no wells in the Cape Helles bridgehead; water had to be brought by sea from the Nile in Egypt, 700 miles away, pumped ashore and carried up to the front by mules. Sometimes the men were down to a third of a gallon of water a day for all purposes, and it was even worse at Anzac, where they were forced to condense salt water from the sea.

In the end probably these discomforts were not too

much, and the men adjusted themselves. But the thing that was absolutely unbearable was the flies. They began to multiply in May; by June they were a plague, and it was a plague of such foulness and persistence that it often seemed more horrible than the war itself. The flies fed on the unburied corpses in no-man's-land, and on the latrines, the refuse and the food of both armies. There was no escape for anybody even when night fell. No tin of food could be opened without it being covered instantly with a thick layer of writhing insects. One ate them with the food and swallowed them with the water. You might burn them off the walls and ceiling of your dugout at night but another horde would be there in the morning. You washed and shaved with flies about your face and hands and eyes, and even to the most toughened soldier it was horribly apparent that they were often bloated with feeding on the blood of dead animals and men. Mosquito nets were almost unknown, and one of the most valuable possessions a soldier could have was a little piece of muslin veiling, which he could put over his face when he ate or slept. To avoid the flies some of the men learned to write their letters home in the darkness of their dug-outs at night.

From June onwards dysenteric diarrhœa spread through the Army and soon every man was infected by it.[1] Many of the soldiers were able to endure it without reporting sick, but some soon became too weak even to drag themselves to the latrines, and by July, when over a thousand men were being evacuated every week, the disease had become far more destructive than the battle itself. Quite apart from the discomfort and the self-disgust it created an overmastering lassitude. 'It fills me,' Hamilton wrote, 'with a desperate longing to lie down and do nothing but rest . . . and this, I think, must be the reason the Greeks were ten long years in taking Troy.'

The flies no doubt were principally to blame for the spread of the disease, but the food can scarcely have helped: the salt and fatty bully beef, the absence of all green vegetables. The N.A.A.F.I. stores of later campaigns did not exist at Gallipoli, and there were no means by which the soldiers could buy small luxuries to vary the monotony of

[1] Dysentery was nothing new on the Gallipoli peninsula. Xerxes' soldiers were infected with it on their return march from Greece to the Hellespont in the fifth century B.C.

their diet. There was a rum ration which was doled out at long intervals, very occasionally they got eggs or perhaps a parcel from home, or even fresh fish (by throwing hand-grenades into the sea), but for the rest it was a monotonous routine of milkless tea, bully beef and plum and apple jam.

The medical services came near to breaking down during this period; they had been organized on the principle that hospitals would be set up on the peninsula soon after the original landing, and when this failed to happen hurried arrangements were made to establish a base under canvas on the island of Lemnos, while the more serious cases were evacuated to Egypt, Malta and even England. Lemnos soon became overwhelmed by the increasing number of casualties and there were never enough hospital ships to cope with the overflow.

And now in June the doctors were faced with this major epidemic of dysentery in the Army. 'Well, you won't die of it,' was the current phrase. But men did die, and the bodies were simply sewn up in blankets and buried in the nearest cemetery. The great majority who survived suffered dreadfully, and perhaps unnecessarily at times. Horse-drawn ambulances bumped down to the beaches with the sick and wounded, and then there would be hours of waiting in the unshaded lighters before they were finally got away. Conditions in the islands were not much better. On Lemnos the patients lay about on the ground in their thick cord breeches and they were pestered by flies. There were no mosquito nets, and often no beds, not even pyjamas.

Trained dentists were unknown at Gallipoli; if a man got toothache, or broke his teeth on the ration biscuits—a thing that happened quite often—he had to put up with it as best he could, unless he was lucky enough to find some hospital orderly who was able to make rough repairs.

These things began to cause a growing resentment in the Army. 'The men are getting pretty tired,' Aubrey Herbert wrote. 'They are not as resigned as their ten thousand brother monks over the way at Mount Athos.'

On June 1 Hamilton had abandoned his cheese-ridden berth aboard the *Arcadian* and had set up his headquarters on the island of Imbros. But the staff there were hardly better off than anybody else, except that they were not under fire. They had put up their tents on a particularly dreary stretch of coast where there was no shade, and the fine biscuit-coloured sand blew into their faces all day.

There existed close by a perfectly good site on level ground among figs and olive trees, but this was deliberately ignored partly because they did not wish to give the camp an air of permanence—the next attack might gain enough ground to allow them to land on the peninsula—and partly because it was felt that the staff should know something of the hardships and miseries of the men at the front. Almost uneatable food was provided to strengthen this illusion. It does not seem to have occurred to the General or any of his senior officers that efficiency mattered more than appearances, and that a man suffering from dysentery— from the flies, the bad food and the heat—was not likely to give his best attention to his work.

And in fact an exasperating muddle began to overtake affairs in the rear areas and along the lines of supply. Most of it was centred on Lemnos and its harbour of Mudros where many of the base installations had been dumped down. Ships arrived without manifests and had to be un-loaded before the transport officers could discover what was in them. Often cargoes were sent in the wrong vessels to the wrong places, or became lost or mixed up with other cargoes. New shells arrived without the new keys which were essential to them. Mail disappeared. A polyglot crowd of men in transit hung about the shore waiting for orders. 'Mingling among them all,' Admiral Wemyss, the Gov-ernor, wrote in his diary,[1] 'is the wily Greek, avaricious and plausible, making much money out of both of the others (the French and the British) hawking every sort of commodity from onions to Turkish Delight and Beecham's Pills.' At the front someone invented a phrase which ex-pressed the soldiers' view of the islands. It was 'Imbros, Mudros and Chaos'.

There was a fantastic difference between the life of the soldiers on shore and that of the sailors in the warships that steamed by, perhaps only a couple of hundred yards out at sea. A ship's wardroom was a kind of wonderland

[1] Perhaps because of its isolation and its strangeness, perhaps because of the lack of other entertainment, the Gallipoli cam-paign produced an extraordinary number of diaries. Every other man seems to have kept one, and no doubt the notebooks still exist in tens of thousands of homes. It was customary to illus-trate them with sketches and photographs, and perhaps some wild flower, a bird's feather, a souvenir like a captured Turkish badge, pressed between the leaves.

for any Army officer who was invited on board. After weeks of enduring the flies, and the lice in his clothes, and with his eyes still filled with the sight and smell of the decaying dead, he would stand and gaze with astonishment at the clean linen on the table, the glasses, the plates, the meat, the fruit and the wine.

These differences were multiplied still more in the case of the ocean liners which were taken over as transports complete with their peacetime crews and furnishings. Henry Nevinson, the war correspondent, has related that he was aboard the liner *Minneapolis* just before a major battle was to be fought. He was to go ashore with the attacking troops in the early dawn, and at 4 a.m. he rang for a cup of tea. 'On this ship,' the steward informed him, 'breakfast is always at 8.30.' A little later when the soldiers were taking to the assault boats the stewards got out their vacuum-cleaners and went to work along the carpets in the corridors in the usual way. Breakfast no doubt was served at eight-thirty, though there were few to eat it, and indeed by that time many of the soldiers were no longer alive.

There was no resentment at all about these things in the Army, for the sailors were known to be eager to get into the fight, and it was a kind of reassurance, a pleasant reminder of the ultimate sanity of life, to have the Navy there with its clean, comfortable ships. 'It has been computed,' Wemyss wrote, 'that in shore fighting it takes several tons of lead to kill one man: at sea one torpedo can cause the death of many hundreds. On shore the soldier is in almost perpetual discomfort, if not misery—at sea the sailor lives in comparative comfort until the moment comes when his life is required of him.'

Yet it seems possible that one can make too much of the hardships of the soldiers at Gallipoli, or rather there is a danger of seeing these hardships out of their right context. With the mere cataloguing of the Army's miseries a sense of dreariness is transmitted, and this is a false impression; at this stage life on the peninsula was anything but dreary. It was ghastly but it was not yet petty or monotonous. There can be no fair comparison with the relatively comfortable lives of the soldiers in the second world war, or even with the lives of these men themselves before they enlisted. Gallipoli swallowed them up and made conditions of its own. With marvellous rapidity the men removed

210

themselves to another plane of existence, the past receded, the future barely existed, and they lived as never before upon the moment, released from the normal weight of human ambitions and regrets. 'It was in some ways,' Herbert says, 'a curiously happy time.' It is a strange remark, but one feels one understands it very well. The men had no cinemas, no music, no radios, no 'entertainment' of any kind, and they never met women or children as the soldiers did behind the lines in France. Yet the very absence of these pleasures created another scale of values. They had a sharp and enormous appetite for the smallest things. Bathing in the sea became an inexpressible joy. To get away from the flies, to wash the dust from one's eyes and mouth, to feel cool again: this was a heightening of sensation which, for the moment, went beyond their dreams of home. The brewing of tea in the evening, the sharing out of a parcel, a cake or a bar of chocolate, the long talks in the starlight talking of what they would do 'when it was all over'—all these things took on an almost mystical emphasis of a kind that became familiar enough in the western desert of Egypt in the second world war, or indeed on any distant front in any war. There were no pin-up girls; no erotic magazines reached them—they were lucky if they even saw a newspaper from home that was under a month old—and there were no nurses or Ensa troupes. Perhaps because of this the sexual instinct seems to have been held in abeyance for the time, or rather it was absorbed in the minutiae of their intensely friendly life, the generous feelings created by the danger all around them. There was very little vice; ordinary crimes became lost in the innocence of the crime of war itself. Certainly there was no possibility of drunkenness,[1] and gambling was not much more than an anaemic pastime in a world where money was the least of things. They craved not soft beds and hot baths but mosquito nets and salt water soap. Promotion counted for a good deal, and so did the word of praise and the medal. General Gouraud, the French commander who had replaced d'Amade, would form his men up in a hollow square in the moonlight and solemnly bestow the *Croix de Guerre* and the accolade upon some young *poilu* who, they all knew, had earned these honours only a few days or even

[1] Except once at Anzac when some barrels of wine were washed ashore from the wreck of the *Triumph*.

a few hours before; and this was much more impressive than any ceremonial in a barracks could have been. They were all keen judges of bravery on that narrow front.

Yet probably it was the small network of habits that grew up in the trenches that made life bearable to the men. There was a deliberate playing down of the dramatic and the dangerous quality of things. The biggest of the Turkish guns that fired from Kum Kale was known as 'Asiatic Annie'; another was called 'Quick Dick', and the most commonplace names were found for the places where the bloodiest actions were fought: 'Clapham Junction', 'The Vineyard', 'Le Haricot'. A kind of defensive mechanism was made out of swearing and a simple, ironical, hard-boiled sense of humour: 'Please God give us victory. But not in *our* sector.' 'Having a good clean-up?' a commanding general said one day to a soldier who was washing himself in a mug of water. 'Yes, sir,' the man answered, 'and I only wish I were a bloody canary.'

Hours were spent in improving their dug-outs, in picking lice out of their clothing, in cooking their food (pancakes made of flour and water soon became a universal thing), in writing their diaries and letters.[1]

Some managed to develop hobbies of a kind. There was, for example, a mild fever for the excavation of antiquities among the French. At Lemnos before the landing they had unearthed a mutilated statue of Eros at the site of the ancient Hephaestia, and on arriving at Cape Helles they were delighted to find that Asiatic Annie was disinterring other relics. Two huge jars with skeletons in them were uncovered in a shell crater, and when the soldiers started to dig their trenches at Hissarlik they came on a series of large stone sarcophagi which resounded dully when struck with a pick. Through the centuries (and at once it was asserted that these finds were as old as Troy), soil had penetrated, grain by grain, into the interior of the tombs, but the soldiers managed to excavate many bones, as well as

[1] The men were issued with a green active service envelope on which was printed, 'I certify on my honour that the contents of this envelope refer to nothing but family matters.' This meant that the letter was censored at the base and not in the regiment.

For the laconic there was also a card with the printed words:
'I am quite well.'
'I have been admitted to hospital, sick, wounded.'
One simply struck out the words that did not apply.

vases, lamps and statues in pottery of men and women. The French doctor wrote again to his wife about one especially beautiful cup: 'Its long handles, almost ethereal in their delicacy, give to this little thing the palpitation of wings.'

Living as they did beneath the ground, many of the men became absorbed in the insect life around them. They set on centipedes and scorpions to fight one another, and hours would go by while they watched the ant-lion digging his small craters in the sand. Round and round he would go, clockwise and then anti-clockwise, scooping up the soil with his great flippers, tossing it on to his head, and then with an upward jerk flipping it over the rim of the crater. When finally the crater was finished, and the ant-lion was lying in hiding at the bottom, the soldiers would drive beetles and other insects up to the rim, and there would be the quick scuffle in the sand, the pounce and then the slow death as the ant-lion sucked his victim dry. In this troglodyte war in the trenches there was perhaps something symbolic about the ant-lion.

A stream of rumours (known on the Anzac bridgehead as 'furphies'), flowed through the trenches, and they were usually based upon something which was heard 'down on the beach', or from someone's batman or cook or signaller at brigade or battalion headquarters. The most lurid stories were passed along: the Turks in one sector had all been dressed as women, Hamilton had been sacked, the Russians had landed on the Bosphorus and had sunk the *Goeben*, Enver had ordered a general offensive to celebrate the first day of Ramadan on July 12, a notorious female spy had been captured in a ship at Mudros.

Unless a battle was in progress one day was very like another; the stand-to in the trenches at 3 a.m., the first shots at dawn rising to a crescendo and dying away again; the morning shelling, the evening bathe, the ritual of brewing tea and the long conversations in the starlight; finally the muffled sound of the mule teams coming up to the front with stores from the beach as soon as darkness fell.

Occasionally the unexpected happened, as when a German and a British aeroplane, flying low like wasps, fought a rifle duel with one another over the trenches, and both armies held their fire to watch it; and again when the Turks sprinkled the Allies' lines with pamphlets in Urdu appealing to the Indian soldiers not to fight their brother Moslems —a device that had very little success with the Gurkhas, who were unable to read Urdu and who, being Hindu by religion, loathed Mahomet.

The Air Force had a particular fascination for the soldiers. Being chained to their trenches, the men could only dream of what it might be like to roam far behind the enemy lines. To see the other side of Achi Baba was to them almost as wonderful as to see the other side of the moon. As for Constantinople, it was lurid fantasy, a vision of minarets and spice bazaars, of caliphs and harems, of jewels and odalisques and whirling dervishes. Constantinople, of course, was not like this at all; but just to have the possibility of winging your way there through the air—this in 1915 had a touch of the magic carpet about it. And there was, in fact, an immense exhilaration in the adventures of these box kites in the sky. Within a day or two Samson had established what would now be called an airstrip at Cape Helles, and although he was shelled every time he took off and landed he continued there, to the admiration of the soldiers, for a week or two. When finally he decided that it was more sensible to make his base on the island of Imbros he left a dummy plane behind, and the Army had the enjoyment of watching the Turks bombarding it for a week on end. Some 500 shells exploded on the field before the machine was demolished.

Samson liked to go up in the first light of the morning, and having waved to the British soldiers in the trenches he flew on up the peninsula to catch the Turks around their cooking fires. Then he would return in the last light of the evening to shoot up the enemy camel teams and bullock carts as they set out on their nightly journey to the front.

Both British and French airmen helped the Allied submarines as they made their passage of the Narrows by flying overhead and distracting the attention of the Turkish gunners; and often they joined Nasmith, Boyle and the others in the attack on the supply lines at the neck of the peninsula. Once a British pilot succeeded in torpedoing a Turkish vessel from the air. There were frequent disasters; a seaplane with a faulty engine would alight perhaps in the straits and then, with enemy bullets churning up the water all around, the machine would limp away across the sea like some maimed bird until it reached the safety of the cliffs.

These were absorbing spectacles for the soldiers in the trenches; in a world where everything was earthbound and without movement the airmen brought a sense of freedom into life.

As at Anzac, the men at Cape Helles had no personal hatred of the Turks, and there was a good deal of sympathy for them when, after one of their disastrous assaults, they asked for an armistice to bury their dead. Hamilton, on the advice of Hunter-Weston's headquarters, refused the request, as it was believed that the Turkish commanders wanted to renew the attack and were having difficulty in inducing their men to charge over ground that was strewn with corpses.

'A bit of hate is just what our men want here,' one of the British colonels wrote. 'They are inclined to look on the Turk as a very bad old comic . . . one feels very sorry for the individual and absolutely bloodthirsty against the mass.' It was a common thing for the soldiers to offer prisoners their waterbottles and packages of cigarettes as soon as they were captured.

After June it was noticed that a psychological change was overtaking the Army. Whenever there was the project of another battle sickness fell off, and if the men were not actually as eager for the fight as their commanders pretended them to be, they were at least unwilling to see others take their place. It was the dogged attitude of the man who, having been obliged to undertake a disagreeable job, is determined to finish it. Always too they hoped that this battle was to be the last. Then, when the attack was over and all their hopes had come to nothing, the reaction set in. More and more men reported sick. Discipline flagged, and a despondent and irritable atmosphere spread through the trenches. To accept risk in idleness, to wait under the constant shelling without plans and hopes—that was the intolerable thing.

After the mid-July battles this attitude towards the campaign became more marked than ever. The number of patients going to the doctors increased in every regiment, and although batches of them were sent off on leave to Imbros so that they would escape the shell fire for a few days the ennui continued, the sense of waste and loss. There were cases of men putting their hands above the parapet so that they would be invalided away with a minor wound, but it was not malingering on a large scale; nearly all were dysentery cases, and without the stimulus of action the soldiers were genuinely unable to find the necessary resistance to fight the disease. Many in fact were so infected that they never returned to the front again.

The situation was not altogether unlike that of the British Army in the Western Desert of Egypt in the summer of 1942 in the second world war. The men were exhausted and dispirited. Nothing ever seemed to go right; they attacked, and always it ended in the same way, the stalemate, the long boring labour of carrying more ammunition up to the front so that they could repeat the same futile proceedings all over again. Many of the soldiers began to say openly that the whole expedition was a blunder; the politicians and brasshats at home had tried to pull off a victory on the cheap, and now that it had failed the expedition was to be abandoned to its fate. This was the real core of their grievances: that they were being neglected and forgotten. The armies in France were to have the favours, and Gallipoli no longer counted for anything at all. It was true that reinforcements were arriving, but they were too late and too few. The casualties had been too heavy.

This was the surface of things, and in a perverse way there was a counter-current working against it. The expedition feeling still persisted, and perhaps it was stronger than ever—the feeling that every man on Gallipoli was a dedicated man, that he was part of an adventure that set him apart from every other soldier. None of the general resentment seems to have been directed upon the commanders on the spot. Hamilton perhaps may have come in for some of the blame, but he was a vague and remote figure whom few of them ever saw, despite the fact that he was constantly going round the trenches, and in any case he too was regarded as a victim of 'the politicians'. The others, the corps and divisional commanders, were too close to the men to attract their criticism. They shared the same dangers and almost the same hardships with the rank and file, and this was something new in the armies of the first world war, when no officer was without his batman and there was a strict division, a class division, between the gentleman with a commission and the worker-soldier in the ranks. At Anzac Birdwood made a point of being in the front line, and the soldiers saw him every day. He was just as much a target for the sniper and the bursting shrapnel as they were themselves. In June General Gouraud had his arm shattered by a shell-burst, and one of his divisional commanders was killed. Hunter-Weston, made haggard by the strain of too much work and too much unrequited optimism, fell ill of the prevailing dysentery and had to be sent home. And there were of course many more casualties among the brigadiers and the colonels.

All this brought the officer and the soldier very close together, and however much they may have criticized the men in the rear areas, the hospital staffs and the transport companies on the line of supply, it was seldom thought that the commander at the front might be wanting in skill and imagination—he simply took orders and did what he was told to do. He was one of them. It was felt that the solution of their problems lay elsewhere, and it was an intangible thing, this mystical recipe for the success that always eluded them. Yet somehow, the men thought, there was a way of breaking the stalemate, of justifying themselves, of proving that the expedition was sound after all. And so underneath all their bitterness and tiredness, the men were perfectly willing to attack again provided they could be given the least glimmering of a chance of success. As with the desert soldiers in 1942 they needed a battle of Alamein.

The Turks, meanwhile, were not much better off than the Allies during these hot months. The official casualty figures issued after the campaign reveal that a total of 85,000 were evacuated sick, and of these 21,000 died of disease. By Western standards the Turkish soldiers were very poorly cared for. According to Liman von Sanders their uniforms were so tattered that the hessian sacks which were sent up to the trenches to be filled with sand were constantly disappearing; the men used the material to patch their trousers. No doubt the Turkish peasants were able to withstand the heat and the dirt more easily than the Europeans, and their simpler vegetable diet—rice, bread and oil—was much better for them than bully beef; but they were not inoculated against typhoid and other diseases as the Allied soldiers were, and their trenches and latrines were kept in a much less hygienic state. By July the Turkish generals were finding it necessary to send increasing numbers of men home on leave to their villages, and it often happened that once a soldier left the front he found means of staying away.

Meanwhile the British submarine campaign was causing

a shortage of ammunition, which was almost as acute as it was with the Allies. 'It was fortunate for us,' Liman wrote, 'that the British attacks never lasted more than one day, and were punctuated by pauses of several days. Otherwise it would have been impossible to replenish our artillery ammunition.' He speaks too of 'the jealousy and lack of co-operation so common among Turkish general officers', and of several changes in the high command which had to be made at this time as a result of their heavy losses.

None of this was more than guessed at in Hamilton's headquarters. It was known, however, from prisoners, from aerial reconnaissance and from agents in Constantinople, that Turkish reinforcements in large numbers were arriving on the peninsula, though whether for attack or simply to make good their losses it was impossible to say. As July ran out both sides settled down to an erratic apprehensive calm, enduring the same blistering sun, the same plague of flies and infected dust, the same ant-like existence in the ground. The Allies waited for the Turks to issue forth from the hills; the Turks waited for the Allies to come up to meet them. It was all very old and very new, a twentieth-century revival of the interminable siege. The Turks had a trench and a machine-gun post among Schliemann's excavations on the site of Troy.

TWELVE

THE soldiers at Gallipoli were wrong in thinking that the campaign had been abandoned and forgotten in London. Directly the new government was in office Churchill circulated a paper to cabinet Ministers in which he argued that while the Allies had neither the men nor the ammunition to bring about a decision in France, a comparatively small addition to Hamilton's forces would make all the difference at Gallipoli.[1] 'It seems most urgent,' he wrote, 'to try to obtain a decision here and wind up the enterprise in a satisfactory manner as soon as possible.' If the Army advanced just three or four miles up the peninsula the Fleet could steam through to the Sea of Marmara and all the old objects could still be realized: the collapse of the Ottoman Empire, the support of Russia, the allegiance of the Balkans. Where else in all the other theatres of war could they look during the next three months for such a victory?

Kitchener himself had for some time been approaching this point of view, and in June he came the whole way. The recruiting and training of his new army in England was now well advanced, but it was not yet ready for a resumption of the offensive in France. 'Such an attack,' he wrote, 'before an adequate supply of guns and high-explosive shell can be provided, would only result in heavy casualties and the capture of another turnip field.'

[1] There were 24 British divisions in France at this time and only 4 in Gallipoli. The remainder of Hamilton's force was made up of 2 French and 2 Anzac divisions—a total of 8 divisions.

It was an indication of this new approach that as soon as the new cabinet was formed the War Council had been reconstructed under the name of the Dardanelles Committee. It met on June 7, and Kitchener and Churchill between them had no difficulty in getting the members to agree to the dispatch of another three divisions to Gallipoli. By the end of the month two more divisions had been added, and three of the largest ocean liners, the *Olympic*, the *Mauretania* and the *Aquitania*, had been chartered to take them to the Mediterranean. By the beginning of July Hamilton was informed that he was to have the ammunition for which he had been so persistently pleading, and a few weeks later the War Office was writing: 'We should like to hear from you after considering your plans whether there is anything further in the way of personnel, guns or ammunition we can send you, as we are most anxious to give you everything you can possibly require and use.'

It was almost an embarrassment of favours. By now Hamilton had either in Gallipoli or in transit an army of thirteen divisions or approximately some 120,000 effective men. This was no longer a distracting novel enterprise: it was the front on which the main British hopes were fixed, and men and shells were being withheld from France to supply it.

The Admiralty, too, was making a large contribution. The monitors arrived to replace the battleships, strange, flat-bottomed boats of 6,000 tons, mounting 14-inch guns of American manufacture. Their most original feature was the blisters or bulges on their sides, designed to ward off the explosions of torpedoes (which the sailors soon discovered made excellent bathing platforms). Almost as important were the Beetles, the landing barges which had been designed by Fisher and which were to be the precursors of the small craft used at Normandy and other landings in the second world war. They were capable of carrying five hundred men or forty horses, and were fitted with armoured plates sufficiently strong to resist shrapnel and machine-gun fire. The name derived from the fact that they were painted black, and the long landing ramps which projected from their bows had the appearance of antennae.

Two more balloon ships, the *Hector* and the *Canning*, were sent out to assist in the artillery spotting, and there were additions to the number of trawlers, auxiliary hospital ships, and other craft. It was a less imposing fleet than the one which had originally sailed to the Dardanelles in the spring, but it was larger and much better suited to an amphibious operation in a narrow sea.

A similar change overtook the Air Force with the arrival of new seaplane carriers and pilots, the French setting themselves up on Tenedos and the British on Imbros. As many as fifteen aircraft were now able to take off together for concentrated raids on the peninsula and the Narrows.

Towards the end of July, when a lull had again settled over the front, most of these new forces were concentrated in the Ægean islands, where they were to be kept in secret until the moment came to commit them to the battle. A new landing on the enemy coast was obviously essential, and all the old arguments came up once again: Bulair was too strongly fortified, the Asiatic coast too distant from their objectives, and at neither place could the Navy give its full support to the Army on the shore. So once again it had to be the peninsula itself. The plan that finally emerged was very largely a repetition of April 25, but it had one vital difference: the emphasis was now removed from Cape Helles and Achi Baba and placed upon the Sari Bair ridge in the centre of the peninsula. Birdwood had been urging this course for some weeks past, and in many ways it appeared to be a promising design. He proposed to break out of the north of the Anzac bridgehead by night and assault Chunuk Bair and the crests of the hills, having first made a major feint at a place called Lone Pine to the south. Simultaneously there was to be a new landing at Suvla Bay, immediately to the north of Anzac, and it was hoped that as soon as the hills there were taken the combined force would push through to the Narrows about four miles away. With the bulk of the Turkish Army then bottled up in the tip of the peninsula, and under heavy pressure from the French and the British at Cape Helles, it was hoped that there would be a quick ending to the campaign, at any rate as far as the Dardanelles was concerned.

There were to be pretended landings at Bulair and from the island of Mytilene on to the Asiatic coast so as to keep Liman in doubt until after the main battle had been joined. Once again surprise was the chief element of the plan; once again the Fleet was to hold its hand until the Army had broken through.

Suvla Bay was an admirable place for the new landing. It offered a safe anchorage for the Fleet, it was backed by low undulating country, and it was known to be very lightly defended. Once ashore the soldiers would quickly join up with the Anzac bridgehead and relieve the congestion in that narrow space. There was a salt lake about a mile and a half wide directly behind the Suvla Bay beaches, but this dried up in summer, and Hamilton in any case planned to avoid it by landing in the first instance on an easy strip of coastline just south of the Bay itself. Everything depended upon the speed with which the soldiers pushed inland to the hills so that they could bring assistance to Birdwood fighting the main battle on Sari Bair. This time there was to be no repetition of the *River Clyde* and the Sedd-el-Bahr disaster for the troops were to come ashore by night without preliminary bombardment.

In addition to the Beetles (which were to be commanded by Commander Unwin, V.C., in the first assault), a great deal of modern equipment had been shipped out to the Ægean. An anti-submarine net, over a mile in length, was to be laid across the mouth of Suvla Bay immediately after the landing. A pontoon pier 300 feet long had been assembled at Imbros, and was to be towed across to the beach. Four 50-ton water lighters were also to be taken over by the water steamer *Krini*, which had another 200 tons on board in addition to pumps and hoses. As a further precaution the Egyptian bazaars were once again ransacked for camel tanks, milk cans, skins—anything that would hold water.

For a time Hamilton debated whether or not he should bring the battered but experienced 29th Division round from Cape Helles to make the first landing at Suvla, but in the end he decided that the operation should be entrusted to the new troops coming out from England. Extreme secrecy was the key to all these arrangements, and there was a special difficulty in reinforcing Birdwood for the battle. The Anzac bridgehead was not much bigger than Regent's Park in London, or Central Park in New York (if one can imagine a park of bare cliffs and peaks), and just as much overlooked. The Navy, however, believed that over a series of nights they could smuggle another 25,000 men ashore without the Turks knowing anything about it.

The Army was finally disposed as follows: the six divisions already in Cape Helles, about 35,000 men, to remain where they were and make a northern thrust against the village of Krithia; Birdwood with his Australians, New

Zealanders and a division and a half of new British and Gurkha troops, about 37,000 men in all, to make the main attack at Anzac, and the remainder of the reinforcements from the United Kingdom, numbering some 25,000, to go ashore at Suvla.

August 6 was fixed as the day of the offensive, since the waning moon, then in its last quarter, would not rise until about 10.30 that night, and the boats on the Suvla landing would thus be able to approach the coast in the darkness. The actual timing of the various attacks was arranged so as to create the maximum confusion in the enemy command. It was a chain reaction, a succession of explosions from south to north, beginning with the first bombardment on the Helles front at 2.30 in the afternoon. There would then follow the Australian feint at Lone Pine at 5.30, the main assault on Chunuk Bair at 9.30 at night, and the landing at Suvla about an hour later. Thus by midnight the whole front would be ablaze.

By the end of June all these plans were well advanced, and Keyes and the Army staff were again involved with their elaborate timetables for the ferrying of the troops and their supplies from the islands to the beaches. Meanwhile a crucial issue had arisen over the question of who was to have command of the new landing at Suvla. Hamilton had two men in mind, Sir Julian Byng and Sir Henry Rawlinson, but when he put their names up to Kitchener he was refused on the grounds that neither could be spared from France. The appointment, Kitchener decided, must go to the most suitable and senior Lieutenant-General who was not already in a field command. This practically narrowed the choice down to the Hon. Sir Frederick Stopford, and he duly arrived at Mudros with his chief staff officer Brigadier-General Reed, on July 11. Hamilton had misgivings about both of them. Stopford was 61, and although he had been in Egypt and the Sudan in the 'eighties, and had served as military secretary to General Buller in the Boer War, he had seen very little actual fighting and had never commanded troops in war. He had a reputation as a teacher of military history, but he had been living in retirement since 1909, and was often in ill-health. Reed, a gunner, had also been in South Africa, and had won a memorable V.C. there, but his recent experiences in France had left him with an obsession for tremendous artillery bombardments, and he could talk of very little else.

The officers commanding the five new divisions were of similar cast: professional soldiers who had made their way upward mostly on the strength of their years of service. Many of them, generals and colonels alike, were men who were well over fifty and who had been in retirement when the war broke out. Major-General Hammersley, the officer who was to lead the 11th Division on the actual assault at Suvla, had suffered a breakdown a year or two before. It was a curious position; while the generals were old Regular Army soldiers, their troops were civilians and very young; and all of them, generals as well as soldiers, were wholly unused to the rough and individual kind of campaigning upon which they were now to be engaged.

Soon after he arrived at Mudros Stopford was sent over to Cape Helles for a few days to accustom himself to conditions at the front, and it was there that he was shown the plan on July 22. He was well satisfied. 'This is the plan which I have always hoped he (Hamilton) would adopt,' he said. 'It is a good plan. I am sure it will succeed and I congratulate whoever has been responsible for framing it.' But the General soon changed his mind.

On the following day he had a talk with Reed, the exponent of artillery bombardments, and on July 25 he went over to Anzac on an afternoon visit so that he could survey the Suvla plain from the slopes of Sari Bair. These experiences unsettled Stopford profoundly. On July 26 he called with Reed at G.H.Q. at Imbros and together they tore the plan to pieces. He must have more artillery, Stopford said, more howitzers to fire into the enemy trenches. It was pointed out to him that at Suvla there were no enemy trenches to speak of; Hamilton himself had been close to the shore in a destroyer and had seen no sign of life there. Samson had flown over within the last day or so and his photographs revealed nothing more than 150 yards of entrenchments between the salt lake and the sea. But Stopford remained only half convinced and Reed was quite tireless in his criticisms. Next they argued that the force should be put ashore within the bay itself. The Navy was all against this, since the water there was shallow and uncharted and no one could say what reefs or shoals might wreck the boats in the darkness. In the end, however, they agreed to land one of the three assaulting brigades inside the bay.

Still another difficulty arose over corps headquarters.

Hamilton, remembering his isolation aboard the *Queen Elizabeth* on April 25, wanted Stopford to remain at Imbros during the early hours of the landing since he would be in touch with the troops by wireless as soon as they were ashore, and soon afterwards a telephone cable was to be laid from Imbros to the Suvla beaches. Stopford insisted that he must remain close to his troops aboard his headquarters ship, the sloop *Jonquil*, and in the end he had his way.

His other objections to the plan were of a vague and more subtle kind. In the original drafting it had been stated quite definitely that, since speed was essential, the assaulting troops were to reach a series of low hills, known as Ismail Oglu Tepe, by daylight. There were good reasons for this. The interrogations of prisoners had gone to show that no more than three enemy battalions were holding the Suvla area, and the whole point of the landing was to overwhelm them and seize the high ground before the Turkish reinforcements could arrive. Since all Liman's forces in the south of the peninsula would already be engaged at Anzac and Helles, it was believed that these reinforcements would have to be brought down from Bulair, some thirty miles away. Yet it was unwise to count on more than fifteen or twenty hours' respite; from the moment the first Allied soldier put his foot ashore the Turks would be on the march. Everything in their bitter three months' experience in Gallipoli had made it plain to Hamilton's headquarters that once the period of surprise was gone there was very little chance of breaking the enemy line. Every hour, even every minute, counted.

Stopford demurred. He would do his best, he said, but there was no guarantee that he could reach the hills by daylight.

Hamilton does not appear to have pressed the point; he was content, he said, to leave it to Stopford's own discretion as to how far he got inland in the first attack. This was a drastic watering-down of the spirit of the original plan, and it had its effect when Stopford came to pass on his instructions to his divisional commanders. The orders which General Hammersley issued to the 11th Division contained no references to speed: the brigade commanders were merely instructed to reach the hills 'if possible'. Hammersley, indeed, seems to have gone into action in complete misunderstanding of his role in the battle; instead of regarding himself as a support to Birdwood's main attack from Anzac, he thought—and actually stated in his orders—that one of the objects of the Anzac attack was to distract the Turks from Suvla Bay while the 11th Division was getting ashore.

General Hammersley was not the only man who was in ignorance of the real objects of the offensive. An extreme secrecy was maintained by G.H.Q. at Imbros up to the very last moment.

Hamilton felt very strongly about this question of security, for he had bitter memories of the indiscretions of the Egyptian Press before the April landing. He feared the exposure of his plan by many means: by garrulous cabinet Ministers in England, by the Greek caiques that were constantly arriving in the islands from the mainland and slipping away again, by wounded officers who, on being invalided back to Egypt, might talk too freely in hospital. There was even a danger that some soldier who knew what was on foot might be captured on Gallipoli and induced by the Turks to give the show away.

In view of all this the plan was confined to a very small group at G.H.Q. throughout June and July, and Hamilton was even cautious in his letters to Kitchener. In the middle of July he sent a sharp telegram to Corps Headquarters at Anzac when he heard that Birdwood had been discussing the matter with General Godley and General Walker. 'I am sorry you have told your divisional generals,' he wrote. 'I have not even informed Stopford or Bailloud (the French corps commander who had succeeded Gouraud). Please find out at once how many staff officers each of them has told, and let me know. Now take early opportunity of telling your divisional generals that whole plan is abandoned. I leave it to you to invent the reason for this abandonment. The operation is secret and must remain secret.'

Stopford himself knew nothing of the plan until three weeks before it was to be put into effect, and it was not until the last week of July that Hammersley was given his orders; Stopford took him up the coast in a destroyer to survey the intended landing places from the sea. On July 30 the brigadiers were briefed at last, and on August 3— three days before the battle was to begin—the brigadiers and their colonels were allowed a quick glimpse of the beaches from the decks of a destroyer. All other reconnaissance from the sea was forbidden lest the suspicions of the Turks should be aroused, and when finally the 11th

Division embarked for the landing on August 6 many of its officers had never seen a map of Suvla Bay.

It was an excess of caution and it was not wise. Liman von Sanders says that in any case he was warned. Early in July he began to hear rumours from the islands that another landing was imminent: some 50,000 men and 140 ships were said to have been assembled at Lemnos. On July 22—the same day that Hamilton was breaking the secret to Stopford—Liman received a telegram from Supreme Headquarters in Germany. 'From reports received here,' it ran, 'it seems probable that at the beginning of August a strong attack will be made on the Dardanelles, perhaps in connection with a landing on the Gulf of Saros (the Bulair area), or on the coast of Asia Minor. It will be well to economize ammunition.'

Liman himself was inclined to agree with this forecast, and he deployed his army accordingly. He now had a force of sixteen small divisions (which was roughly equivalent to Hamilton's thirteen), and three of these he posted at Bulair, three opposite the Anzac bridgehead, five at Cape Helles, and the remaining three at Kum Kale on the Asiatic side of the straits. As for the Suvla area, the British were very nearly right in their estimate of the Turkish garrison there. Liman did not consider it a danger point, and he stationed only three weak battalions—about 1,800 men—around the bay. They had no barbed wire and no machine-guns.

There were then three main Turkish battle groups on the peninsula: the Bulair force in the north commanded by Feizi Bey, the force opposite Anzac in the centre commanded by Essad Pasha, and the southern force at Cape Helles commanded by Wehib Pasha (a younger brother of Essad Pasha). Mustafa Kemal was in a somewhat dubious position at this time. Liman respected him very much as a soldier, and would have promoted him, but he found him quarrelsome and difficult to control. A major row had developed in June when Enver, arriving on one of his periodical visits from Constantinople, cancelled an attack which Kemal had planned to launch on Anzac. Kemal, he said, was too much given to the squandering of troops, and Kemal at once resigned. Liman managed to restore peace between them, but when the attack turned out to be a complete disaster recriminations broke out afresh. Kemal declared that Enver's interference had spoiled his plans, and

227

Enver retaliated by making an address to the soldiers in which he praised them for the way they had fought under such poor leadership. It was another and violent example of the 'jealousy and lack of co-operation so common among Turkish general officers'. Kemal once more resigned in a sour rage, and it was only when Enver left the peninsula that he calmed down and agreed to continue with his division—the old 19th. He was still with it on the north of the Anzac front in August, a senior divisional commander but no more.

It seems possible that Liman was to some extent taken in by the British feint on the island of Mytilene, the ancient Lesbos, for it was very thoroughly done. In July a British officer made ostentatious inquiries among the local population of Turks and Greeks about the water supply and sites for encampments; and a little later a brigade of troops actually arrived. Maps of the Asiatic coast were freely distributed through the Army, and on August 3 Hamilton himself came over to the island to inspect the troops: an indication they were on the eve of going into battle, as indeed they were, but not in Asia. These moves can hardly have failed to have been reported to the Turks, for there were many people on the island who were hostile to the Allies, and a fantasy of espionage and counter-espionage was going on. In particular there was one family named Vassilaki of two brothers and three alleged beautiful sisters, which was the talk of the islands. The brothers kept eluding the British intelligence officers, and it was all very enjoyable in an *opéra bouffe* kind of way.

Birdwood's plan of deception at Anzac was of a more practical nature and very daring. There were a number of miners in the Australian forces, and these threw out an underground tunnel, over 500 yards in length, in no-man's-land at Lone Pine.[1] From this the Australians planned to issue forth like disturbed ants at zero hour on the afternoon of August 6. A more elaborate scheme had been worked out to pave the way for the main assault on Chunuk Bair

---

[1] Lone Pine had its name from the fact that the Turks, though supplied with charcoal for their cooking, had cut down for firewood all but a single tree on the ridge. It so happened that on the very morning of the attack this last tree was also felled.

that night. For some weeks almost every night a destroyer had posted herself off Anzac, and with the aid of her search-lights had bombarded a line of Turkish trenches known as Post 3. This action always began precisely at 9 p.m. and continued for half an hour, and it was calculated that the Turks, being human, would fall into a habit of retiring from the trench at 9 p.m. and of returning to it when the bombardment was over. On the night of the attack the Anzac troops planned to creep up to the position in the deep darkness on either side of the searchlight's beam and then leap into the empty trenches directly the barrage was lifted.

But Birdwood's main concern was the secret disembark-ment at Anzac of his additional 25,000 men with their stores and equipment. In every valley which was not over-looked by the enemy long terraces were dug and new caves were driven into the rocks. Here the incoming troops were to be secreted. Orders were issued that the men, on reach-ing the shore, were to remain in strict hiding throughout the day, no swimming was allowed until after nightfall, and if German aircraft passed over they were not to turn their faces to the sky. No boat with the reinforcements on board was to approach the shore in the daylight, none was to be in sight of land when dawn broke. In the darkness tens of thousands of gallons of water had to be pumped ashore, new hospitals, ammunition dumps, guns and food stores hidden away. All horses were to be landed with full nose-bags, and each man was to carry a full waterbottle and one day's iron ration.

The movement began on August 4 and continued on three successive nights until August 6. Except that on one occasion a group of lighters was delayed until after dawn and was shelled and driven away the operation was carried out with complete success. There were moments at Bird-wood's headquarters when they felt sure that the Turks must have heard the rattling of anchor chains in the bay, and the shouted orders of the officers on the beach. But the enemy apparently suspected nothing. By August 6 there was scarcely standing room for another man at Anzac.

Meanwhile the last reinforcements from England were arriving in the islands, and it was already something of a victory that all five divisions were brought through the

Mediterranean without the loss of a single man. They moved into tented cities on Mytilene, Lemnos and Imbros, and there they waited, in the eyes of the veterans a pale and hesitant lot, for the moment when they were to be re-embarked and taken to the battle.

It was a strange atmosphere. Among the older soldiers on the peninsula the approaching struggle had acted as a stimulus. Fewer and fewer men reported sick, and everything which in idleness had seemed so insupportable—the flies, the heat and the dust—became apparently much easier to bear. But for the new troops this period of suspense was a depressing experience. They were in a halfway house; while they themselves had never been in battle they still did not have the luxury of the ignorance in which the older soldiers had set out to make the first landing on April 25. They knew what the veterans had not known—that a landing could be a terrible thing, that the Turks were a stubborn enemy, and that all might easily end in wounds or death. This was no jaunt to Constantinople and the harems. It so happened that the War Office had published Hamilton's first dispatch from Gallipoli just at the time that the new drafts were leaving England, and they had all been discussing that tragic story on the voyage out. And so they knew and did not know. Whenever they could they asked tentative questions of the older soldiers. What was it *like* on the peninsula? Would there be guides to lead them when they got ashore, and if no guides how would they know where to go? What about the shelling? And the sniping? And the Turks? And finally there was the question they could not ask: what was it like to kill a man and to stand up to be killed oneself?

All this was as old as war itself, but these early August days were frightfully hot, the flies and the mosquitoes leapt on to the men's pink skins and they caught the endemic dysentery very quickly. While they waited they gossiped, and the rumours that went about were not of the hopeful kind. By August 6 the constricting sense of endless waiting had become as bad as if not worse than the prospect of the battle itself. They wanted to get it over.

Upon G.H.Q. at Imbros the strain was of a different kind, for it was perfectly obvious to everybody that this was a gambler's chance, and probably their last chance. Mentally they might have persuaded themselves that, within reason, every eventuality had been foreseen, that the plan was good, that there was no reason why it should not succeed; but when so many things had gone wrong before it was difficult to feel an emotional enthusiasm. Hamilton was always at his best at these moments. He was courteous, patient, and apparently full of intelligent confidence; he spread an aura of authority round him, he was very much respected. But the crust was thin, and not unnaturally there were occasional disputes at headquarters. The French were not entirely liked, nor were the newcomers who were arriving from England. The staff, too, was on guard against any show of superiority in officers who were serving at the front, and they were often irritated as well by the men in the rear echelons behind them.

Despite the reinforcements, there was still a feeling that the Dardanelles was a poor relation to the French front, and an interminable telegram battle with the War Office went on. In July Churchill had been expected to come to Gallipoli, and he was awaited with much eagerness. At the last moment, however, the visit was blocked by Churchill's political opponents in cabinet, and Colonel Maurice Hankey, the Secretary of the Committee of Imperial Defence, was sent out instead. Hamilton at first found it difficult to suppress a feeling of antipathy towards this relatively junior officer who was to report directly to the cabinet at home, and it was not until Hankey had been a week or more on Imbros that the staff realized that he was anxious only to use his exceptional talents for their good.

Mackenzie records an odd scene when he was lunching one day with the generals at their mess at G.H.Q. 'The one next to me,' he says, 'was Sir Frederick Stopford, a man of great kindliness and personal charm, whose conversation at lunch left me at the end of the meal completely without hope of victory at Suvla. The reason for this apprehension was his inability to quash the new General opposite, who was one of the Brigadiers in his Army Corps. This Brigadier was holding forth almost truculently about the folly of the plan of operations drawn up by the General Staff, while Sir Frederick Stopford appeared to be trying to reassure him in a fatherly way. I looked along the table to where Aspinall and Dawnay (two of Hamilton's general staff officers) were sitting near General Braithwaite; but they were out of earshot and the dogmatic Brigadier continued unchallenged to enumerate the various military axioms which were being ignored by the Suvla plan of operations. For one thing, he vowed, most certainly he was not going to advance a single yard until all the Divisional Artillery was ashore. I longed for Sir Frederick to rebuke his disagreeable and discouraging junior; but he was deprecating, courteous, fatherly, anything except the Commander of an Army Corps which had been entrusted with a major operation that might change the whole course of the war in twenty-four hours.'

Hamilton's position at this time is difficult to understand, for by now he had broken nearly all the rules which were subsequently evolved by Field-Marshal Montgomery in the second world war for operations of this kind. He had allowed his junior commanders to criticize and change his plan, and he had never conveyed to them by word of mouth exactly what he wanted them to do. Instead of keeping the control of the battle under his own hand, his generals and brigadiers were to act on their own discretion; they were to get forward 'if possible'. In the same way Hamilton had failed to impress his will on Kitchener and the War Office; he had not wanted these new commanders, they were charming men of his own world, but they were old and they had a fatal lack of experience. Nevertheless, he had accepted them. What was wanted was young commanders with seasoned troops, but at Suvla it was the other way about.

Had Hamilton but known it there existed in his Army a man of quite exceptional ability who would have been the ideal commander for the Suvla operation. This was a brigadier-general named John Monash. Monash is something of an enigma in the first world war, for although Hamilton had noticed that he was an able officer, no one, either at Imbros or at Anzac or anywhere else, seems to have divined his peculiar talents as a leader. He was an Australian Jew, already fifty years of age, and his attainments were extraordinary: he was a Doctor of Engineering, and had also graduated in Arts and Law, in addition to being deeply read in music, in medicine and in German literature. Soldiering had been merely a hobby for Monash but for years he had been enthusiastic about it, and when he had volunteered for service at the outbreak of the war he had been made a colonel. He took a brigade ashore at Anzac in the April landing, and had since done well within the limits of that narrow front, but he had not advanced beyond the rank of brigadier.

This was the man who was soon to rise to the command of an army corps in France, and who towards the end of the war was to be considered as a possible successor to Haig as Commander-in-Chief of all the British Armies in France.

'Unfortunately,' Lloyd George wrote in his memoirs, 'the British did not bring into prominence any commander who, taking all round, was more conspicuously fitted for this post (than Haig). No doubt Monash would, if the opportunity had been given him, have risen to the height of it, but the greatness of his abilities was not brought to the attention of the cabinet in any of the Despatches. Professional soldiers could hardly be expected to advertise the fact that the greatest strategist in the Army was a civilian when the war began, and they they were being surpassed by a man who had not received any of their advantages in training and teaching. . . . Monash was . . . the most resourceful general in the whole British Army.'

But in August 1915 no one had thought of Monash in such terms as these, and indeed he had never been heard of outside his own narrow circle. In the coming battle he was confined to the role of taking one of the Anzac columns on a roundabout route up Sari Bair.

The plan itself was open to serious criticism; except for the Suvla landing it did not force the Turks to react to the British, it was the British who were reacting to the Turks. They were proposing to direct their main attack upon Chunuk Bair, the enemy's strongest point, and it was not to be one concentrated blow on a broad manageable front, but the most congested of battles in which only a few men could take part at one time, and in the most difficult country where anything and everything could go wrong. The Anzac bridgehead was perfectly safe, and the Turks never had a hope of dislodging the Allies from it. It was an ideal training ground, and the new troops coming out from the United Kingdom might very well have been put in there to hold the line while the main attack was delivered not at Chunuk Bair but at Suvla.

The Australians and New Zealanders were by now the

most aggressive fighters in the whole peninsula. They had not been heavily engaged through June and July like the British and the French at Cape Helles. They were eager for action, they wanted space and movement after all these claustrophobic months under the ground, and the Suvla landing, with a broad flanking movement round Sari Bair, was precisely the sort of adventure to which they would have responded. They knew the ground—from their perches in the bridgehead they looked down on it every day—they knew the Turks, and their commanders had all the experience of the April landing behind them.

But apparently neither Hamilton nor Birdwood ever contemplated this course, and it was left to the new soldiers who had never been to war before—who had never been abroad before—to land on the strange dark shore against a trained enemy, without knowing clearly what they had to do. And that perhaps was asking too much.

Yet when all this is said it has to be remembered that very similar errors were committed all over again in the second world war especially in the Italian campaign, and with almost painful fidelity at the time of the landing at Anzio, south of Rome, in 1944. At Gallipoli nothing was yet established, nothing was clear, not even the one principle that the campaign itself was already revealing—that everything which was done by stealth and imagination was a success, while everything that was done by means of the headlong frontal attack was foredoomed to failure. Hamilton was beset by problems that seldom became so acute in the second world war: the rub of the old Regular Army ideas against the new soldier; the preoccupation of the high command with the other front in France; the novelty of the whole conception of an amphibious operation; the hazards of maintaining morale among the troops of so many different nationalities in that distant and difficult place.

Yet despite the hesitations of the new commanders and the complications of the plan there were very good hopes of success as the first week of August ran out. The tired troops at Cape Helles were very ready to try again. At Anzac the spirit of the soldiers was high. The Fleet was more than eager; and the weather held good. Moreover, the Turks on their side were just as prone to error as the British, just as uncertain and no better equipped. Liman at this stage had no new ideas, no clear view of how he might gain the victory. He could think of nothing but to reinforce, to dig in and to hold on. Admiral von Usedom, the German commander of the defences of the Dardanelles, wrote to the Kaiser on July 30: 'How long the Fifth Army can hold the enemy is more than I can prophesy. If no ammunition comes through from Germany, it can only be a question of a short time . . . it is a matter of life and death. The opinion of the Turkish General Headquarters appears to me to incline to a hazardous optimism.'

The German Supreme Command was seriously disturbed about Liman von Sanders at this time. On July 26 they sent a message ordering him to hand over his command to Field-Marshal von der Goltz and to come home to Germany to report. Liman managed to stave off this decision, but he was forced to accept on his staff a certain Colonel von Lossow who was to keep an eye on his superior, and even take a hand in the planning of operations.

But the battle itself soon swallowed up all disagreements and doubts on either side. On August 4 Samson went out on a last reconnaissance over Suvla, and reported that no Turks were on the move there. A shell was fired into the gleaming white surface of the salt lake. This was an unauthorized act which annoyed Hamilton very much, but it did prove that men could walk and even ride a horse on the caked and salty mud. The last intelligence appreciations of the situation were issued to commanders, and some attempt was made to provide them with an idea of the kind of country they would encounter as they made their way inland; they would find water once they got to the hills, they were told, but their progress might be impeded by the thick six-foot-high scrub that was cut only by goat tracks.

Nasmith set off on his August cruise which a few days later was to bring its first result in the sinking of the battleship *Barbarossa Harradin*. And in the islands the invasion fleet assembled: the black beetles, the Isle of Man paddlesteamers, the North Sea trawlers, the yachts, the Thames tugs, the drifters, the monitors, the cruisers and destroyers.

Only bad weather or a Turkish attack could now delay or change the plans. At zero hour de Robeck was to go to Suvla in his new flagship, the light cruiser *Chatham*, but Hamilton this time elected to remain on shore at Imbros, where he was connected by submarine telephone to Cape Helles, ten miles, and Anzac, fifteen miles, away.

August 6 was a day of calm, hard, glaring sunshine, and in the afternoon when the soldiers were embarking at Imbros they could clearly hear the roar of the guns at Anzac and Cape Helles where the battle had already begun. Bright little stabbing flashes sparkled in the sky. As night fell a few minutes after seven a brilliant crimson sunset expanded along the horizon. Then it was black darkness, with no light showing in the Fleet. The island with its thousands of empty tents and its silence took on an air of terrible desolation. 'The day before the start is the worst day for a commander,' Hamilton wrote. 'The operation overhangs him as the thought of another sort of operation troubles the mind of a sick man in hospital.' He was restless, and walked down to the beach to see the 11th Division go off. The men, packed like herrings in the beetles and on the decks of the destroyers, were silent and listless: 'These new men seem subdued when I recall the blaze of enthusiasm in which the old lot started out of Mudros harbour on that April afternoon.' For a moment he debated whether or not he should have cruised round the invasion fleet in a motor launch, saying a few encouraging words to each unit as he went along, but he dismissed the idea when he remembered that the men did not know him by sight; and in any case several hours were to go by before they arrived on the beaches, and that was too long an interval for his words to survive.

He looked for Stopford and Reed, hoping that they might have done something to enthuse their soldiers, but they were nowhere to be seen; and he returned to his hut. Nothing to do but to wait.

Stopford had been lying on his valise spread out on the floor of his tent, and Colonel Aspinall found him there. The General had slipped and sprained his knee that morning and was not feeling very well. 'I want you to tell Sir Ian Hamilton,' he said, 'that I am going to do my best, and that I hope to be successful. But he must realize that if the enemy proves to be holding a strong line of continuous entrenchments I shall be unable to dislodge him till more guns are landed.' Glumly he went on to quote his chief-of-staff: 'All the teaching of the campaign in France,' he said, 'proves that continuous trenches cannot be attacked without the assistance of large numbers of howitzers.'

He rose soon afterwards, and getting aboard the *Jonquil* with Rear-Admiral Christian, steamed away.

In the darkness Hamilton strolled down to the beach

again and saw the ships moving, ghostlike and silent, to the boom across the mouth of the harbour. 'This empty harbour frightens me,' he wrote later. 'Nothing in legend is stranger or more terrible than the silent departure of this silent Army.'

Then he went back to his tent to keep a vigil with his telephones through the night.

THIRTEEN

~~~~~~

MUSTAFA KEMAL kept a record of his own activities during the campaign, and it is quite unlike anything else that has been written about Gallipoli. It is a kind of day book, half pamphlet and half military history, a mixture of the intensely egoistical and the very practical. Long arid passages about the movements of regiments are followed by outbursts of almost childish jingoism (the equivalent of the Allies' 'One of our men is worth half a dozen Turks'). At times he breaks off to moralize: 'What a fine mirror history is. . . . In great events which pass to the bosom of history how clearly do the conduct and acts of those who take an active part in these events show their moral character.' There is a strong suggestion throughout that the other commanders are wrong while he is right, and his approach to all but a few of his superior officers is at once obsequious and contemptuous. Yet he argues very closely, he always sees the battle from a fresh point of view, and he is very precise about such things as dates and place-names and the movements of troops.

There is no reason to think that this document has been edited or changed by others with an eye to the General's later career as the dictator of Turkey; the original notebook is preserved by the Historical Branch of the Turkish General Staff at Ankara, and most of it is filled with Kemal's own handwriting in the fine arabic script which he later abolished in Turkey in favour of the more practical and much less beautiful Latin alphabet. The rest of the notebook has been dictated to an assistant either on the battlefield itself or shortly afterwards.

There is one very interesting passage dealing with the period immediately before the Suvla landing. As so often happened, Kemal was involved in a dispute with his commanding officer—in this case Essad Pasha, the Corps Commander opposite Anzac. It had been decided to extend Kemal's divisional front in the north of the Anzac bridgehead so as to take in part of a ravine known as Sazlidere. Kemal at once protested that this was too much responsibility for him to undertake. He went on and on about it, writing letter after letter (which he quotes) to Corps Headquarters. Essad took the line that this was all very unimportant, but, since Kemal wished it, he would remove the area from the 19th divisional front and take it under his own command. This did not suit Kemal at all. He replied that the Sazlidere area was so important that it must be put under a strong independent command; did they not realize that it was quite possible for the enemy to advance by day up to the very foot of Sari Bair under the cover of this deep ravine? Essad answered that he was in fact establishing an independent command from Suvla to the north of Anzac, and a German officer was coming out to take charge of it. The dividing line between his and Kemal's command would be the Sazlidere ravine—or at any rate the upper part of it, since the mouth was already occupied by the enemy.

Once again Kemal protested; a dividing line between two commands, he said, was always the weakest point. The responsibility for Sazlidere must be made perfectly clear, and strong forces posted there. Essad was growing weary of the argument. 'Little valleys like this,' he wrote, 'cannot be inclusive or exclusive of either side.' However, he agreed to come down one day with his chief-of-staff to survey the position. Kemal led them to his advance headquarters on a plateau known to the British as Battleship Hill, and from there they looked down, as from an aircraft, at the coastline to the north of Anzac, the salt lake glistening in the distance by the sea, the empty bay at Suvla, the hills to the east, and in between, the flat plain reaching up to the tangle of foothills around Sazlidere at their feet. The three crests of Sari Bair—Chunuk Bair, Hill Q and Koja Chemen Tepe—with their apparently unclimbable slopes, rose up above them immediately to their right.

Kemal reports the discussion that followed in these

239

words: 'Seeing this view, the Chief-of-Staff of the Corps said, "Only raiding parties could cross this ground."

'The Corps Commander turned to me and said, "Where will the enemy come from?" Pointing with my hand in the direction of Ari Burnu, and along the whole shore as far as Suvla, I said, "From here".

' "Very well, supposing he does come from there, how will he advance?" Again pointing towards Ari Burnu, I moved my hand in a semi-circle towards Koja Chemen Tepe. "He will advance from here," I said. The Corps Commander smiled and patted my shoulder. "Don't you worry, he can't do it," he said. Seeing that it was impossible to convince him I felt it unnecessary to prolong the argument any further. I confined myself to saying, "God willing, sir, things will turn out as you expect".'

In short, Kemal had anticipated the general lines of Hamilton's attack—the landing at Suvla, the advance up Sazlidere and the neighbouring ravines to the crests of Sari Bair—and perhaps it was only human that Kemal later should have written in his journal: 'When from the 6th August onwards the enemy's plans turned out just as I expected and tried to explain, I could not imagine the feelings of those who, two months before, had insisted on not accepting my explanations. Events were to show that they had been mentally unprepared and that due to insufficient measures in the face of hostile action, they had allowed the whole situation to become critical and the nation to be exposed to very great danger.'

From the British point of view the important thing was that Kemal at this stage had no power to enforce his ideas, and while he fumed and complained on Battleship Hill all the broken ground from Sazlidere to the north-east remained virtually unoccupied by the Turks, and the Suvla plain was left to the care of only three weak battalions. However, the German officer arrived to take command of the area, a Major Willmer of the Bavarian cavalry, a tall, spare figure with a duelling scar on his cheek, and he proved to be a very capable man indeed. When the salt lake dried up in July, Willmer saw that it was no use posting his 1,800 men along the coast, since there was no hope of preventing an enemy landing there. Just two outposts were left beside the sea: one of them on a patch of rising ground known as Hill Ten, to the north of the salt lake, and the other at Lala Baba, a 200-foot hillock between the salt lake and the bay. In the event of a landing being made, these men were told to resist as long as they could, but not to get cut off: they were to retire to the hills some three miles inland where the bulk of the little force was entrenched. And there, somehow or other, Willmer hoped to hold on until help reached him from Bulair in the north.

At the end of July Willmer received the warning issued to all Turkish army commanders that an enemy offensive was to be expected at any time, and he took care to conceal his men as much as possible by day and to push on with the digging of his entrenchments by night.

On August 6 the Major went down to the coast to inspect his outpost at Lala Baba, and it was there, late in the afternoon, that he heard the tremendous barrage of guns starting up at Anzac. Shortly afterwards he received an order from Liman to send one of his battalions there. The men were put on the road, but Willmer himself remained at Lala Baba to watch the horizon for any sign of approaching enemy ships. He saw the crimson sun go down on a flat and empty sea, and then, giving orders to his men to remain in instant readiness through the night, he rode home to his headquarters in the hills. He had hardly arrived there when he had word from Lala Baba that enemy soldiers were coming ashore on the beach below them in the darkness. At once he sent off a signal to Liman asking for the return of the battalion which was on the march to Anzac. Liman refused and Willmer was now left with a force of less than 1,500 men to hold the whole area around Suvla Bay.

The night was pitch dark, and for some time the outpost at Lala Baba could not make out what was going on. Had they been able to see out to sea they would have been much more alarmed than they were, for the British fleet had carried through the first part of the plan with remarkable timing. There were three echelons: the 10,000 men from Imbros who, in three brigades, were to make the first landing, one of them inside the bay and the other two on the open beach to the south of it, and then, following on behind, the 6,000 men from Mytilene and the 4,000 from Mudros. Precisely at 9.30 p.m. the leading destroyers in line abreast came to a stop five hundred yards out from B Beach—the beach to the south of the lake—and quietly eased their anchors into the sea. The beetles and the picket boats which they had been towing were then cast off and made towards the shore.

At Lala Baba the Turks held their fire, for they could still see nothing, and in a fresh and gentle breeze the boats ran up to the beach and dropped their ramps on the sand. Within a few minutes some 7,000 men had walked ashore without getting their feet wet, and they were disturbed only by a single rifle shot which killed a sailor on the beach. As they marched inland for half a mile, two Turkish sentries rose in the darkness, fired their rifles and fled, but there was no other opposition; the invaders were in possession of an empty countryside.

But now a red flare went up from Lala Baba on their left, and the two battalions of Yorkshire soldiers who were advancing in that direction came under heavy rifle fire. This was the first time that Kitchener's new civilian army had faced the enemy, and the conditions were very difficult: they had been on their feet for seventeen hours, they could see hardly more than a yard or two ahead, and they were under orders to use only their bayonets until the day broke. A third of the men and all but three of their officers were hit, but the remainder kept trudging on until they had driven the Turks off the top of the hill and had pursued them down to the salt lake on the opposite side. It was now midnight, and the survivors looked around for the third brigade which was supposed to have landed inside the bay, at a place called A Beach, and to have kept a rendezvous with them at Lala Baba. But of these others there was nothing to be seen; and so the men sat down to wait.

The Navy had been all too well justified in their dislike of the unknown waters in the bay. In the darkness the landing craft had lost their way, and those which had not fouled hidden reefs had come ashore at least a thousand yards to the south of the place where they were intended to be. It was not until well after midnight that the first troops of this third brigade began to line up on the beach, and nobody knew quite where they were or what they were supposed to do. However, the moon came up at 2 a.m. and by that pale light one column made a dash at a hill which they imagined to be Hill Ten (and which was not), while another struggled up the slopes of Kiretch Tepe to the north, and still another sat down and waited on the beach. As day began to break at 4.30 a.m. the advance everywhere had stopped. Hill Ten had still not been attacked or even found, disorganized groups were firing raggedly at any target that happened to present itself, and the utmost confusion spread along the shore. Officers everywhere were shouting to one another for information, arguing over their orders and sending off messengers who never returned. It was not the enemy fire that defeated them, for it was not very heavy, but their own physical exhaustion, the unfamiliar maps which seemed to bear no relation to the landscape, and the absence of anyone in high authority to give a clear command.

General Hammersley had come ashore soon after midnight, and he spent the remaining hours of darkness vainly trying to find out what was going on. It was not until dawn that he realized that, far from reaching the hills, his soldiers had merely seized the two arms of the bay.

General Stopford was in somewhat easier circumstances. On the voyage across from Imbros he had confided to Admiral Christian his misgivings about the whole adventure, but his spirits rose as they approached the coast. Very little firing was to be heard on shore, and it even seemed that the landing had been made unopposed. In the very early hours of the morning the *Jonquil* dropped anchor just inside the bay. The night was warm, and the General had his mattress brought up on deck close under the bridge; and there he went to sleep. No one was sent ashore to inquire for news, no one came out to the *Jonquil* from the beach, and no message was sent to G.H.Q. at Imbros. It was not until 4 a.m. that Commander Unwin, who had been very busy through the night, came on board to urge the Admiral that the monitors should open fire to hearten the troops who were still held up in confusion on the shore.

On Imbros Hamilton and his staff were finding the absence of news almost insupportable. The General kept pacing back and forth from his hut to the signals tent, and although Anzac and Helles sent him their news, from Suvla there was not a word. The cable ship *Levant* had gone off with the invasion fleet, paying out its cable on the way, and it was arranged that the first message that was to come through would announce that the troops were ashore. There was a dial face in the signals tent at the Imbros end of the cable, and through the midnight hours the headquarters staff kept watching it. At last at 2 a.m. the needle on the dial began to move and a telegraphist spelt out the message: 'A little shelling at A has now ceased. All quiet at B.'

243

There was no signature—it was simply the signaller on board the *Levant* passing a private message to his mate at the Imbros end—but it did at least serve to reassure the Commander-in-Chief's mind. 'Now, thank God,' he wrote, 'the deadliest of the perils is past. The New Army are fairly ashore.'

It was quite true. Nearly 20,000 men had been landed and the casualties had been very light. This time Liman had been caught completely off his guard. It was also unfortunately true that at this moment all three senior British generals—Hammersley at Suvla, Stopford in the *Jonquil* and Hamilton on Imbros—were in almost total ignorance of what was really happening, and the hills which they (or Hamilton, at any rate) had so much hoped to have by dawn, were still several miles away. But even so the situation was not too dangerous; the confusing darkness of the night had gone, no Turkish reinforcements had yet arrived, and there was still time for the Suvla troops to bring help to Birdwood in his frightful struggle for Sari Bair. All depended on the dispatch with which Stopford disentangled his forces on the shore and got them moving inland.

It had been Stopford's original intention to go ashore with his headquarters on the morning of August 7, but he changed his mind when he heard that his signals unit had not yet arrived. He could better control the battle, he decided, from the decks of the *Jonquil,* and it was here, soon after daybreak, that he received a visit from Brigadier-General Hill, the commander of the 6,000 troops who had just come in from Mytilene. Hill was not the least bewildered man at Suvla that morning. For nearly a month he and his men had been incarcerated in their transports, and they might have been living on the moon for all they knew about Gallipoli. On the previous day they had received orders to move from their peaceful anchorage in Mytilene harbour. They had no idea where they were going, no plan had been given to the Brigadier, and no map had been shown to him. He was surprised therefore to wake on this hot sunny morning and find himself on a strange coast with hostile shells falling into the sea around him; and he now wished to know what he was to do.

Stopford, on the advice of Unwin, was inclined to think that Hill had better get his ships out of the shellfire in Suvla Bay and go round to the safe outer beach beyond Nibrunesi Point where he could attach himself to General

Hammersley for the time being. This would mean that the men would have to march for a mile or more under enemy fire to get back to their appointed landing-place inside the bay; still, it could not be helped. The two generals were still debating the matter when Keyes burst in upon them. Keyes had observed the hesitations and delays on the shore, and he had come across from the *Chatham* 'in a fever of resentment at these leisurely proceedings' to say that shellfire or no shellfire Hill should land his men inside the bay at once. It was decided, however, that another change of plan would cause too much confusion, and so Hill went off with his men around Nibrunesi Point. Arriving on shore his orders were instantly countermanded by Hammersley; instead of marching north towards Hill Ten he was now to march east towards a rise known as Chocolate Hill, where the Turks were still entrenched. Later on these orders were again cancelled. Still later the plans were altered again.

It was typical of much else that happened on this day. Indeed, it requires a more than average interest in the minutiae of military history to follow the marches and the counter-marches that now began, the stream of orders, each one cancelling out the last, the misunderstandings between the various headquarters, the long silences and the sudden frantic changes of front. The best part of two divisions had now come ashore, the 11th under Hammersley and the 10th under Mahon, and hardly anyone was where he was supposed to be. Companies, battalions and even whole brigades were hopelessly mixed up together, and any resolute action that did occur was usually the work of some junior commander who took affairs into his own hands on a limited front.

General Hammersley, now perched on the end of Nibrunesi Point, was feeling the heat very much, and he was further upset when a shell fell on his headquarters and killed several of his staff. Three times in the course of the morning he changed his plans, and no sooner had an order gone out than it was followed by another giving other objectives with other combinations of troops and at a later time. About 7 a.m. there was a rush for Hill Ten, which had been found at last, and the hundred odd Turks who were defending it were driven off the top. Now was the time to turn east to the hills—in particular to seize Chocolate Hill and the long spur running out into the plain from Anafarta Sagir, and then to move on to the heights of

Tekke Tepe on the ridge beyond. Instead, many of the troops went streaming north in the general direction of Kiretch Tepe, and even here the impetus soon expended itself. Here and there a brigadier or a colonel was ready enough to go forward provided someone gave him an order, but even in this there was another complication. The maps which had been issued at the last minute to the officers were marked in some instances with the Turkish names for the features on the plain. Hammersley's orders, on the other hand, used the English names for these places; and so it sometimes happened that units advanced to quite the wrong objectives. Other commanders merely succumbed to what Keyes described as 'the ghastly inertia', and refused to move anywhere until their troops were rested. The heat was very great—about ninety degrees in the shade—and it was often too much for men who had been inoculated against cholera only two days before and whose water bottles had given out. Near the shore many hundreds went down to the sea to bathe.

In the bay at Suvla the scene was hardly less disordered than on the land. Everywhere the disembarkation programme was breaking down, partly because of the hidden reefs in the sea, and partly because a sudden thunderstorm lashed up the surface water for an hour or two. Not a single gun was landed on this day, and hardly fifty mules were got ashore. But the most serious deficiency was in the water supply. The Navy had never expected that it would have to provide for two whole divisions—it was thought that the soldiers would advance inland, where it was known there were many wells. Even so the situation might have been saved had not two of the water lighters grounded far out in the bay, and had not many of the soldiers, frantic with thirst, come crowding down to the shore. They were quite desperate, their tongues blackened, their faces smeared with dust and sweat, and they simply could not wait; they had to drink. Some waded into the sea and drank the salt water, others slashed the canvas hoses through which the watership *Krini* was pumping out her tanks to the shore. The warships did what they could; one destroyer captain cut out his water tank and sent it ashore along with his canvas bath and kept both full with his pumps, and later in the day all the other vessels in the bay were ordered to follow suit. But still it was not enough.

At dawn a juncture had been made with the Anzac

bridgehead on the shore, and soon afterwards some of Birdwood's signallers ran a telephone line around to Hammersley's headquarters. In the middle of the morning a message came through on this line to say that from the heights of Anzac it had been observed that there were signs of a general retirement of the enemy on Suvla plain—carts had been seen making for the hills, guns were being moved back. Heartened perhaps by this, Hammersley got out orders for an advance which was to proceed at least as far as Chocolate Hill. But he was still only half convinced that he was not confronted by large enemy entrenchments, he was still in doubt about the position of his own forces, and so the orders which he gave were not very clear. At mid-day the attack had not started, and the brigadier who was supposed to be leading it was tramping back through the heavy sand to make sure that he understood his instructions. At last in the middle of the afternoon the advance began, but it was stopped almost at once as the General had decided on second thoughts to delay until 5.30 p.m. when he would be in a position to mount a stronger attack.

And so it goes on, hour after hour, an extraordinary scene in which 1,500 Turks with a few howitzers and not a machine-gun among them were harrying an army of 20,000 men backwards and forwards across the empty plain. The British soldiers were very inexperienced. Major Willmer remarked in a message to Liman that they marched 'bolt upright' without attempting to use the cover of the scrub, and he added, 'No energetic attacks on the enemy's part have taken place. On the contrary, the enemy is advancing timidly.' But it was not a situation which could continue indefinitely, and he begged Liman to hasten the reinforcements which were coming down from Bulair in the north.

It was dusk on August 7 when at last the British began to move across the salt lake, but they did take Chocolate Hill. They took it very bravely, considering all the hesitations and frustrations of the day, and they went on for another quarter of a mile and took Green Hill as well. They were now within a mile or two of the main heights which were the object of the whole attack, and the Turkish outposts were streaming away before them. It so happened, however, that none of the three British brigadiers who were concerned in this action came forward with the leading troops. They remained two miles in the rear. And so the troops received no further orders; instead of pursuing the

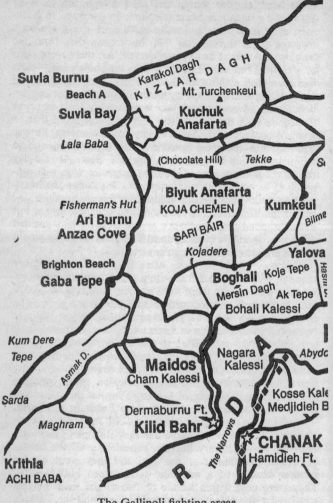

The Gallipoli fighting areas

Turks they sat down and waited. When night fell all contact with the enemy had been lost.

The chain of command had now broken down entirely. General Hammersley could not have taken any resolute decision even if he had wished to do so, for he did not know that Chocolate Hill had been captured until well after midnight, and the news about Green Hill never reached him till the following morning. Stopford continued in virtual isolation aboard the *Jonquil* all day, and G.H.Q. at Imbros was even more out of touch. Hamilton, immensely relieved that the new army had got ashore, had naturally presumed that it would advance to the hills in the first light of the morning on August 7, and the second-hand news he received from Anzac and from ships returning from Suvla did, in fact, give him the impression that all was going well. It was, then, something of a shock when Stopford's first message came in at mid-day. 'As you see,' it said, 'we have been able to advance little beyond the beach.' It hardly seemed possible. But Hamilton was reassured when he observed that the message had taken some time to reach him and dealt only with the situation as it was soon after daybreak on August 7; surely since then, he reasoned, the advance must have begun. But when no further message came in from the *Jonquil* he began to grow anxious. A little after 4 p.m. he sent off a signal to Stopford urging him to push on. To this there was no answer.

Thus at the end of the first twenty-four hours at Suvla there had been very little change; the troops were barely two miles inland and the generals were in exactly the same places—Hammersley on the beach, Stopford on the *Jonquil* and Hamilton on Imbros. The only really new factor was that the Turks, having inflicted some 1,600 casualties on the British, which was rather more than the total number of their own force, had retired and the Suvla plain was now empty.

There is something so mocking about this situation, something so wrong, that one feels that it is not explained by all the errors and mischances that had occurred: by the commander-in-chief pacing about his headquarters at Imbros when he might just as well have been asleep, by Stopford lying in bed at sea when he should have been wide awake on shore, by the landing of raw troops at night instead of experienced men at dawn, by the appointment of elderly inefficient commanders, by the excessive secrecy that had kept them so much in the dark, by the thirst and the heat and the uncharted reefs beneath the sea. In the face of so much mismanagement things were bound to go wrong, yet not so wrong as all this. Somewhere, one feels, there must be some missing factor which has not been brought to light—some element of luck neglected, some supernatural accident, some evil chain of coincidence that nobody could have anticipated. And yet it was quite unlike the April landing. One does not have the feeling that it was touch and go at Suvla, that some slight shifting of the pattern would have put things right again. There is instead a strong sense of inevitability; each event leads on quite inexorably to the next, and it cannot have mattered, one feels, whether Hamilton went to bed or not, whether Stopford got ashore or stayed aboard the *Jonquil*, whether the brigadiers marched in this or that direction—the results would have been just the same. Given this set of conditions everything was bound to continue to its fated end.

But that end was not nearly in sight as night fell on August 7. Nobody had given up hope: it was quite the other way about. A feeling of intense relief had followed the successful landing, and the generals were sure that given a little time to straighten things out they would be able to move on again.

The night was cold and absolutely still. Away to the south at Anzac the artillery was rumbling steadily, but at Suvla not a gun was fired. No attempt was made to push patrols forward either from Chocolate Hill or along Kiretch Tepe, and no contact was made with the enemy anywhere. Soon after 5 a.m. on August 8, when the blazing sun came up, the scene remained as it was on the previous evening; the plain was still empty, no sound of rifle fire was heard, and there were still no Turks on the heights of Tekke Tepe. Willmer had concentrated his men around Anafarta Sagir further to the south, certain that the real, concentrated blow of the British was about to fall on him at any moment.

Hammersley, in fact, had something of the sort in mind, and he set off early on this second morning at Suvla to consult his brigadiers. He was much discouraged, however, by what they told him; the soldiers, they said, were too tired to go on—and when the General heard nothing from Stopford he gave up the idea of making an advance .

Stopford's actions during this morning of August 8 were almost as simple: a few minutes after 7 a.m. he signalled

General Mahon on Kiretch Tepe to entrench. At 9.30 he sent a message of congratulation to his generals and at 10 he communicated his satisfaction to Hamilton. 'Consider,' he said, 'Major-General Hammersley and troops under him deserve great credit for result attained against strenuous opposition and great difficulty.' And he added, 'I must now consolidate.'

Hamilton was baffled. What on earth was happening at Suvla? Over 20,000 men had now been on shore for more than twenty-four hours, and he knew from the reports of the Naval Air Service that there was no serious opposition in front of them. Stopford seemed quite contented, but still he did not push on. It had been estimated that the Turks would take about thirty-six hours to get their reinforcements down from Bulair, and now, on the morning of August 8, there were at the most six or seven hours to go. He sent for Colonel Aspinall and told him to get over to Suvla and find out what was going on.

Aspinall got his orders shortly before 6 a.m., and he at once went down to the docks at Imbros with Colonel Hankey, but it was not until 9.30 a.m. that they managed to find a trawler to take them to the mainland. Another two hours went by before they reached Suvla Bay, and there they surveyed with astonishment the scene along the shore. It was, they reported later, like an August Bank Holiday in England. Hardly a sound disturbed the quivering summer air. Many boats were bobbing about on the gentle swell in the bay, and on the beach naked troops were bathing in hundreds and tending their cooking fires. Inland beyond the salt lake there was perfect peace. No one was in a hurry, no one seemed to be very busy, unless it was the group of soldiers who were digging a large entrenchment along the coast. 'You seem to be making yourselves snug,' Hankey said to a staff officer standing by. 'We expect to be here a long time,' was the reply.

There could be only one explanation of this cheerful atmosphere—the hills had been taken and the front was a long way off—and Aspinall and Hankey went ashore in a much happier frame of mind. Leaving Hankey on the beach, Aspinall at once struck inland in search of Stopford. He had gone only a few paces, however, when an artillery officer came running after him to say that, if he did not take care, he would find himself in front of the front line. It was only a hundred yards away.

'But where are the Turks?' Aspinall asked.

'There aren't any; but no orders have been issued for an advance and the corps commander is still aboard the *Jonquil*.'

It seemed then to Aspinall that the best thing to do was to find the headquarters of the 11th Division, and they were directed to a stretch of sand on the south side of the bay. Here in a moment they learned the full disillusioning truth. General Hammersley was lying full length on the ground with his head in his hands, and it was evident that he was still very much upset by the shelling of his headquarters and the rush of events since the landing. His chief-of-staff explained despondently that the Army was still pinned to the shore. It so happened that a message had just come in from Stopford asking them to advance, but it had stated, 'In view of want of adequate artillery support I do not want you to attack an entrenched position held in strength.' In these circumstances both Hammersley and Mahon had decided that it was perhaps wiser not to go forward until the guns *did* arrive. The troops were dead-beat, Hammersley said, they had suffered many casualties. Perhaps they might get ahead on the following day.

It was now well after noon, and Aspinall, thoroughly alarmed, set off to see Stopford aboard the *Jonquil*. The scene that followed is one of the anti-climaxes of the campaign, and it has been described by Aspinall himself in his official history:

'Arriving on board the *Jonquil,* about 3 o'clock, Aspinall found General Stopford on deck. He was in excellent spirits, and at once came forward to greet the new arrival. "Well, Aspinall," he said, "the men have done splendidly, and have been magnificent." "But they haven't reached the hills, sir," said Aspinall. "No," replied the General, "but they are ashore."

'Aspinall urged that he was sure Sir Ian would be disappointed that the high ground had not yet been occupied, and he begged him to issue orders for an immediate advance before the enemy's troops from Bulair could forestall him.

'General Stopford replied that he fully realized the importance of losing no time, but that it was impossible to move till the men had rested, and till more guns

252

were ashore. He intended to order a fresh advance next day.'

Aspinall was in a delicate position. He could not himself insist further to a senior officer, and while it was essential to get word to Hamilton immediately, he could hardly put through Stopford's signals office the highly critical message he had in mind. He solved the difficulty by making off— 'in despair' he says—to de Robeck's flagship, the *Chatham*, on the other side of the bay. There he found both Keyes and the Admiral in a similar state of tense anxiety about the delay. Keyes was furious. He himself had just been over to the *Jonquil*, and the visit, he wrote later, 'nearly drove me to open mutiny.' De Robeck had already sent a signal to Hamilton urging him to come to Suvla and now Aspinall added his word. 'Just been ashore,' his message ran, 'where I found all quiet. No rifle fire, no artillery fire, and apparently no Turks. IX Corps resting. Feel confident that golden opportunities are being lost and look upon situation as serious.'

It so happened that Hamilton did not receive either of these messages; the Admiral's went permanently astray and Aspinall's did not turn up till the following morning. But this hardly mattered, for Hamilton was on his way at last. He had waited for news with increasing impatience all through the morning. At 10 he had been momentarily reassured by Stopford's message saying that Hammersley and his men deserved much credit for their work, and he had replied, 'You and your troops have indeed done splendidly. Please tell Hammersley how much we hope from his able and rapid advance.' But soon afterwards his doubts set in again. Where was Aspinall? It was only an hour's run to Suvla and he had set off shortly after daybreak. Why were there no more messages from Stopford? Why was he consolidating? At 11 a.m. Hamilton had been unable to stand it any longer: he ordered his duty destroyer, an Italian-built Portuguese vessel called the *Arno*, to stand by to take him to the mainland. And now the evil fate of Suvla added to itself a touch that was perfectly ironic. The *Arno* was not ready. She had developed boiler trouble, her fires had been drawn, and she would not be able to sail before evening. Then another ship? The Navy was sorry but there was no other ship.

Through the heat of the day Hamilton remained there, a

253

prisoner on his island, until at last at 4.30 in the afternoon the *Triad* arrived and took him on board. An hour and a half later the yacht ran up alongside the *Chatham* in Suvla Bay, and Hamilton found de Robeck, Keyes and Aspinall waiting for him there. A few new moves had taken place during the latter part of the afternoon, but they were very largely a repetition of the morning's events, a further shuffling round in the bemused coil in which they had all been caught from the first moment of the landing. It took Hamilton only a few minutes to hear the outlines of the dismal story, and he then jumped into a fast motor-boat with Roger Keyes and Aspinall and headed across the bay for the *Jonquil*.

Stopford meanwhile had been ashore for the first time. He had intended to visit Hammersley on the beach at 5 p.m. but he had been a little worried by Aspinall's visit, and the distinct breeze of impatience that appeared to be blowing from G.H.Q., and so he had put the time forward by an hour. When he arrived on the beach he found that Hammersley was out, but the divisional staff assured him that plans were well advanced for an attack on the following day. Content with this, the General returned to the *Jonquil*. Yet another message from G.H.Q. was waiting for him there. Reconnaissance planes had been ranging over the peninsula again, and they reported there were still no signs of the enemy on Tekke Tepe. On the other hand, reinforcements of an ominous size had been seen marching down from Bulair, and they were clearly headed for Suvla Bay. Stopford sent another signal to the shore ordering a general advance on the hills, but leaving it to Hammersley to fix the time for the start. He had barely completed these arrangements when Hamilton arrived.

The interview was balanced on a thin edge of courtesy and was very brief. Where were the troops, Hamilton asked, and why weren't they in the hills? The men were exhausted, Stopford said. They must have artillery to support them. After a night's rest they would attack in the morning. Why not tonight? Well, for one thing Hammersley was all against a night attack.

'We must occupy the heights at once,' Hamilton insisted. 'It is imperative we get to Ismail Oglu Tepe and Tekke Tepe *now*.' But it was insistence in a void, an argument that no longer had any point, in this strange headquarters in the sea. It might have had a point if it had taken place

254

before the landing, had Hamilton driven it home quite ruthlessly and clearly to the generals and the brigadiers and the colonels that there was only one object before them, and that was to get inland. But he had not pressed the argument then, he had left things to Stopford's discretion, and in the intervening two days his plan had become nothing more than a vague hope hanging in the air. The colonels had told the brigadiers they could not get forward, the brigadiers had passed this on to the divisions, and now he was talking to a tired general who had foreseen it all from the beginning. Stopford had known all along that the plan would not work: you had to have guns.

Hamilton said shortly that he himself would go ashore and talk to Hammersley and the brigadiers.

'Stopford agreed,' Hamilton wrote that night in his diary. 'Nothing, he said, would please him more than if I could succeed where he had failed, and would I excuse him from accompanying me; he had not been very fit; he had just returned from a visit to the shore and he wanted to give his leg a chance. He pointed out Hammersley's headquarters about 400 yards off and said he, Hammersley, would be able to direct me to the Brigades.

'So I nipped down the *Jonquil's* ladder, tumbled into Roger Keyes' racing motor-boat and with him and Aspinall we simply shot across the water to Lala Baba. Every moment was priceless. I had not been five minutes on the *Jonquil* and in another two I was with Hammersley.

'Under the low cliffs by the sea was a small half-moon of a beach about 100 by 40 yards. At the north end of the half-moon was Hammersley. Asked to give me an idea of the situation he gave me much the same story as Stopford.'

So now they had the same argument all over again. They simply could not do it, Hammersley said, not until eight the following morning. Tomorrow was too late, Hamilton said, were there no troops whatever ready to march? They were asked only to cover two and a half miles, and there were no Turks in front of them. No, Hammersley said, there were no troops ready—unless just possibly the 32nd Brigade. 'Then tell them,' Hamilton said, 'to advance at once and dig themselves in on the crestline.'

It was now 6.30 p.m. on August 8, and the time allowed for the arrival of the enemy reinforcements had long since gone by. And yet, astonishingly, there was still no sign of any new formations gathering on the heights. Nine hours of darkness still lay before them; it was going to be a race, but surely there was time for the 32nd Brigade to gather itself together and march the two and a half miles to the top of Tekke Tepe. If they got just one battalion dug in before dawn it would be enough: the rest of the division could follow later.

Hamilton went back to the *Triad*. He did not communicate again with Stopford, and no one else bothered to inform Corps Headquarters in the *Jonquil* that by the commander-in-chief's orders the plans had been changed and the troops were on the march.

Towards midnight Hamilton walked out on to the deck. The night—this third night on the Suvla beaches—was absolutely still. Somewhere in the hills now the soldiers were creeping upward through the scrub.

FOURTEEN

AT Anzac on August 6 there was no confusion over the plans; the commanders knew exactly what they had to do. During the afternoon the Australians were to attack at Lone Pine in the south of the bridgehead, so as to give the Turks the impression that the main assault was coming from that direction, and then, after nightfall, the bulk of Birdwood's forces were to march up the ravines towards Sari Bair. They hoped to take the crest of the ridge by morning.

The charge at Lone Pine was a particularly desperate adventure, since it was to take place in broad daylight and on a narrow front of only 220 yards where the Turks could concentrate their fire. Yet the soldiers believed in the plan. They believed in it so well and were so eager to fight that guards had to be posted in the rear trenches to prevent unauthorized men from attempting to take part. This was a wise precaution, because when the fighting did begin it created a frenzy that was not far from madness, and men were to be seen offering sums of five pounds or more for the privilege of getting a place in the front line.

Through the midday hours the soldiers committed to the first assault filed quietly into the secret underground tunnel which had been dug about fifty yards in advance of the front line and parallel to it through no-man's-land. The sandbags plugging the holes from which they were to emerge were loosened, and they lay waiting there in darkness and in fearful heat, while the artillery barrage thundered over their heads. At 5.30 p.m. whistles sounded the attack along the line. It was the strangest of battles; soldiers erupting from the ground into the bright sunlight, others leaping up from the trenches behind them, and all of them with shouts and yells running forward into the scrub. They had about a hundred yards to go, and when they arrived at the Turkish line they found that the trenches had been roofed over with heavy pine logs. Some of the men dropped their rifles and started to claw these logs aside with their hands, others simply fired down through the chinks into the Turks below, others again went running on to the open communication trenches and there they sprang down to take the enemy in the rear. In the semi-darkness under the pine logs there was very little space to shoot; on both sides they fought with bayonets and sometimes without any weapons at all, kicking and struggling on the ground, trying to throttle one another with their hands.

Although in after years the action at Lone Pine was very carefully chronicled—the attacks and counter-attacks that followed one another through the day and night for a week on end—it is not really possible to comprehend what happened. All dissolves into the confused impression of a riot, of a vicious street-fight in the back alleys of a city, and the metaphor of the stirred-up ant-heap persists; it was the same frantic movement to and fro, the agitated jerking and rushing and the apparent absence of all meaning except that contained in the idea of mutual destruction. It was the kind of fighting which General Stopford could hardly have understood.

Seven Victoria Crosses were won at Lone Pine, and in the first few days' fighting alone something like 4,000 men were killed there. On this first evening, however, the important thing was that by 6 p.m. the Australians had captured the Turkish front line and were resisting every effort to turn them out. If they did not altogether deceive Essad Pasha as to the true direction of Birdwood's main attack, at least they made it impossible for him to obtain reinforcements from this part of his line. By nightfall the way was clear for the main assault on Sari Bair ridge to begin.

Mustafa Kemal made one error in his anticipation of Birdwood's plan; he did not believe that the British would ever have attempted to climb these hills by night. Yet here again the commanders were very confident. A New Zealand major named Overton had been secretly reconnoitring the ground through the latter part of July and early August, and he had organized a troop of guides who were to lead

258

the soldiers over the fantastically broken country to their objectives. They had an excellent map of the area which had been taken from the dead body of a Turkish officer after the May 19 assault. Twenty thousand men, under the command of Major-General Godley, were to be engaged, and they were divided into two columns. The first of these, made up chiefly of New Zealanders, was to advance up Sazlidere and a neighbouring ravine to the top of Chunuk Bair. The second, comprising British, Australian and Indian troops, was to march on a roundabout course to the north of the bridgehead, where it was to split into two halves for the assault of Hill Q and Koja Chemen Tepe.

The first column's offensive opened brilliantly soon after night had fallen. Faithfully at 9 p.m. the British destroyer shelled the Turks at Old Post 3 in the usual way, and at 9.30 the New Zealanders rushing alongside the searchlight beam occupied the position before the enemy could get back to it. There developed almost at once some of the most brutal fighting of the campaign along the side of Sazlidere, but the Turks, as Kemal had predicted, were not strong enough to hold. They fell back along a ridge known to the British as Rhododendron Spur,[1] and for a time the New Zealanders found themselves advancing through unoccupied country behind the enemy lines. 'It was a curious sensation,' one of their officers related later, 'to be marching along that valley in bright moonlight, far within the Turkish lines, without opposition of any kind. One Turk, who rushed out ahead of the advanced guard, I shot dead with my pistol. He was the only Turk seen that night.'

Soon after midnight, however, things began to go wrong. The guides faltered, stopped, and finally admitted they were lost. One part of the column having marched—or rather climbed and descended—all through the night found itself back at its starting point. The part which did succeed in finding its way to the top of Rhododendron Spur sat down to wait for the lost battalions, and when dawn broke the assault of the final summit of Chunuk Bair had still not begun.

But this was nothing to the difficulties in which the second column on the left found itself almost from the outset.

---

[1] Brilliant crimson oleanders, mistaken by the British for rhododendrons, were flowering there.

The men had been set to march a distance of about three and a half miles in three hours, and no doubt it might have been done if they had been on a walking expedition in peacetime, and if they had travelled in daylight with good maps and without baggage of any kind. But many of them were weakened by months of dysentery, they were heavily burdened, it was very dark and they had to fight the Turks on the way. Moreover, the guides were so confident that at the last minute they chose to take a short cut. Instead of following the easy roundabout route on the low ground to the north, they led the column into a ravine at Aghyldere, and here the Turks poured down their fire upon them. At once the whole column came to a halt, and it was not very helpful that the men had been ordered to march with unloaded rifles so as to confine their fighting to the silent bayonet. In this wilderness there was now no silence, and there was no one whom they could see to bayonet. When the commanding officer was wounded panic began to spread along the line. Some of the men, believing the opposition to be far worse than it was, started to scatter and retreat; others pressed on in broken groups into dark valleys that led nowhere, and every ridge was the beginning of another ridge beyond. They were soon exhausted. Many of the men dropped in their tracks and fell asleep, and it was difficult for the officers to harry them on since they themselves were without orders, and were bewildered by the unaccountable delays in the movement of the column. It was like a caterpillar, undulating at the centre, but without forward motion, its head and tail rooted to the ground. Daylight on August 7 found them still groping about in the ravines; and the crests of Hill Q and Koja Chemen Tepe, which they had hoped to rush at 3 a.m., were a mile or more away.

There was still one more forfeit to pay for the folly of attempting this night march. In the expectation that the Sari Bair ridge would have fallen by dawn it had been arranged that the Australian Light Horse should carry out a frontal attack just below Kemal's headquarters on Battleship Hill, so as to prevent the enemy from enfilading on that flank. The Light Horsemen were an aggressive lot, and Birdwood at one stage had even contemplated putting them back on their horses so that they could make a cavalry charge into the rear of the Turkish lines, somewhat in the manner of the Light Brigade in the Crimean campaign.

That colourful idea, however, had been dismissed, and the Light Horsemen now found themselves dismounted in the trenches below Battleship Hill. The Sari Bair ridge had not been taken but they decided to charge just the same. 'You have ten minutes to live,' one of the officers said to his men while they waited, and this proved to be very nearly accurate, for it did not take the Turks long to destroy 650 out of the 1,250 who came over the top, one wave following another, the living stumbling for a few seconds over the bodies of the dead until they too were dead. Only a handful reached the Turkish trenches and there they fired their green and red rockets as the signal for the others to come on. But there were none to follow them.

Other small attacks along the line came to no better end and an unnatural quiet began to spread along the front through the early hours of the morning of August 7. On the Turkish side the commanders had survived the surprise of the first shock of the offensive, but they had had no time as yet to re-group their men to meet the next assault. The British, like the crew of a ship which has barely weathered a bad storm in the night, were still dazed and uncertain. Those New Zealanders who had gained the crest of Rhododendron Spur looked down and saw far below them to the north-west Stopford's soldiers strolling about in the sunshine at Suvla Bay. From the lefthand Anzac column, still beleaguered in the hills, there was no sound; nor was there any movement in the direction of Battleship Hill, since the Australian attack here had failed and so many were dead. The fight at Lone Pine further to the south was still going on, but apart from this the battle had stopped. Not unnaturally the New Zealanders began to feel isolated in their high perch under Chunuk Bair—they alone seemed to have penetrated into the enemy lines, and there was no knowing whether or not they were about to be entirely cut off. There was still no sign of the other units who were expected to join them there, and the plan was now running many hours behind schedule.

Presently, however, two companies of Gurkhas who had been lost all night came straggling up the spur, and with these reinforcements the New Zealanders made a rush for the summit of Chunuk Bair in the middle of this morning of August 7. It was several hours too late. By now a German Colonel named Kannengiesser had arrived on the hilltop, and although he was wounded he roused the Turkish outpost there and they drove back the attack. This was the last heavy fighting on Anzac on August 7. The rest of the day went by while the left hand column extricated itself from the frightful muddle it had got into during the night, and nothing more could be done on Rhododendron Spur until the New Zealanders were reinforced.

General Godley now decided to reorganize his force for a new attack at dawn on August 8. Through the night five columns were assembled, and their objectives were the same as before—the three main peaks on Sari Bair. It was a confused affair, for the troops were still not properly rested or supplied—most of them had been wandering about half the night in the hopeless maze of gullies and ravines, and had not even reached the start line when the attack began. But there were two encouraging events: a British Major named Allanson, in command of a battalion of Gurkhas, found himself far out in front near the center of the line, and instead of waiting for support to reach him he elected to go on and see whether he could take Hill Q on his own initiative. He very nearly succeeded. It chanced that he struck a gap in the enemy defences, and he had actually advanced to within 300 feet of the crest before he was fired on. He then scrambled back down the cliffs in search of reinforcements, and having gathered in some British infantry managed to hoist his little force another hundred feet towards his goal: and there they perched all day on ledges and crannies in the rocks under the fire of Turkish snipers, until, at dusk, they clambered on to a better position a little higher up. It was not so much fighting as mountaineering. They were quite cut off, and at Godley's headquarters that night nothing was known about them.

The other success was on Chunuk Bair, and here too there was another inexplicable gap in the Turkish line. A Lieut.-Colonel Malone made a rush for the summit with two companies of New Zealanders, and they surprised the Turkish outpost there asleep. One does not know why it was that these exhausted Turks had not been relieved or reinforced, but it was so, and Malone and his New Zealanders contrived to dig in just below the crest. But they had very little chance of survival: there was no cover on the open hilltop, and from either side the Turks shot shells and machine-gun bullets into them all through the day. Several times the Gloucestershire regiment and others tried

262

to get through to them without success, and when night fell Malone and nearly all his men were dead.

Thus on the evening of August 8, forty-eight hours after the offensive had begun, the Allies had reached none of their main objectives. The Suvla plan, which was a good plan, had failed because the wrong commanders and soldiers had been employed, and at Anzac the best officers and men were employed upon a plan that would not work. And both attacks had been bedevilled at the outset by the difficulties of advancing through a strange country in the night. Even at Helles the battle had gone wrong, for the British there had launched their diversionary attack against Krithia at the very moment when the Turks were also massing for an assault. And so the Allies were thrown back to their own trenches with heavy casualties and apparently nothing gained.

It was the nadir of the campaign. And yet in a perverse way, when everything seemed to have gone wrong, when the vital element of surprise had been lost, a change was taking place at this instant and hope began again. It came chiefly from the commanders. Hamilton was now at Suvla, arguing, persuading, and finally insisting that the new army should march to the hills, and something of the same sort was happening at Anzac. Birdwood and Godley were a long way from abandoning their offensive. Instead they simplified it: they planned still another dawn attack on August 9, but this time they ignored Koja Chemen Tepe and aimed simply for Chunuk Bair and the narrow saddle of land connecting it to Hill Q—the point where Allanson and a little handful of survivors were still clinging to the cliffs. The main assault was entrusted to a General Baldwin, who was in command of four British battalions which had not yet taken part in the battle. At 4.30 a.m. in the first light of the morning every gun at Anzac, at sea or on the shore, was to fire at the crestline, and at 5.15 a.m. the infantry were to get up and charge.

The night again passed in comparative quiet at the front, but with much agitated movement behind the lines. General Baldwin was particularly unlucky. He was given two guides who were supposed to be reliable, but they led him and his column at first in one direction and then in another, until eventually they finished up against the blank wall of a precipice. When the guns opened up at 4.30 a.m. Baldwin was still roaming about some distance from the front, and three quarters of an hour later, when he should have been attacking, he was only beginning to march in the right direction. The rest of the line went into the assault without him, and it was a slow uncertain movement. Perhaps it ought never to have been begun with troops who were so tired and so utterly confused, perhaps Birdwood and his staff were no longer making any sense out of their maps and plans and were guided only by a dull persistence. Yet the crest was very near; so long as there was any hope they had to try again. And in fact, in the most unexpected way, their hope was justified.

Major Allanson, on his eyrie on the ridge, had made contact with the main body of the British during the night and had obtained a reinforcement of Lancashire troops for the new attack—a total of about 450 men in all. He had his orders direct from General Godley: he was to keep his head down until the bombardment was over and then he was to rush the Turkish trenches on the ridge.

'I had only fifteen minutes left,' Allanson wrote in the report he made two days later. 'The roar of the artillery preparation was enormous; the hill, which was almost perpendicular, seemed to leap underneath one. I recognized that if we flew up the hill the moment it stopped, we ought to get to the top. I put the three (Lancashire) companies into the trenches among my men, and said that the moment they saw me go forward carrying a red flag, everyone was to start. I had my watch out, 5.15. I never saw such artillery preparation; the trenches were being torn to pieces; the accuracy was marvellous, as we were only just below. At 5.18 it had not stopped, and I wondered if my watch was wrong. 5.20 silence. I waited three minutes to be certain, great as the risk was. Then off we dashed, all hand in hand, a most perfect advance, and a wonderful sight. . . . At the top we met the Turks; Le Marchand was down, a bayonet through the heart. I got one through the leg, and then for about what appeared to be ten minutes, we fought hand to hand, we bit and fisted, and used rifles and pistols as clubs; and then the Turks turned and fled, and I felt a very proud man; the key of the whole peninsula was ours, and our losses had not been so very great for such a result. Below I saw the straits, motors and wheeled transport on the roads leading to Achi Baba. As I looked round I saw that we were not being supported, and thought I could help best by going after those who had retreated in

264

front of us. We dashed down towards Maidos, but had only got about 100 feet down when suddenly our own Navy put six twelve-inch monitor shells into us, and all was terrible confusion. It was a deplorable disaster; we were obviously mistaken for Turks, and we had to get back. It was an appalling sight: the first hit a Gurkha in the face: the place was a mass of blood and limbs and screams, and we all flew back to the summit and to our old position just below. I remained on the crest with about fifteen men; it was a wonderful view; below were the straits, reinforcements coming over from the Asia Minor side, motor-cars flying. We commanded Kilid Bahr, and the rear of Achi Baba and the communications to all their Army there.'

There is some doubt about the shells that fell on Allanson. The Navy deny that they were theirs, and even those soldiers who, from just below, were observers of the skirmish, were not quite certain what had happened. They saw that Allanson, on reaching the summit, had caught the Turks in the open as they were running back to their trenches after the bombardment. They saw the hand-to-hand fighting with the bayonet, and at the end of it they saw the excited and triumphant figures of the Gurkhas and the British waving on the skyline.[1] Then as they disappeared over the other side the thunderclap occurred, but it was impossible to know the direction from which the shells had come or who had fired them.

Yet the incident was not absolutely disastrous. Allanson was still on the top, and although wounded was prepared to hold on there until reinforcements arrived. And it was indeed a wonderful view, the best that any Allied soldier had ever had on Gallipoli. After three and a half months of the bitterest fighting the Turks were now displaced from the heights, and in effect their army was cut in half. 'Koja Chemen Tepe not yet,' Hamilton wrote in his diary. 'But Chunuk Bair will do: with that, we win.'

Liman von Sanders had had an exasperating time during these first three days of the battle. He was at Gallipoli town on the evening of August 6 when he first heard of the break-

---

[1] Field Marshal Sir William Slim, who subsequently became Governor-General of Australia, was one of the few young officers who, though severely wounded, survived the assault.

out from Anzac and the Suvla landing, and he seems to have appreciated very rapidly that his expectations had been wrong—that the Allies had no intention of landing either at Bulair or in Asia, and were in fact putting their main attack into the centre of the peninsula itself. The Bulair group, consisting of the 7th and the 12th Turkish divisions under Ahmed Feizi Bey, was standing by in reserve at the neck of the peninsula, and he ordered it to get ready to move. At the same time two of the divisions in Asia were told to come up to Chanak so that they could cross to Gallipoli in boats. Still another division was instructed to move round to the north of the Anzac bridgehead where the attack appeared to be growing more and more menacing.

Feizi Bey had been ill, and he was asleep in bed when he was woken at a quarter to two in the morning on August 7 with an order to march his two divisions south with all speed to Suvla. Soon after daylight the first battalions were on the road—they had a distance of some thirty-five miles to go—and Feizi Bey went on ahead by car to reconnoitre the position at the front. Towards two in the afternoon he found Liman at the village of Yalova, just north of the Narrows, and a conference was held around a small table at the local police station. It was apparent by now that a major landing had taken place at Suvla, and that Willmer with his three battalions could not be expected to hold out much longer. How long would it be before the Saros group arrived? Feizi Bey was anxious to please and he committed the error of saying not what he knew to be true but what he believed Liman wanted to hear. The soldiers, he said, were making a double march; they would arrive before the end of the afternoon. Liman was much surprised and pleased at this, and at once ordered that an attack should be made on Suvla at dawn on the following day.

After the conference Feizi Bey abandoned his car and set off on horseback into the hills. Sunset found him at Willmer's headquarters on the heights above the Suvla plain, and it was there that he learned that he had been much too optimistic: his troops were still on the road a long way to the north. However, he continued to hope that he would be able to give battle in the morning, and he sat up all night with his staff drawing up his plans.

Before daybreak on August 8 Liman rode out towards

the Suvla plain to watch the attack, and was a good deal annoyed to find that nothing whatever was happening. No soldiers had reached the startline, and except for the British clustering around the Suvla beaches there was no sign of movement anywhere. After an hour or two a staff officer turned up and explained that there had been a delay—the Bulair troops could not be expected for several hours. Liman curtly ordered the attack to be put in at sunset and went off to see what was happening at Anzac.

At 2 p.m. Feizi Bey had a conference with his staff, and they agreed that it was now too late for anything to be done that day; the men were exhausted after their long march, many had still not arrived, and to attack across exposed ground with the setting sun shining in their eyes would mean certain disaster. The battle was put off until dawn on the following day, August 9.

Liman was extremely impatient when he heard this news. He said over the telephone that the situation had become very serious, and that it was absolutely essential that the Saros group should attack that night. Willmer's small forces might crack at any moment and the British would gain the heights. Feizi Bey replied he would do what he could but he was back on the telephone to Liman again a little later. An immediate attack, he said, was quite impossible. His generals were against it and so were his staff. The men had been without sleep for two nights, they were short of guns and supplies of every kind. They were without water. Tomorrow morning was the very earliest moment that a move could be made.

It was absurdly like the scene that was being played out at this instant just a few miles away on the Suvla coast between Hamilton and Stopford. Feizi's arguments were precisely Stopford's, and there was nothing that Hamilton was saying that Liman left unsaid. One has a glimpse of a strange pattern of enemies here. Had the circumstances permitted it, General Stopford and Feizi Bey might have found much to commune with together, for Stopford too had not enjoyed his harrying from G.H.Q. nor Hamilton's direct interference in the battle. It even seems possible that Hamilton and Liman might have felt themselves closer to each other than to their reluctant generals, for they had a common emotion of frustration and impotence; each thought he was being baulked, not by bad luck or any fault in his plans, but by the incompetence of his corps commander.

Yet on balance Liman's situation was worse than Hamilton's—even much worse. Hamilton at least had his men on the spot, and at that moment was getting out orders for them to advance to the vital ridge at Tekke Tepe. At Anzac Birdwood was preparing still another onslaught on Sari Bair, and Allanson and the New Zealanders at the spearhead were getting ready for their final rush to the summit. The Turks on Chunuk Bair were in a more critical position than anyone on the British side had guessed. Their casualties had been appalling: one after another the senior officers had been killed or wounded, and they had been forced to put a certain Lieut.-Colonel Potrih in command. He can hardly have been a really useful commander, for he was the Director of Railways at Constantinople, and it was only by chance that he was visiting the front at this moment. Then too, in the course of the fighting the battalions had become scarcely less mixed up than the British, and their battle order was now chaotic. A stream of agitated messages was coming in from the junior officers in the line. 'An attack has been ordered on Chunuk Bair,' one message ran. 'To whom should I give this order? I am looking for the battalion commanders but I cannot find them. Everything is in a muddle.' And again: 'I have received no information about what is going on. All the officers are killed and wounded. I do not even know the name of the place where I am. I cannot see anything by observation. I request in the name of the safety of the nation that an officer be appointed who knows the area well.' And still again—'At dawn some troops withdrew from Sahinsirt towards Chunuk Bair and they are digging in on Chunuk Bair but it is not known whether they are friends or enemies.'

These were the men upon whom Allanson was preparing to rush at first light in the morning.

At Helles too things had suddenly become very sinister for the Turks. Although the British did not know it, their holding attack had extended the Turkish defence to the edge of its endurance, and the German chief-of-staff there had lost his nerve. He had sent a signal to Liman urging that the whole tip of the peninsula should be abandoned— that the troops there should be evacuated across the Dardanelles to Asia 'while there is still time to extricate them'.

But Liman's methods were a good deal more ruthless than those of the British Commander-in-Chief, and in this triple crisis he acted very promptly. He removed the German chief-of-staff from his post at Cape Helles, and instructed the commanding general there that in no circumstances whatever was a single yard of ground to be given up. As for the unfortunate Feizi Bey, who had failed to make his attack at Suvla, he was dismissed out of hand. He was woken out of his sleep at 11 p.m. that night and bundled off to Constantinople. A new command was created embracing the whole battle area from Chunuk Bair to Suvla, and it was given to Mustafa Kemal.

In his account of the campaign Liman gives no explanation of why his choice fell on Kemal. He simply says, 'That evening I gave command of all the troops in the Anafarta section to Colonel Mustafa Kemal . . . I had full confidence in his energy.' Yet it was a surprising appointment to make. One can only conclude that Liman had long since divined Kemal's abilities, but had been prevented by Enver from promoting him. But now in this extreme crisis he could afford to ignore Enver.

Kemal had been in the heaviest of the fighting on the Anzac front from the beginning. His 19th Division had met the first shock of the New Zealand advance; it had demolished the Australian Light Horse on August 7 and it had been fighting night and day ever since. In Kemal's view the Turkish position had, by then, become 'extremely delicate', and he told Liman's chief-of-staff so over the telephone on August 8. Unless something was quickly done to straighten out the tangle on Chunuk Bair, he said, they might be forced to evacuate the whole ridge. A unified command on the front was essential. 'There is no other course,' he went on, 'but to put all the available troops under my command.'

Liman's chief-of-staff at that stage had no notion that Kemal, who was always a troublesome figure at headquarters, was about to be promoted, and he permitted himself to say ironically, 'Won't that be too many troops?'

'It will be too few,' Kemal replied.

So now, after he had been awake for two nights at Anzac and continually in the front line, Kemal suddenly found himself in charge of the battle. He seems to have been not at all dismayed. Having calmly given orders to his successor in command of the 19th Division on Battleship Hill, he got on his horse and rode across the dark hills to Suvla. One has a vivid picture of him on this solitary midnight ride. Physically he was quite worn out, and his divisional doctor was giving him doses to keep him going. He had grown very thin, his eyes were bloodshot, his voice grating with fatigue, and the battle had brought him to a state of nervous tension which was perhaps not far from fanaticism, except that it was fanaticism of a cold and calculating kind.

With his doctor and an A.D.C. following on behind, he turned up at Willmer's headquarters in the Suvla hills soon after midnight, and spent the next two hours making himself familiar with the front. No one was able to tell him very much about the movements of the British, but he decided to make a general attack along the whole line from Tekke Tepe to the Sari Bair ridge in the morning. The Bulair force had now arrived, and at 4 a.m. orders were sent out to the commanders telling them to be ready to start in half an hour; they were to advance directly to the heights and then charge down into the Suvla plain on the other side. As dawn was about to break the Tekke Tepe ridge was still empty. The British 32nd Brigade had not got under way so promptly as Hamilton had hoped on the previous night. Seven hours had gone by while the men groped about in the thick scrub, constantly losing themselves in the winding goat tracks, and it was not until 3.30 a.m. that the brigade was assembled below the summit. At 4 a.m. it advanced at last, and it was just half an hour too late; as the men in the leading company went forward the Turks burst over the rise above them. It was a tumultuous charge, and it annihilated the British. Within a few minutes all their officers were killed, battalion and brigade headquarters were over-run, and men were scattering everywhere in wild disorder. In the intense heat of the machine-gun fire the scrub burst into flames, and the soldiers who had secreted themselves there came bolting into the open like rabbits, with the smoke and flames billowing out behind them. At sunrise Hamilton, watching from the deck of the *Triad*, was presented with an awful sight. His men were streaming back across the plain in thousands, and at 6 a.m., only an hour and a half after the battle had begun, there seemed to be a general collapse. Not only were the hills lost, but some of the soldiers in their headlong retreat did not stop until they reached the salt lake and the sea. 'My heart has grown tough amidst the struggles of the peninsula,' he wrote in his diary that night, 'but the misery of this scene wellnigh broke it. . . . Words are no use.'

Another two hours went by before the Turkish fire slackened and the British began to rally themselves on a line across the centre of the plain. Hamilton then went ashore to look for Stopford, who had landed overnight at a place called Ghazi Baba, close to the extreme tip of the northern arm of the bay. 'We found Stopford,' he says, 'about four or five hundred yards to the east of Ghazi Baba, busy with part of a Field Company of engineers supervising the building of some splinterproof headquarters huts for himself and his staff. He was absorbed in the work, and he said it would be well to make a thorough good job of the dug-outs as we should probably be here for a very long time. . . . As to this morning's hold-up, Stopford took it very philosophically.'

And still the polite façade between the two men did not fail. Since headquarters was without news of the left flank on Kiretch Tepe Hamilton suggested that it might be a good thing if he went off on a reconnaissance in that direction. Stopford agreed, but thought that he himself had better stay at headquarters to deal with the messages coming in. Upon this Hamilton set off with an A.D.C. on a long walk towards the hills and the Corps Commander returned to the building of his huts.

Later that day Stopford sent out a message to one of his divisional generals congratulating him on his stand. 'Do not try any more today,' he added, 'unless the enemy gives you a favourable chance.'

Kemal had watched the battle from a hilltop behind the front line, and by midday he was satisfied that he had nothing more to fear from the British on the Suvla front. But by now alarming messages had reached him from Sari Bair: Allanson had gained the ridge and the centre of crisis had obviously shifted there. At 3 p.m. Kemal went off on horseback through the blazing heat, and having called in on Liman's headquarters on the way, reached Chunuk Bair just as the evening light was failing. The situation there had grown worse. Allanson and his men had been withdrawn, but other British troops had taken up their positions

271

on the hill; a fresh Turkish regiment which was due to come up from Helles had not arrived, and the troops in the line were to some extent demoralized by the British artillery fire and the continuing strain of the battle. Kemal, who was now spending his fourth night on his feet, at once ordered an attack for four-thirty on the following morning, August 10. His staff protested that the men were incapable of further effort, but Kemal merely repeated his order and went off on a personal reconnaissance along the front.

It was the last gasp of the battle, the final spasm that was to decide the issue one way or another. On both sides the men had been fighting for three days and nights without sleep, and with very little water or food. The trenches behind them were choked with dead and wounded, and most of those who were still living looked out on their hideous surroundings through a fog of exhaustion. They lay on the ground, they waited, and they responded to their orders like robots with dull mechanical movements. They were ready enough to go on fighting, but some of them hardly knew what they were doing, and the end of the nightmare in which they were living was now becoming more important to them than the idea of victory. It had been so hot through the day that water had begun to seem like the one last luxury in the world, more urgent even than sleep, and when water mules went by men ran forward to lick the moisture off the canvas buckets.

On Chunuk Bair the trenches were barely thirty yards apart, and Kemal got two regiments into his front line very quietly through the night. All depended on whether or not the British guns fired on this mass of closely-packed men before they could charge with the light of the morning sun behind them.

When there were still a few minutes to go before daybreak Kemal crept out into no-man's-land and softly called out a few last words of encouragement to his men as he crawled along. 'Don't hurry. Let me go first. Wait until you see me raise my whip and then all rush forward together.'

At four-thirty he stood up between the opposing trenches. A bullet smashed his wrist watch but he raised his whip and walked towards the British line. Four hours later not an Allied soldier remained on Sari Bair.

It had been a fiercer charge than the one at Suvla, more

compact and much more desperate, and most of the Turks who took part in it were obliterated by the British artillery on the open slopes. But they managed to win back their lost trenches, and by midday on August 10 not a single height of any importance at Suvla or Anzac was in British hands. At Cape Helles the battle subsided to a fitful end.

FIFTEEN

~~~~~~

'BRUTUS: *Art thou anything?*
Art thou some god, some angel, or some
*   devil,*
That mak'st my blood cold, and my hair
*   to stare?*
Speak to me what thou art.
GHOST: *Thy evil spirit, Brutus.'*
JULIUS CAESAR, Act IV, Scene 3.

THE Suvla-Anzac battles dragged on until the last week in August and, in the way of things at Gallipoli, there were at least two moments when just possibly the British might have broken through. On August 15, Irish troops thrust along the Kiretch Tepe ridge where the main enemy ammunition dump happened to be established. Liman regarded this attack as very dangerous. 'If,' he wrote, 'on August 15 and 16 the British had taken the Kiretch Tepe they would have outflanked the entire Fifth Army and final success might have fallen to them.'

But the British had no such great objects in view. The attack was no more than a chance afterthought of Stopford's, and the men were so ill-provided with ammunition that they were reduced at one stage to throwing rocks and stones at the Turks; and so in a day or two it petered out.

Then on August 21 Hamilton delivered a major assault on Scimitar Hill and Hill 60 on the south-east of the Suvla plain, and the 29th Division was brought round from Cape Helles to lead it. The soldiers fought in an unseasonable fog which obscured the hills from the British artillery at

274

the opening of the battle, and as the day went on scrub fires broke out, filling the air with acrid smoke. In terms of numbers of men engaged this was the greatest battle fought in the Gallipoli campaign, and the last Turkish reserves were used up in bringing the Allies to a halt at nightfall. Yet in reality the issue had been decided on August 10, when Kemal recaptured the heights of Tekke Tepe and Chunuk Bair, and these later engagements were merely a restatement of the fact that when surprise was lost so too was the battle. There were no serious alterations in the front line.

Stopford continued adamant for inaction and entrenchment to the end. He protested in a series of messages to G.H.Q. that his New Army troops had let him down, that he was still without sufficient water and guns. On August 13, when the full bitterness of his failure was becoming apparent, Hamilton asked himself, 'Ought I to have resigned sooner than allow generals old and yet inexperienced to be foisted on me?' But he still took no action about Stopford, and it was Kitchener who extricated him from the skein of chivalry in which he was enmeshed. 'If you deem it necessary to replace Stopford, Mahon and Hammersley,' Kitchener cabled on August 14, 'have you any competent generals to take their place? From your report I think Stopford ought to come home.' A few hours later the Field Marshal cabled again, saying that General Byng, one of the men for whom Hamilton had pleaded in vain before the offensive began, was now to come out to Gallipoli from France. And he added, 'I hope Stopford has been relieved by you already.'

Next day Hamilton sent for General de Lisle, the commander of the 29th Division, and told him to take over from Stopford at Suvla. General Mahon of the 10th Division was senior to de Lisle, and Hamilton wrote him a tactful note asking him to accept de Lisle's orders until Byng arrived. But Mahon would have none of this. 'I respectfully decline,' he replied, 'to waive my seniority and to serve under the officer you mention. Please let me know to whom I am to hand over the command of the Division.' He was sent to cool off on the island of Lemnos, and the other elderly generals were dispatched with less ceremony; one of them who came to Hamilton and frankly admitted that he was not competent was found a job at the base, another was returned to England with Stopford, and on August 23

275

Hammersley was taken off the peninsula in a state of collapse.

They were all angry, disillusioned and exhausted. 'An ugly dream came to me last night,' Hamilton wrote. '. . . I was being drowned, held violently under the Hellespont. The grip of a hand was still on my throat, the waters were closing over my head as I broke away and found myself wide awake. I was trembling and carried back with me into the realms of consciousness an idea that some uncanny visitor had entered my tent . . . never have I suffered from so fearful a dream. For hours afterwards I was haunted by the thought that the Dardanelles were fatal: that something sinister was afoot: that we, all of us, were predoomed.'

For others, matters had already gone beyond dreams and Philippian visions; some 45,000 Allied soldiers had fallen in these August battles, and the hospital services which had never been organized to deal with such an avalanche of wounded were for a few days in almost as bad a state as anything which Florence Nightingale had found at the Crimea. Even private yachts which had turned up from England were pressed into service as hospital ships. But it was the collapse of the Army's hopes which was the demoralizing thing. When all was over the gains amounted, in General Godley's phrase, to 'five hundred acres of bad grazing ground'; they had enlarged their hold on the peninsula to about eight square miles, perhaps a little less. Now, with Suvla added to their responsibilities, they had 'three sieges to contend with instead of two'.

A dull, implacable ennui began to settle on the Allied Army. It was not exactly hopelessness, nor cynicism, it was an absence of purpose in their lives, a mechanical focusing down of their minds on to the simplest and the nearest things, the next meal, the last mail from home. The 'awful, horrible, lethargic flies' persisted, and the high dry wind of the early autumn sent the dust billowing through the air. Once more the soldiers began to report sick. Many of them were so weak with dysentery they moved at no faster pace than a crawl, and on the Anzac sector in particular it was noticed that the former *panache* had gone; the men looked old and drawn, and with any exertion quickly lost their breath. They were sent in brigades to rest camps on Imbros and Lemnos, but they did not recover; they came back into the line again looking very much as though they

276

had never been away. The Indian soldiers, with their simple vegetable diet, stood the heat very well, but the others continued with their bully beef and they hated it. Within a few weeks 800 sick men were being evacuated from the peninsula every day, and it was one more sign of the aimless strain with which they were suffering life rather than living it that the horses which before had been indifferent to shellfire now screamed and trembled at the report of a distant gun.

Hamilton began a weary struggle to obtain reinforcements from Egypt, where a garrison of 70,000 men was immobilized, but General Maxwell, the commander there, was very reluctant. He was much concerned, he said, over the movements of the Senoussi tribesmen in the Libyan desert: they might attack at any moment. He could release no troops. Hamilton persisted and got the War Office to agree to the dispatch of two battalions. 'That was yesterday,' he wrote in his diary. 'But the Senoussi must have heard of it at once, for Maxwell forthwith cables, "The attitude of the Senoussi is distinctly dangerous, and his people have been latterly executing night manœuvres round our post at Sollum" . . . I have renounced the two battalions with apologies, and now I daresay the Senoussi will retire from his night manœuvres round Sollum and resume his old strategic position up Maxwell's sleeve.' Hamilton, too, was becoming bitter.

The Turks did not attack. Half their entire army was now in the peninsula, but they too had suffered heavily in August, and were numbed by the same lethargy and weariness. It was the spent atmosphere of convalescence—perhaps hardly as yet convalescence—which had followed the assault on Anzac in May and all the other major battles. For the time being they had had enough of mass killing. Once more gifts of food and cigarettes were thrown back and forth between the trenches, and the war ceased to be a matter of rage, of pitched battle in the open, but of individual professional skill. They sniped. They dug tunnels under each other's lines and exploded mines in them. They made small raids and feints.

In many ways the men in the opposing trenches must have felt mentally and emotionally closer to one another than to the shadowy figures of the commanding generals and the politicians in the rear. Like poverty, the extreme danger and hardship of the trenches reduced them all,

British and Turks alike, to a bare level of existence, and they were set apart from the rest of the world. They may have hated it, but it drew them together, and now more than ever they had for one another the friendly cruelty of the very poor. This was an exact and prescribed arena, and until they were released from it and made safe and comfortable again they were hardly likely to know much about the propaganda animosities and the vicious fears of those who, being behind the lines, endured the war only at second-hand. For the moment the shared misery of dysentery, of flies, of dirt and lice was all.

Herbert records a curious instance of this detached and clinical attitude in the trenches. 'The fact is,' a Turkish prisoner said one day, 'you are just a bit above our trenches. If you could only get your fire rather lower you will be right into them, and here exactly is the dugout of our captain, Risa Kiazim Bey, a poor, good man. You miss him all the time. If you will take a line on that pine tree you will get him.'

Sometimes the Turks would parley with Herbert across the front lines, but they resented as a rule being cajoled by deserters who had gone over to the British. Once for a few minutes they listened in silence and then a voice replied: 'There are still Turks here and sons of Turks. Who are you? A prisoner? Then go away and don't talk.'

The end of Ramadan, the Moslem period of fasting, came, and it was expected that the Turks might celebrate it with a new attack. But nothing happened. Instead, the Turkish soldiers made what shift they could to hold a feast in the trenches, and the British at some places sent them gifts.

By September it was already growing cold at night. A strong west wind would drive the sea into the salt lake at Suvla and hold it there until, after a few hours, the water drained out again. Once or twice there were sharp showers of rain accompanied by vivid lightning, and then on October 8 a gale blew up. It was an ominous warning for the British. At Suvla some of the provisioning barges broke loose and carried away ninety feet of the pier; and there was other damage to the improvised wharves at Anzac. 'Both sides,' Herbert wrote, 'sat down grimly to wait for the winter.'

The Allies were waiting for something else as well, and it was even more serious than the winter. What was to become of them? Were they to attack again or stay where they were? *Could* they stay if Bulgaria came into the war against the Allies? If that happened—and it seemed quite likely now that the Suvla offensive had failed—Germany would have a through railway to Turkey. New guns and ammunition, perhaps even German and Bulgarian troops, could be brought down to the peninsula. Where were the reinforcements to meet them? And whether they were reinforced or not, how was the Navy to keep supplying the peninsula in heavy seas?

The soldiers in the ranks were aware that their fate was being decided in London and Paris, and they discussed the matter interminably in their dugouts. But there was never any definite news. They simply waited.

Hamilton knew what was going on in London, but it was so secret, so sensational and it so often blew hot and cold from week to week that he was not even able to confide in his corps commanders. In August he admitted to Kitchener that he had failed and could do no more unless he was reinforced again: and he needed another 95,000 men. Kitchener in reply said, in effect, that Gallipoli had been given its chance and lost it. The War Cabinet was now turning its mind back to France, and he had agreed to support Joffre in a vast offensive on the western front in September. Seventy French and British divisions were to be employed, and this meant that apart from normal replacements nothing more could be done for Gallipoli at the moment.

Then on September 2 a message arrived at Imbros saying that everything was changed. The French had suddenly and quite unpredictably come forward with an offer to send out a new army to the Dardanelles under the command of General Sarrail. Four French divisions were to be embarked at Marseilles to join the two already at Cape Helles, and they were to be landed on the Asiatic side. The British government would replace the French taken from Cape Helles with two fresh divisions of their own. Hamilton could scarcely believe it when he read the cable. 'From bankrupt to millionaire in twenty-four hours,' he wrote. 'The enormous spin of fortune's wheel makes me giddy.' Now they were bound to get through; the Turks had had the go knocked out of them already and this new attack in Asia would be the finish. He himself would offer to serve under Sarrail if that would help to buttress this wonderful piece of news.

The appointment of Sarrail was a devious affair with roots reaching back as far as the Dreyfus case. Sarrail, a Radical-Socialist, an anti-cleric, had been relieved of his command at Verdun by Joffre, but he was politically strong enough to force the French government to find him another appointment. And so he was to have this new independent command in the Near East. Joffre was not in a position to block the appointment, but he could delay and weaken it, and this he was already doing by the time Hamilton got his cable. The four French divisions, he insisted, were not to go to the Dardanelles until after the September offensive had been fought on the western front.

Hamilton got this news on September 14. The earliest date on which the new soldiers could arrive, Kitchener now told him, was mid-November. 'Postponed!' the entry runs in Hamilton's diary. 'The word is like a knell.' There was worse to follow.

In the last week of September Bulgaria mobilized, and it was apparent that within a matter of days she would be marching with the Germans and Austrians against Serbia. There was only one way of bringing help to the Serbians, and that was by attacking Bulgaria through Greece. But the Greek government was now insisting that if she was to enter the war she must be supported by an Allied force at Salonika. There was not much time. Kitchener and Joffre agreed that two divisions, one French and the other British, must be sent from Gallipoli to Salonika at once. If necessary Hamilton would have to abandon Suvla and again confine himself to the bridgeheads at Anzac and Cape Helles.

This blow fell on Imbros on September 26, and Hamilton forced himself to take it philosophically. He wrote in his diary early in October, 'At whose door will history leave the blame for the helpless, hopeless fix we are left in—rotting with disease and told to take it easy.' But he loyally sent off the two divisions to Salonika and fitted them out as well as he could before they left.

By now, however, events had come to a crisis where two divisions could make little difference one way or another. Joffre's offensive in the west failed with the loss of a quarter of a million men. Then on October 9 the Germans and Austrians fell on Belgrade, while on the following day the Bulgarians attacked Serbia from the east. The Allies' force at Salonika was too small, too disorganized and too far away to do anything but to look on helplessly. And it was one more galling twist that the removal of the two divisions from Gallipoli had precisely the reverse effect on Greece to the one anticipated. Seeing Hamilton's army reduced like this, King Constantine at once made up his mind that the Allies were about to abandon Gallipoli. He dismissed his anti-German Prime Minister, Venizelos, and decided upon a neutrality which, if not actively hostile to the Allies, was at least not helpful.

There was but one ray of hope for Gallipoli in all this. Keyes wanted the Fleet to assault the Narrows again. He had argued for it after the August battles had failed, he argued all through September, and with a new ally—Admiral Wemyss, the Commander-in-Chief at Lemnos—he was still arguing in October. De Robeck was still opposed but he allowed Keyes to draw up a new plan and propound it to a group of senior admirals at the Dardanelles. They were caught again in the old half-emotional dilemma. They felt deeply about the losses of the Army, they wanted to attack, and they again half believed that in the end the Admiralty would order them to do so. But still they could not clearly see how it was to be done. Eventually a compromise was decided upon: Keyes was to go to London and put the matter personally to the Admiralty and the War Cabinet.

But this for the moment was a side-issue, a single current moving against a turning tide. After the September offensive Joffre still withheld the four divisions earmarked for the Dardanelles, and the longer he delayed the more French opinion began to swing against the Asiatic landing altogether. With Serbia falling, Salonika appeared to be the more crucial strategic point for a new offensive. In London, too, Lloyd George and Carson,[1] the Attorney-General, were openly pushing their campaign against Kitchener, and the issue was rapidly narrowing down to a simple alternative: Salonika or Gallipoli, which was it to be? Hamilton's army was now down to half its strength and the campaign was at a stalemate. Was it really worth while throwing good money after bad?

---

[1] Carson resigned soon afterwards over the failure of the Government to send adequate help to Serbia. 'The Dardanelles operations,' he told the House of Commons, 'hang like a millstone round our necks, and have brought upon us the most vast disaster that has happened in the course of the war.'

On October 11 Kitchener felt bound to acknowledge the pressure of these questions. He cabled Hamilton, 'What is your estimate of the probable losses which would be entailed to your force if the evacuation of the Gallipoli Peninsula was decided upon and carried out in the most careful manner? No decision has been arrived at yet on this question of evacuation, but I feel I ought to have your views.'

When he read this Hamilton burst out, 'If they do this they make the Dardanelles into the bloodiest tragedy of the world . . . I won't touch it.' Could they not understand that the Turks were worn out, that the Allied soldiers were reviving now in the cooler weather, that they had only to be supported at Gallipoli and they would get through? And what if a gale came up half way through the evacuation? It might cause a disaster only equalled in history by that of the Athenians at Syracuse.

The headquarters at Imbros was not the best of places in which to take calm decisions. Hamilton was suffering miserably from dysentery, and German aircraft had begun to raid the island. On this very day a quiverful of iron spikes had come rattling down about the General's head.

In the morning, however, he sent off a sober reply. They must reckon on the loss of half the men, and all their guns and stores, he said. 'One quarter would probably get off quite easily, then the trouble would begin. We might be very lucky and lose considerably less than I have estimated. On the other hand, with all these raw troops at Suvla and all these Senegalese at Cape Helles, we might have a veritable catastrophe.'

Privately Hamilton believed that the losses would be less than half—between 35 and 45 per cent. was his estimate—but his staff were in favour of the higher figure, and he adopted it to make his opposition to the evacuation absolutely clear. But there was more in Kitchener's query than a balancing of estimates about evacuation: the whole question of Hamilton's command was involved. Already there had been rumblings. On October 4 Kitchener had sent a private cable to Hamilton warning him that there had been a 'flow of unofficial reports from Gallipoli' adversely criticizing G.H.Q. at Imbros. Should they not make some changes, Kitchener suggested. Perhaps Braithwaite should come home.

Hamilton had indignantly refused. But it was clear now that he himself and everyone on Imbros were under fire.

Then on October 11, the same day that Kitchener had sent his cable about evacuation, the Dardanelles Committee approached the matter in an oblique but very definite way. They decided that reinforcements should be dispatched to the Near East, but they were not to go directly to Gallipoli; they were to be held in Egypt while a senior general, Haig or Kitchener himself—someone at any rate who was of Hamilton's rank—went out and decided between Gallipoli and Salonika.

The truth was that Hamilton was diminishing fast in everybody's estimation. He was the general who always nearly succeeded. He had badly mismanaged Suvla, and General Stopford, who had recently come home, was making some very serious charges about the interference of G.H.Q. in the battle. The headquarters staff, Stopford wrote in a report to the War Office, 'lived on an island at some distance from the peninsula' and had been greatly misinformed about the Turkish strength at Suvla. There was another factor. Hamilton was Kitchener's man, and it was beginning to seem that Kitchener might be covering him up. The Committee waited now with some impatience to see whether anything hopeful or useful would come in reply to Kitchener's cable. It chanced, too, that just at this time the German zeppelins were having a particular success in their raids on London: 176 people had been killed in two successive nights. Between the falling bombs on London and the falling spikes on Imbros everybody's nerves were on edge.

But it was not the bombs, nor Stopford's criticisms, not even the growing opposition to Kitchener and all his plans and protégés which was the immediate factor in the undoing of Hamilton's reputation at this moment. It was an Australian journalist named Keith Murdoch. His entry into the explosive scene is one of the oddest incidents in the Gallipoli campaign.

The trouble had begun far back in April with Ashmead-Bartlett, the war correspondent who represented the London press at the Dardanelles. According to Compton Mackenzie, who was in a position to know, Ashmead-Bartlett was not liked at headquarters. He was the stranger in the camp, a solitary civilian among professional and amateur soldiers. He was never captivated by Hamilton as the others were, but remained instead the detached hostile critic. He resented the censorship at G.H.Q., he disagreed with all their plans, and, worst of all, he was for ever predicting failure. Things grew to such a pitch that on one occasion, according to Mackenzie, the officers at Corps Headquarters at Cape Helles went into hiding in the rocks when Ashmead-Bartlett approached to avoid having to ask him to lunch.

Despite its self-imposed discomfort and its devotion, Imbros was not a very inspiring place for an outsider. Of necessity it was a club. There was a disguised but inescapable atmosphere of privilege, of the old school and the old regiment, of breeding and manners. Hamilton found some of the most devoted of his admirers among the many young men of good family who had recently joined his staff. To strangers they sometimes conveyed an impression of superiority and complacency, and their good humour and politeness were often mistaken for dilettantism. No one questioned their courage; from Hamilton downwards senior officers made a point of deliberately and nonchalantly exposing themselves to enemy fire when they were at the front. Still, there was something lacking: a toughness, a roughness, the reassurance of the common touch. Among the troops it was rumoured that Hamilton wrote poetry in his spare time, and he was supposed to be very much under Braithwaite's thumb. His charm, his integrity and his subtle intelligence were recognized by those who met him, but somehow these qualities did not work at a distance—and the soldiers were always at a distance. In brief, he seemed soft.

It was against these things that Ashmead-Bartlett, burning with his own ideas, waged his private war. Hamilton's outward attitude to him was polite and helpful, but he felt privately that Ashmead-Bartlett had too much power and that his depressing attitude was damaging the expedition. Ashmead-Bartlett's persistent theme was that the Army should have landed at Bulair, and with this Hamilton did not agree. Nor was he very encouraging when Ashmead-Bartlett came to him one day with the suggestion that the Turkish soldiers in the trenches should be induced to desert by the offer of ten shillings and a free pardon. 'This makes one wonder,' Hamilton wrote after the interview, 'what would Ashmead-Bartlett himself do if he were offered ten shillings and a good supper by a Mahommedan when he was feeling a bit hungry and hard-up among the Christians.' In May, when Ashmead-Bartlett went home on leave, Hamilton appointed Mackenzie to fill his place and tried to make the arrangement permanent, but neither Mackenzie nor the authorities in London were enthusiastic. Ashmead-Bartlett came back and was more glum and despondent than ever.

Mackenzie's description of him at their first meeting is of 'a slim man in khaki with a soft felt hat the colour of verdigris, a camera slung around his shoulders, and an unrelaxing expression of nervous exasperation.'

He 'walked along the deck with the air of one convinced that his presence there annoyed everybody, and that we all wanted a jolly good dose of physic. Presently he came away from an interview with Sir Ian Hamilton, looking the way Cassandra must have often looked some three thousand years before. After telling me that the whole expedition was doomed to failure, and that he expected to be torpedoed aboard the *Majestic* (in which he was about to sail) he left the ship.'

Yet the really irritating thing about Ashmead-Bartlett was that he was so often right. He *was* torpedoed aboard the *Majestic* that same night. And there was indeed a great deal to criticize in the generals' plans since they so frequently did end in disaster. Moreover, he could not be ignored. In London he had the ear of a number of important people in the cabinet, and however much he was disliked on Imbros the soldiers at the front were glad enough to see him, and he was often at the front. As a war correspondent, Ashmead-Bartlett was extremely capable.

He was still with the expedition and more exasperated than ever when at the conclusion of the August battles Murdoch arrived.

Murdoch was not really a war correspondent at all. He was on his way to London to act as the representative of various Australian newspapers there, and had been given a temporary official mission by his government to call in at Egypt and report upon the postal arrangements for the Australian troops. He was carrying letters of introduction from the Australian Prime Minister, Andrew Fisher, and the Australian Minister for Defence, Senator Pearce.

On August 17 Murdoch wrote to Hamilton from Cairo saying that he was finding it difficult to complete his inquiries in Egypt. He asked for permission to come to Gallipoli, and added, 'I should like to go across in only a semi-

285

official capacity, so that I might record censored impressions in the London and Australian newspapers I represent, but any conditions you impose I should, of course, faithfully observe. . . . May I add that I had the honour of meeting you at the Melbourne Town Hall, and wrote fully of your visit in the *Sydney Sun* and *Melbourne Punch;*[1] also may I say that my anxiety as an Australian to visit the sacred shores of Gallipoli while our army is there is intense.'

Hamilton says that he was not much impressed at having been written up in the *Sun* and *Punch,* but he sent off the necessary permission and on September 2 Murdoch arrived. Hamilton, at their single meeting, found him 'a sensible man'. He was to prove, however, much more than that: so far as Hamilton was concerned he was a very dangerous man.

Murdoch signed the usual war correspondent's declaration saying that he would submit all he wrote to the censor at headquarters, and then made a brief visit to the Anzac bridgehead. On his return to Imbros he set up at the Press Camp, and there found Ashmead-Bartlett. The two at once discovered that they had much in common.

Murdoch had been genuinely appalled by what he had heard and seen at Anzac: the danger and the squalor of the men's lives, the sickness, the monotonous food, the general air of depression. The Australians he talked to were extremely critical of G.H.Q., and they said that they dreaded the approach of winter. Ashmead-Bartlett was able to corroborate all this and add a good deal more. He gave it as his opinion that a major catastrophe was about to occur unless something was done. The authorities and the public at home, he said, were in complete ignorance of what was going on, and under the existing censorship at Imbros there was no way of enlightening them—unless, of course, one broke the rules and sent out an uncensored letter. After some discussion they agreed that this must be done. Murdoch was due to leave for England in a day or two; it was arranged that he would take a letter written by Ashmead-Bartlett and get it into the hands of the authorities in London.

While they were waiting for the next ship for Marseilles, Ashmead-Bartlett wrote his letter, and then coached Mur-

[1] Hamilton had made a visit to Australia shortly before the war.

doch very fully in the mistakes and dangers of the campaign so that Murdoch would be able to furnish information on his own account on his arrival in London. 'I further,' Ashmead-Bartlett says in his book *The Uncensored Dardanelles*, 'gave Murdoch letters of introduction to others who might be useful in organizing a campaign to save the Army on Gallipoli, and arranged for him to see Harry Lawson[1] to urge him to allow me to return. I promised him that if he was held up in his mission, or if the authorities refused to listen to his warnings, I would at once resign and join forces with him in London.'

Early in the second week of September Murdoch set off. When he arrived at Marseilles a few days later he was met on the quay by a British officer with an escort of British troops and French gendarmes. They proceeded to place him under arrest, and it was not until he had handed over Ashmead-Bartlett's letter that he was released and allowed to go on his way to London.

Long afterwards, when the war was over, Ashmead-Bartlett and Murdoch learned how they were given away: they had been overheard in their discussions at Imbros by another correspondent (Henry Nevinson) who sent a letter to Hamilton warning him of what was afoot. Hamilton was inclined to be amused at first, and he wrote, 'I had begun to wonder what had come over Mr. Murdoch and now it seems he has come over me!' But he acted very quickly. A cable was sent off to the War Office in London asking them to intercept Murdoch on his journey; and on September 28 Ashmead-Bartlett at Imbros was sent for by Braithwaite and told that he must leave the Army.

Hamilton's informant had been wrong in one respect. The letter had not been addressed to Lawson as he thought, but to Asquith, the Prime Minister. Hamilton was not dismayed when he heard this news from London: 'I do not for one moment believe Mr. Asquith would employ such agencies and for sure he will turn Murdoch and his wares into the wastepaper basket. . . . Tittle-tattle will effect no lodgement in the Asquith brain.'

But here again he was wrong, for Murdoch had by no means given up the hunt. He had lost Ashmead-Bartlett's letter, but he had his own pen. On his arrival in England

---

[1] The proprietor of Ashmead-Bartlett's newspaper the *Daily Telegraph*.

he wrote an 8,000-word report on Gallipoli, and addressed it to the Australian Prime Minister, Andrew Fisher. Ashmead-Bartlett's letter, which was now safely pouched in the War Office, had said that Hamilton and his staff were openly referred to by the troops at Gallipolli with derision, and that morale in the Army had collapsed; but this was the mildest pin-pricking compared with the views that Murdoch now disclosed. Part of his report was a eulogy of the Australian soldiers: his criticism was reserved for the English. Braithwaite, he informed the Australian Prime Minister, was 'more cordially detested in our forces than Enver Pasha'. Birdwood 'had not the fighting qualities or the big brain of a great general'. Kitchener 'has a terrible task in getting pure work from the General Staff of the British Army, whose motives can never be pure, for they are unchangeably selfish'. Murdoch had seen one of Hamilton's staff officers 'wallowing' in ice while wounded men were dying of heat a few hundred yards away. As for the British soldiers of the New Army, they were 'merely a lot of childish youths without strength to endure or brains to improve their conditions'. One would refuse to believe that these could be British soldiers at all, their physique was so much below that of the Turks. 'From what I saw of the Turk,' the report went on, 'I am convinced he is . . . a better man than those opposed to him.'

On the question of the morale of the soldiers Murdoch was equally trenchant. 'Sedition,' he wrote, 'is talked around every tin of bully beef on the peninsula.' And again, 'I shall always remember the stricken face of a young English lieutenant when I told him he must make up his mind for a winter campaign.' And finally, 'I do not like to dictate this sentence, even for your eyes, but the fact is that after the first day at Suvla an order had to be issued to officers to shoot without mercy any soldier who lagged behind or loitered in an advance.'

There was perhaps some excuse for this amazing document, despite the fact that Murdoch had been only for a few hours at the front and could hardly have seen very much of the Turks. Overstatement is not such a rare thing in time of war, and any journalist would recognize here the desire to tell a good story, to present the facts in the most brisk and colourful way.

To the inexperienced and confident eye of a young man who had been brought up in a remote dominion, who knew very little about other kinds of people and their ways, and still less about war, this first sight of the battlefield had been a terrible thing; and no doubt Murdoch was genuinely indignant. He felt that it was his duty to break 'the conspiracy of silence' on Imbros.

And there was some substance in the report; not in the frantic and reckless details about sedition and the shooting of lagging soldiers, but in the general theme. G.H.Q. was being criticized, things had been mismanaged, and Murdoch was telling the plain truth when he said so. At all events, it was the truth as he saw it, and in wartime there is a definite place for the reports of fresh eye-witnesses of this kind. They serve to remind politicians and headquarters planners that they are dealing with human beings who in the end are much more important than machines and elaborate plans. Such documents can hardly be used as state papers, as evidence upon which policy can be decided, and Murdoch's letter should have remained what it was— a private letter to his Government which required checking from other sources.

But Lloyd George saw it. It is only fair to assume that Lloyd George was sincerely moved by its terms, but he was also an opponent of Lord Kitchener, and he had always preferred Salonika to Gallipoli. He urged Murdoch to send a copy to Mr. Asquith.

If up to this point an explanation can be made of Murdoch's motives, it is more difficult to find an excuse for the action which the Prime Minister now took. He did not send the report to Hamilton for his comments. He did not wait until Kitchener had studied it. He had it printed as a state paper on the duck-egg blue stationery of the Committee of Imperial Defence, and circulated it to the members of the Dardanelles Committee. This was the paper they had before them, when on October 11 they decided to send either Haig or Kitchener to Gallipoli to find out what Hamilton and his headquarters were up to. This was the origin of the 'flow of unofficial reports' about which Kitchener had warned Hamilton earlier in the week.

On this same day, too, October 11, Ashmead-Bartlett arrived in London fresh from his dismissal from G.H.Q. at Imbros. He lost no time in seeing Lord Northcliffe, the proprietor of *The Times* and the *Daily Mail,* and in making arrangements for a full, uncensored exposure of the Gallipoli question in the columns of the *Sunday Times.* Both

Murdoch and Ashmead-Bartlett were very busy in Whitehall and Fleet Street during the next few days, and it soon became known that they had Northcliffe's backing. Northcliffe by now was convinced that Gallipoli must be evacuated.

On October 14 the Dardanelles Committee assembled again, and Hamilton's reply to Kitchener's evacuation cable was put before them. It was, as they feared, an unhelpful and depressing message—merely this despondent reference to losses of fifty per cent. Churchill was still for supporting Gallipoli, but with the failure of the August battles his reputation had taken a further downward plunge—after all, was he not the author of the whole disastrous adventure?—and the Salonika group was very active. They insisted that Hamilton should go. It was left to Kitchener to break the news to him.

At Gallipoli the weather had turned bitterly cold, and October 15 on Imbros was a depressing day. Headquarters was on the point of moving across to winter quarters on the other side of the island. A new stone shack, something like a Greek shepherd's hut, had been built for Hamilton, and he was sleeping in his tent for the last time. He was already in bed when an officer came to him with a message from Kitchener marked 'Secret and Personal', telling him that when the next message arrived he should decipher it himself. Hamilton had a fair idea of what his next message was going to be, but he allowed himself one final gesture. No, he said, he did not want to be woken when the message came in: it was to be brought to him at the usual hour in the morning.

Next day the message was put before him, and he got to work with the cipher book. Word by word he spelled out:

'The War Council held last night decided that though the Government fully appreciate your work and the gallant manner in which you personally have struggled to make the enterprise a success in face of the terrible difficulties you have had to contend against, they, all the same, wish to make a change in the command which will give them an opportunity of seeing you.'

General Sir Charles Monro, one of the Army commanders on the Western front, was to supersede him, and Monro was to bring out a new chief-of-staff in place of Braithwaite. Birdwood was to be in temporary command until Monro arrived. Perhaps, the message added, Hamilton might like to visit Salonika and Egypt on his way home so that he could make a report on those places.

No, he decided, he would not like to visit either Egypt or Salonika. He would go home at once and tell them that it was still not too late. Let them send Kitchener out to take command with an adequate force—a force that would hardly be missed in France—and they would have Constantinople within one month. He would buttonhole every Minister from Lloyd George to Asquith, grovel at their feet if necessary, and persuade them that Gallipoli was not lost. They could still win.

It was another cold and windy day. Birdwood and the other Corps Commanders came over to the island to say good-bye, and Hamilton was grateful to the French for their lightness of touch. There was a farewell dinner with de Robeck and Keyes in the *Triad,* and on the following day a last ride across the island for a last word with the staff. In the afternoon with Braithwaite and his A.D.C.'s he went aboard the cruiser *Chatham* which was to take him home. He was very tired. Now that it was all over it was a little too much to remain on deck and watch Imbros fade from view, and he went down to his cabin. Presently, however, when the anchor was weighed, a message was sent to him from de Robeck asking him to come up on to the quarter-deck of the *Chatham,* and because he had never wanted for courage he felt bound to go. As he came on deck he found the *Chatham* steering on a corkscrew course between the anchored vessels of the Fleet. And as he passed each ship the sailors stood and cheered him on his way.

SIXTEEN

LIEUT.-GENERAL SIR CHARLES MONRO had already achieved something of a reputation as a cool and determined commander on the western front when he went out to Gallipoli. He was fifty-five, a methodical and authoritative man, one of the kind who accepts the rules and excels in them. There was nothing speculative about him, nothing amateur. Of all the generals who served at Gallipoli one is most tempted to compare him with Liman von Sanders, for he had the same dispassionate and professional air, the same aura of calm responsibility. 'He was born,' Hamilton wrote, 'with another sort of mind from me.'

Monro had quite made up his mind about the general strategy of the war. It could be won, he believed, on the western front, and nowhere else, and any other campaign could only be justified provided that it did not divert men or materials from France. To kill Germans had become with him an act of faith: Turks did not count.

It was apparent then—or rather it should have been apparent—that some unusually bright prospect of success would have to be demonstrated to him at Gallipoli if he was to recommend that the campaign should go on. The terms of his appointment were very clear: he was to advise on whether or not the Army was to be evacuated; and if it was not, he was to estimate what reinforcements were required to carry the peninsula, to keep the straits open and to capture Constantinople.

The new commander did not hurry to the Dardanelles. He spent several days in London studying the problem at the War Office, and it was not until October 28—ten days after Hamilton's departure—that he arrived on Imbros with his chief of staff Major-General Lynden-Bell.[1] He was met by Birdwood and the three officers who had recently been promoted to the command of the three corps at the front: Byng, at Suvla, Godley at Anzac, and Lieut.-General Sir Francis Davies at Cape Helles.

Churchill in his account of the campaign says that Monro was 'an officer of quick decision. He came, he saw, he capitulated'. But this is not entirely fair, for Kitchener was impatiently pressing for a decision. 'Please send me as soon as possible,' he cabled, 'your report on the main issue, namely, leaving or staying.' Monro got this message at Imbros within twenty-four hours of his arrival and on October 30 he set out for the peninsula. Lynden-Bell complained of a sprained knee, and his place on the trip was taken by Colonel Aspinall.

No commander as yet had succeeded in visiting Suvla, Anzac and Cape Helles in a single day, but Monro achieved this feat in a destroyer in a matter of six hours. At each of the three bridgeheads the divisional generals met him on the beach, and he put to each of them in turn an identical set of questions: could their men attack and capture the Turkish positions? If the Turks were reinforced with heavy guns could they hold out through the winter?

The British guns at this time were down to a ration of two shells a day, no winter clothing had arrived, and during the stalemate of the past two months many units had dwindled to half their strength. Yet there had been no thought of evacuation among the troops. Evacuation was a kind of death, and no one imagined that Monro had come to Gallipoli to discuss it. He had arrived like some eminent specialist called down to the country from London when the local doctors had failed, and it was thought that he would suggest new remedies and ways of treatment, perhaps even some bold act of surgery which would make all well again. But there was no hint of this in his questions. No mention was made of any reinforcements being sent to the peninsula. It was very depressing. The generals replied

---

[1] Churchill saw them off at dawn in London on October 22. As the train was drawing out of the station he threw a bundle of papers into Monro's compartment and declared, 'Remember that a withdrawal from Gallipoli would be as great a disaster as Corunna.'

that the men might keep up an attack for twenty-four hours, but if the Turks made a counter-offensive with unlimited shells and fresh troops—well then they could only do their best. They could say no more.

But Monro hardly needed to hear the generals' replies. One glance at the beaches had been enough: the ramshackle piers, the spiritless gangs of men hanging about with their carts and donkeys, the shanty-town dug-outs in the cliffs, the untidiness of it all. At Anzac the General glanced at Aspinall with a specialist's rueful smile. 'Like Alice in Wonderland,' he said. 'Curiouser and curiouser.'

On the following day he sent Kitchener a message recommending the evacuation of the peninsula. Only the Anzac Corps, he said, was in a fit condition to carry on. What the men needed was rest, re-organization and training. The best thing to do was to get as many as possible back to Egypt where after a few months they might be ready for action again. He followed this with a second message saying that he estimated the losses in an evacuation at between thirty and forty per cent: in other words some 40,000 men.

Here it was then in black and white: the end of the campaign. So many dead and all for nothing, and another 40,000 men to be lost. For the cabinet in London who had to take the final decision it posed an intolerable dilemma, and even those who had been advocating the Salonika adventure were sobered by it. They had asked the professional expert for his opinion, and now they had got it: and it was unthinkable. They hesitated. And while they hesitated the thing they most wished for happened: a new factor came into the scene.

Roger Keyes was still a small man in these affairs. He was no more than a young commodore, his admiral was against him, and for the past eight months he had been isolated from the great political and military issues of the west. But he had one advantage. When nearly everyone was wavering and hesitating about the Dardanelles his views had the clarity that comes from a long pent-up exasperation. His blood was up, he knew what he wanted, and he was every bit as determined as General Monro to whom he was implacably opposed. There is a remarkable counterpoise in the movements of the two men during these few days.

On October 28, when Monro arrived at Imbros, Keyes reached London. Although it was nine o'clock at night he went straight to the Admiralty hoping to get in to see the admirals then and there, but they put him off until the following morning. At 10.30 a.m. on October 29, when Monro was examining the problems of evacuation at Imbros, Keyes had his plan in the hands of Admiral Oliver, the chief of the War Staff, and from there he went on to Sir Henry Jackson, the First Sea Lord. Soon the other admirals were brought in, and at five in the evening he went off to see the First Lord, Arthur Balfour. Next day, when Monro was preparing his evacuation report after his visit to the beaches, Keyes had a second interview with Balfour. They continued for two hours, Balfour lying back full-length in his armchair listening, Keyes talking resolutely on. At a quarter to five in the afternoon Balfour sustained himself with a cup of tea, and at twenty past five he rose and said, 'It is not often that when one examines a hazardous enterprise—and you will admit it has its hazards—the more one considers it the better one likes it.' He sent Keyes back to talk to the admirals again.

There was a break then when Keyes went off to see his wife and children in the country. But he was back in the Admiralty on November 2. The next morning he was with Churchill, and in the afternoon he found himself with Kitchener at last.

The plan which Keyes was propounding was quite simply a headlong assault on the Narrows with the battleships and cruisers which had been lying in harbour in the Ægean Islands since May. The attacking fleet was to be divided into two main squadrons. The first of these, with minesweepers and destroyers in the van, was to steam straight at the Narrows just before dawn under the cover of a smoke screen; and come what might, whether the Turkish guns were silenced or not, whether or not all the mines were swept, they were to keep on until some, at least, of the ships got through. Keyes asked for permission to lead this squadron himself. The other squadron, meanwhile—and it was to consist of the monitors and the newer battleships—was to pin down the Turkish shore batteries with a furious bombardment from the mouth of the straits. Once in the Marmara the surviving vessels were to steam directly to the Bulair Isthmus, where they were to cut the single road which was supplying the twenty Turkish divisions now stationed in the peninsula.

Keyes had effective arguments to support his plan. Many

of the enemy guns on the straits, he said, had been taken away by the Turkish Army, and a naval attack was not expected. The minefields had now been fully reconnoitred. In every respect, and especially in the support it would get from the new seaplane carriers, the Fleet had been immeasurably improved since March, and the Allied Army was now ashore to do its part in distracting the enemy fire. Already the Turks were finding difficulty in supplying their large Army on a single road—and he pointed to the success of the Allied submarines, three of which were in the Sea of Marmara and dominating it at that moment. Cut the neck at Bulair and the Turks were lost. The French, he added, were all for the new attempt and had offered new warships to take part in it.[1] It was true that Admiral de Robeck was still against the idea, but Admiral Wemyss, who was senior to de Robeck and who had been all this time at Mudros, was not. He was very much for it. He should be given the command to carry it through.

Finally, what was the sane and rational decision to take? To risk a few old battleships with a chance of winning the campaign? Or to evacuate, to give up everything with the loss of 40,000 men?

By November 3 Keyes had made headway with these arguments. Jackson, the First Sea Lord, had said he was in favour provided that the Army attacked at the same time. Balfour had all but committed himself. Churchill had needed no persuading. 'I believe,' he had written in a recent cabinet paper urging a new attempt, 'we have been all these months in the position of the Spanish prisoner who languished for twenty years in a dungeon until one morning the idea struck him to push the door which had been open all the time.' And now Keyes found himself with Kitchener.

Kitchener had been appalled by Monro's message. He could not bring himself to believe, he said, that a responsible officer could have recommended to the Government so drastic a course as evacuation. He had replied curtly by asking Monro for the opinion of the corps commanders, and Monro had answered that both Davies and Byng were

---

[1] Keyes had mentioned the scheme to Admiral Guépratte before he came to London, and Guépratte had said, 'I think always of Nasmith. I think always of Boyle; if (thumping his chest) I were permitted to do this, I would think also of myself, moi, Guépratte.'

for evacuation, while Birdwood was against it (but only because he feared the loss of prestige in the East). And then there had been this devastating estimate of the loss in cold blood of 40,000 men. Angrily, resentfully, realizing at last how much he was committed to the Dardanelles, Kitchener had been passing between the War Office and the cabinet room saying that he himself would never sign the evacuation order, and that if the Government insisted on it he himself would go out and take command, and that he would be the last man off. Keyes came in like a fresh wind at this moment, and Kitchener seized upon his plan. He told Keyes to return to the Admiralty and get some sort of a definite undertaking from them.

Keyes now was hot on the trail. He was back with Kitchener after dinner with the news that the First Sea Lord had given at least a partial promise: if the Army would attack, then the Navy would probably agree to force the straits at the same time.

While Keyes had been away Kitchener himself had taken a drastic decision which committed him more deeply than ever to the Dardanelles. It was a thunderblast in the old Olympian manner, impulsive, imperious, and absolute. He sent the following message to Birdwood, his follower of former days:

'Most secret. Decipher yourself. Tell no one. You know Monro's report. I leave here tomorrow night to come out to you. Have seen Commodore Keyes, and the Admiralty will, I believe, agree naval attempt to force straits. We must do what we can to assist them, and I think as soon as ships are in the Marmara we should seize and hold the isthmus (i.e. Bulair) so as to supply them if Turks hold out. Examine very carefully best position for landing near marsh at head of Gulf of Xeros, so that we could get a line across at isthmus with ships on both sides. To find troops for this purpose we should have to reduce to lowest possible numbers the men in all the trenches, and perhaps evacuate positions at Suvla. All the best fighting men that could be spared, including your boys from Anzac and reinforcements I can sweep up in Egypt, might be concentrated at Mudros ready for this enterprise. The admiral will probably be changed and Wemyss given command to carry through the naval part of the work. As regards command you would have the whole force and should carefully select your commanders and troops. I would suggest Maude, Fanshawe,

Marshall, Peyton (all new commanders recently sent out from England), Godley and Cox, leaving others to hold the lines. Work out plans for this or alternate plans as you think best. We must do it right this time. I absolutely refuse to sign order for evacuation, which I think would be the greatest disaster and would condemn a large percentage of our men to death or imprisonment. Monro will be appointed to command the Salonika force.'[1]

This was followed by a War Office signal officially appointing Birdwood to the command of the Expedition and directing Monro to Salonika.

The Field Marshal was up till midnight with Keyes making his plans, and it was arranged that he was to leave for the Dardanelles on the following day. Keyes was to go with him provided that first he got the guarantee of certain naval reinforcements for his attempt on the Narrows.

This was on November 3. November 4 was a still more agitated day. In the morning Keyes got his reinforcements. Four battleships, *Hibernia, Zealandia, Albemarle* and *Russell,* 4 destroyers and 24 more trawlers were ordered to the Dardanelles. In the afternoon Balfour sent off a tactful message to de Robeck saying that he had heard that he was not well and in need of a rest; he must come home on leave. 'In making arrangements for your substitute during your absence,' the message went on, 'please bear in mind the possibility that an urgent appeal from the Army to co-operate with them in a great effort may make it necessary for the Fleet to attempt to force the straits. The admiral left in charge should therefore be capable of organizing this critical operation and should be in full agreement with the policy.'

Then in the evening there was a setback. At a farewell meeting with the cabinet Kitchener found the other Ministers still divided between Gallipoli and Salonika. Bonar Law was actually threatening resignation unless the peninsula was evacuated, and Balfour made it absolutely clear

---

[1] When this message arrived at Imbros at 2 a.m. the following morning the signals officer on duty began to decode it in the usual way. He stopped however, at the words 'Decipher yourself' and took the message to Colonel Aspinall. Aspinall then began decoding but baulked at the words 'Tell no one' and woke Birdwood. Birdwood, however, was unable to handle the cipher and Aspinall, having been pledged to secrecy, finished the message for him by the light of a hurricane lamp.

that the Navy would do nothing at the Dardanelles unless the Army also attacked. Could the Army attack? Kitchener was forced to say he did not know. After the meeting he sent off a gloomy cable to Birdwood cancelling his previous message. 'I fear,' he said, 'the Navy may not play up. . . . The more I look at the problem the less I see my way through, so you had better very quietly and very secretly work out any scheme for getting the troops off.'

Then he set off, taking the overland route through France to Marseilles, where the *Dartmouth* was waiting to transport him to the Dardanelles. However, there was better news waiting for the Field Marshal in Paris, where he stopped that night to consult with the French government; the French told him that they were opposed to evacuation. On hearing this, Kitchener cabled Birdwood once again saying that he yet might be reinforced, and another message was despatched to Keyes in London telling him to proceed at once to Marseilles to join the *Dartmouth* so that they could discuss the joint naval and Army attack on their voyage to Gallipoli.

Keyes never got this message. It arrived at the Admiralty in London, but the officer on duty there decided (quite erroneously) that there was no point in sending it on to the Commodore since he had no hope of getting to Marseilles before the *Dartmouth* sailed.

Now they were all at sixes and sevens. When Keyes failed to turn up at Marseilles Kitchener concluded that the naval plan must have fallen through, and he sailed despondently without him. Keyes meanwhile, knowing nothing about all this, was jubilant. He went across to Paris, got a promise of six more warships from the French Minister of Marine, and hurried off after Kitchener, confident that all was well. At the Dardanelles de Robeck was getting ready to pack his bags, believing that he was about to be superseded by Wemyss; and Monro, who had been on a trip to Egypt, was confronted with the baffling news that Kitchener had been secretly arranging for his removal to Salonika. Birdwood perhaps was the most perplexed man of all. Kitchener was thrusting greatness upon him, and he was not at all sure that he wanted it. He did not believe that the Army would have a ghost of a chance in making a fresh landing in the vicinity of the Bulair isthmus, and he had no wish to become Commander-in-Chief. He suppressed the

War Office cable announcing his appointment, and cabled Kitchener saying that he hoped Monro would remain in command.

And still in London the tug of war between Gallipoli and Salonika went on among the politicians.

But it was the uncertainty of Kitchener's own position which was the most unsettling aspect of these confused events. Outwardly his prestige remained untouched, the generals and the politicians still revolved around him; yet it was becoming every day more apparent that his former steadiness was deserting him, that he too was being sucked into the fatal limbo of the Dardanelles. As the commanders at Gallipoli and the cabinet Ministers in London were pulled first in one way and then in another, he drifted with the rest and it began to seem that he was no more capable of finding a solution than anybody else. And in fact by the beginning of November only two men appeared to be standing on firm ground. One was Keyes and the other Monro, and the real issue—whether to stay or to go, to attack or retreat—was bound to be decided between them. These two were the champions of the two great opposing camps, and it was simply a question of which was going to be more successful in imposing his will. Kitchener, in other words, was going to Gallipoli not as a leader but as an umpire, and it was a game in which there were no precedents at all.

At first Keyes did not stand a chance. He was still far away on his outward journey to the Dardanelles when Kitchener arrived at Lemnos. The Field Marshal was met by Monro, de Robeck, Birdwood, General Maxwell, the Commander-in-Chief in Egypt, and Sir Henry MacMahon, the Egyptian High Commissioner. Maxwell and MacMahon had come over to express their fears about the safety of Egypt in the event of the Gallipoli evacuation taking place, and in the course of their journey they had reached an agreement with Monro. They were prepared to back an evacuation, they told him, provided he made a new landing on the Asiatic coast of Turkey at Ayas Bay in the Gulf of Iskanderun. This was to prevent the Turks from advancing on the Suez Canal. Monro did not think much of the plan, but he was ready to fall in with it provided he got the troops out of Gallipoli. These three, then, formed a solid block. De Robeck concerned himself chiefly with the technical problems of the Navy. He could get the troops off Suvla and Anzac, he said, but he wanted Cape Helles retained as a base to assist him in blockading the Dardanelles. Birdwood too was coming round to the idea of evacuation, but was absolutely opposed to the Ayas Bay scheme. No one spoke in favour of the Navy making a new attempt on the Narrows—de Robeck indeed expressly repeated that he regarded it as folly.

So now they were all evacuators, all eager to find some way of getting out without losing too much face, and the safety of Egypt had become more important than the capture of Constantinople.

But Kitchener was still not persuaded. He liked the Ayas Bay idea, and sent off a cable to London saying so; but he held his hand about evacuation. After two days of argument on Imbros he went off to the peninsula and methodically inspected the three bridgeheads, giving a full day to each one.

Like Monro he was depressed by the difficulties of the country, and the precarious hold of the Army on the beaches. But he was not quite so hopeless; he believed they might hold on through the winter, and that, if forced to evacuate, they might get out with fewer casualties than had been anticipated, perhaps no more than 25,000 men. He said all this in a cable to London on his return to Imbros on November 15, but still made no recommendation one way or another as to what should be done. By now a week had gone by.

It was the General Staff at the War Office in London which brought a note of reality into this drifting scene. The Ayas Bay scheme they turned down flat, pointing out that with two fronts already on their hands at Salonika and Gallipoli it was unwise to add a third, and that if the Turks were going to attack Egypt it was much better to meet them after they had crossed the desert than at the outset of their journey. The French in any case hated the idea, since they regarded Ayas Bay and the Alexandretta area as their own sphere of influence. It was many months since anyone, least of all the General Staff, had rejected Kitchener's advice in such terms as these.

And now more troubles arose. The Salonika force had accomplished nothing in Bulgaria—it had not even made contact with the Serbs—and was now about to fall back into Greece. King Constantine spoke of disarming the troops as they crossed the border. In haste Kitchener set off with Monro on November 16 for Salonika to see what could be done; and it was there at last on the following day that Keyes caught up with him. They met aboard the *Dartmouth*.

'Well, I have seen the place,' Kitchener began. 'It is an awful place and you will never get through.' Keyes attacked this at once. What had happened to change Lord Kitchener's mind? Why had he dropped his support of the naval plan? Nothing had altered since they had left London; if anything the position was even better than it was before. The naval reinforcements were arriving. It was agreed that de Robeck, who was a sick man, should go home and that Wemyss should take his place. As for the Dardanelles being such an awful place, Kitchener had had no opportunity of studying it. He, Keyes, had been there eight months. He knew the possibilities intimately and he knew they could get through. All the Navy needed was the word to go ahead.

To Kitchener, who wanted to believe it, yet saw no escape from his ever-increasing difficulties, this was a siren's song and scarcely bearable. He got up and walked into his sleeping cabin, closing the door behind him. 'I could not help feeling sorry for him,' Keyes wrote that night in his diary. 'He loked so terribly weary and harassed.'

That night they steamed back to Mudros to take up the argument all over again. Keyes lost no time in heartening the reluctant generals. Any argument served: on November 17 a heavy southerly gale had again wrecked the piers at Cape Helles, and he pointed out to General Davies that evacuation had become too dangerous. To MacMahon, the Egyptian High Commissioner, he said, 'If we fight the Turk and beat him in Gallipoli isn't that the best way to defend Egypt?' MacMahon was forced to agree, and said he would approach Kitchener again. A General Horne had been brought out by Kitchener as an adviser, and Keyes tackled him with, 'If you western-front generals don't like the idea of attacking, at least be ready to take advantage of our naval attack when we deliver it.' Horne, according to Keyes, was 'enthusiastic before I finished'. Then there was Birdwood. Keyes braced him with a preliminary harangue, and then left it to Admiral Wemyss to continue the argument.

By November 21, when the generals assembled again at Mudros for a final conference, Birdwood had been brought round. He was reassured, no doubt, by the fact that his own officers at Anzac had now come out definitely against evacuation, while at Cape Helles a new Turkish attack had collapsed. It collapsed because the Turkish soldiers, having jumped up from their trenches, absolutely refused to go forward against the British fire. They fell back with heavy loss. Keyes began to feel that he had recovered all his lost ground at last.

Yet the truth was that Monro with his slow persistence had by now begun to dominate them all. The subordinate generals might privately agree with Keyes, but they were still unable to stand up to Monro—and it was to Monro and not Kitchener that they were turning for the last word. Birdwood was perfectly clear about this. He said to Keyes, 'Everything depends upon Monro.' It was time now for the two adversaries to meet.

Monro had broken his ankle getting into a boat at Salonika and Keyes found him lying on a sofa aboard the *Chatham*. Lynden-Bell was with him. The argument began quite pleasantly and it was not until the end that Keyes burst out with, 'If *you* don't want to share in the glory, then there are some soldiers who will.'

'Look out, Lynden-Bell,' Monro said. 'The Commodore is going to attack us. I can't get up.'

With a rather heavy reference to the General's 'cold feet' Keyes got up and left.

But he had gained nothing. Kitchener, who had been off to Athens to placate the King of Greece, returned to Mudros that day, and he had found no arguments with which to withstand Monro while he had been away. Birdwood and the others were quickly overborne. On November 22 Kitchener cabled London recommending that Suvla and Anzac should be evacuated while Cape Helles should be held 'for the time being'. Monro was to remain at Lemnos as Commander-in-Chief of both Gallipoli and Salonika. Birdwood was to take charge of the withdrawal. De Robeck was to go home on sick leave, and Wemyss was to take his place. On November 24 Kitchener sailed for England, and on the following day de Robeck too was gone.

'Thus,' says Keyes, 'the Admiral and the General who were really entirely responsible for the lamentable policy

303

of evacuation left the execution of this unpleasant task to an Admiral and a General who were strongly opposed to it.'

Yet it was still not the end—not at any rate so far as Keyes and Wemyss were concerned—for now suddenly at the end of November the weather intervened. There had been ample warning of the winter. Twice the piers had been washed away in gales. For the past few days flocks of ducks and other birds migrating south from Russia had been passing over the peninsula, and although both armies, first the Turks and then the Allies, had enjoyed themselves blazing away with their rifles into the sky,[1] it was clear that cold weather was soon coming. Yet no one—and certainly not the meteorologists who had been saying that November was the best month of the year—could have anticipated the horror and severity of the blizzard that swept down on the Dardanelles on November 27. Nothing like it had been known there for forty years.

For the first twenty-four hours rain poured down and violent thunderstorms raged over the peninsula. Then, as the wind veered round to the north and rose to hurricane force there followed two days of snow and icy sleet. After this there were two nights of frost.

At Anzac and Cape Helles the soldiers were well dug in, and there was some small protection from the surrounding hills, but at Suvla the men were defenceless. The earth there was so stony that in place of trenches stone parapets had been built above the ground. These burst open in the first deluge, and a torrent came rushing down to the Salt Lake carrying with it the bodies of Turks who had been drowned in the hills. Soon the lake was four feet deep, and on both sides the war was forgotten. Turks and British alike jumped up on what was left of the parapets in full view of one another, and there they perched, numb and shivering, while the flood went by. Then, overnight, when the landscape turned to a universal white, dysentery vanished along with the flies and the dust, but the cold was past all bearing. At Anzac, where many of the Australians and Indians were seeing snow for the first time, the dugouts were knee-deep

[1] Thousands of ducks were shot down, and it was said after the campaign was over, with how much truth one cannot know, that several years went by before the migrating birds settled again on Gallipoli.

in slush, and the soldiers, still without winter kit,[1] wrapped themselves in their sodden blankets. The freeze that followed was worse than any shelling. Triggers were jammed and rifles refused to fire. At Helles sentries were found in the morning still standing, their rifles in their hands, but they were frozen to death. Blankets and bedding were so congealed with cold they could be stood on end. Everywhere mud had turned to ice and the roofs of the dugouts were lined with icicles as hard as iron. A tacit truce prevailed along the front while the men gave themselves up to the simple struggle of finding enough warmth to remain alive. Nevinson, the war correspondent, describes how he saw men staggering down to the beaches from the trenches: 'They could neither hear nor speak, but stared about them like bewildered bullocks.' It was rather worse for the Allies than for the Turks, since for three days no boat could approach the shore, and the beaches were strewn with wreckage of every kind. At Imbros where three steamers had been sunk as a breakwater the raging sea broke through, and smashed most of the small craft in the harbour. Even a submarine went down to the shallow bottom, and the only sign that life remained within her was the shifting of the periscope from time to time.

On November 30, when the wind had blown itself out at last, a reckoning was made, and it was found that the Allied Army had lost one tenth of its strength. Two hundred soldiers had been drowned, 5,000 were suffering from frostbite, and another 5,000 were casualties of one sort or another. It raised once more, and in an ominous way, the whole question of evacuation. Many of those who before had wanted to remain could now think of nothing but of getting away from the accursed place. But could they get off? Were they not now bound to stay and fight it out? Keyes thought so. He was not nearly defeated yet.

Directly de Robeck had gone he and Wemyss returned to the naval plan, and another cable was sent to the Admiralty urging its adoption. Then they tackled Monro directly. Monro was patient and polite, but no argument could shake his overriding conviction that the war must be fought in France. 'Well,' he said in the course of one of his

[1] A certain amount of winter clothing had been landed on the peninsula but it had been taken off again in view of the plans for evacuation.

long discussions with Keyes, 'if all succeeds, you go through the straits into the Marmara and we occupy Constantinople, what good is it going to do? What then? It won't help us win the war; France is the only place in which Germany can be beaten. Every man not employed in killing Germans in France and Flanders is wasted.'

Keyes reminded him that if the Gallipoli Army was to be evacuated it would not go to Germany but to Egypt. Monro said he did not believe that Egypt was in any danger. No more do I, Keyes replied, yet the Government would be bound to send the Army there.

After his one brief visit Monro had not returned to the peninsula, and his chief-of-staff never set foot on the beaches at all. Yet they held strong views on the tactical situation there. The Allies' position lacked depth, they said. Keyes answered that the sea was very deep; where else could they use the Navy to deploy their men so secretly and rapidly? Even so, Monro said, it was now too late to think of attacking. It would not have been too late, Keyes replied, if Monro had acted when he had first arrived a month ago; and it was still not too late.

And so it went round and round, and no one was persuaded. After one of his outbursts Keyes attempted to relieve the tension by asking after the General's foot. 'It will be well enough soon,' Monro said, 'to get up and kick somebody's——stern.' He meant the Turks of course, Keyes said. But Monro did not mean the Turks.

Having failed at G.H.Q. Wemyss and Keyes tried their hands again with Birdwood and the subordinate generals. Here they were more successful, for the soldiers had been badly shaken by the storm and were coming round to the idea that the risks of going were greater than the risks of staying. Moreover, many deserters were coming in from the Turkish lines, and it was obvious that the enemy's morale had fallen very low.

At a conference at Imbros several of the commanders said they were prepared to reconsider their ideas about withdrawal. Monro retaliated to these manœuvres by forbidding Birdwood and the other generals to hold any further discussion with Wemyss and Keyes without his knowledge.

But it was in London that the two sailors found their real allies. Lord Curzon, who was a member of the Dardanelles Committee (now renamed once more the War Committee), had suddenly become very active. He was appalled at the prospect of the casualties in an evacuation, and in a forceful paper he reminded the cabinet that there was no real agreement among the generals at Gallipoli. Monro was firm, Curzon said, but he had made up his mind within forty-eight hours of his arrival, after a cursory inspection of the front. The other generals had changed their opinion more than once and might do so again.

This was buttressed by a second paper from Hankey, who was now back at his post as Secretary of the War Committee. If they withdrew, Hankey argued, Turkey was free to turn all her forces on to Russia and the British possessions in the Near East. There was even a danger that Russia might sign a separate peace. He urged that since the Salonika landing had failed, the fresh divisions which had been sent out to reinforce it should be diverted instead to Gallipoli. It was an idea that appealed to Kitchener; even at this eleventh hour he too was prepared to change once more, and cables were sent out to Wemyss asking him if he could transport the troops from Salonika to Gallipoli. Keyes hurried to Salonika to make the arrangements.

Bluntly Monro held on. No, he said, he still could not attack. Even if he was given these reinforcements he could not employ them. Nevertheless, for the first time he was shaken, and in an unguarded moment Lynden-Bell said to Keyes, 'Well, we are in for it—we are going to do it; you have got your way.' This was on December 4, and for a little longer the agony was to be maintained, while still in London the cabinet hesitated and waited for a lead.

It was the French and the Russians who cast the deciding vote at last; they informed the British that Salonika could not be abandoned, and on December 7 the cabinet decided definitely to 'shorten the front by evacuating Anzac and Suvla'. Wemyss was astonished when he heard the news. He sent off a battery of cables to London saying that if necessary the Fleet was now prepared to 'go it alone'. 'What is offered the Army, therefore,' he wrote, 'is the practical complete severance of the Turkish lines of communication accomplished by the destruction of the large supply depots on the shore of the Dardanelles.' The idea of evacuation, he told Balfour, was now being ridiculed by the soldiers at Gallipoli, especially at Anzac. Birdwood ought to be consulted.

But it was too late. The Admiralty was not prepared to

act alone, especially as de Robeck was now in London and giving his advice against it. On December 10 Wemyss was turned down once more; and although he continued to argue for several days in effect he was beaten and Monro had won. Depressed and uncertain, the soldiers and the sailors turned together to the plans for their retreat.

Except for Birdwood, Keyes and one or two others nearly all the pioneers had now gone. Hamilton and de Robeck were in England, Kitchener was no longer the leader he had been at the time of the April landings, and it was becoming clear to his opponents that, with the failure of the Dardanelles, they could bring him down at last. Churchill, his reputation at the lowest ebb ever touched in his career, was bundled into retirement in the wake of Fisher and with even less regret. During these final negotiations over Gallipoli Asquith reformed the War Committee, and there was no place on it for the man who, at that moment, seemed most responsible for the tragedy they were about to face. Churchill made a last speech in the House in November, and then went off to France to fight in the trenches.

On the Turkish side Liman remained but Kemal had gone. After the August battles Kemal had been made a Pasha, and he had continued to lead a charmed life at the front. He was convinced that he would never be hit, and it did indeed appear that nothing could destroy him. While other men died he walked casually among the bullets. Samson very nearly killed him one day. Flying low behind the Turkish lines, the air commodore saw a staff car with three people inside, one of whom at least seemed to be a general (it was in fact Kemal). Samson dived and launched two bombs. At once the car stopped and the three men inside got out and ran to a ditch. Samson then drew off and cruised about for twenty minutes until he saw the Turks return to the car. Then again he dived, and actually succeeded in splintering the windscreen. But it was the chauffeur who was hit: Kemal remained untouched. Soon afterwards, however, his health broke down through exhaustion and nervous strain, and no amount of pills or injections could revive him. Early in December he was evacuated from the peninsula.

There was another casualty which was even closer to the nemesis of the Dardanelles. Wangenheim—Churchill's ultimate rival, the man who had begun it all by getting the *Goeben* into the Sea of Marmara—was dead. His health had been failing all through the early summer and in July he went back to Germany on leave. When he returned to Constantinople in October his face was twitching, one of his eyes was covered with a black patch, and he was nervous and depressed. He came to the American Embassy, and Morgenthau describes the end of this, their last meeting: 'Wangenheim rose to leave. As he did so he gave a gasp and his legs shot from under him. I jumped and caught him just as he was falling.' Morgenthau helped him out to his car. Two days later Wangenheim had a stroke at the dinner table, and never again regained consciousness. He died on October 24, and was buried in the park of the German summer embassy at Therapia, that same nook on the Bosphorus where in the old days the ambassador, his telegrams in his hand, had so often bobbed in and out of view according to the changes in the German political weather.

Enver remained, with his pert confident air, but he was in secret no longer confident. Through these last days of November and early December he more than once came to Morgenthau asking him to appeal to President Wilson to use his influence to end the war. He admitted that Turkey had drifted into a critical state at the end of this first twelve months of hostilities, its farms uncultivated, its business at a standstill. The campaign at Gallipoli was swallowing them all. At this time neither Enver nor Liman nor anyone else had any notion of what was afoot in the British camp. They saw nothing ahead but limitless war, and the withdrawal of the Allies from the peninsula never entered their minds.

For the Allies at Gallipoli there was at least one small particle of relief in the hateful situation. They had definite orders at last; in place of demoralizing delay they now had something practical to do, even if it was nothing more than to arrange a humiliating retreat.

Yet there remained the overwhelming question of the casualties. What were they going to be? Kitchener had taken up a surprising line. Just as he was about to leave Gallipoli to return to England he had turned suddenly to Colonel Aspinall and had said, 'I don't believe a word about those 25,000 casualties (this was the latest estimate of the staff) . . . you'll just step off without losing a man, and without the Turks knowing anything about it.' It was another of his impulsive, inspirational flashes, and it was based on nothing definite: a guess, in fact, in the blue.

Lord Curzon in his paper to the cabinet saw the evacuation in another light. 'I wish to draw it in no impressionist colours,' he said, 'but as it must in all probability arise. The evacuation and the final scenes will be enacted at night. Our guns will continue firing until the last moment . . . but the trenches will have been taken one by one, and a moment must come when a final *sauve qui peut* takes place, and when a disorganized crowd will press in despairing tumult on to the shore and into the boats. Shells will be falling and bullets ploughing their way into the mass of retreating humanity. . . . Conceive the crowding into the boats of thousands of half-crazy men, the swamping of craft, the nocturnal panic, the agony of the wounded, the hecatombs of slain. It requires no imagination to create a scene that, when it is told, will be burned into the hearts and consciences of the British people for generations to come.'

Between these two, the wishful guess and the fearful nightmare, there were a dozen other conjectures, all equally guesses, all equally at the mercy of luck and the weather.

They were to depart, in fact, in the same way as they had arrived: as adventurers into the unknown.

SEVENTEEN

~~~~~~

> *'. . . But this same day*
> *Must end that work the ides of March begun.'*
> JULIUS CAESAR, Act V, Scene 1.

THE weather was superb. For three weeks after the storm
the sun rose on a placid, gently-moving sea and went down
again at five in the evening in a red blaze behind Mount
Athos and Samothrace. Through the long night the men
slept in relative peace. There might be sudden alarms in
the starlight, a mine exploding, an outburst of small-arms
fire, and by day a desultory shelling; but neither side made
any attempt to take the offensive.

With the cooler weather the soldiers' health grew better.
There was enough water at last and the food improved; a
bakery was set up on Imbros and occasionally they saw
fresh bread. Sometimes for brief intervals a canteen appeared, and the men tried to squander their months of
unspent pay before its supplies gave out. Blankets, trench
boots, and even oil stoves were issued to the units, and
there was a fever of preparation for the winter. Like hiber-
nating animals they went underground, roofing over their
dugouts with timber and galvanized iron, digging deeper
and deeper into the rocks. There was an air of permanence
in the traffic that flowed back and forth between the
wharves and the network of trenches at the front. Each day
at the same hour the mule carts passed by, the sentries
were posted, the fatigue parties made their way to the shore
and those who were being sent off on leave to the islands
waited for the evening ferry to arrive from Imbros. Each

day, with the regularity of dockers and miners taking over a shift, gangs of men went to work on the wharves and underground entrenchments. It was a waiting game, and there was a sense of security in these repeated habits, in building things rather than destroying them.

By now Gallipoli had an established reputation in the outside world. It had ceased to be the Constantinople Expedition or even an expedition at all; it was Gallipoli, a name repeated over and over again in the newspapers. A picture had been built up in people's minds at home just as once perhaps they built up pictures of the garrisons on the northwest frontier of India, of Kitchener and Gordon in the Sudan, of the African veldt in the Boer War. They saw, or thought they saw, the trenches in the cliffs and the blue Mediterranean below, the lurid turbanned Turks—hardly very different surely from the Pathans, the Fuzzy-wuzzies, the 'natives'—and they knew the names of all the generals and the admirals. They knew, too, that things had 'gone wrong' at Gallipoli, that something would have to be done about it, and although the battlefield was so unlike any other in the war it had an agonizing reality for every family that awaited a letter from the front.

But the clearest picture of Gallipoli at this time is not given by the newspapers, nor by the generals' dispatches, nor even by the letters and diaries of the veterans who had been there for months: it comes from the young soldiers who were still being sent out as replacements or reinforcements. Many of them had never been abroad before, and they saw it all with the clear and frightened eye of the child who for the first time in his life leaves his family and sets off alone for school. He might have been told all about Gallipoli just as once he was told all about the school to which he was being sent; but it remained terrible to him because he had never seen himself in that context before. He did not know whether or not he would have the courage of the others, and the absence of the unknown in the adventure—the fact that tens of thousands of others had gone to Gallipoli before him—was no real reassurance; it merely emphasized the unknown within himself.

These no doubt might have been the emotions of any young soldier going to war, but Gallipoli occupied a special place, since it was so far away and already so fixed in a popular myth. No one who went there ever came back on leave.

But there was at least, at the outset, the excitement and the respite of the journey. For the English soldier it began at some dim port like Liverpool, often in the rain and often aboard the *Olympic* or some other transatlantic liner. Here the strings with home and normality still remained, the clean food, the peacetime order on the decks, the uneventful days. A thousand letters home described the first sight of Gibraltar, the Mediterranean sunshine, the glimpse of Malta and Tunis, the U-boat scare that came to nothing. After a fortnight of this there was the arrival at Mudros, and Mudros, like every transit camp in every war, was awful: a city of dusty tents, the dreary anonymous hutments on the wharves, the appalling canteen food eaten among strangers. The spirits of the new arrivals fell sharply at Mudros while they waited for their posting to one of the three fronts on the peninsula. Anzac had the worst reputation for danger and discomfort, and there was little to choose, it was said, between Suvla and Helles.

As a rule the men revived again once they set off from Mudros and the climax of their adventure lay clear before them. They travelled by night on steamers brought out from the English Channel (the peacetime notices in French and English still painted on the gangways), and in silence and darkness they stood on deck straining their eyes for a first sight of the fabulous coast. If they were bound for Helles they saw, away to the starboard, the glare of the enemy searchlights sweeping the Dardanelles, and perhaps a starshell coming up from Asia. Then, as the rotten, sweet smell of the battlefield came out towards them, a voice, shouting in the darkness, would tell them that they were now within range, that there was to be no smoking, all torches to be extinguished. Two red lights shone on the masthead, and presently an answering light would come out from the shore. Then, all at once, they were touching something solid in the blackness, a pier or a lighter in the bay, and a gang of Indian porters, coughing dismally in the bitter cold, would come swarming on to the decks.

Waking next morning, stiff and uncomfortable on the ground, the young soldier found himself looking out on a scene which was probably much less dramatic than he had imagined, at any rate as far as the general prospect was concerned. He was in the midst of a vast dishevelled dumping ground, a slum of piled-up boxes and crates, of discoloured tents and dusty carts, of the debris of broken

313

boats and vehicles that seemed to have been cast up like wreckage by some violent storm in the night. There was a stony football field; a few squalid huts were standing by the shore, and the legendary *River Clyde* was an old hulk in the bay. Smoke drifted up from cooking fires as from the back streets of an industrial town. Not a green thing grew, and although all kinds of soldiers were moving about from their holes in the ground and among the tents, they imparted somehow that air of fatigue, of staleness and physical boredom, which overtakes the homeward-going crowd in a great city railway station at the end of a long Sunday in the summer. Of Troy and the Hellespont, of the raging Turks and the crashing artillery, of death itself, there was usually nothing to be seen.

But then, as the recruit waited to be told what to do, like a boy in the quadrangle on his first morning at school, the others ignoring him as they went by on their own mysterious and definite occupations, the morning shelling would begin, the long scream, the shuddering crump in the ground, and at once he would discover a sense of identity; his nerves touched the hidden current by which, under an air of matter-of-factness, they were all animated and controlled, and there was a sort of reassurance in this experience. When at last he got his orders to go to this or that sector in the line, when he found himself actually on the road and marching, as it were, towards a precipice, his fear was often swallowed up in a delirious fatalism, a sort of bated recklessness. Now finally he was committed, from this moment his past life had gone, and he ran blindly forward or galloped his horse when he was told to hurry across the exposed ground. Obediently he dived down in the wake of his guide into the gullies and the underground city on the plain, acutely aware of the strange sights about him but in reality seeing nothing but himself. And again at the front, a mile or two away from the coast, anticlimax intervened. For long periods it was very quiet in the trenches, but there was an uninhibited air, almost a sense of freedom, which was much less constricting than the atmosphere of the headquarters and the base depots on the beach. Men strolled about in the sunshine, apparently in full view of the Turks. They were incurious but friendly. 'Ah yes, we've been expecting you. Don't know where you're going to sleep. Perhaps over there.' Over there might be a neolithic hut of stones, a blanket stretched across a

314

hole in the side of a trench, some blind alley where a group of men were playing cards. They did not move or look up when a machine-gun snapped out somewhere in the open field ahead, a field like any other field but dry and characterless in the flat sunlight.

Then days would elapse while the new soldier, emerging from his private foreboding, still marvelled at things which had long since ceased to be remarkable to the other men: the way, for instance, a French soldier would perch on the cliffs and sound a hunting horn as a warning to the soldiers bathing in the sea below that a shell was coming over from Asia. Or it would be some surprising act of military punctilio, a pipe band parading on the shore, an immaculate colonel, looking like some animated tin soldier from the nursery, raising his hand to salute the flag at sunset. It was the casual thing done in these bizarre surroundings which was so unexpected, the very fact that they could play football at all, that the men could abandon themselves to the simplest pastimes, that they could sit, as some of them did, for hours on end oblivious of the world, happily shooting with a catapult at sparrows coming across from the Turkish lines. And always to the fresh eye there were recurring moments of release and wonder at the slanting luminous light in the early mornings and the evenings, in the marvellous colour of the sea.

But in the end, inevitably, these things ceased to be remarkable any more, they became part of an accepted background, and soon the new soldier would be filling his diary with jottings about food, about the latest parcel from home, about the hour at which he went to sleep on the previous night, about food again.

It was many months now since any of the older soldiers had seen a woman, and although the usual kind of story went around—the Turks had women in *their* trenches, B Company had quite definitely heard them squealing last night—sex was not a subject that generally obsessed them. It was very secondary to food. In a book called *Letters from Helles,* which a Colonel Darlington published long after the war, there is recorded an incident which reveals a not too painful detachment, almost a Robinson Crusoe submission to the inevitable, which was probably the general thing.

An orderly announced in an awed voice one day, 'There's women in that boat, Colonel.' The Colonel 'went out and sure enough there was a party of Australian nurses being shown around the shore to see how the wild soldier lives and sleeps. I got my glasses to see the unusual sight and much to all our Tommies' annoyance a young nut of a staff officer with much ostentation put his arm round one of the nurses' waists, struck an attitude and waved his hand to us. We all shook our fists at him, which caused great amusement on the launch.'

Up to the end of November there was very little talk of evacuation. It was discussed in the trenches like any other possibility, but in a detached way, and few of the men really believed that it could happen. The physical presence of the Army, its air of permanence, was all around them; too much had been committed here, too many were dead, to make it possible for them to go away. And in any case there was at this stage no plan for withdrawing from Helles at all.

At the beginning of December, however, the men at Anzac and Suvla began to notice that something unusual was going on. Soldiers who reported sick with some minor ailment were not treated at the hospitals on the bridgehead but were at once sent off to the islands and were seen no more. In increasing numbers companies and battalions were taken off *en bloc*, and those who remained behind did not altogether believe the official explanation that this was part of the new 'winter policy of thinning out the bridgehead'. They thought for the most part that a new landing was to be made.

The problem was one of frightful complexity. There were some 83,000 men in the Suvla-Anzac bridgehead, and to these were added 5,000 animals, 2,000 vehicles, nearly 200 guns and vast quantities of stores. It was quite impractical to think of getting the whole of this army off in a single night, since there was neither room for them on the beaches nor sufficient boats to get them across to the islands. Equally a fighting withdrawal was out of the question: in a moment the enemy guns firing from the hills above would have wrecked all hope of embarkation.

The plan that was finally adopted was very largely the work of Colonel Aspinall, who was now serving as a brigadier-general on Birdwood's staff, and of Lieut.-Colonel White, an Australian at Anzac. They proposed a gradual and secret withdrawal which was to take place during successive nights until at last only a small garrison was left;

316

and these last, the 'bravest and the steadiest men', were then to take their chance on getting away before the Turks discovered what was happening. This meant that the operation would rise to an acute point of tension during the last hours—a rough sea would ruin all, a Turkish attack would expose them to a slaughter—but still there seemed no other way.

There now began a period of intensive preparation. Once again a fleet of small boats was assembled in the islands. Twelve thousand hospital beds were got ready in Egypt, and fifty-six temporary hospital ships were ordered to stand ready to take the wounded off the beaches—the larger liners, the *Mauretania,* the *Aquitania* and the *Britannic,* to sail directly to England. Gangs of engineers were put to work to repair the piers destroyed in the November storms,[1] and an elaborate time-table was worked out so that every man would know precisely what he had to do.

Clearly everything would depend on secrecy and the weather. Secrecy was even more vital now than it had been in the days before the landings, and it was a constant anxiety in Birdwood's headquarters that some soldier, wittingly or unwittingly, might give the plans away. A naval patrol sealed off the islands from Greek caiques trading with the mainland, and on Imbros a cordon was placed round the civilian village on the pretext that an outbreak of smallpox was suspected there.

In the midst of these arrangements Lord Milner and others chose to discuss openly the whole question of evacuation in the House of Lords in London. It was common knowledge, Lord Milner said, that General Monro had recommended evacuation. Had Kitchener gone out to the Dardanelles to give a second opinion? Or was Kitchener himself to command the operation? It was part of the old zany carelessness which had led people to address letters to 'The Constantinople Force' when Hamilton was first assembling the Army in Egypt, and on Imbros Birdwood's planning staff could do nothing but listen in despair. For-

---

[1] Several ships were sunk to form breakwaters at this time, and on Imbros Admiral Wemyss even proposed to use an old battleship in this way. Eventually, however, he requisitioned a collier which had just steamed in from England with 1,500 tons of coal on board. The captain protested but down the ship went to the bottom. The vessel was pumped out after the evacuation and sailed away apparently none the worse for her immersion.

tunately, however, the Turks and the Germans simply could not bring themselves to believe that the British would give away their plans in this casual way; they revealed later that they regarded the debate in the House of Lords as propaganda.

Over the weather there could be even less control; the meteorologists said that it ought to hold until the end of the year, and one could only pray that they were right. One good southerly blow on the final night would wreck the whole adventure.

There remained one other imponderable, and that was the behaviour of the Army itself. On December 12 the soldiers at Suvla and Anzac were told for the first time that they were to be taken off, that this for them was the end of the campaign. There seems to have been a moment of stupefaction. Even those who had guessed that something of the sort was about to happen were astonished, and perhaps it was something more than astonishment, a dull awe, a feeling that this was a shaming and unnatural reversal of the order of things. Among the majority, no doubt, these thoughts were soon overtaken by a sense of relief, and they were content simply to accept instructions and to get away. Others, and there were very many of them, remained indignant. They, too, like Rupert Brooke, had seen a vision of Constantinople and had perhaps exclaimed, as he had, when they had first set out from Egypt only eight months before, 'Oh God! I've never been quite so happy before.' All this was now an embarrassment to remember, an absurd and childish excitement, and it was made more bitter by the endless disappointments, the death and the wastage that had intervened.

There was a simple and immediate reaction, and possibly it was a desire to remove the stigma of defeat, to create artificially a chance of heroism since the plan provided none: the men came to their officers in hundreds and asked to be the last to leave the shore. It was nothing more than a gesture, something for the pride to feed on, a kind of tribute to their friends who were already dead, but they were intensely serious about it. The veterans argued that they had earned this right, the newer arrivals insisted that they should be given this one last opportunity of distinguishing themselves. And so there was no need to call for volunteers to man the trenches at the end; it was a matter of selection.

318

But for the moment there was more need of cunning and discipline than heroism. In the second week of December the first stage of the evacuation began. Each evening after dusk flotillas of barges and small boats crept into Anzac Cove and Suvla Bay and there was a fever of activity all night as troops and animals and guns were got on board. The sick and wounded came first, the prisoners-of-war, and then, in increasing numbers, the infantry. The men walked silently down from the trenches, their boots wrapped in sacking, their footfall deadened by layers of blankets laid along the piers. In the morning the little fleet had vanished and all was normal again. Men and stores were being disembarked in the usual way, the same mule teams laden with boxes were toiling up to the front from the beaches, and there was no way for the Turks to know that the boxes on the mules were empty or that the disembarking men were a special group whose job was to go aboard the boats each night in the darkness and then return ostentatiously to the shore in the morning. Another deception was carried out with the guns. They ceased to fire soon after dark each night, so that the Turks should grow accustomed to silence and should not guess that anything was amiss on the final night when the last men were leaving the trenches. In the same way the infantry were ordered to hold back their rifle and machine-gun fire.

By the end of the second week of December these preliminary stages of the evacuation were well advanced. The weather held. The Turks apparently still suspected nothing and made no attempt to attack. But the British ranks were becoming very thin, and in order to keep up the deception it was necessary to march columns of men and animals like a stage army round and round the dusty tracks along the shore. No tents were struck, the gunners that remained fired twice as many rounds and kept moving their batteries from place to place; and thousands of extra cooking fires were lit in the morning and the evening. Throughout the daylight hours Allied aircraft flew along the coast in readiness to drive back any German aircraft that came out on reconnaissance.

On December 15 an acceleration of the programme began. All through the night channel steamers and barges shuttled back and forth between the islands and the coast, and even a battleship was called in to act as a transport. On the beaches huge piles of clothing, blankets, boots, water bottles, woollen gloves, tarpaulin sheets, motor cycles, tinned food and ammunition were made ready to be destroyed. Acid was poured over hundreds of unwanted sacks of flour, and, as a precaution against drunkenness, the commanders of units poured their stores of liquor into the sea.

By the morning of December 18 the beachmasters were able to report that half the force in the bridgehead, some 40,000 men, and most of their equipment had been taken off. Both Anzac and Suvla now were honeycombs of silent, half-deserted trenches, and the men that remained in them were utterly exposed to enemy attack. 'It's getting terribly lonely at night,' one of the English soldiers wrote in his diary. 'Not a soul about. Only the excitement keeps us from getting tired.'

All was now ready for the final stage. Twenty thousand men were to be taken off on the night of Saturday, December 19, and on Sunday—known as 'Z' night in the plan—the last 20,000 were to go. There was one thought in everybody's mind: 'If only the weather holds.' Through all this period the soldiers in the Cape Helles bridgehead, only thirteen miles away, knew nothing of what was going on.

Saturday morning broke with a mild breeze and a flat calm on the sea. There had been a short alarm at Anzac during the night when one of the storage dumps on the shore accidentally took fire, and everywhere the embarking men stood stock-still waiting to see if they were discovered at last. But nothing happened.

Through the long day the men went silently about their final preparations. A ton of high explosive was placed in a tunnel under the Turkish lines on the foothills of Chunuk Bair and made ready for detonation. Mines and booby traps were hidden in the soil, and to make certain that the troops avoided them on the final night long white lines of flour and salt and sugar were laid down from the trenches to the beach. The hard floor of the trenches themselves was dug up with picks to soften the noise of the final departure, and at places nearest the Turkish line torn blankets were laid on the ground.

Anzac posed a fantastic problem. At some places the British trenches were no more than ten yards from the Turks. Yet somehow the men had to be got out of them and down to the shore without the enemy knowing anything about it. They hit upon the device of the self-firing rifle. This was a contraption that involved the use of two kerosene tins. The upper tin was filled with water which dripped through a hole in the bottom into the empty tin below. Directly the lower tin became sufficiently weighted with water it over-balanced and fired a rifle by pulling a string attached to the trigger. There were several versions of this gadget: in place of water some men preferred to use fuses and candles that would burn through the string and release a weight on the rifle trigger, but the principle remained the same, and it was hoped that spasmodic shots would still be sounding along the line for half an hour or more after the last troops had gone. Thus it was believed that all might have at least a chance of getting away. Saturday went by in perfecting these arrangements. That night another 20,000 men crept down to the beaches at Suvla and Anzac and got away.

On Sunday morning the Turks shelled the coast rather more heavily than usual, and with new shells which evidently had been brought through Bulgaria from Germany. The Navy and such of the British guns as were left on shore replied. It was an intolerable strain, and the tension increased as the day went on. Now finally these last 20,000 men had returned to the conditions of the first landings in April. There was nothing more that the generals or the admirals could do to help them; as on the first day they were on their own in a limbo where no one knew what was going to happen, where only the individual will of the soldier could ruin or save them all. They waited very quietly. Many went for the last time to the graves of their friends and erected new crosses there; made little lines of stones and tidied up the ground; this apparently they minded more than anything, this leaving of their friends behind, and it was something better than sentimentality that made one soldier say to his officer, 'I hope *they* won't hear us going down to the beaches.'

On the shore the medical staff waited. They were to remain behind with the seriously wounded, and they had a letter written in French and addressed to the enemy commander-in-chief requesting a British hospital ship be allowed to embark them on the following day. Still, no one could be sure how this would be received, or indeed be sure of anything. They were on their own.

In the afternoon some went down to the horse lines and cut the throats of the animals which they knew could not

321

be got away. Others threw five millions rounds of rifle ammunition into the sea, together with twenty thousand rations in wooden cases. Others again kept up the pretence that the Army was still there in its tens of thousands by driving about in carts, a last surrealist ride in a vacuum. Birdwood and Keyes came ashore for the last time and went away again. Up at the front the remaining men who held the line—at some places no more than ten against a thousand Turks—went from one loophole to another firing their rifles, filling up the kerosene tins with water, making as much of a show as they could. It amused some of them to lay out a meal in their dugouts in readiness for the Turks when they came. But most preferred to wreck the places which they had dug and furnished with so much care.

At last at five the day ended and a wet moon came up, misted over with clouds and drifting fog. There was a slight drizzle of rain. Except for the occasional crack of a rifle shot and the distant rumble of the guns at Helles an absolute silence fell along the front. The men on the flanks and in the rear were the first to go. Each as he left the trenches fired his rifle for the last time, fell into line and marched in Indian file down the white lines to the beach. They came down from the hills in batches of four hundred and the boats were waiting. The last act of each man before he embarked was to take the two hand-grenades he was carrying and cast them silently into the sea.

Within an hour of nightfall both sectors at Anzac and Suvla were contracting rapidly towards their centres, and everywhere, from dozens of little gullies and ravines, like streams pouring softly down to join a river, men were moving to the shore. No one ran. Not smoking or talking, each group, when it reached the sea, stood quietly waiting for its turn to embark. At Anzac only 5,000 men were left at 8 p.m. At 10 p.m. the trenches at the front were manned by less than 1,500 men. This was the point of extreme danger; now, more than ever, every rifle shot seemed the beginning of an enemy attack. For several nights previously a destroyer had shone its searchlight across the southern end of the bridgehead to block the Turks' vision of the beach, and now again the light went on. Apart from this and the occasional gleam of the moon through the drifting clouds no other light was showing. Midnight passed and there was still no movement from the enemy. The handful of soldiers now left at the front moved quietly from loophole to loophole, occasionally firing their rifles, but more often simply standing and waiting until, with excruciating slowness, the moment came for them to go. The last men began to leave the trenches at 3 a.m. Fifteen minutes later Lone Pine was evacuated, and the men turned their backs on the Turks a dozen yards away. They had a mile or more to go before they reached the beach. As they went they drew cages of barbed wire across the paths behind them, and lit the fuses which an hour later would explode hidden mines beneath the ground. On the beach the hospital staff was told that, since there were no wounded, they too could leave. A private named Pollard who had gone to sleep at the front and had woken to find himself alone came stumbling nervously down to the shore and was gathered in.

They waited ten more minutes to make sure that none had been left behind. Then at 4 a.m., when the first faint streaks of dawn were beginning, they set fire to the dumps on the shore. On the hills above they could hear the automatic rifles going off and the noise of the Turks firing back spasmodically at the deserted trenches. At ten past four a sailor gave the final order, 'Let go all over—right away', and the last boat put out to sea. At that instant the mine below Chunuk Bair went off with a tearing, cataclysmic roar, and a huge cloud, lit from beneath with a red glow, rolled upward over the peninsula. Immediately a hurricane of Turkish rifle fire swept the bay.

At Suvla a similar scene was going on, but it continued a little longer. It was not until ten past five that Commodore Unwin, of the *River Clyde*, pushed off in the last boat. A soldier fell overboard as they were leaving, and the Commodore dived in and fished him out. 'You really must do something about Unwin,' General Byng said to Keyes, who was watching from his own ship off the shore. 'You should send him home; we want several little Unwins.'

And now a naval steamboat ran along the coast, an officer on board calling and calling to the shore for stragglers. But there were none. At Suvla every man and animal had been got off. At Anzac two soldiers were wounded during the night. There were no other casualties. Just before they vanished hull down over the horizon at 7 a.m. the soldiers in the last boats looked back towards the shore across the oily sea and saw the Turks come out of the foothills and run like madmen along the empty beach. At once the Navy opened fire on them, and a destroyer rushed in to ignite with its shells the unburnt piles of stores that had remained behind. On board the boats, where generals and privates were packed in together, a wild hilarity broke out, the men shaking one another's hands, shouting and crying. But before they reached the islands most of them had subsided to the deck and were asleep.

That night, sixteen hours after the last man had been taken off, a violent storm blew up with torrents of rain and washed away the piers.

Liman von Sanders says that he found great booty at Suvla and Anzac; five small steamers and sixty boats abandoned on the beaches, dumps of artillery and ammunition, railway lines and whole cities of standing tents, medicines and instruments of every kind, vast stacks of clothing, bully beef and flour, mountains of timber. And on the shore some hundreds of dead horses lay in rows. The ragged, hungry Turkish soldiers, who patched their uniforms with sacking and who subsisted on a daily handful of olives and a slice of bread, fell on this treasure like men who had lost their wits. Sentries were unable to hold them back; the soldiers rushed upon the food, and for weeks afterwards they were to be seen in the strangest uniforms, Australian hats, puttees wound round their stomachs, breeches cut from flags and tarpaulins, British trench boots of odd sizes on their feet. They carried in their knapsacks the most useless and futile things that they had picked up, but it was all glorious because it was loot, it was free and it was theirs. And they had won.

Liman von Sanders says too that he was planning a major attack on the Suvla and Anzac positions when he was forestalled by the evacuation, and he admits that right up to the early hours of Sunday, December 20, he had no notion of what was happening at the front. Confusing reports came to him at his headquarters through the night, and these were made still more confusing by sea mist. At 4 a.m., however, he ordered a general alarm. Yet there were still delays. The Turkish soldiers advanced very gingerly into the foremost trenches where there had only been instant death for so many months before. After a little while they paused, fearing that some trick was being played, and an hour or more went by before their commanders, woken from their sleep, came up to the front and told them to go on again. Even the final advance to the beaches was very slow, because the troops were held up by barbed wire and booby traps; and on the shore itself they were shelled from the sea. And so an army slipped away.

Liman's first reaction was the obvious one: he immediately set about gathering up his best divisions—there were now twenty-one under his command—and marching them south for an assault on the last remaining British bridgehead at Cape Helles. 'It was thought possible,' he says, 'that the enemy might hang on there for some time. That could not be permitted.' While his preparations for the attack were going forward patrols were sent out into no-man's-land each night, and the Turkish commanders at the front were ordered to keep a constant watch on every movement in the British lines.

It was an impossible position for the British. They had four divisions in Cape Helles. If they stayed they knew it could not be long before the Turks mounted a major attack against them; if they attempted to go they were hardly likely to outwit the Turks a second time. Monro as ever was in no doubt at all as to what should be done. Directly the Anzac-Suvla evacuation was completed he sent a message to London urging that Helles should be given up as well; and this time he found an ally in Admiral Wemyss. Birdwood too was eager to be off. And eventually on December 27 the cabinet agreed.

There followed a rapid series of changes in the high command. On December 22 de Robeck came back from London to resume control of the Fleet and Wemyss was posted off to the East Indies. A few days later Monro himself was gone; a signal arrived appointing him to the command of the First Army in France, the place where in all the world he most wished to be. On New Year's Day he sailed for Egypt and Gallipoli saw him no more. Now everyone was averting their eyes from this graveyard of men and their reputations, and this last act seemed likely to be the most painful of all. It was left to Birdwood, de Robeck and Keyes, the three men who had been there from the beginning, to clean up the mess.

There was not much time. With every day the weather grew more threatening and the Turks more likely to attack; they were shelling now with terrible accuracy with their new German guns and ammunition. There were 35,000 men in the Helles bridgehead, nearly 4,000 animals and almost as many guns and stores as there had been at

Suvla and Anzac. Once again it was decided that half the garrison should be evacuated secretly over a series of nights. General Davies, the corps commander, insisted that on January 9, the final night, he should be left with sufficient men to hold off the Turks for a week in case, at the last moment, he was cut off by foul weather. He fixed on the total of 17,000 as the minimum of soldiers required for this rearguard, and this also happened to be the maximum number that the Navy could take off in a single night. By January 1, 1916, all was agreed and the movement began.

The French were the first to go, and they left such a yawning gap in the line that there was nothing for it but to bring back the British 29th Division, to take their places. There was not much left of the 29th. The division had been badly cut up in the August battles and when they were evacuated from Suvla they were down to less than half their strength. One thing however remained to them, and that was a reputation of great bravery and steadiness; so now, after a few brief days' respite in the islands, they found themselves landing again beside the *River Clyde* and marching back to the trenches which they had first occupied eight months before. Among so many anticlimaxes this, perhaps, was the hardest of all.

There was a constricting feeling in the British trenches at Cape Helles at this time. At first the soldiers had no idea that the bridgehead was to be evacuated—indeed they were given a printed order of the day specifically saying that they were to remain. They hated this prospect, and in particular they feared that they might become prisoners of war—a fear that was all the more lurid because a rumour got about that the Turks would castrate them.

About five days before the final night it became generally known that the bridgehead was to be evacuated, and then the period of real tension began. But still excitement was the drug and a fatalism intervened. Four divisions against twenty-one was a monstrosity even on such a narrow front as this, but there was nothing that anyone could do about it. And so they played football, they waited, they made a kind of security out of the accustomed routine in the trenches, and they saw no further than the day ahead. Night by night the battalions went away and no one questioned the order of withdrawal; one simply waited for the summons and it was absurdly like the atmosphere of a dentist's waiting room. 'You're next,' and another regiment vanished. The others, feeling neither lucky nor unlucky, but fixed simply in an unalterable succession of events, remained behind and waited as the last patients wait, amid vague smells of carbolic and grisly secret apprehensions, in the silence of an emptying room.

There were a number of alarms and misadventures. High winds blew up, and they had to throw in cases of bully beef and other stores to repair the breaches in the causeway at Sedd-el-Bahr. Once when a sailor flashed a torch on a lighter full of mules there was a stampede, and for a long time the animals were snorting and screaming in the sea. Another night the French battleship *Suffren* ran down a large transport and sent her to the bottom. The U-boat scare began again. Yet by January 7 they had got the garrison down to 19,000; and now at last, at this instant of greatest danger for the British, Liman von Sanders delivered his attack.

He had been much delayed. All had been ready forty-eight hours before, but Enver had chosen that moment to send a message from Constantinople ordering nine of the Gallipoli divisions to Thrace. It was Enver's last gesture in the campaign, and Liman countered it in the usual way; he sent in his resignation. In the usual way, too, Enver backed down. The order was countermanded and now, in the early afternoon on January 7, the Turks came in for the kill. They were equipped with wooden ramps to throw across the British trenches, and special squads carried inflammable materials with which they were to burn the British boats on the shore. This was to be the final coup.

The attack began with the heaviest artillery bombardment of the campaign, and it went on steadily for four and a half hours. There was a lull for a few minutes and then it recommenced. In the British trenches the soldiers waited for the inevitable rush that would follow the bombardment; and in the early evening it began. The Turkish infantry had a hundred yards or more to go before they reached the first British trenches, and they jumped up with their old cries of *Allah, Allah,* and *Voor, Voor*—strike, strike. Perhaps there was something of desperation in the answering fire of the British defence. It was so murderous, so concentrated and steady, that when only a few minutes had gone by the soldiers saw a thing which had scarcely ever happened before—the Turkish infantry were refusing to charge. Their officers could be seen shouting and striking at the men, urging them up and out into the open where so many were already dead. But the men would not move. By nightfall it was all over. Not a single enemy soldier had broken into the British lines.

Liman admits that this disastrous attack convinced him that the British were not going to evacuate Cape Helles after all, and nothing further was done to molest them all through that night and the following day.

There were now just 17,000 men left, and January 8 was another calm spring-like day. Once again as at Suvla and Anzac great piles of stores and ammunition were got ready for destruction. Landmines were laid, and the self-firing rifles set in position in the trenches. Once again the sad mules lay dead in rows.

During the day the wind shifted round to the south-west and freshened a little, but it was still calm when at dusk the long lines of boats and warships set out for the peninsula for the last time. From Clapham Junction, from the Vineyard and *Le Haricot*, and the other famous places which soon would not even be mentioned on the maps, the men came marching to the sea, a distance of three miles or so.

The thing that the soldiers afterwards remembered with particular vividness was the curious alternation of silence and of deafening noise that went on through the day. At Sedd-el-Bahr they crouched under the corner of the battered fort waiting for their turn to embark, and in the overwhelming stillness of their private fear they heard nothing but the footfall of the men who had gone ahead; the clop, clop, clop of their boots as they ran across the pontoons to the *River Clyde* where lighters were waiting to embark them. Then, in an instant, all was dissolved in the shattering explosion of enemy shells erupting in the sea. Then again the clop, clop, clop of the boots as the line of running men took up its course again. To see safety so near and to know that with every second it might be lost—this was the hardest trial of all to bear, and it crushed the waiting soldier with nightmares of loneliness.

Apart from the spasmodic shelling there was no movement in the Turkish lines, and as the night advanced the Turks very largely ceased to count; it was the weather which engrossed everybody's mind. By 8 p.m. the glass was falling, and at nine when the waning moon went down the wind had risen to thirty-five miles an hour. The *River*

Clyde held firmly enough—all through these nights the men had been passing under her lee to the boats—but the crazy piers in the bay strained and groaned as heavy seas came smashing up against them. Soon an alarm went up. Two lighters broke adrift and crashed through the flimsy timber. All further embarkation then was stopped while a gang of engineers, working in the black and icy sea, put things to rights again. Then when another 3,000 men had been got off the pier collapsed once more, and again there was another hour's delay.

By midnight when the last troops began to leave the trenches on their long walk to the shore the wind was rising with every minute that went by, and in the starlight there was nothing to be seen at sea but a waste of racing water. Two white rockets went up from the battleship *Prince George*—the signal that she was being attacked by a submarine. Two thousand men had just got aboard the ship, and de Robeck and Keyes in the *Chatham* rushed towards her. But it was nothing—the vessel had merely bumped some wreckage in the water.

Now everything depended upon the speed with which the last men could be got away. At 2 a.m. 3,200 still remained. Through the next hour most of them managed to reach the boats, and barely 200 were then waiting to be embarked. These, however, were in a critical situation. Under the charge of General Maude, the commander of the 13th Division who had insisted on being among the last to leave, they had made their way to Gully Beach, an isolated landing place on the west coast, only to find that the lighter which was to take them off had run aground. By now the trenches had been empty for two and a half hours, and it was apparent that they could not stay where they were. One hope remained: to march on another two miles to 'W' beach at the tip of the peninsula on the chance that they might still be in time to find another boat. They set off soon after 2 a.m. and had been on the road for some ten minutes when the General discovered with consternation that his valise had been left behind on the stranded lighter. Nothing, he announced, would induce him to leave without it, and so while the rest of the column went on he turned back with another officer to Gully Beach. Here they retrieved the lost valise, and placing it on a wheeled stretcher set off once more along the deserted shore. Meanwhile the others had reached 'W' beach, where the last barge was waiting to push off. They felt, however, that they could not leave until the General arrived—a decision which required some courage, for the storm had now risen to half a gale, and the main ammunition dump, the fuse of which had already been lighted, was due to explode in under half an hour.[1] After twenty minutes the commander of the boat announced that he could wait no more; in another five minutes all further embarkation would become impossible. It was at this moment that the General emerged from the darkness with his companion and came trundling his valise down the pier.

It was just a quarter to four in the morning when they pushed off, and ten minutes later the first of the ammunition dumps went up with a colossal roar. As the soldiers and sailors in the last boats looked back towards the shore they saw hundreds of red rockets going up from Achi Baba and the cliffs in Asia, and immediately afterwards Turkish shells began to burst and crash along the beach. The fire in the burning dumps of stores took a stronger hold, and presently all the sky to the north was reddened with a false dawn. Not a man had been left behind.

It had been a fantastic, and unbelievable success, a victory of a sort at a moment when hope itself had almost gone. Decorations were awarded to General Monro and his chief-of-staff who had so firmly insisted upon the evacuation.

No special medal, however, was given to the soldiers who fought in the Gallipoli campaign.

[1] The incident inspired the exasperated embarkation officer to compose the following lines:

'Come into the lighter, Maude,
For the fuse has long been lit.
Hop into the lighter, Maude,
And never mind your kit.'

An alernative version runs:

'Come into the lighter, Maude,
For the night is nearly flown.
Come into the lighter, Maude,
And leave your bag alone.'

330

EPILOGUE

'You will hardly fade away until the sun fades out of the sky and the earth sinks into the universal blackness. For already you form part of that great tradition of the Dardanelles which began with Hector and Achilles. In another few thousand years the two stories will have blended into one, and whether when "the iron roaring went up to the vault of heaven through the unharvested sky", as Homer tells us, it was the spear of Achilles or whether it was a 100-lb shell from Asiatic Annie won't make much odds to the Almighty.'

GENERAL HAMILTON in a preface
addressed to the Gallipoli soldiers.

THE war never returned to Gallipoli. Soon after the campaign most of the Turkish soldiers were removed to other fronts, and within a few years nearly all the debris of the battlefield had been taken away.[1] In successive winter storms the remnants of the wharves and jetties were destroyed, and the trenches in the hills above fell in upon themselves and lost all pattern. Already by 1918 a thick growth of camel thorn and wild thyme, of saltbush and

---

[1] According to Liman von Sanders the booty at Cape Helles was enormous and took two years to gather up. Whole shiploads of conserves, flour and timber were sent to Constantinople.

myrtle, had covered the scarred ground where for nine months there had been nothing but dust or mud.

On January 20, 1918, the *Goeben* emerged at last. Shortly before dawn she came out of the straits with the *Breslau* and headed through the Ægean towards Imbros. For two years a British flotilla had been waiting there for just this opportunity, but it chanced that the *Lord Nelson* and the *Agamemnon,* the only two ships which were capable of sinking the *Goeben,* were away at Salonika that day; and so it was left to a group of destroyers and monitors to engage. They had very little chance. The monitor *Raglan* and another British ship soon went down, and for the Germans it might have been a supremely successful day had they not run on to a minefield off Imbros. The *Breslau* sank instantly, and the *Goeben* with a hole in her side struggled back to the Narrows where she beached herself. The vessel was repeatedly attacked from the air during the next few days, but she managed to right herself and escaped to Constantinople. Under the name of *Yavus* she is still serving with the Turkish Fleet.

Had the war continued into 1919 the British Fleet would have made another attempt to force the Dardanelles. In 1918 Admiral Wemyss had been installed as First Sea Lord, and Keyes was in command of the Dover Patrol. They had obtained the cabinet's consent to the new assault, and were actually engaged in assembling the ships when they were forestalled by the Armistice. It was signed with the Turks in the harbour of Mudros on October 30, 1918, twelve days before the cessation of hostilities in France. A fortnight later an Allied flotilla steamed up the Dardanelles, a long grey line of silent ships watched silently by the Turkish gunners on the cliffs, and an occupation force was put ashore.

Talaat and Enver did not wait for the end. Shortly before the Armistice they were ousted by a provisional government, and while all the waterfront at Constantinople was hung with Greek flags in expectation of the arrival of the Allied Fleet they fled to Germany. Talaat made his home under another name in Berlin, and from there in 1921 he sent a message to Aubrey Herbert in England suggesting that they should meet. The rendezvous took place at Hamm in Germany, and Talaat proposed an Anglo-Turkish alliance. He agreed that he had made mistakes—that the

332

Young Turks should never have joined the Germans—but that, he said, was past and done with; the important thing was that Britain was losing everything she had gained in Turkey by failing to come to an agreement with Mustafa Kemal.

The two men talked at great length, and it did not seem to Herbert that Talaat, even in these circumstances when his voice could only be a voice in a void, was absurd or even particularly pathetic. He was thinner and he was obviously poor, but the shrewdness remained, the hardness and the subtlety. Herbert said he could do no more than report to the Foreign Office, and Talaat went off in the Berlin train.

Talaat was wrong in one important aspect of his argument, for the past was not nearly done with yet. A few days later he felt a tap on his shoulder as he was walking in the street in Berlin, and turning round he saw the strained white face of a young Armenian student. This boy, Solomon Telririam by name, was in that instant the apotheosis of the ruined Armenian race. As a child he had seen his father stripped and murdered by the Turks, his mother and sisters put on the road for the Mesopotamian desert only to be raped and butchered by their guards. Someone had picked him up unconscious from the ground, and somehow he had made his way through Russia to Berlin. There, he said later, he had a vision: his mother was standing over him saying, 'You know Talaat is here. But you seem quite heartless and are not my son.' And now in the street, having looked for a second into the gypsy face, the boy took a revolver from his pocket and blew out Talaat's brains.

Both Liman, who was now living in retirement in Germany, and Talaat's widow gave evidence at the trial—Liman to defend the reputation of himself and the German soldiers who were in Turkey at the time of the Armenian massacres, and the widow to plead for her husband's name. Yet no one had the ghost of a chance of exonerating Talaat on this issue. One of the telegrams sent to a provincial Turkish commander was read in court. The officer had asked for the name of the place to which he was to send the Armenians whom he had rounded up. Talaat replied, 'The place where they are being sent to is nowhere.'

Enver too had set out for Germany at the collapse in 1918, and soon after he was gone he was condemned to death in Constantinople. He made his way across the Black Sea to Odessa, and thence overland through the chaos of the Balkans to Berlin. He soon grew tired of the wretched life of a refugee in a defeated capital, and in 1919 he returned to Russia to try his fortune with the Soviets. For a while he was with General Denikin in the struggle for the independence of the Caucasus, but when Denikin negotiated with the Allies he went to Azerbaijan. During 1920 and 1921 he was employed at Moscow as the director of the Asiatic department of the Soviet government, and attended a conference at Baku as the leader of the communist movement in the Middle East. From this point on the story grows obscure; he was constantly reported dead only to appear again. In the end, however, it appears that he turned against the Russians, and he is said to have met his death leading a cavalry charge against them in the mountains of Russian Turkestan in 1922. He was then in his early forties.

Liman remained in command of the Turkish Army on the southern front in Syria until he was defeated by Allenby in 1918, when he handed over the command to Kemal and returned to Constantinople. There he surrendered to the Allies, and was interned in Malta until the summer of 1919. In the ten years that were left to him (he was already sixty at Gallipoli), he enjoyed a dignified and respected retirement, and the private rages which, one feels, lie just below the surface in such a controlled character were his own affair. He died a few years before Hitler came to power and left a name as a military strategist which was hardly less admired in Britain than it was in Germany.

Of Kemal's own fabulous rise to power there are of course very full accounts, but perhaps his first triumphs at the Dardanelles were as important to him as any others. When towards the end of the campaign he arrived in Constantinople ill and exhausted not even Enver's opposition could prevent the Turkish newspapers from greeting him as 'The Saviour of Gallipoli'.

In August 1916 a Royal Commission was set up in London to investigate the Gallipoli campaign. General Monro, who was then on his way to India to become Commander-in-Chief, was the first witness, and in the ensuing year nearly 200 others were called to give evidence: Churchill and Hamilton, de Robeck and Keyes, Stopford and Fisher, all the generals and admirals, and finally the war correspondents, Nevinson, Ashmead-Bartlett and Murdoch. Kitchener, who by then was dead,[1] was the only major figure who did not put his case. At the end of 1917 the Commission's report came out, and it stated its general conclusions very clearly: '. . . from the outset the risks of failure attending the enterprise outweighed its chances of success.' General Monro was congratulated upon the evacuation: it was, the Commission said, 'A wise and courageous decision.'

Dealing with the Suvla landing, the Commissioners expressed the view that General Stopford might have kept in closer touch with his troops, but Hamilton, they thought, had only increased his difficulties by intervening on August 8. 'We regard the intervention,' the report stated, 'as well-intentioned but injudicious.' In short, the general conclusion was that the campaign was a mistake, and that even with better luck and better management, it could hardly have succeeded.

In 1917 the Dardanelles Commissioners were not ideally placed for taking an historical view of the campaign, for there was then still another year of trench warfare to be fought in France, and the Russian revolution had not yet taken its full effect; and so it may not have been altogether apparent then that there were worse things in the world than the loss of half a dozen old battleships in the Dardanelles, or the weakening of the French front by a few extra divisions which might have made all the difference at Gallipoli.

It was apparent only that the Allies had been incomparably the losers. During the 259 days that elapsed between the first landings in April 1915 and the final withdrawal in January 1916 they sent half a million men to Gallipoli, and slightly more than half of these became casualties. There is some doubt about the exact number of the Turkish losses, but they are officially computed at 251,000, which is just one thousand less than those suffered by the Allies; and this

---

[1] On June 5, 1916, he sailed in the *Hampshire* on an official visit to Russia, and was drowned when the ship struck a mine off the Orkneys.

perhaps is the best indication of how closely the struggle was fought.[1]

As for the strategic consequences of the defeat, they scarcely bore thinking about. Twenty Turkish divisions were set free to attack Russia and to threaten Egypt. All contact with Russia and Rumania was lost, and the war dragged on in the Near East for another three years while another Allied army, infinitely greater in size than the one employed at Gallipoli, slowly and painfully made good the ground that had been lost. Before the Ottoman Empire fell in 1918 nearly three-quarters of a million Allied soldiers were sent to Salonika, and another 280,000 fought their way northwards across the desert from Egypt to Jerusalem and Damascus. Except for the Anzac troops few of the men who were evacuated from Gallipoli were ever employed against the Germans as General Monro had hoped they would be; most of them remained in the East until the end of the war.

The campaign had been a mighty destroyer of reputations. When Kitchener returned to England at the end of 1915 he was forced to reinstate the General Staff in the War Office, and he was no longer a semi-dictatorial figure in the cabinet. He was sixty-five, Gallipoli seemed to have deprived him of his old oracular powers of taking decisions, and Lloyd George, Bonar Law and others began a concerted move to get him out. At his death six months later his influence was rapidly falling away. In the years that followed it was demonstrated over and over again in many books that the sinking of the *Hampshire* had saved Kitchener from a sad and inevitable decline. Yet he was so revered by the public in England that for a long time people simply could not bring themselves to believe that he

---

[1] The official figures were:

	ALLIES		TURKS	
Soldiers engaged:	British	410,000	Soldiers engaged:	
	French	79,000	Approximately	500,000
		489,000	Casualties:	
			Killed	55,127
Casualties:	British	205,000	Wounded	100,177
	French	47,000	Missing	10,067
		252,000	Died of disease	21,498
			Evacuated sick	64,440
				251,309

336

was dead, and there was a persistent rumour that he was a prisoner of the Germans.

And still the aura persists, his name still rises above that of any other British general in the first world war, and it is not clear that these others managed any better than he would have done had he lived and remained in office. He delayed and vacillated over Gallipoli, and in the end it was his undoing; yet he understood the campaign with a better strategical sense than most of his contemporaries, and for a time at least—that time when he persuaded the British and the French Governments to give priority to Gallipoli—he had the courage of his imagination.

It was the same with Churchill, except that in his case he lived on and had to fight his way back. It was not until 1917 that Lloyd George, the new Prime Minister, felt that he was able to bring him into the Government again as Minister of Munitions, and even then there was much opposition to it. As late as the general election of 1923 there were cries of 'What about the Dardanelles?' whenever he addressed a public meeting. That was the year when the Lloyd George coalition fell, and Churchill was defeated in the election—his first defeat since he had entered the House of Commons nearly a quarter of a century before. His eclipse seemed to be complete. In a study of the Gallipoli campaign an American staff officer wrote, 'It is doubtful if even Great Britain could survive another world war and another Churchill.' And the Australian Official History which appeared about this time contained these words: 'So through a Churchill's lack of imagination, a layman's ignorance of artillery, and the fatal power of a young enthusiasm to convince older and slower brains, the tragedy of Gallipoli was born.' Somewhere in the painful fields of memory the ghost of Fisher was still repeating, 'Damn the Dardanelles. They will be our grave.'

Then in the nineteen-twenties the reaction began to set in. The first surprise came from the Turkish General Staff when they admitted that on March 19, 1915, nearly all their ammunition at the Narrows had been shot away, and that a renewed attack on that day might very well have been decisive. The whole conception of the naval attack was now seen, if not in a new light, in a more controversial way. Other evidence followed—evidence of the extreme political tension in Constantinople at that time, and of the

337

fact that Turkey possessed only two arsenals which the Allied Fleet might easily have destroyed.

In its report the Turkish staff stated: 'A naval attack executed with rapidity and vigour at the outbreak of the war might have been successful . . . if the Entente Fleets had appeared before Constantinople the eight divisions retained there would have been impotent to defend it.' And so that first and much derided directive: 'The Admiralty should prepare for a naval expedition in February to bombard and take the Gallipoli peninsula with Constantinople as its objective,' was not so fanciful after all.

Roger Keyes, not surprisingly, needed very little persuading about the importance of these revelations. In 1925, when he was in command of the Mediterranean Fleet, he steamed through the Dardanelles and, according to Aspinall, who was with him, he could hardly speak for emotion. 'My God,' he said at last, 'it would have been even easier than I thought; we simply *couldn't* have failed . . . and because we didn't try, another million lives were thrown away and the war went on for another three years.'

Other experts—and they were still in a majority—remained unconvinced. Yet no one could altogether ignore the admission of Liman von Sanders and the Turkish commanders that more than once the divisional generals at Cape Helles had wanted to withdraw behind Achi Baba; that on at least two occasions, at the original landing at Anzac in April and again at Suvla in August, the Allies were on the very edge of breaking through and were only prevented from doing so by the intervention of Mustafa Kemal.

Gradually too with the passing of time the great events of the war and its aftermath were falling into perspective, and the Gallipoli adventure was seen, not in isolation, but as a part of the general strategy; not as a sideshow, but as an alternative to the fearful three years of slaughter that followed in the trenches in France, to the long campaign against the Turks in Mesopotamia, and to the expedition to Salonika. It was even perhaps not too much to say that if the Allies had succeeded in penetrating the Dardanelles in 1915 or 1916 the Russians would not have signed a separate peace, and that the revolution might not have followed, not at all events so soon, or possibly so drastically.

Seen in this new light the Gallipoli campaign was no longer a blunder or a reckless gamble; it was the most imaginative conception of the war, and its potentialities were almost beyond reckoning. It might even have been regarded, as Rupert Brooke had hoped, as a turning point in history. Certainly in its strictly military aspect its influence was enormous. It was the greatest amphibious operation which mankind had known up till then, and it took place in circumstances in which nearly everything was experimental: in the use of submarines and aircraft, in the trial of modern naval guns against artillery on the shore, in the manœuvre of landing armies in small boats on a hostile coast, in the use of radio, of the aerial bomb, the land mine, and many other novel devices. These things led on through Dunkirk and the Mediterranean landings to the invasion of Normandy in the second world war. In 1940 there was very little the Allied commanders could learn from the long struggle against the Kaiser's armies in the trenches in France. But Gallipoli was a mine of information about the complexities of the modern war of manœuvre, of the combined operation by land and sea and sky; and the correction of the errors made then was the basis of the victory of 1945. The next time, as Kitchener had once hoped, 'they got it right.'

It was Churchill himself who first restored the reputation of the Gallipoli campaign with the publication in the twenties of *The World Crisis,* his study of the first world war. He had never really been heard before, and now, step by step, he took the story through the political and military events which led up to the campaign: the controversy with Fisher, the arguments in cabinet, the long struggle to win support for Gallipoli from Joffre and the trench-warfare generals in France, the agonizing delays that hung on Kitchener's word, the trembling balance of politics in the Balkans, and finally the crises of the battle itself, when just for a few moments, in a vacuum of indecision, all depended upon the inspiration of a single act of faith.

There followed the admirable official history prepared by Brigadier Aspinall, and it amply confirmed all Churchill had written.

Meanwhile the authors who had served in the campaign had been at work. There were Hamilton's own diaries, Compton Mackenzie's *Gallipoli Memories,* Henry Nevinson's graceful and accomplished account of the operations, a short book from the Poet Laureate, John Masefield, and two novels that were widely read, *The Secret Battle* by

Alan Herbert, and *Tell England* by Ernest Raymond. By the nineteen-thirties a large library had grown up, British, French, Turkish and German, and although there was general criticism of the tactics no serious student now questioned the wisdom of the Allies going to the Dardanelles.

An astonishing number of the Gallipoli commanders survived to see this vindication. Birdwood lived on until his ninety-seventh year, and Keyes, having served as Director of Combined Operations in the second world war, died in 1945, leaving behind him an endless speculation as to what might have happened had he been the admiral in command in the Dardanelles and de Robeck his chief-of-staff. Nasmith of the E 11 went on to become the youngest admiral afloat. Others took up careers that could never have been predicted: Allanson became the British consul at Monte Carlo, Murdoch, the Australian journalist, became the owner of a powerful chain of newspapers and radio stations, Unwin resigned from the Navy almost at once and became a well-known yachtsman; he had three children. Others again were young and obscure when they fought at Gallipoli, but later the world knew them very well. Among these there were Clement Attlee, then a spruce young captain of thirty-two, and three future field marshals, Slim, Harding and the Australian, Blamey. Of the group of friends who buried Rupert Brooke on Skyros only Freyberg and Arthur Asquith survived. Freyberg fought through the second world war, a V.C. with three bars to his D.S.O., and subsequently Governor-General of New Zealand. De Robeck, Monro and Stopford died at the end of the nineteen-twenties.

Hamilton was not asked to serve in the field again after the campaign, but his later career was in some ways the most remarkable of all. In 1918 he became Lieutenant of the Tower of London, and in 1932 Rector of Edinburgh University. Year after year, while all but a few of his Gallipoli contemporaries reached the ends of their lives, he continued into a distinguished and sensitive old age, the nimbus of Gallipoli always overhanging his name but never daunting him. His *Gallipoli Diary*, which appeared in 1920, was followed by a prophetic study of the trend of modern war and several books of reminiscence. The second world war passed, and he was still there in his pleasant home at Hyde Park Gardens in London, surrounded by his books, his military trophies and by many friends; a tall thin figure,

340

very well dressed, and it was still a groomed and supple mind. If he was not entirely vidicated at least he was loved and respected. All the great opponents of Gallipoli were gone, Monro and the generals of the western front, Bonar Law, Carson and Northcliffe. When the General died on October 12, 1947, he had reached the great age of ninety-four, and a large congregation of the leading people in Britain gathered at a service in Westminster Abbey to honour his memory.

It was the silence of the Gallipoli peninsula which most surprised and awed the survivors of the campaign who returned there after the war, the stillness of the cliffs and beaches where nothing much remained of the battle except the awful sight of the white bones of unburied soldiers and the rusting guns along the shore. Of the sunken battleships nothing was to be seen; the *Majestic* was broken up by an Italian company and sold for scrap, and the other vessels, the *Triumph,* the *Irresistible,* the *Bouvet* and the *Ocean* lay too deep for salvage. The *River Clyde* was gone. Although she had been shelled a thousand times they towed her off the beach at Sedd-el-Bahr and at Malta engineers soon patched up her broken plates. In 1920 she was sold to a Spanish owner, and in the nineteen-fifties she was still sailing the Mediterranean under the name of *Muruja Y Aurora.*

The peninsula itself was cordoned off as a military area by the Turks, but the peasants came back and replanted the land about Cape Helles and Maidos and Suvla Bay. At the Narrows the Allied occupation force dismantled the guns, but the two mediæval castle-fortresses still stood. Chanak was rebuilt, was shattered by an earthquake and was rebuilt again; and little by little the other towns on the peninsula were restored to what they were. All the rest of the wild and lonely coast remained unchanged, and the second world war passed over it without making any difference. Today the hills are as deserted as ever, and packs of wolves still appear from time to time. In a cold winter they descend to the valleys to attack the flocks, and they have even been known to bring a donkey down.

Today one needs a guide to find one's way around the battlefields. At Sedd-el-Bahr one recognizes at once the shattered fortress, the half-moon beach and the ledge of sand under which the first survivors of the *River Clyde* waited all day on April 25, 1915; but beyond this, on the long slopes to Achi Baba all traces of the fighting have gone. Just occasionally a farmer ploughing deeply will turn up a rusted bullet or a piece of shrapnel, and it is not unknown for a hand-grenade to burst beneath the bullocks' hooves.

At Anzac, where the land is too broken up for any cultivation to be possible, there is much more evidence of the battle. Here the trenches, growing shallower and shallower every year, can yet be seen; the holes of the old tunnels still vanish into darkness, and one has only to kick the dust to turn up jagged pieces of metal, the remains of a pannikin or a hobnailed boot, perhaps a broken segment of a rum jar with the makers' name still on it. The scene of the past fighting is evoked very easily: the mule teams winding up from the beach, the city of dugouts perched on the sides of the cliffs, the soldiers bathing in the sea, the heat and the flies and the fearful racket of shellfire re-echoing in every valley. But it is still hardly possible to bring oneself to believe that for nearly nine months men could have lived and fought at such places as Quinn's Post. One jump brings you from the Turkish trench to the Allied lines; it is too close, too savage, too intimate to be entirely credible to an age that only knows the enemy at a distance, and as a disembodied figure in a machine.

The cemeteries at Gallipoli are unlike those of any other battlefield in Europe. As soon as the Armistice was signed an Allied war graves commission arrived, and it was decided that the dead as far as possible should be buried where they fell. Consequently a score or more of cemeteries were made, some with only a hundred graves, others with thousands, and they lie on every height where the fighting reached its zenith. Each is surrounded by a bank of pines, and the graves themselves, which are not marked by crosses but by marble plaques in the ground, are thickly planted with cypresses and junipers, arbutus and rosemary and such flowering shrubs as the Judas tree. In winter moss and grass cover the ground, and in summer a thick carpet of pine needles deadens the footfall. There is no sound except for the wind in the trees and the calls of the migrating birds who have found these places the safest sanctuary on the peninsula. The effect upon the visitor's mind is not that of tragedy or death but of an immense tranquillity, of the continuity of things.

The highest of these cemeteries lies on Chunuk Bair at the spot where the New Zealanders reached the crest and Allanson and his men looked briefly down upon Maidos and the Narrows. Here perhaps more than anywhere else the Gallipoli campaign is revealed, for as the eye roams round from west to east it falls on the salt lake at Suvla, and then on the cascade of hills and ravines around Anzac Cove, and finally on the high stone pillar which has been erected on Cape Helles just above the beach where the 29th Division came ashore. These scenes are in the immediate foreground, and they are set, as it were, in a frame of other older battlefields in the Ægean Islands, the Troad and the Hellespont.

For nearly forty years the cemeteries have been tended with great devotion by a Major Millington, an old Australian soldier. He has a curious existence, for at Chanak on the Narrows, where he has his house, he is in a Turkish military area and may not move more than a thousand paces in any direction without escort. However, the young Turkish conscripts accompany him willingly enough as he goes over to the peninsula month by month and year by year to supervise his staff of local stonemasons and gardeners. The Turks find this preoccupation with the dead somewhat strange, since their own soldiers who died at Gallipoli were buried in anonymous communal graves, and until recently almost their only memorial was a legend picked out in large white letters on the hillside above Chanak. It reads, 'March 18, 1915'—a reminder to all passing ships that that was the day when the Allied Fleet was defeated. However, the Turkish gardeners work well; no wall around the French and British cemeteries is allowed to crumble, no weed is anywhere allowed to grow, and now in the nineteen-fifties the gardens are more beautiful than ever. Yet hardly anyone ever visits them. Except for occasional organized tours not more than half a dozen visitors arrive from one year's end to the other. Often for months at a time nothing of any consequence happens, lizards scuttle about the tombstones in the sunshine and time goes by in an endless dream.

The most fascinating people and events of World War II